Jury Nullification

A Cato Institute Book

Jury Nullification

The Evolution of a Doctrine

Clay S. Conrad

CAROLINA ACADEMIC PRESS
Durham, North Carolina

ISBN 0-89089-702-6
LCCN 98-87688

CAROLINA ACADEMIC PRESS
700 Kent Street
Durham, North Carolina 27701
Telephone (919) 489-7486
Fax (919) 493-5668
E-mail: cap@cap-press.com
www.cap-press.com

Printed in the United States of America

To the Defenders

This book is dedicated to those warriors, old and new, who have the temerity to fight for justice in American courtrooms from the Supreme Court itself to the lowest municipal or justice of the peace court. But for their efforts, the guarantees of liberty the Founding Fathers enshrined in the Bill of Rights would be no more than paper promises which the lowest bureaucrat could ignore at whim, and which the powerful and well-placed could safely thumb their noses at with impunity.

Contents

Table of Cases

Preface

That is what a jury trial is all about—justice.
See that it be done.
Nancy Lord

My first introduction to the doctrine of jury nullification occurred during the summer of 1990, when I heard Dr. Larry Dodge, founder of the Fully Informed Jury Association (FIJA), speak in New York. It was the first time I had ever been exposed to the ideas discussed in this book, and quite frankly my opinion was that they were bizarre and horrific. The public was endorsing—even demanding—all sorts of draconian criminal laws and sanctions. National Drug Czar William Bennett had recently gone so far as to state publicly that he had no moral qualms about public executions for drug dealers—by beheading, no less—and there was no public outcry or condemnation. Public opinion polls showed that a frightening number of people were more than willing, they were anxious, to trade away essential liberties for the illusion of increased security. What would these people do when sitting as jurors, given the authority to make up the law as they go? Could we trust the conscience of the community when it was increasingly apparent that the community was bitter with revenge, and weary of talk about rights, justice and mercy?

Out of curiosity, however, I did take some of the FIJA literature home with me. I read it, then re-read it, then re-read it again. I kept turning these ideas over in my mind. I was growing curious about the history, development and purpose of the criminal trial jury. The ability of juries to protect a minority was new to me; I had never really understood why juries were essential to our system of government. Like most Americans, I accepted that juries were somehow important, but I never understood or questioned how or why. I had never learned the role of the jury as a check on the excesses of a democratic government, or the reasons why jury trial was so rare outside of the United States. I had never realized how the role of the jury had been minimized, as the power of government had increased.

We live in an America where more and more well-meaning, law abiding citizens find themselves the targets of some criminal law or another, often with serious consequences. More and more frequently, juries are finding that the laws they are asked to enforce are questionable, or even repugnant. Jurors are too often leaving courtrooms horrified at the sentences handed down as a result of their verdict. Judges are spending a growing proportion of their time "controlling" and "selecting" juries, and the amount of information kept from juries is often greater than the amount they are allowed to consider. Specifically in capital cases, the fear of jury nullification has forced courts to empanel special "death-qualified" juries, which are widely understood to be unfairly biased towards conviction. This is because the alternatives—to abandon the death penalty altogether, or to use separate juries during the punishment and guilt/innocence phases of the trial—have both been found unacceptable to our lawmakers. Have we actually become willing to openly and officially endorse biased juries, and in the most serious criminal cases, merely in order to prevent jury nullification of the law? I began to see that something is wrong, very wrong, with the way we try criminal cases in this country, and that our sporadic piecemeal attempts at reform—as piecemeal reforms are wont to do—are only making matters worse.

Our country presently has over one million people in prison, the highest per-capita incarceration rate of any industrialized nation. Millions more are under the control and supervision of the criminal justice system through parole, probation, community supervision, or deferred adjudication. The vast majority of these prisoners are incarcerated for non-violent crimes, with well over half imprisoned for drug offenses alone. Even though we have spent billions and billions of dollars building prisons and courtrooms, hiring police, prosecutors, jailers and judges and otherwise fighting the "war on crime," the streets are not significantly safer than they were before this vast "war on crime" began—and the marginal reduction in crime we have experienced is more attributable to an aging population than to any law enforcement efforts.

The criminal sanction is only one tool available to shape public policy, and it is a dumb, blunt, dangerous weapon of a tool. It is a hammer. And as fine a tool as a hammer may be for some purposes, you cannot use it to fix your television set. You cannot use it to tighten your doorknob or mow your lawn. And yet, in America in the 1990s, we have come to believe that this hammer—the criminal sanction—is the tool of first choice for fixing any social problem. We have lost the appreciation that there are legitimate limits to the use of the criminal sanction. We have abandoned the creativity necessary to find ways to solve social problems other than locking one of our less conventional or less fortunate neighbors in a cage.

We are becoming an increasingly divided society, and a decreasingly tolerant one. Although many people believe that with the widespread acceptance of the goals of the civil rights movement social intolerance has become an aberration, in a broader context the growing intolerance in American society is not surprising. Can there be any act more appropriately symbolic of social intolerance than to incarcerate someone for a victimless "crime?" This relentless resort to the criminal sanction as a means of social control is balkanizing our society, especially our inner cities, as thousands of young people—disproportionately minority males—despair of succeeding in a society all too anxious to brand them as criminals. As the next millenium begins, there are more young black men in prison than in college. Those left on the streets are increasingly likely to be on parole or probation. They are finding fewer opportunities, fewer jobs, and increasing apprehension and hostility among a white majority grown inured to thinking of young black men as dangerous, uneducated criminals.

Band-aid solutions to the problems of our criminal justice system have merely led to layers upon layers of incompatible and often contradictory or nonsensical laws and procedures. These laws are neither routinely enforced, understood, nor followed. The edifice has become too ponderous for substantial legislative reform, as each successive legislative session adds additional layers without fundamentally rethinking what has gone before. What is needed is not to reform, but to remove—to remove the layers, remove out-moded or unsupportable laws, remove procedural barricades that place form over substance, procedure over justice. In order to accomplish this creative demolition, we require a target, a specific goal.

The only sensible goal of enlightened penal reform is to limit the criminal sanction to the punishment of those acts (and only those acts) which are broadly and uniformly condemned by the vast majority of Americans. We need to ensure that criminal law is no longer controlled by special interest politics, so that criminal law is no longer a source of divisiveness in society. We should be confident that criminal punishments are not destroying the lives of productive, useful Americans who merely engage in unpopular but victimless activities. But how are we to do this, in an era when the most dangerous addiction in America seems to be to the use of the criminal sanction itself?

And this is where jury nullification presents itself. Jury nullification, the act of a criminal trial jury in deciding not to enforce a law where they believe it would be unjust or misguided to do so, allows average citizens, through deliberations, to limit the scope of the criminal sanction. History shows juries have taken this enormous power very seriously, and used it responsibly. But this history has rarely been developed. That is why this book was written.

In writing this book, I was overwhelmed with the quantity of material available. The sheer volume of cases, articles, books and essays dealing with jury nullification was astounding—a quick computer search in 1993 listed over 400 law journal articles discussing the topic, and an even greater number of cases and newspaper articles. By 1998, there were closer to six hundred articles listed. Few of these articles, however, discussed independent juries in much depth. One could read that jury nullification was influential in ending slavery, but not see any cases cited as support for that conclusion. One could read about juries being influential in the labor movement, in the freedom of religion and of the press, or in ending prohibition—but with no cases cited as support for those conclusions. Alternatively, one could read that juries routinely acquitted lynch mobs and civil rights murderers, especially in the South. Again, that conclusion would stand unsupported in the vast majority of articles or cases, or the same cases would be cited again and again—often with no analysis justifying the conclusions.

The hung juries in the trials of the Menendez brothers in Los Angeles gave rise to a fierce movement in California to eliminate that state's unanimous jury requirement. Even though not a single juror voted to acquit either brother, and there was no majority on either side (the jury was evenly split between first and second degree murder convictions), conventional wisdom concerning the number of dangerous persons freed through successive hung juries was fed through rumors and usually inaccurate anecdotal evidence. California Governor Pete Wilson campaigned vigorously for non-unanimous verdicts in his state, with surprising media support.

Unquestionably, the most spectacular (and possibly least relevant) event was the verdict in the O.J. Simpson murder trial. When the Simpson jury deliberated only briefly before reaching a verdict of acquittal, it seemed every pundit in the country was assuming the verdict was premised on jury nullification. Defense attorney Johnny Cochran was alternately chastised and praised for his "send them a message" defense argument; Marcia Clark and Christopher Darden wrote books and went on speaking tours across the country condemning the jurors and taking no responsibility for their loss themselves; and black law professors including Lani Guinier and Paul Butler began praising the doctrine of jury independence in the media and in law reviews. The media could not force themselves to let go of the case. Long after the verdict was old news, talk shows and commentators were referring to the supposedly widespread racial split in interpreting the verdict as though public opinion polls had some relevance to determining the true guilt or innocence of O.J. Simpson, or anyone else.

Amidst this commentary, probably less than one in ten articles in the popular media showed even a basic understanding of what jury nullification *is*, much less whether it was involved in the Simpson case. Nobody was paying attention to what the Simpson jury said, the evidence they were and were not allowed to see, the circumstances under which they reached their conclusions, or the background and life experiences they took into consideration in reaching their verdict. The Simpson jury was simply scapegoated for the gross failures and mistakes of the Los Angeles District Attorney's office. Indeed, Los Angeles District Attorney Gil Garcetti placed responsibility for his office's defeat squarely on the jury, angrily complaining that "[a]pparently (the jury's) verdict was based on emotion that over-came their reason."[1] For an elected official to have spoken so conde-scendingly, and with so little respect, towards any other group of voters would be unthinkable. This group, however, Garcetti could openly condemn with no fear of reprisal: they were a jury, and juries are almost always safe targets.

The Senate and Congressional hearings into the Ruby Ridge and Waco operations of the Bureau of Alcohol, Tobacco and Firearms and the Fed-eral Bureau of Investigation, combined with the bombing of the Murrah Federal Center in Oklahoma City, revealed opposed but related concerns about excesses of government and of the burgeoning militia movement in the country. Jury independence (and particularly FIJA) was falsely identi-fied with the "militia movement" and the extreme far-right in a number of television and radio broadcasts, in spite of the fact that many prominent left-leaning attorneys and judges including Alan Scheflin, William Kun-stler, Leonard Weinglass, Michael Tigar, David Kairys, Tony Serra and David Bazelon have promoted and praised jury independence as an impor-tant bulwark of American liberty. While jury nullification may have become headline news it was almost always inaccurately portrayed, and occa-sionally wrongly identified with a political ideology which was often its antithesis.

As an institution the jury has received a great deal of criticism, much of it unwarranted. This criticism tends to come from an elitist perspective: jurors are variously described as being "dumb," "racist," "irrational," "uneducated," "lazy," "irresponsible," "ignorant," or "emotional." Of course, these same critics are confident that they would never be selected for jury duty: they are too "intelligent," "objective," "informed," or "edu-cated." In fact, none of these criticisms is borne out by statistics: jurors, on the average, have a few more months of education than the average Amer-ican. Jurors tend to take their jobs with a profound sense of responsibili-ty, apply themselves with a great deal of energy and sincerity, and show less racial disparity in their decisions than any of the other actors in the crim-inal justice system—police, prosecutors, or judges. Yet it has become arro-gantly fashionable to scapegoat the jury for any outcome in the legal sys-tem with which we are dissatisfied.

We seem to forget that the same people who sit as jurors are the same people who elect our politicians, sheriffs, judges and prosecutors. If citi-zens are not qualified to serve as jurors, how can they be qualified to elect the judge who would necessarily decide the case in the absence of a jury? Criticisms of the jury are radically undemocratic, striking at the very root

---

1. *In Wake of Simpson Trial, Garcetti Talks About Judicial Reform*, SEATTLE POST-INTELLIGENCER, November 8, 1995 at A13.

of citizen autonomy and self-government: the ability of the average citizen to make good, informed, rational and unprejudicial judgments. If, as a citizenry, we are not qualified to serve as jurors, then we are not qualified to govern ourselves.

None of the prejudices against jurors is borne out by the statistics or by the experience of most good trial attorneys. The best attorneys usually sing the jury's praises, and believe juries are fairer and more open-minded than judges. Houston attorney Dick DeGuerin, for example, has referred to a bench trial as "a long, sustained plea of guilty," believing judges are rarely able to hear both sides of a case with an open and unjaundiced mind. A lawyer who is able to explain his case to a jury will rarely complain that the jury was not capable or not willing to understand his case. The lawyer who is unable to explain his case to a jury may not really understand it himself. We should perhaps take his complaints with a large grain of salt.

Of course, criticisms of the jury usually come from the losing side, and stink of sour grapes. Instead of reflecting the lack of responsibility of jurors, these criticisms reflect upon the lack of responsibility of those attorneys, judges and politicians who have failed to prove their cases, adjudicate fairly, or write just, intelligible laws. Even worse, these criticisms are aimed at an institution and at a group of people who are rarely able to defend themselves. The jury scatters after a trial. They have no office, no spokesperson, no press secretary, no fax machines, post office boxes or telephone numbers. And no attorney to argue in defense of their integrity, their reputation, their rights.

If this short work is successful at all, perhaps some of these myths may finally be laid to rest. The history of independent juries, and the available social science research, show that jurors are profoundly responsible, dedicated and serious about their tasks. They show that bad lawyering, bad laws, and bad judging are more often responsible for bad verdicts than bad juries could ever be, and that most of the criticism aimed at juries are not only misguided, but are often deliberate scapegoating.

This book will show that jury independence is neither "left" nor "right," neither "anarchist" nor "fascist" nor "anti-democratic." What jury nullification *is* about is particularized justice; it is about citizen oversight of prosecutorial discretion; and it is about limiting the power and intrusiveness of the legislature and of the criminal sanction. Properly understood, instructed, and empowered, juries can reduce social intolerance and divisiveness, reduce unnecessary incarceration, and redirect our criminal justice system to social protection, as opposed to social engineering. That is an ambitious order, but history shows American juries have performed it in the past. American juries have the same powers today. If only they knew them.

I cannot even begin to list all of the people I have to thank for their assistance, inspiration, encouragement and support in writing this book. Timothy Lynch and David Boaz of the Cato Institute encouraged me, gave me invaluable assistance and advice, and helped champion this project into a book. Larry Dodge and Don Doig inspired me, and got me started on research and investigation. The entire staff of the Tarlton Law Library at the University of Texas School of Law is superb, and without their excellent resources and assistance I would never have dared begin this project. Professors George Dix, James Treece, Elizabeth Chambliss and Lynn Blaise at the University of Texas School of Law indulged my obssessions on this topic and helped steer me towards the most fruitful avenues of inquiry. Dr. Chambliss in particular I must thank for her help with the chapter titled "Scapegoating the Jury."

The Texas Forum on Civil Liberties and Civil Rights and the Cornell Journal of Law and Politics originally published parts of this book, in edited versions, and generously allowed them to be reprinted here, and for that I am extremely grateful. Additionally, I would like to thank Elena and Eugenia Arakelova, John C. Boston, Debbie Collins, Lucille Douglass, John Farah, Rachanee "Gip" Kongsomrand, Paul C. Looney, Carol Meltzer, Pat Moore, Irina and Robert Plumlee, Professor Michael Saks, Professor Alan Scheflin and Steve Terry, all of whom inspired, encouraged or supported me in this effort. I really have to thank all of those hundreds of students, lawyers, professors, friends and acquaintances with whom I have discussed this subject. Finally, I wish to thank my wife, Yekaterina Lvovna Conrad, who has helped me in countless ways to maintain my perspective, sanity and focus.

Clay S. Conrad
Houston, TX
1998

Jury Nullification

Chapter One

Introduction

> *Trust in the jury is, after all, one of the cornerstones*
> *of our entire criminal jurisprudence, and if that*
> *trust is without foundation we must re-examine a*
> *great deal more than just the nullification doctrine.*
> *Judge David L. Bazelon*

There may be no feature more distinctive of American legal culture than the criminal trial jury. Americans have a deep and stubborn devotion to the belief that the guilt or innocence of a person accused of crime can only be judged fairly by a "jury of his peers." This notion is a particularly American one, although it was inherited from English common law during the Colonial era. While throughout the last century those European countries which had adopted them have steadily reduced or eliminated the role of trial juries,[1] we Americans have steadfastly continued using trial juries in both civil and criminal cases. Even England, where our common law system of trial by jury first evolved, has almost eliminated civil jury trials and

---

1. An exception to this trend may be occurring in Russia. Czarist Russia not only employed trial juries from 1864–1917, but had a proud history of jury independence (although they rarely employed juries in political trials). Vera Zasulich was acquitted by a jury in 1878 after attempting to assassinate General Trepov, the Governor of St. Petersburg. The jury found that although she had "perpetrated" the crime, she was not "guilty." Zasulich admitted shooting Trepov, but justified doing so because nothing had been done after Trepov ordered a prisoner at the Peter-Paul Fortress beaten half to death for failing to take off his cap when Trepov walked by. The prisoner, despairing of his situation, later committed suicide. Zasulich asserted at trial that "I didn't find, I couldn't find any other means to direct attention to this event. I didn't see any other means…It is terrible to raise one's hand against one's fellow man, but I decided this was what I had to do." *See* GODFREY LEHMAN, WE, THE JURY: THE IMPACT OF JURORS ON OUR BASIC FREEDOMS, 116 (1997).

General Trepov was considered a great favorite of Czar Alexander. Following the verdict acquitting Zasulich, Alexander eliminated the option of jury trials in political cases, although juries in Czarist Russia still decided all other criminal cases.

Soviet Russia completely eliminated jury trials following the Revolution. Since the breakup of the Soviet Union, however, Russia has again turned to trial juries in order to re-establish a link between legal authority and community values, and held its first jury trial in more than 76 years in December, 1993. *See* Stephen C. Thaman, *The Resurrection of Trial by Jury in Russia*, 31 STAN. J. INT'L L. 61 (1995).

has taken large measures to restrict the role of the jury in criminal cases.[2] We in America are far less willing to relinquish our right to have our disputes settled by a jury of our peers.

It would be exceedingly difficult to completely eliminate the institution of trial by jury in America. Besides the fact that jury trial is deeply ingrained in American tradition, history and popular culture, the right to have a jury hear and decide legal disputes is guaranteed by Art. III, § 2 of the Constitution and the Sixth Amendment in criminal cases, and by the Seventh Amendment in civil cases. Jury trial is also guaranteed in the Constitutions of every state in the Union. The Founding Fathers on both sides of the ratification debate had abundant faith in the power of the criminal trial jury to prevent governmental overreaching, as was best expressed by Alexander Hamilton:

> The friends and adversaries of the plan of the convention, if they agree on nothing else, concur at least in the value they set upon the trial by jury; or if there is any difference between them it consists of this: the former regard it as a valuable safeguard to liberty, the latter represent it as the very palladium of free government.[3]

American history is replete with similar references to the prophylactic role of the criminal trial jury. Moreover, the jury's history as an essential safeguard of liberty began centuries before the American revolution. Long before the Battle of Runnymede led to the signing of the Magna Charta in 1215, Anglo-Saxon juries were acting as the final arbiter of the guilt or innocence of the accused. British courts, after a long history of persecuting jurors for acquitting against the wishes of the Crown, finally guaranteed the independence of criminal trial juries in 1670. Early American jurors had frequently refused to enforce the acts of Parliament in order to protect the autonomy of the Colonies. The Founding Fathers inherited a well-evolved view of the role of the jury, and both adopted it and adapted it for use in the new Nation.

Even though Americans maintain a practically religious devotion to the institution of trial by jury, we remain ambivalent about what juries in criminal cases are supposed to do. We want them to impartially judge the evidence in the case before them, and to decide the case solely on the facts according to the instructions given to them by the judge. They are supposed to be able to put their personal feelings aside, and use their common sense and experience to objectively determine whether witnesses are

---

2. *See* HARRIET HARMAN AND JOHN GRIFFITH, JUSTICE DESERTED: THE SUBVERSION OF THE JURY (National Council for Civil Liberties 1979).

3. Federalist 83 (Hamilton), in ROSSITER, ED., THE FEDERALIST PAPERS, 491, 499 (Penguin 1961).

believable, whether the evidence makes sense, and whether or not the prosecution has proven its case beyond the requisite reasonable doubt. According to this model, juries are supposed to act dispassionately, almost mechanically, and apply the law given to them by the Judge without question. And, according to this "jury as fact-finder" model, that is all juries are supposed to do.

In analyzing the evidence, we want jurors to act as independent, autonomous, self-motivated individuals, deciding the facts according to their own ability, belief and understanding. Jurors are expected to be independent actors, beholden to none. However, we also find it important to ensure that all segments of society have an equal chance of participating in the process. We speak of "representative" juries, while being none too clear about who the jurors are representing, or how they are supposed to represent them. Is the straight black female Christian juror to represent the views of heterosexuals, of African-Americans, of Christians, of women, or merely her own views after hearing the facts and law involved in the case before her? We have no touchstone to measure whether the jury we have is in fact a representative one, but we do know that nothing less than the Constitution demands that it be so. Even more confusing, in some cases we are none too clear as to whether fairness and impartiality or representativeness is the more important value.

Finally, and most importantly for our purposes, we want juries to act as Alexander Hamilton's "valuable safeguard to liberty," and as the "conscience of the community."[4] The first job of a juror is to see that justice is done, or at least that injustice is prevented. We want juries to act as a safety valve, limiting the ability of the courts and legislatures to impose punishment on well meaning or morally blameless defendants, and to protect their neighbors from overreaching or oppressive laws or law enforcement. Juries do this by rendering an independent verdict, acquitting a defendant who may be factually guilty when they believe that it would be unjust, unfair or pointless to enter a conviction. In order for juries to do this, they must go beyond the "jury as fact-finder" paradigm and form an independent view of what it will take for justice to be done.

We are unable to be too clear about when jurors are supposed to judge just the facts, and when they are supposed to conscientiously intervene on behalf of the defendant. The borderline is fuzzy, and the more intently we examine it, the fuzzier it gets. We want juries to intervene on occasion; we just want them to do it on their own initiative, without any guidance, without us telling them about their power to do so and without their telling

---

4. *See* Taylor v. Louisiana, 419 U.S. 522, 529–531 (1975); *see also* United States v. Spock, 416 F.2d 165, 182 (1st Cir. 1969).

us about their decision to do so. Our awareness of the practice is somehow believed to cheapen it, to take away its dignity.

Yet hiding the jury's decision to look beyond the letter of the law miscasts it as a shameful act, something that must be kept "behind closed doors." Shouldn't juries be proud of their integrity, of their willingness to stand up for justice, even in those exceptional cases where justice and law come into conflict? Does our silence concerning the independent powers of the jury discourage jurors from returning nullification verdicts in appropriate cases? Moreover, does the clandestine nature of jury independence make it more or less likely that jurors will set the law aside in inappropriate cases, for racist, prejudicial or political reasons having nothing to do with justice?

When jurors decide not to enforce the written law and to "do justice" instead, we say that they have "nullified" the law. The power of juries to go beyond acting as mere finders of fact has been variously referred to as "jury mercy," "jury lawlessness," "jury justice," "jury nullification" or "jury veto power." In this writing I will use the terms "jury nullification" and "jury independence" interchangeably. One source reports that "Despite its routine usage in law-journal prose, the phrase [jury nullification] is both inaccurate and improperly pejorative."[5] The media has also routinely used and mis-used the term jury nullification. Whatever its defects, "jury nullification" is the term most often employed to identify this power of the jury.

It is both derisive and deceptive to refer to the discretionary powers of the jury as "jury nullification." It is derisive because it gives a very negative description of what the jury does, and it assumes that the jury is acting outside their legal powers. However, the law assumes — and occasionally, in some very important circumstances, demands — that juries do just this. Why should we describe the jury's exercise of lenity solely in negative terms? "Jury independence" provides a more descriptive and positive term to refer to the powers of the jury to reach outside the written law in deciding their verdict.

The term "jury nullification" is also deceptive. When a jury decides not to enforce a law it is the jury which nullifies that particular application of the statute, and not the jury which is nullified. And the statute is nullified only in the instant case the jury is judging; the statute itself is not struck from the books or made forever inapplicable. Perhaps the most accurate term to describe jury nullification is in fact "prosecutorial nullification." This is because when a jury returns a verdict of acquittal, it eliminates the power of the prosecutor to pursue charges against the defendant, for those acts on which they refused to convict. The awesome power of the government

---

5. JOHN GUINTHER, THE JURY IN AMERICA, 220 (1988).

over that individual, for that act, is what has been nullified by the jury's discretionary provision of lenity.

What Jury Independence Is All About

Jury independence is a simple doctrine, although in individual applications it has occasionally had dramatic and wide-ranging implications. The doctrine states that jurors in criminal trials have the right to refuse to convict if they believe that a conviction would be in some way unjust. If jurors believe enforcing the law in a specific case would cause an injustice, it is their prerogative to acquit. If they believe a law is unjust, or misapplied, or that it never was, or never should have been, intended to cover a case such as the one they are facing, it is their duty to see justice done.

In this book, I will not examine the law-judging role of civil trial juries. Jury law-judging is especially problematic in civil cases, due to the powers of judges in civil cases to direct verdicts or grant new trials. The decisions of civil juries are not final; a judge may decide to grant a judgment notwithstanding the verdict (*non obstante veredicto*, or simply "*N.O.V.*"), or to grant a "remittiture," effectively reducing the size of the jury's award. Although in a criminal case the double jeopardy clause of the Fifth Amendment to the United States Constitution prevents a defendant who has been acquitted from being prosecuted anew, there is no similar protection given in civil cases. Although the legal doctrines of *res judicata*[6] and collateral estoppel[7] may prevent an issue from being relitigated in some cases, there are no instances where a civil jury verdict is absolute and unimpeachable, as a jury acquittal in a criminal case unquestionably is.

The basis of the doctrine of jury independence is the fundamental power of criminal trial juries to deliver a general verdict of either "guilty" or "not guilty." Jurors are not obliged to justify their conclusion to the court. The verdict in a criminal case does not rest on certain "findings of fact" by the jury, as it may in civil cases; there is no need for the jury to elaborate on or justify their verdict in any way. The prosecution cannot re-indict a defendant who has been acquitted due to jury independence, without violating the constitutional prohibition against double jeopardy. Once a defendant has been acquitted, he is legally (although perhaps not factually) not guilty

---

6. *Res Judicata* means, literally, "a thing adjudicated," and is the doctrine that a final judgment is conclusive of the litigation between the parties involved.

7. Collateral estoppel, or issue preclusion, is the doctrine that the determination of facts litigated between two parties is binding on those parties in any future proceedings between them.

of the charges against him and cannot be required to stand trial for those charges again.[8]

The court may never, regardless of the strength of the evidence against the accused, direct a jury to convict. This is true even when no material fact is in dispute and the only hope for an acquittal is through the jury's mercy. The Supreme Court has held that "... although a judge may direct a verdict for the defendant if the evidence is legally insufficient to establish guilt, he may not direct a verdict for the State, no matter how overwhelming the evidence."[9] Even where there are no material (or even immaterial) facts in dispute, the decision to convict belongs solely to the jury, not to the court. The court may not so much as inquire whether the jury acquitted the defendant due to doubts about an essential element or fact, or their doubt about the justness of the law. So long as the defendant cannot be subjected to double jeopardy, it will remain within the discretion of jurors to provide absolute and irreviewable clemency. As Supreme Court Justice Oliver Wendell Holmes observed, "The judge cannot direct a verdict it is true, and the jury has the power to bring in a verdict in the teeth of both law and facts."[10]

There is probably no doctrine in the study of criminal law that is more controversial than the doctrine of jury independence. Hundreds of law journal articles on jury independence have been published; several times as many newspaper articles have appeared. While academic interest in the role of the jury has been steadily increasing in recent years, grass roots organizations have either formed specifically to promote jury independence, or participated in promoting jury independence to their members. The largest such organization is the Montana-based Fully Informed Jury Association (FIJA), formed in 1989 with affilliated organizations in 46 states. As this work will show, this debate is essentially a political and not a strictly academic or legal one, and has been raging for nearly 800 years. There is no reason to anticipate that it will ever be fully resolved, nor can it be expected to simply "go away" at any time in the foreseeable future.

Considered from a different perspective, jury independence is not controversial at all. Nobody questions what jury nullification is, or that modern courts consider it a power that juries possess, but may not rightfully

---

8. The one exception to this rule is the Dual-Sovereignty Doctrine, which allows the federal government to pursue charges against a defendant already tried on state charges stemming from the same activities. *See* United States v. Lanza, 260 U.S. 377 (1922); Abbate v. United States, 359 U.S. 187 (1959).

9. Sullivan v. Louisiana, 508 U.S. 275, 277 (1993). *See also* United States v. Martin Linen Supply Co., 430 U.S. 564, 572–573 (1977); Carpenters v. United States, 330 U.S. 395, 410 (1947).

10. Horning v. District of Columbia, 254 U.S. 135, 138 (1920).

exercise. On the surface, it appears well established that jury independence is not supposed to play any role whatsoever in modern criminal law. Jurors are expected to follow the "jury as fact-finder" model, and to mechanically apply the facts to the law as given to them by the judge. Judges admonish jurors to follow the courts' instructions to the absolute limits of their ability, and consider it a violation of their oaths when they refuse to. Every exercise of jury independence is considered wrongful, an example of "juror lawlessness" which left unchecked could lead to "anarchy." In the study of law, there are few black letter rules more firmly established than these.

Still, this alleged lawlessness by jurors remains not only unpunishable, but irreviewable and absolute. There is a dichotomy between widespread judicial distrust of the ability, motives and intelligence of jurors, and the enormous power and responsibility entrusted to them. Due to this tension, the idea has developed that juries have the "power," but not the "right," to nullify the written law. According to this position, the raw power of a jury to deliver an independent verdict is an artifact of the American guarantee of trial by jury, but it is an unfortunate artifact, and we should do whatever is possible within the Constitution to control juries and discourage the exercise of their nullification powers.[11] If jury nullification were a "right," then courts would be required to inform juries that they may nullify and would be obliged to refrain from interfering with their exercise of this right. By framing jury nullification as a dangerous raw power, courts are free from the obligation to be so candid. This work examines whether this rights/power dichotomy is either sensible or sustainable, considering the current grass-roots movements to inform jurors of their absolute discretion to refuse to convict on conscientious grounds. Further, it raises questions whether such a posture is in the interests of justice, even if it is sustainable.

We shall also examine the long history of the doctrine of jury independence, from the Magna Charta to present, with an eye toward understanding the evolutionary changes and constant pressures that exist between the legislature, the judiciary and the jury. We will trace the history of jury independence through important British precedents, across the ocean to the Colonies, and later, to the United States. We will look at the development and the authority of the juror's oath, and whether that oath is at odds with either the power of juries to nullify, or with the numerous other obligations confronting jurors. The cyclical re-emergence of jury independence in resisting unpopular and unjust laws in America will be investigated.

We shall also inquire into whether the prevailing legal view, established by the United States Supreme Court in the landmark 1895 case *Sparf et al.*

---

11. *See* United States v. Thomas et al., 116 F.3d 606, 608 (2nd Cir. 1997).

v. United States,[12] is really widely accepted, or if that decision still remains controversial. We will examine whether continuing pressure to revise judicial practices is having any effect in the courtrooms of America, and whether those changes improve or dampen the likelihood of a given verdict being a just one. We shall look at the views of many leading cases and commentators, both favoring and opposing jury independence, with the purpose of facilitating the development of a realistic, sensible and prudent set of procedures that would empower juries to exercise their important historical role as 'the valuable safeguard of liberty,' when appropriate, while being made aware of the enormous gravity of a decision to nullify the written law.

Additionally, we must examine the "dark side" of jury nullification, the recurrent charges that juries cannot be trusted in cases involving racial violence. Conventional wisdom is that Southern juries routinely acquitted lynch mobs and the murderers of civil rights workers, primarily because of the racist sentiments of those white men sitting as jurors. In this book we will take a close look at that view, with an eye towards finding out if it is exaggerated or erroneous. We shall also examine the tools that can be employed to reduce the potential for racist or otherwise partial or biased decision-making, without restraining the power of the jury to deliver an independent verdict. And because juries do not operate in a vacuum, we will examine how the behavior of juries compares with the behavior of judges, police and prosecutors, and attempt to discover whether racist outcomes are the result of racist juries, as is commonly alleged, or the result of actions taken by those other participants in the criminal justice system.

We will also need to look at the special concerns independent juries raise in capital cases. Juries have a long and often noble history of refusing to convict in capital cases, and of finding defendants facing capital charges guilty only of lesser included non-capital offenses. From the "Bloody Codes" of Elizabethan England, to our present "death-qualified" jury requirements, to the constitutional necessity of individualized sentencing, to the peculiar circumstances of *Penry v. Lynaugh*[13] and the "clumsy attempts at jury nullification"[14] made in Texas courts in order to rescue Texas capital punishment procedures from their Constitutional infirmities, the realities of independent juries have shaped and fashioned both the practices and policies of capital punishment law in America.

As important as the historical and theoretical debates may be, we must attempt to put this entire debate into a current perspective. The events of

---

12. 156 U.S. 51 (1895).
13. 492 U.S. 302 (1989).
14. *See* Rios v. State, 846 S.W.2d 310, 316–317 (Tex.Crim.App. 1992).

recent years—notably the activities of the Fully Informed Jury Association (FIJA)—have changed the nature of our debate. FIJA volunteers have distributed well over two million "True or False" brochures informing potential jurors of their power to judge the law. Organizations like the National Organization for Reform of Marijuana Laws (NORML), Operation Rescue, and Gun Owners of America have printed an unknown number of similar brochures for distribution. Newspaper articles, television news reports, talk radio programs and other educational efforts have all contributed to a growing flow of information concerning jury independence. A backlash against independent minded jurors and FIJA activists has resulted in several criminal prosecutions against both jurors and leafleters, with almost all of the cases eventually being dismissed or ending in acquittal.

Trying to keep juries in the 1990s from finding out about their power to nullify laws they find morally objectionable is like trying to keep teenagers from finding out about sex: if they do not learn about it from a responsible source, they are increasingly likely to learn about it on the streets. The debate over the role of jury independence in the criminal justice system, as it has been couched in the past, is becoming increasingly moot. Therefore, this book discusses why and how the system must come to grips with the power of jurors to judge the law. We will look at recent popular and legislative efforts to require courts to either inform jurors of their powers to nullify the law, or to allow criminal defense attorneys to do the same. There has been a landslide of jury independence legislation filed throughout this country since 1989, and the bills introduced have become increasingly sophisticated within that short period. While these bills have not yet passed both houses of any state legislature and been signed into law, it appears to be only a matter of time before one does.

Finally, we will examine the procedures and strategies criminal defense lawyers can employ under present laws to encourage independent verdicts, and what considerations are involved in designing and mounting a jury nullification defense. While the purpose of this book is not to be a "how-to" manual for criminal defense lawyers, the present system allows lawyers sufficient maneuvering room to successfully seek an independent verdict, if the lawyer is adequately prepared to take advantage of those procedures that are available. Although there has been a great deal of academic dialogue concerning jury independence as an abstraction, there has been very little dialogue concerning how the criminal defense attorney may best take advantage of the powers of the jury under present legal constraints. It is unfair and somewhat ironic that those few who are fortunate enough to be able to afford the most ingenious and creative defense counsel can take advantage of this essentially populist doctrine, while those who are left to more meager resources must oftentimes throw themselves on the mercy of the state. By having lawyers utilize procedures that are presently available, we can encourage courts and legislatures to adopt better, more straightforward methods of empowering the jury to do that task which they were intended by the Founding Fathers to perform, and which the Supreme Court has recognized as the enduring purpose of the criminal jury trial: preventing oppression by the government.

Chapter Two

The Origins of the Doctrine

It is far better that ten guilty escape
than that one innocent suffer.
Sir William Blackstone

Pre-Revolutionary History

While the origins of jury nullification are unknown, it is obvious that the doctrine has an ancient history within the common law. It is reasonable to presume that juries were independently refusing to enforce the edicts of British kings long before the Battle of Runnymede led to the signing of the Magna Charta in 1215. The nineteenth-century lawyer and historian Lysander Spooner described the pre-Magna Charta role of juries as follows:

> It is manifest from all the accounts we have of the courts in which juries sat, prior to the Magna Charta, such as the court-baron, the hundred court, the court-leet, and the county court, that they were mere courts of conscience, and that the juries were the judges, deciding causes according to their own notions of equity, and not according to any laws of the king, unless they thought them just.[1]

In his landmark work *An Essay on the Trial by Jury*, Spooner traced independent juries to the period preceding the Norman Conquest.[2] John Proffatt, a contemporary of Spooner, reported in his *Treatise on Trial by Jury, Including Questions of Law and Fact* that in early Anglo-Saxon practice there was "one body discharging the functions of both judge and jury."[3] According to one popular recent text, juries were rarely used in criminal trials before the Magna Charta, and juries of that period seldom had the

---

1. Lysander Spooner, An Essay on The Trial by Jury, 64 (1852)(emphasis in original).

2. *Id.* at 51-85.

3. John Proffatt, A Treatise on Trial by Jury, Including Questions of Law and Fact, 14 (1877) (Reprinted 1986).

right to judge the law.[4] However, the high number of the court sessions (up to nine hundred in a month), the illiteracy of the people, the fact that the few written copies of laws available were almost entirely in French and Latin, and the lack of regular and knowledgeable judicial supervision show that ancient juries by necessity would have had nothing to refer to but their own sense of justice, equity and conscience.[5]

The earliest insight we have into the operation of jury trials before Magna Charta comes from *A Treatise on the Laws and Customs of the Realm of England* written by Ranulph de Glanvill, one of the first *justiciars* appointed by William the Conqueror. Glanvill's treatise was written in 1181 during the reign of Henry II, one year after Glanvill began his nine year administration as the Chief Justiciar of England.[6]

Glanvill's treatise dealt only with the king's court. It had little to do with criminal cases except those that violated the rights of the king or the king's peace—specifically, fraudulently concealing treasure trove, homicide, arson, robbery, rape, and 'falsifying' (forgery). In criminal cases, the king's court allowed an accused to choose between disproving the charges against him in an inquest—the functional equivalent of an early grand jury or jury trial—or undergoing trial by ordeal or wager of battle.[7]

Trial by ordeal was perhaps the most often used form of trial under medieval law, and it remains as the earliest known common law form of trial. Its use in Europe dates back at least to the fourth or fifth centuries. The defendant was required to participate in some sort of painful or dangerous experiment or "ordeal" to conclusively establish his guilt or innocence. Common ordeals included the ordeals of fire, hot iron, boiling water, cold water, poison, balance, the *cornsœd* (or ordeal of the cursed morsel), and several others.[8]

Trial by ordeal typically required the accused to perform some dangerous act, such as placing his arm up to the elbow in boiling water, carrying a piece of red-hot iron in his bare hands, swallowing poison, or walking through fire. Those who were innocent, supposedly, would not be harmed by these acts, while those who were guilty would be injured or even killed. These trials were premised on a belief that divine intervention would pre-

---

4. Lloyd E. Moore, The Jury: Tool of Kings, Palladium of Liberty, 2d Edition, 39-40 (1988).

5. Spooner, *supra* note 1, 64-66.

6. Moore, *supra* note 4, 35.

7. Ranulph de Glanvill, The Treatise on the Laws and Customs of the Realm of England Commonly Called Glanvill, translated from the latin by G.D.G. Hall, Book XIV, Chapters I–VIII (1181) (Reprinted 1983).

8. See Henry Charles Lea, The Ordeal, (1973)(originally published as Part III of Henry Charles Lea, Superstition and Force, 1866).

vent harm to, or punishment of, an innocent man. The ordeal of boiling water, for example, was supposedly performed on a Catholic Priest named Jacintus in the seventh century, who reportedly kept his arm in a caldron of boiling water for two hours retrieving a floating ring. When he finally grasped the ring, he claimed that the water was cold at the bottom of the caldron, and comfortably warm at the top. When his adversary attempted to perform the same feat, the flesh was reportedly boiled off of his arm up to the elbow within moments.[9]

Other ordeals were based more clearly on the power of the faith of the accused. The *cornsœd*, for example, involved having the accused attempt to eat a small morsel of food which had been blessed through religious ceremonies, and apparently depended on the faith of the accused and his sensitivity to the exhortations of the cleric overseeing the ordeal for its efficacy.[10] If the accused was able to swallow the morsel, he was acquitted. As harmless as the *cornsœd* would appear, it is reported to have caused the death of Earl Godwin on April 15, 1053. While dining with Edward the Confessor, Godwin was accused of his brother's murder. "May god cause this morsel to choke me if I am guilty of the crime!" exclaimed Godwin. After the King blessed the bread; Godwin was unable to swallow it, and reportedly choked to death.[11]

The ordeal of the lot or of chance, on the other hand, depended on the random selection of marked tokens to determine guilt or innocence, or on some other random occurrence. Supernatural forces or the unseen hand of God were supposed to protect the righteous and punish the wicked. The ordeal of chance was actually resorted to in occasional cases well into the nineteenth century.[12]

The ordeal of cold water dates back at least to the Code of Hammurabi.[13] This ordeal was frequently applied to witches, on the principle that "It appears that God hath appointed for a supernatural sign of the monstrous impiety of witches, that the water shall refuse to receive them in her bosom that have shaken off them the sacred water of baptism."[14] Guilty people were supposed to float, innocent people to sink. Unfortunately, people who sink could potentially drown and occasionally did so, their "innocence" affirmed.

Whereas trial by ordeal was premised on a belief of divine or supernatural intervention, the wager of battle might appear to be grounded on

9. *Id.* at 32-33.

10. *Id.* at 95.

11. Francis Watt, The Law's Lumber Room, 103-105 (1896).

12. Lea, *supra* note 8, 106-112.

13. Hugh Goitein, Primitive Ordeal and the Modern Law, 54-55 (1923).

14. *Id.* at 57-58.

the primitive belief that might makes right. That appearance may be deceiving, however: Frederic William Maitland, one of England's most renowned historians, described the wager of battle as "an appeal to the God of Battles."[15] Although the wager of battle or judicial duel reportedly came to England with the Norman Conquest,[16] it was originally considered low and ungentlemanly in England, and was considered "the Frenchman's mode of trial, and not the Englishman's."[17] The first known use of the wager of battle in England was in 1077,[18] yet it only gained widespread usage after the abolition of other forms of trial by ordeal in 1215. Wager of battle as a legal form of trial was not entirely abolished in England until 1819.[19]

A final ancient form of trial was by the "wager of law," or the oaths of compurgators. The compurgators were in themselves an early form of jury, as the accused could clear himself by providing a number of 'oath-worthy' witnesses to his innocence. The usual number of witnesses required was twelve,[20] although the number could reach as high as the court felt were required. In one fifteenth century felony case, the defendant was required to provide thirty-six compurgators in order to "prove" her innocence.[21]

The wager of law was possibly the longest lived of the ancient forms of trial. The wager of law survived in England until it was officially abolished by Parliament in 1833,[22] although it was seldom resorted to after the middle of the eighteenth century. The wager of law was considered safer for the defendant than a jury trial, because the defendant was able to select his own compurgators. If an adequate number of people could be found who would swear that the defendant was innocent, he was acquitted.

During the reign of Henry II, the defendant "accused of murder, robbery, arson, coining, or harboring of felons" could not be put to trial by ordeal except by "the oaths of twelve knights of the hundred, or in default of knights by the oaths of twelve free and lawful men..."[23] The accusers were in effect another form of ancient jury (or more accurately, a precursor to

---

15. FREDERIC WILLIAM MAITLAND, THE COLLECTED PAPERS OF FREDERIC WILLIAM MAITLAND, H.A.L. Fisher, Ed. Vol. II, p. 448 (1911).

16. JAMES BRADLEY THAYER, A PRELIMINARY TREATISE ON EVIDENCE AT THE COMMON LAW, 7 (1898).

17. *Id.* at 40.

18. *Id.*

19. *Id.* at 45.

20. PROFFATT, *supra* note 3, 23-25.

21. THAYER, *supra* note 16, 26-27.

22. PROFFATT, *supra* note 3, 34.

23. *Id.* at 42.

the grand jury,[24]) required to swear to the truth of their accusation.[25] Because the accusers lacked the benefit of judicial instruction and could swear only to the facts as they knew or perceived them to be crimes, they would by necessity have had to judge the criminality of the defendant's acts according to their own perception of the law.

Although the use of the jury in criminal trials in England was encouraged by the Assize of Clarendon in 1166, it was not until after 1215 that juries were routinely used in the trial of criminal cases.[26] This was the result of two events: Pope Innocent III condemned the entire system of trials by ordeal and prohibited clerics from participation in them in the decree of the Fourth Lateran Council in Rome,[27] and the Magna Charta was signed, incorporating significant provisions guaranteeing the trial by jury. The end of the clerical participation in the trial by ordeal robbed it of its theological legitimacy, and created the need for its replacement by some other method of trial. Trial by jury apparently developed as the most acceptable substitute.[28]

To understand jury trial as guaranteed in the Magna Charta, it is important to consider the history that led King John to sign it. John is not remembered as the kindest or gentlest of English kings. One phrase characteristic of John's reign was his boast that "the law is in my mouth." Whatever the king said was the law. King John could make whatever laws he wished at any time, with or without the consent of Parliament. Judges served at the pleasure of the king and could be summarily removed at the king's whim. The English barons' intent in drafting the Magna Charta was to limit the powers of the king, which before the Magna Charta were virtually absolute.

The only substantive limitation on the power of the king before the Magna Charta, if it can be considered one, was the king's oath to maintain the "law of the land," or the common law. However, there being no impartial tribunal authorized to enforce this oath, the king was left upon his honor to obey it. When the tyranny of the king's unlimited power became,

---

24. Sir Patrick Devlin, Trial by Jury, 9 (3rd ed. 1966)(Reprinted 1988); See also Richard D. Younger, The People's Panel: The Grand Jury in the United States 1641-1941, 1 (1963).

25. Proffatt, *supra* note 3, 42.

26. Devlin, *supra* note 24, 9; Proffatt, *supra* note 3, 41; Roger D. Groot, The Early-Thirteenth-Century Criminal Jury, 5, from J.S. Cockburn and Thomas A. Green, Eds., Twelve Good Men and True (1988).

27. See Lea, *supra* note 8, 37; Watt, *supra* note 11, 104-105; Moore, *supra* note 4, 50; Devlin, *supra* note 24, 9.

28. Groot, *supra* note 26, 5.

in the case of King John, so oppressive that the barons and the people rose against him and forced him to sign the Magna Charta, we can safely assume that their intention was to place something other than an illusory limitation on the king's arbitrary power.[29]

Lysander Spooner put the question accordingly:

> Whether those haughty and victorious barons, when they had their tyrant king at their feet, gave back to him his throne, with full power to enact any tyrannical laws he might please, reserving only to a jury ("the country") the contemptible and servile privilege of ascertaining, (under the dictation of the king, or his judges, as to the laws of evidence), the simple fact whether those laws had been transgressed? Was this the only restraint, which, when they had all power in their hands, they placed upon the tyranny of a king, whose oppressions they had risen in arms to resist? ... No. ... On the contrary, when they required him to renounce forever the power to punish any freeman, unless by the consent of his peers, they intended those peers should judge of, and try, the whole case on its merits, independently of all arbitrary legislation, or judicial authority on the part of the king. In this way they took the liberties of each individual—and thus the liberties of the whole people—entirely out of the hands of the king, and out of the power of his laws, and placed them in the keeping of the people themselves. And this it was that made the trial by jury the palladium of their liberties.[30]

Various translations of the Magna Charta have been made. The original Latin text reads:

> *Nullus liber homo capiatur, vel imprisonetur, aut disseisetur, aut utlagetur, aut exuletur, aut aliquo modo destruatur; nec super eum ibimus, nec super eum mittemus, nisi per legale judicium parium suorum, vel per legem terrae.*

One authoritative translation of Article 39, the clause that nineteenth-century scholars read as supporting the trial by jury, made in 1854 by Francis Bowen, Harvard University Professor of Civil Polity and Moral Philosophy, reads as follows:

> No freeman shall be taken, or imprisoned, or disseized, or outlawed, or banished, or anyways injured; nor will we pass upon him, nor send upon him, unless by the legal judgment of his peers, or by the law of the land.[31]

Spooner notes that the words "nec super eum ibimus, nec super eum mittemus" are more properly translated as "nor will we (the king) proceed against him, nor send anyone against him with force or arms," as there is nothing in them referring to judicial action, but merely to physical or exec-

---

29. SPOONER, *supra* note 1, 20-23.

30. *Id.* at 23.

31. FRANCIS BOWEN, DOCUMENTS OF THE CONSTITUTION OF ENGLAND AND AMERICA, 11 (1854).

utive action.[32] This clause eliminates the power of the king to impose arbitrary punishment. No action can be taken against the accused (except to summon him to a trial by jury) without the prior consent of a jury of his peers.

This interpretation is supported by the words "*nisi per legale judicium parium suorum, vel per legem terrae,*" which Spooner translates as "except according to the judgment of the peers and by the law of the land." This clause grants to the peers — the jury — the power to fix the sentence, but only to the extent allowed "by the law of the land," or the common law.[33] "By the law of the land" as it is used in the Magna Charta, is best defined as the equivalent of the modern phrase "by due process of law":

> Nisi per legem terrae. But by the law of the land. For the true sense and exposition of these words, see the statute of 37 Edward III, cap. 8, where the words, *by the law of the land* are rendered *without due process of law*; for there it is said, though it be contained in the Great Charter, that no man be taken, imprisoned, or put out of his freehold, *without due process of the law; that is, by indictment, or presentment of good and lawful men, where such deeds be done in due manner, or by writ original of the common law.* Without being brought in to answer but by due process of the common law. No man be put to answer without presentment before justices, or thing of record, or by due process, or by writ original, *according to the old law of the land.*[34]

Spooner cites common-law treatises by Hallam, Coke and Blackstone to support the proposition that *vel* should be read as requiring "concurrence both of the judgment of the peers *and* the law of the land," which plainly gives peers the power to veto the law of the land.[35] By this interpretation, a jury verdict of guilty that is not in accordance with the law of the land may not lead to a judgment against the accused. The clause limits the power of a jury to enact *ex post facto* laws, while allowing the jury their full measure of authority to reach an independent verdict.

Spooner's final translation of article 39 of the Magna Charta reads as follows:

> No freeman shall be arrested, or imprisoned, or deprived of his freehold, or his liberties, or free customs, or be outlawed, or exiled, or in any manner destroyed (harmed), nor will we (the king) proceed against him, nor send any one against him, by force or arms, unless according to (that is, in execution of) the sentence of his peers, *and* (or *or*, as the case may require) the Common Law of England, (as it was at the time of Magna Carta, in 1215.)[36]

---

32. SPOONER, *supra* note 1, 26-29.
33. *Id.* at 31-33.
34. COKE, 2 INST., 50, quoted in SPOONER, *supra* note 1, 44-45 (emphasis in original).
35. SPOONER, *supra* note 1, 46-49.
36. *Id.* at 49-50.

Even when jurors were in agreement with the law, the harsh nature of medieval penalties often gave medieval English jurors an incentive to deliver an independent verdict. All felony offenses, and many misdemeanor thefts, were punishable by death, which jurors often believed was unjustly severe. Consequently, the conviction rate in the thirteenth and fourteenth centuries was very low. Although many acquittals were likely due either to failure to prove guilt, to bribery, or fear of retribution by the defendant's relations, many appear to have resulted from a reluctance to impose the death penalty for minor or forgivable offenses.[37]

In cases where the defendant had killed his victim after premeditation, convictions were obtained in about half of all cases. Where the killer had acted out of sudden provocation or in circumstances that aroused the jury's sympathies (such as the killing of the defendant's wife's paramour), jurors often altered the facts to find "self-defense," thereby granting the killer a pardon *de corsu* ("of course").[38] This "pious perjury" of refusing to convict a defendant facing what the jury considers an unjust or draconian sentence has continued to this day, and is often a factor in modern cases where mandatory minimum sentences have been imposed.[39]

The English trial by jury was not fully developed or widely accepted by the mere signing of the Magna Charta. It was at least two hundred years before it was to develop into a form easily recognizable to modern investigators, although it quickly became the regular or preferred mode for deciding guilt or innocence in routine criminal cases. The institution of the trial jury spread rapidly following the signing of the Magna Charta.[40] It was not until the mid-fourteenth century that the law required trial juries to be composed of individuals who had not served on the presenting jury[41] (a precursor to the modern Grand Jury).[42] Public prosecution and investigation began to take the place of private criminal complaints only in the mid-fifteenth century. This increasing specialization and professionalism in law enforcement and prosecution allowed the court to take more control over judicial proceedings, and partially accounted for an increase in con-

---

37. Thomas Andrew Green, Verdict According to Conscience: Perspectives on the English Criminal Trial Jury 1200-1800, 28-35, 64 (1985).

38. *Id.* at 39-46.

39. Some modern judges have allowed defendants to argue the injustice of minimum sentences to the jury, possibly as a protest against harsh mandatory sentencing guidelines. *See* United States v. Datcher, 830 F.Supp 411 (M.D. Tenn. 1993).

40. *See* Roger D. Groot, *supra* note 26, 34. ("In the short period from 1216-1222, the true trial jury was born.")

41. 25 Edward III, stat 5, c. 3 (1352).

42. Jon M. Van Dyke, Jury Selection Procedures: Our Uncertain Commitment to Representative Panels, 4 (1977).

viction rates. Jurors, however, were responsible for conducting their own investigation into the facts of the case until the mid-sixteenth century,[43] and were expected to use their own knowledge of the case in reaching a verdict well into the seventeenth century.[44]

Because early jurors were expected to be witnesses, an "incorrect" verdict was considered perjury. A trial jury delivering an erroneous verdict in a civil case could be subjected to an "attaint." An attaint was a writ to inquire as to whether a trial jury had given a false verdict, and to reverse that verdict, if false. Attaints were tried by a grand assise, consisting of twenty-four jurors. The attaint jury would receive the same evidence that was heard by the trial jury. Should the attaint jury reach a conclusion contrary to that reached by the trial jury, the trial jury could be harshly punished for its "error." An attaint could be demanded by any party suspecting an erroneous verdict in the earlier trial.[45] Attaints could be quite drastic. According to one source:

> [T]he punishment of the jury first impaneled was severe; they were immediately arrested and imprisoned, their lands and chattels were forfeited to the king, and they became for the future unworthy of credit.... Still later a more severe punishment was inflicted, that their wives and children should be turned out of their houses, which were to be demolished and their trees and meadows destroyed...[46]

Although criminal juries were not subject to the attaint, they were subject to the contempt powers of the court.[47] At least by the end of the fifteenth century and with increasing frequency during that court's existence, unfortunate jurors could be brought to answer for their verdict before the court of the Star Chamber. Juries could be harshly dealt with for a refusal to convict, although they were rarely punished for failing to acquit.[48] The Star Chamber's contempt powers were generously exercised, especially in libel cases and other cases with political overtones.

In the 1554 case of *The Trial of Sir Nicholas Throckmorton*,[49] the defendant, a knight who had openly participated in Wyatt's Rebellion, was

---

43. GREEN, *supra* note 37, 109-110.

44. One of the bases for the decision in Bushell's Case, Howell's State Trials (hereinafter referred to as How.St.Tr.) 6:999 (1670), was that the jury may have evidence not given in court.

45. *See* ANDREW HORNE, MIRROUR OF JUSTICES, 175 (early fourteenth century)(Reprinted 1903).

46. PROFFATT, *supra* note 3, 47.

47. MOORE, *supra* note 4, 71.

48. *Id.* at 72-73.

49. How. St.Tr. 1:869 (1554).

acquitted of high treason for "conspiring and imagining the death of the queen, and intending to depose and deprive her of her royal estate, and also traitorously devising to take violently the Tower of London."[50] After acquitting Throckmorton, the jurors were bound over to answer for their verdict in the Star Chamber, "whensoever they shall be charged or called."[51] The foreman of the jury beseeched the court

> I pray on, my lords, be good unto us, let us not be molested for discharging our consciences truly? We be poor merchant-men, and have great charge upon our hands, and our livings do depend upon our travails; therefore it may please you to appoint us a certain day for our appearance, because perhaps else some of us may be in foreign parts about our business.[52]

The jurors were committed to prison, and four later confessed that the verdict had been wrong. The remaining eight members of the jury were fined as much as £2,000 apiece for their intransigence.[53] These punishments inflicted on one set of jurors were predictably effective in intimidating future juries. According to the official report of the case, "[This] rigour executed upon the Jury was fatal to Sir John Throckmorton, who was found guilty upon the same evidence on which his brother had been acquitted."[54]

Throckmorton was not an isolated case. One may wonder why anyone would be willing to sit as a juror at all, considering the personal risks. The practice of punishing criminal juries for returning verdicts unsatisfactory to the Crown continued almost unabated until the 1670 trial of *Bushell's Case*.[55] This was in spite of the fact that the court of the Star Chamber was abolished in 1635, and a 1667 resolution of the Commons was passed stating "[t]hat the precedents and practices of fining or imprisoning jurors, for verdicts is illegal."[56]

---

50. PROFFATT, *supra* note 3, 53-54.

51. *Throckmorton's Case, supra* note 49, 900.

52. *Id.*

53. The reports disagree on the amounts of the fines. Proffatt writes that "[t]hree were adjudged to pay 2,000 pounds each, and the rest £200 each," (PROFFATT, *supra* note 3, 56) whereas Moore reports that "[t]he foreman and another juror…were fined £2,000 each and committed to prison. Six of the jurors were fined 1,000 marks each and sent to prison," (MOORE, *supra* note 4, 73). The report in Howell's is that three jurors were fined £2,000 each, and the other five 1,000 marks each. *Throckmorton's Case, supra* note 49, 901. Godfrey Lehman reports that the foreman and two other jurors were fined £2,000 and the other nine jurors fined £500. GODFREY LEHMAN, WE, THE JURY: THE IMPACT OF JURORS ON OUR BASIC FREEDOMS, 93-94 (1997).

54. *Throckmorton's Case, supra* note 49, 902.

55. *Bushell's Case, supra* note 44.

56. How. St.Tr. 6:995 (1667).

The power of juries to correct oppressive or unjust laws was just beginning to be explicitly recognized by the mid-seventeenth century. The first explicit argument that jurors were judges of law as well as fact was made in 1649, by the Leveller John "Free-born John" Lilburn in his trial on charges of high treason.[57] The Levellers published and distributed a large number of political tracts declaring the rights of jurors to vote according to conscience.[58] Professor Paul G. Willis has commented that

> The jury appears to have emerged as a significant check on governmental action for the first time in 1649, when John Lilburne, the Leveller leader, persuaded the jurors who tried him that the bill of attainder by which he was to be put to death was an *ultra vires* act on the part of the legislature and that they, as the representatives of the people, should deprive it of effect by acquitting him.[59]

The Levellers were considered fanatical for their opposition to a permanent government executive and their "impossible" demands for representative government chosen through universal male suffrage, broader parliamentary representation, elimination of the privileges granted to nobles and commercial monopolies, and religious tolerance. They demanded that trials be conducted in English, and that Latin and French phrases used by judges be translated so that the accused and the jurors could properly understand the proceedings. The Levellers argued that the people were the original source of all political power. They presented their proposals in a written constitution called "The Agreement of the People," which was in many ways a percursor to the Constitution of the United States.[60] The Levellers have frequently been credited with formulating "virtually all the ideas of the American Constitution and nineteenth-century democracy, including the theory of a written constitution and reserved powers, although these ideas were too new to gain widespread support immediately."[61]

---

57. GREEN, *supra* note 37, 153-199.

58. For reprints of some of the Leveller tracts see WILLIAM HALLER AND GODFREY DAVIES, THE LEVELLER TRACTS 1647-1653 (1944). Other mid-seventeenth century authors contributed to the literature urging jury independence. Among the most important were JUDGES JUDGED OUT OF THEIR OWN MOUTHES (1650) and JURORS JUDGES OF LAW AND FACT (1650) by John Jones, and JURIES JUSTIFIED (1651) by the Leveller William Walwin.

59. Paul G. Willis, *Juries and Judicial Review*, 3 WEST. POL. Q. 66 (1950).

60. COLIN RHYS LOWELL, ENGLISH CONSTITUTIONAL AND ENGLISH HISTORY, 338 (1962).

61. M.N. KNAPPER, CONSTITUTIONAL AND LEGAL HISTORY OF ENGLAND, 436 (1942).

Lilburne had twelve years earlier been brought before the Star Chamber on charges of printing and publishing seditious books.[62] After being convicted of those charges, Lilburne was tied to a cart and whipped through the streets of London, and then pilloried for two hours. During his treason trial, Lilburne had been denied an opportunity to question witnesses, and was also denied counsel after numerous requests. Lilburne believed he had no other option than to address himself to "the jury, my countrymen, upon whose conscience, integrity and honesty, my life, and the lives and liberties of the honest men of this nation, now lies; you are in law judges of law as well as fact, and [the judges] only the pronouncers of their sentence, will and mind."[63]

After one of the trial judges, Lord Keble, interjected that the jury are not judges of law, Lilburne further pressed his point, insisting that "[t]he jury by law are not only judges of fact, but of law also: and you that call yourselves judges of the law are no more but Norman intruders; and in deed and in truth, if the jury please, are no more but cyphers, to pronounce their verdict."[64] Lilburne ended his argument by exhorting "[y]ou, Gentlemen of the Jury, who now are my sole judges, I pray you take notice of [your power to judge the law]."[65] Lilburne's argument apparently provoked Justice Jermin, who complained of "how short [Lilburne's] pretended answers are of real satisfaction." It also apparently provoked the jury, who, after deliberating for only three-quarters of an hour, acquitted Lilburne of all charges.[66]

Bushell's Case: Recognition for Jury Independence

Bushell's Case was the result of a writ of *Habeas Corpus ad Subjiciendum*, brought by Edward Bushell, one of the twelve jurors who in 1670 acquitted the Quakers William Penn and William Mead of the capital offenses of unlawful and tumultuous assembly, disturbance of the peace and riot. Penn and Mead were charged with these crimes as a result of Penn's having preached in Grace Church Street to a meeting of three to

---

62. The Trial of John Lilburne and John Wharton for Printing and Publishing Seditious Books. In the Star Chamber, How.St.Tr. 3:1315 (1637).

63. The Trial of Lieutenant-Colonel John Lilburne at the Guildhall of London, for High Treason, How. St.Tr. 4:1269, 1379 (1649).

64. *Id.*

65. *Id.* at 1403.

66. *Id.*

four hundred Quakers. The meeting was held in the street because the congregation had been locked out of their meeting house by the police: in 1670 England, the Quaker religion was illegal.[67]

Official persecution of Quakers was not unusual in seventeenth century England. The 1664 Conventicles Act,[68] which modified the 1662 Quaker Act,[69] made it a crime to attend a religious meeting of five or more people unless it complied with the teachings and practices of the Anglican Church.[70] Quakers responded, in part, by writing and distributing tracts encouraging potential jurors to form their own interpretation of the law,[71] much as the Leveller John Lilburne had done more than a decade before.

There were several startling irregularities during Penn's trial.[72] Penn was denied an opportunity to read the indictment against him before entering his plea. At the beginning of the proceedings, the Lord Mayor of London Sir Samuel Starling, who also served as the presiding Judge, ordered the bailiff to place Penn and Mead's hats upon their heads. Penn and Mead were then immediately fined 40 marks apiece for disrespectfully having their hats on in court. On several occasions during the course of the trial Penn and Mead were gagged, bound or put into the 'bale-dock' for making legal arguments displeasing to the bench.[73]

Perhaps most remarkable were the jury instructions Lord Mayor Starling gave the jury:

---

67. The Tryal of Wm. Penn and Wm. Mead for Causing a Tumult..., How. St.Tr. 6:951 (1670).

The Quaker religion was even more severely repressed in the American Colonies at this time, particularly in Massachusetts. The penalty for a first offense was a severe whipping and confinement in the house of corrections with hard labor in 1654. The penalties were gradually increased, and by 1658 persons accused of being members of "this cursed sect of Quakers" were sentenced to death by hanging. JOHN D. LAWSON, LL.D., ED., 1 AMERICAN STATE TRIALS: A COLLECTION OF THE IMPORTANT AND INTERESTING CRIMINAL TRIALS WHICH HAVE TAKEN PLACE IN THE UNITED STATES, FROM THE BEGINNING OF OUR GOVERNMENT TO THE PRESENT DAYS (WITH NOTES AND ANNOTATIONS) 814-816 (1915).

68. Stat. 16 Chas. 2, c. 4 (1664).

69. Stat. 14 Chas. 2, c. 1 (1662).

70. GREEN, supra note 37, 202.

71. Id. at 203-208.

72. The trial of Penn and Mead, and the treatment Bushell and his fellow jurors were subjected to, have been dramatized in a historical novel by a modern historian. See GODFREY LEHMAN, THE ORDEAL OF EDWARD BUSHELL (1988).

73. The Tryal of Wm. Penn and Wm. Mead..., supra note 67, 955-956.

You have heard what the indictment is, It is for preaching to the People, and drawing a tumultuous Company after them, and Mr. *Penn* was speaking; if they should not be dispursed, you see they will go on; there are three or four witnesses that have proved this, that did preach there; that Mr. *Mead* did allow of it; after this, you have heard by substantial witnesses what is said against them. Now we are upon Matter of Fact, which you are to keep to, and observe as what hath been fully sworn, at your peril.[74]

The first time the jury returned with a verdict, they were divided eight for conviction to four in favor of an acquittal. Several of the justices responded by menacing the jurors and singling out Bushell in particular as a target for their insults.[75] The jury deliberated further and returned with a verdict of "Guilty of speaking in Grace-Church Street only." The Recorder, Thomas Howell, refused to accept that verdict, and the jury again retired. The third verdict was to find Penn guilty only of speaking to an assembly, and to completely acquit Mead.[76]

Recorder Howell again refused to accept the jury's verdict, and ordered the jury imprisoned "without meat, drink, fire, and tobacco" until it returned with a verdict he would accept. The next day the jury repeated its third verdict two more times, and each time it was rejected by the court. The jury in turn rejected an opportunity to return a "special verdict," telling the Court what facts they found proven, and leaving the decision as to guilt or innocence with the judges. The court refused to accept the acquittal of Mead, because it would not allow Mead to be acquitted of conspiracy and leave Penn with nobody to have conspired with.[77] On this point Penn responded that "If Not Guilty be not a verdict, then you make of the jury and Magna Charta but a mere nose of wax."[78]

The jury was again sent off to arrive at a verdict satisfactory to the court, after being threatened by the bench with starvation. On the next

---

74. *Id.* at 960-961.

75. Threats and insults addressed from the bench to Bushell include the following:

Mayor: "Sir, you are the cause of this disturbance, and manifestly shew yourself an abettor of faction. I shall set a mark upon you, Sir."

Mayor: "Sirrah, you are an impudent fellow, I will put a mark upon you." (To jury) "What, will you be led by such a silly fellow as Bushel? an impudent canting fellow?"

Mayor: "That conscience of yours would cut my throat."

Bushel: "No, my lord, it never shall."

Mayor: "But I will cut yours so soon as I can." (To jury): "Have you no more wit than to be led by such an impudent fellow? I will cut his nose."

Id. at 961-965.

76. *Id.* at 961-962.

77. *Id.* at 961-966.

78. *Id.* at 964.

day, the third without food, drink, or toilet facilities, the jury finally acquitted both Penn and Mead. Recorder Howell then exclaimed "God keep my life out of your hands,"[79] and fined the jurors forty marks apiece, ordering them imprisoned until the fine was paid. Eight of the jurors paid the fine — stiff in seventeenth-century England — and went home. Edward Bushell, along with fellow jurors John Bailey, John Hammond and Charles Milson, refused to pay the fine. All four jurors were imprisoned.

Bushell made out a writ of *Habeas Corpus ad Subjiciendum*, which was decided two and one-half months later in the Court of Common Pleas, in an opinion authored by that Court's Chief Justice John Vaughan. Chief Justice Vaughan's decision was not an unqualified acknowledgment of the right and power of juries to judge the law, however, but merely affirmed the unremarkable power of juries to decide the facts in a criminal case. The opinion was premised on the presumption that the jurors acquitted Penn and Mead because they disagreed with the court on the facts, and that the court had no authority to decide the facts of the case. Because the jury could legitimately disagree with the court over the trustworthiness of witnesses, and may have knowledge of the case not available to the court, the court could not say that the jury decided the case contrary to their legal instructions.[80] Jurors were still permitted to have some knowledge of the case learned from outside the courtroom. Nowhere in the case does Vaughan discuss what measures, if any, would be appropriate if the jury were to decide the case contrary to their legal instructions. Instead, the Justice made it plain that courts could never know whether that had or had not occurred.

Vaughan observed that if the court could punish the jury for disagreeing with the court's finding of fact, juries would be worthless:

> To what end must they undergo the heavy punishment of the villainous judgment, if after all this they implicitly must give a verdict by the dictates and authority of another man, under pain of fines and imprisonment, when sworn to do it according to the best of their own knowledge? A man cannot see by anothers eye, nor hear by anothers ear, no more can a man conclude or infer the thing to be resolved by anothers understanding or reasoning; and though the verdict be right the jury give, yet they being not assured it is so from their own understanding, are forsworn, at least *in foro conscientiae*.[81]

If the court cannot tell what facts the jury found, it cannot detect whether the jury verdict was contrary to the courts' instructions on the law. The

---

79. *Id.* at 966-967.
80. *Bushell's Case, supra* note 44, 1006, 1012.
81. *Id.* at 1012.

opinion in *Bushell's Case* held no more than that a juror could never be punished for his verdict unless it could be proven that he delivered it in bad faith. Absent evidence of bribery or perjury on the part of the juror, the only way this could be established by the prosecution would be a sworn admission on the part of the acquitting juror that he really believed the defendant had been guilty at the time he delivered his vote.

Vaughan studiously avoided addressing the issue of jury law-finding. Historian Thomas Andrew Green has commented that "Vaughan's opinion...is remarkable for how little it addressed the most volatile issues of the day...The opinion contains no hint of the struggle between bench and jury that typified many Quaker prosecutions."[82] Jurors in earlier prosecutions against Quakers under the Conventicles Act had been fined for failing to bring in a conviction, although in at least two of those cases the fines were reversed on grounds similar to those Lord Chief Justice John Vaughan was to rely on in *Bushell's Case*.[83] Even if Vaughan would not address the issue directly, his decision guaranteed jurors the practical power to deliver a verdict based on their concepts of justice, disguised within the general verdict as a finding of fact. The decision in *Bushell's Case* became a primary authority for advocates of jury independence, who tended to miss many of the details in Vaughan's subtle arguments concerning the irreviewability of jury fact-finding, and rush headlong into the implicit protection given to the practice of jury law-finding.

Fox's Libel Act: British Juries Change the Law

Vaughan's decision in *Bushell's Case* ushered in what historian John M. Beattie has referred to as "the heroic age of the English jury" during which "trial by jury emerged as the principal defense of English liberties."[84] The English bench, however, did not willingly acquiesce in the authority of jurors to deliver irreviewable acquittals free from judicial coercion. Courts rigorously separated issues of law from issues of fact, and the practice of insisting on special verdicts in criminal cases as a means of controlling and manipulating juries became increasingly routine. This practice was especially prominent in cases with political overtones — the most common of which concerned accusations of seditious libel.

---

82. GREEN, *supra* note 37, 239.

83. THAYER, *supra* note 16, 164-165, discussing Leech's Case, Th. Raymond, Rep., 98 (1664) and Wagstaffe's Case, J. Kelyng, Rep. 3d ed. 69 (1665).

84. J.M. BEATTIE, LONDON JURIES IN THE 1690's, 214, from J.S. COCKBURN AND THOMAS A. GREEN, EDS., TWELVE GOOD MEN AND TRUE (1988).

English seditious libel law considered the fact of publication the only element of a libel prosecution that concerned the jury. Whether a given publication was libelous was deemed a matter of law to be determined by the court, not the jury. Many cases, both before and after *Bushell's Case*, found the bench and the jury at loggerheads as juries stubbornly insisted on returning general verdicts. In *Rex v. Harris*[85] and *Rex v. Care*,[86] two 1680 seditious libel trials, the court instructed the jury that they had nothing to do with deciding whether the books involved were libelous or not. In *Care*, the court instructed the jurors that "If you find him guilty, and say what he is guilty of, we will judge whether the thing imports malice or no...if it doth, so that it concerns you not one farthing, whether malicious or not malicious, is plain."[87] Harris was denied an opportunity to speak to the jury;[88] it is not unlikely that he intended to attempt to persuade them to deliver a general verdict based on their view of the criminality of his actions, and not to convict him merely on the basis of his having published and sold the book at issue.

This assumption is reasonable because Harris, following in the footsteps of John Lilburne and William Penn, had published a book informing jurors of their right to judge the law.[89] The unpopular application and prosecution of seditious libel cases, alongside the acknowledged power of the jury to enter a general verdict against the instructions of the court, spawned a virtual cottage industry producing pamphlets advising jurors of their power in criminal cases. While the most often cited of these pamphlets is probably Sir John Hawles' *The Englishman's Right* (1680), many others followed. Care published *English Liberties: or the Free Born Subject's Inheritance*.[90] Many other pro-jury independence tracts were published during the late seventeenth century: *A Guide to Juries, setting forth their Antiquity, Power and Duty* (1699); first published as *A Guide to English Juries* (1682); Lord John Somers, *The Security of Englishmen's Lives, or the Trust, Power and Duty of the Grand Jurys of England* (1681); Sir John Hawles, *The Grand-Jury-man's Oath and Office Explained; and the Rights of English-Men Asserted* (1680).

These and other treatises built on the two trends of jury law-finding that had been developed since the Magna Charta: the use of juries to ame-

---

85. How. St. Tr. 7:925 (1680).

86. How. St. Tr. 7:1111 (1680).

87. *Id.* at 1128.

88. *Rex v. Harris, supra* note 85, 931.

89. HARRIS, TWENTY-FOUR SOBER QUERIES OFFERED TO BE SERIOUSLY CONSIDERED BY ALL JURIES IN CITY AND COUNTRY (1680).

90. GREEN, *supra* note 37, 258.

liorate what were commonly considered to be overly harsh penalties, and the more radical true law-finding view endorsed by William Penn and the Levellers. Often the two theories were so intertwined as to become inseparable. In *The Englishman's Right*, which Hawles wrote as a dialogue between a barrister and a potential juror, the jury is portrayed as the guardian of the Magna Charta and the laws of England; the judges and Parliament are portrayed as unreliable and subject to influence and corruption. Hawles made plain the need for juries to stand ready to override acts of Parliament that might violate traditional English liberties:

> As Juries have ever been *vested* with such *power* by Law, so to exclude them from, or *disseize* them of the same, were utterly *to defeat the end of their institution*. For then if a person should be Indicted for doing any common innocent act, if it be but clothed and disguised in the Indictment with the name of Treason, or some other high crime, and prov'd by Witnesses to have been done by him; the Jury though satisfied in Conscience that the fact is not such offense as 'tis called, yet because (according to this fond opinion) they have no power to judge of *law*, and the *fact* charg'd is fully *prov'd*, they should at this rate be bound to find him *guilty*. And being so found, the Judge pronounce sentence upon him; for he finds a convicted Traytor, &c. by his peers. And thus a certain Physician boasted, That he had *kill'd one of his patients with the best method in the world*; So here we should find an *innocent* man hang'd, drawn, and quarter'd, and all *according to law*.[91]

More conventional academic and legal treatise writers also began to accept and promulgate the doctrine of jury independence. The second edition of Giles Duncombe's *Tryals Per Pais: or the Law of England Concerning Juries by Nisi Prius &c., with a Compleat Treatise on the Law of Evidence*, published in 1682, stated with approval that :

> "[A]nd that question which has made such a noise, viz. whether a jury is finable for going against their evidence in court, or the direction of the judge? I look upon that question, as dead and buried, since Bushell's Case, in my Lord Vaughan's reports" (p. 443).[92]

The 1739 edition of the same treatise repeated the citation above, adding that "This court cannot refuse a general Verdict, if the Jury will find it; it

---

91. Sir John Hawles, The Englishman's Right: A Dialogue between A Barrister At Law and a Jury-Man, 12 (1680)(Reprinted 1978).

92. Giles Duncombe, Tryals Per Pais: or the Law of England Concerning Juries by Nisi Prius &c., with a Compleat Treatise on the Law of Evidence (2nd rev. ed., 1682), cited in Green, *supra* note 37, 260.

was so held before Justice *Wyndham*, Lent Assizes, 1681, in *Verdon's* Case, at Cambridge."[93]

Although jury refusal to enforce laws was still rare in the late seventeenth century, it was not so rare as to give the bench a feeling of security. Cases of independently-minded juries still arose often enough to give encouragement to the tract writers, and to pose a threat to the power of the judiciary. Occasionally, incidents of jury law-finding could not be avoided, as occurred in the *Seven Bishops Case*.[94] In this 1688 case the four judges on the bench were evenly divided as to whether it was libelous for seven Anglican bishops to present a petition to King James II, questioning his authority to require them to read his Declaration of Indulgence in church. While the Declaration of Indulgence superficially appeared to release Britons from the strict controls of a State church, many believed it was the first step in King James II's plans to convert England to Catholicism. Because the judges could not agree, the jury was left to decide the matter for itself after hearing the advice of the bench. The acquittal verdict was considered by many to be a vindication of the right of jurors to judge the law and return a general verdict in seditious libel cases.[95] It also made it clear that King James II's subjects would not brook royal interference with the acts of Parliament, as the Declaration of Indulgence was thought to illegally suspend laws which had been legally passed by that body.

The *Seven Bishops Case* was perhaps more important politically than almost any other in English history. Less than a year after the trial, King James II was forced to abdicate his throne and go into exile as a result of the Glorious Revolution, which culminated when James' successor (and cousin) King William III signed the "Declaration of Rights." The Declaration of Rights not only reaffirmed the rights to trial by jury, freedom of speech and freedom of religion, but further declared "that the pretended power of suspending of laws or the execution of laws by regal authority without consent of the Parliament is illegal."[96]

The early part of the eighteenth century saw a reduced number of publications advocating jury independence, alongside a reduced number of

---

93. GILES DUNCOMBE, TRIALS PER PAIS: OR, THE LAW OF ENGLAND CONCERNING JURIES BY NISI PRIUS, &C., WITH A COMPLEAT TREATISE OF THE LAW OF EVIDENCE, 250 (7th ed., 1739). From the Harry Ransom Collection, University of Texas, Austin, TX.

94. The Trial of the Seven Bishops, How. St.Tr. 12:183 (1688).

95. R.H. HELMHOLZ AND THOMAS ANDREW GREEN, JURIES, LIBEL & JUSTICE: THE ROLE OF ENGLISH JURIES IN SEVENTEENTH- AND EIGHTEENTH-CENTURY TRIALS FOR LIBEL AND SLANDER, 42-43 (1984).

96. LEHMAN, *supra* note 53, 96-99.

prosecutions for seditious libel. The 1731 conviction of a publisher named Richard Francklin for seditious libel [97] led to the reprinting of Hawles' *The Englishman's Right*, and it appeared that the debate was about to be refreshed.[98] Soon afterword, however, the Colonial New York case *Rex v. Zenger*[99] became so intertwined with English law on jury independence as to give a definite renewal to the arguments on both sides of this debate, as well as to mark jury independence as an accepted part of the American law for the next several generations.

Zenger's case was not the first Colonial case involving jury independence. Such arguments had been made in a number of earlier Colonial cases, including at least one involving a political prosecution of importance to the Crown. Unfortunately, in the treason trial of Nicholas Bayard, the jury consisted largely of Dutch-speaking New Yorkers who neither understood the law nor the evidence, as both were in English. The unfortunate defendant was quickly convicted of treason and sentenced to

> Be carried to the place from whence you came; that from thence you be carried upon an hurdle to the place of execution; that there you be hanged by the neck: that being alive you be cut down upon the earth, and that your bowels be taken from your belly, and that your privy-members be cut off, and you being alive they be burnt before your face: and that your head be cut off, and that your body be divided into four quarters; and that your head and quarters be placed where our lord the king shall assign.[100]

The 1735 trial of the German printer John Peter Zenger for seditious libel gave rise to a radical argument for jury law-finding by the celebrated Philadelphia attorney Andrew Hamilton.[101] The charges against Zenger stemmed from his printing of *The New York Weekly Journal*, which was probably written by Zenger's attorney James Alexander and others. The paper was harshly critical of William Cosby, the royally appointed Colonial Governor of New York, and of his appointments to the Supreme Court

---

97. Rex. v. Richard Francklin, How. St.Tr. 17:625 (1731).

98. GREEN, *supra* note 37, 321.

99. How. St. Tr. 17:675 (1735).

100. The Trial of Colonel Nicholas Bayard, How. St.Tr. 14:471, 502-505, 516 (1702).

101. Many law journal and newspaper articles have erroneously attributed the defense of this case to Alexander Hamilton; *see*, e.g., David C. Brody, *Sparf and Dougherty Revisited: Why the Court Should Instruct the Jury of its Nullification Right*, 33 AM.CRIM.L.REV. 89, 94 (1995). However, Alexander Hamilton was no relation to Andrew Hamilton and was not born until 1755, twenty years after Rex v. Zenger was tried.

of New York. Unable to prove the authorship of the offensive sections, the Attorney General brought seditious libel charges against the printer Zenger before the Grand Jury.

The Attorney General's problems began with the Grand Jury, which steadfastly refused to issue an indictment. Not to be discouraged, he entered an information for libel, and the New York Assembly ordered Zenger's papers burnt in public. Because the public hangman refused to perform the function, the Attorney General had his own slave set fire to Zenger's papers. Zenger himself was arrested and imprisoned for several months before trial.

Zenger was originally represented by James Alexander and William Smith, both of whom were vocal opponents of the Governor's administration. The arraignment ended quickly, when Alexander and Smith entered a motion objecting to the commissions of the Supreme Court Justices, as they were appointed to serve at the "will and pleasure" of the Governor. Smith argued that such a commission biased the Justices, and made them little more than agents of the Governor—in effect, parties to the case.[102] Chief Justice Delancey answered those arguments by disbarring Smith and Alexander, commenting that "you have brought it to that point, that either we must go from the bench, or you from the bar; therefore we exclude you and Mr. Alexander from the bar..."[103] John Chambers, a member of the Governor's party, was appointed to represent Zenger. A jury trial was scheduled for almost four months later. Zenger was sent back to his cell to await trial.

Under New York law, jurors names were supposed to have been selected out of the 'freeholder's book,' in the presence of Zenger's attorney. At first, the clerk of courts gave Chambers a list of pre-selected names that he claimed were drawn from that book. Many of them were not freeholders; included were the Governor's appointees and servants and persons who had been criticized in Zenger's *Journal*. Chambers had to appeal to the court to receive a jury selected according to law. At trial, the list was again tampered with, and once again Zenger's attorney had to apply to the court for a jury that was not 'stacked.'[104]

Andrew Hamilton was asked to travel from Philadelphia to defend Zenger, and he agreed. He was regarded as the most skilled attorney in the Colonies; and was purportedly the only American admitted to the Inns of Court in London. His credentials included serving as Speaker of the

---

102. *Rex v. Zenger, supra* note 99, 683-686.
103. *Id.* at 686.
104. *Id.* at 689-690.

Assembly in Pennsylvania, representing the family of William Penn, and designing the building now known as Independence Hall in Philadelphia.[105] His arguments in the Zenger case drew from the radical side of the jury independence arguments. Hamilton left it to the jury to decide whether the law which Zenger was accused of violating was in fact the law of the land.

Hamilton began the trial by admitting what the court considered to be the only relevant fact in the case: that Zenger published *The New York Weekly Journal*. Hamilton, however, denied that there was anything libelous in the *Journal*, and thus asserted that his client had to be acquitted. According to Chief Justice Delancey, it was up to the bench, and not the jury, to determine whether the *Journal* was in fact libelous, so Hamilton by necessity addressed his arguments to the jury. As the information accused Zenger of publishing "a certain false, malicious, seditious and scandalous libel," Hamilton argued that the prosecution needed to prove that the statements in the *Journal* were in fact false. "This word false must have some meaning, or else how came it there?"[106] Should the Attorney General be able to prove the statements false, Hamilton was willing to concede they were malicious, seditious and scandalous. When the Attorney General was not willing or able to prove the statements false, Hamilton offered to prove them true.

Chief Justice Delancey ruled that "You can not be admitted...to give the truth of a libel in evidence, a libel is not to be justified; for it is nevertheless a libel that it is true."[107] In fact, the court was of the opinion that the truth of a libel aggravated the crime. Hamilton turned his arguments to the jury. If he could not present his evidence and prove the facts at issue, the jury, according to Hamilton, owed it to his client to give him the benefit of the doubt. They should consider the fact to have been proven:

> Then, gentlemen of the jury, it is to you we must now appeal, for witnesses to the truth of the facts we have offered, and are denied the liberty to prove; and let it not seem strange, that I apply myself to you in this manner; I am warranted so to do, both by law and reason. The law supposes you to be summoned out of the neighbourhood where the fact is alleged to be committed; and the reason of your being taken out of the neighbourhood is, because you are supposed to have the best knowledge of the fact that is to be tried. And were you to find a verdict against my client, you must take upon you to say, the papers referred to in the information, and which we acknowledge we printed and published, are false, scandalous and seditious; but of this I can have no apprehension. You are

---

105. VINCENT BURANELLI, THE TRIAL OF PETER ZENGER, 51-52 (1975).
106. *Rex v. Zenger, supra* note 99.
107. *Id.* at 699.

citizens of New York: you are really, what the law supposes you to be, honest and lawful men; and according to my brief, the facts which we offer to prove were not committed in a corner; they are notoriously known to be true; and therefore in your justice lies our safety.[108]

The Court attempted to instruct the jury to return a special verdict on the question of whether Zenger actually published the papers. Hamilton was adamant that the jury could not be bound by this instruction:

Mr. Chief Justice. No, Mr. Hamilton, the jury may find that Mr. Zenger printed and published those papers, and leave it to the Court to judge whether they are libellous. You know this is very common: it is in the nature of a Special Verdict, where the jury leave the matter of law to the Court.

Mr. Hamilton. I know, may it please your honour, the jury may do so; but I do likewise know they may do otherwise. I know they have the right, beyond all dispute, to determine both the law and the fact; and where they do not doubt of the law, they ought to do so. This of leaving it to the judgment of the Court, whether the words are libellous or not, in effect renders juries useless (to say no worse) in many cases.... [109]

Turning his attention to the jurors, Hamilton continued:

Gentlemen, the danger is great, in proportion to the mischief that may happen through our too great credulity. A proper confidence in a court is commendable; but as the verdict (whatever it is) will be yours, you ought to refer no part of your duty to the direction of other persons. If you should be of opinion, that there is no falsehood in Mr. Zenger's papers, you will, nay, (pardon me for the expression) you ought to say so; because you don't know whether others (I mean the Court) may be of that opinion. It is your right to do so, and there is much depending upon your resolution, as well as upon your integrity.[110]

Chief Justice Delancey was vexed by Hamilton's unorthodox arguments. Delancey's control over the jury had been minimized by several factors, Hamilton's eloquence being perhaps the least of them. The Court of the Star Chamber, which had been eliminated less than one hundred years before, was still a powerful legend, with many American immigrants having fled England to avoid the style of "justice" that particular court represented. American independence and stubbornness, and the Colonial desire to be free of English domination and royally appointed governors were still in the fledgling stages, but were certainly not without influence. The unpopularity of the governor and his administration, as well as the popularity

---

108. *Id.* at 703-704.
109. *Id.* at 706.
110. *Id.* at 719-720.

of Zenger's paper itself, guaranteed a good deal of sympathy from the jury. By the end of the trial, the court had foregone their insistence on a special verdict, although not abandoning all hopes for one:

> Gentleman of the jury, the great pains Mr. Hamilton has taken to shew how little regard juries are to pay to the opinion of judges, and his insisting so much upon the conduct of some judges in trials of this kind, is done, no doubt, with a design you should take but very little notice of what I may say upon this occasion. I shall therefore only observe to you, that as the facts or words in the information are confessed, the only thing that can come in question before you is, whether the words, as set forth in the information, make a libel: and that is a matter of law, no doubt, and which you may leave to the Court....
>
> Now you are to consider, whether these words I have read to you do not tend to beget an ill opinion of the administration of the government; to tell us, that those that are employed know nothing of the matter, and those that do know are not employed. Men are not adapted to offices, but offices to men, out of a particular regard to their interest, and not of their fitness for the places. This is the purport of these papers.[111]

The jury acquitted Zenger after only brief deliberations. James Alexander's account of the case, *A Brief Narrative on the Case and Tryal of John Peter Zenger, Printer of the New York Weekly Journal,* was first published in 1736.[112] It contained the most complete transcript available of the trial,[113] and is essentially the same report of the trial that appears in the official record.[114] According to the editor of the most widely circulated recent American reprint, Alexander's *Brief Narrative* was "the most famous publication issued in America" in the Colonial era.[115]

The reverberations of Hamilton's defense arguments continued both in America and in England for many years. Up through the early post-Revolutionary years Hamilton's view of the role of juries gained wide acceptance in America among both the public and the courts, for reasons that will be discussed later. In England, one of the immediate repercussions of

---

111. *Id.* at 722-723.

112. Paul Finkelman, The Zenger Case: Prototype of a Political Trial, 36, from American Political Trials, Michael R. Belknap, Ed. (1981).

113. *Id.*

114. *Rex v. Zenger, supra* note 99, contains these remarks in a footnote: "This trial (or rather part of a trial) published by Mr. Zenger himself, having made a great noise in the world, is here inserted; though the doctrines advanced by Mr. Hamilton in his speeches, are not allowed in the courts to be law."

115. *See* James Alexander, A Brief Narrative on the Case and Trial of John Peter Zenger, Stanley Katz, Ed., 37 (2d ed., 1972).

these arguments was a renewal of the tract literature of the middle and late seventeenth century.

One of the first and most powerful rejoinders to Hamilton's arguments in defense of Zenger was written by an author who only identified himself as Anglo-Americanus, and appeared in the July, 1737 edition of Keimer's *Barbados Gazette*. Anglo-Americanus discussed Hamilton's arguments from the viewpoint of a moderate British lawyer. This attack was based more on Hamilton's view that the truth could be used as a defense in a charge of libel than on Hamilton's addressing himself primarily to the jury, and not the court. He criticized Hamilton's use of precedent and history, accusing the trial judge of being too young and inexperienced to stand up to the elder and more knowledgeable Hamilton. Anglo-Americanus correctly recognized that Hamilton's defense of Zenger was aimed more at the political than at the legal sensibilities of the jury, and argued that Colonial subjects should file suit in the courts of London for redress when subjected to a bad administration at home, an argument Hamilton had addressed and rejected at trial.[116] This was followed by a second letter on the same theme written by Indus-Brittanicus, which reportedly "lack[ed] the quality and erudition of the first."[117]

James Alexander answered Anglo-Americanus' criticisms with a series of articles appearing in Benjamin Franklin's *Philadelphia Gazette* from November 10 to December 8, 1737. Unlike his adversary, Alexander thought it was legitimate to rely on the political aspects of the case. Alexander emphasized the fundamentally political nature of liberty of the press, the evil results emanating from strict libel prosecutions, and the inviolability of natural rights and liberties.[118] The shape of the jury independence doctrine espoused by Hamilton was becoming clearer through the arguments it engendered than it would have if it had itself been the subject of dispute: Hamilton was claiming for the jurors the right to refuse to be a part of a manifest injustice, according to their own consciences and perspectives. To exercise this independent ethical judgment, as both Anglo-Americanus and James Alexander implicitly acknowledged, is to exercise a political power. The essentially political nature of the argument was underlined in a letter published in Franklin's *Philadelphia Gazette* from a British lawyer who wrote of Hamilton's argument that "[i]f it is not law, it is better than law, it ought to be law, and will always be law wherever justice prevails."[119]

---

116. ALEXANDER, *supra* note 115, 152-180.
117. FINKELMAN, *supra* note 112, 36.
118. ALEXANDER, *supra* note 115, 181-202.
119. BURANELLI, *supra* note 105, 53.

In England, news of Zenger's trial spread through the Inns of Court and was considered an anomaly, albeit a dangerous one. Anglo-Americanus' retorts from the *Barbados Gazette* were reprinted in America in a 1737 pamphlet entitled *Remarks on Zenger's Tryal, taken out of the Barbados Gazette for the Benefit of Students in Law, and others in North America*, and reprinted again the next year in London under the title *Remarks on the Trial of John-Peter Zenger*.[120] It is questionable whether the single British printing of that pamphlet was very effective, in light of the fact that Alexander's *Brief Narrative* was available in at least four, and possibly five, British editions in that year, with a total of at least nine editions appearing in Britain before 1784.[121]

Prosecutions for seditious libel began to falter with increasing consistency. Of several major late eighteenth-century English libel prosecutions,[122] the prosecution was able to obtain convictions in only two cases, in spite of "clear evidence of publication" in at least one of the acquittals.[123] In the meantime, possibly spurred on by the demand for copies of Alexander's *Brief Narrative*, the trickle of tract literature that had begun to reappear during the early part of the century had turned into a flood.

One well-known pair of tracts attributed to the same author are *A Letter concerning Libels, Seizure of Papers, and Sureties for the Peace or Behaviour*, and *An Enquiry into the Doctrine Lately Propagated Concerning Libels, Warrants and the Seizure of Papers* reportedly written by 'The Father of Candor,' variously speculated to be John Almon, Lord Chancellor Camden and/or Lord Ashburton.[124] Joseph Towers' *An Enquiry into the question Whether Juries are, or are not, Judges of Law As well as of Fact, With a particular reference to The Case of Libels* was printed in 1765, followed by his *Observations on the Rights and Duty of Juries in Trials for Libels* (1786). Many other tracts, urging wider jury powers in libel cases, were written by authors such as John Almon, John Wilkes, Francis Maseres, Henry Woodfall, John Lambert, Morris Robert, Will Owen, George Rous, Thomas Leach and others. Many of these authors had personally been defendants in prosecutions for seditious libels. Typical of the tracts insisting on general verdicts in libel prosecutions was the Father of Candor's statement that

---

120. FINKELMAN, *supra* note 112, 36-37.

121. *Id.* at 37.

122. Rex v. Owens, How. St.Tr. 18:1203 (1752)(acquittal), Rex v. Wilkes, How. St.Tr. 19:1075 (1770)(conviction), Rex v. Almon, How. St.Tr. 20:803 (1770)(conviction), Rex v. Woodfall, How. St.Tr. 19:895 (1770)(hung jury—never retried), Rex v. Miller, How. St.Tr. 20:869 (1770)(acquittal), Rex v. Stockdale, How. St.Tr. 22:237 (1789)(acquittal).

123. GREEN, *supra* note 37, 322-324.

124. *Rex v. Zenger*, *supra* note 99, 725-726 (1735).

In good faith, no Englishman should be construed or innuendoed into a fine or a jail even by a Jury, much less by a Judge, without any trial whatever by his peers. Who is meant or what is meant by any writer is in every case to be resolved by his Country. No affidavits will serve the purpose. And, whenever a contrary doctrine shall take place, the Constitution of this Country will soon be destroyed, and the liberty of every man in it lie at the mercy of his Majesty's Judges. Is this what any man desires or will yet a while endure?[125]

This tract warfare was waged with formidable offensives from both sides. W. Nicoll responded to the Father of Candor:

I cannot therefore approve of any Instance where the Jury, contrary to the Directions of the Judge in Point of Law (for I think Directions ought to be confined solely to Points of Law) pronounces a general Verdict; it is acting contrary to what as to them is the Law, or at least the best Evidence of it; it is therefore contrary to their Oath. If it were possible in any Case to suppose not only the Judges of *England*, and even the House of Lords, to be in any Matter of Law corrupt, or under other Undue Influence; yet even that would not authorize a Jury to assume to themselves a jurisdiction which the Law does not allow to them, or to pronounce contrary to that Evidence, to which they are bound by their Oath. Much, therefore, as I revere those excellent Qualities of private Virtue, by which Juries were activated, in the Case of the seven Bishops, to step forth, in Opposition to arbitrary Power, as the Guardians of persecuted Innocence, yet even there I must think they acted *illegally and unconstitutionally*, by giving a general Verdict on the Law (for the Facts were not disputed) contrary to the Directions of the Judge. They ought to have given a special Verdict; and if they had, we may be well assured from the Temper of Parliament at that Time, that the Bishops would have received, constitutionally, from the House of Lords, the same Justice, of which the well-meant Zeal of the Jury had assumed to themselves the Distribution.[126]

Nicoll was apparently on the losing side of this argument, at least insofar as prosecutions for seditious libel were concerned. Even by responding in the negative he gave additional publicity and acknowledgement to the opposing side of the argument. By the time Nicoll's tract was published, almost one and one-half centuries had passed since the Levellers

---

125. Father of Candor, A Letter concerning Libels, Seizure of Papers, and Sureties for the Peace or Behaviour, 157 (1771).

126. W. Nicoll, Considerations on the Legality of General Warrants and the Propriety of a Parliamentary Regulation of the Same; To Which is Added a Postscript on a Late Pamphlet concerning Juries, Libels, & C. 42-43 (3d Ed., 1765). From the Harry Ransom Collection, University of Texas, Austin, TX.

had first attempted to sway public opinion, and thus the opinions of jurors, by firing the first salvos in this tract warfare. Events across the sea had added to the fray, and there had still been no clear winner, if one could be imagined. But in a sense there had been a clear winner and that had been pro-jury rights, at least in seditious libel prosecutions. Because one juror could block a conviction, it was not necessary to gain a resounding legal victory. Thus, it was somewhat amazing that the government managed to obtain a conviction (that was later overturned for defects in the indict-ment) in the unusual case of *Rex v. Shipley*,[127] popularly known as the *Dean of St. Asaph's Case.*

William Davies Shipley, otherwise known as the dean of St. Asaph's, was arrested for selling a book written by his brother in law, Sir William Jones. At the time of the trial Sir William was acting as a Justice for the Crown in Bengal, a position from which he presumably would have been removed had he in fact been the author of a seditious writing. Sir William was not charged with libel, but his brother-in-law, the seller, was. The jury originally returned a verdict of "guilty of publishing only," which left the dean not guilty of seditious libel. After pressure was applied from the bench, this general verdict was changed to a special verdict, "guilty of pub-lishing, but whether a libel or not the jury do not find."[128] The defense attorney, the Honourable Thomas Erskine, in his motion for a new trial, gave a resounding argument in favor of the rights of juries which occu-pies over one hundred pages in his collected speeches.[129]

Erskine's argument focused on the respective responsibilities of the judge and the jury in libel cases. The principal grounds of his arguments were that the jury could not enter a verdict of guilty unless all the elements of which guilt necessarily consisted had been put forth for their consideration. Because the court had refused to allow the jury to consider the issues of fal-sity, intent and malice, the jury could not enter a valid general verdict of guilty. No evidence had been allowed to go to the jury for its consideration on these points.

The *Dean of St. Asaph's Case* is most notable for Lord Mansfield's sep-aration of the concepts of 'power' and 'right', in describing the juror's pre-rogative to judge of the law. Mansfield admitted that it could be admirable for jurors, in an especially egregious prosecution, to exercise this confessed power of rendering an independent verdict, but he would not admit that

---

127. How. St.Tr. 21:847 (1785).

128. *Id.* at 950-955.

129. 1 Speeches of the Honourable Thomas Erskine on the Liberty of the Press, James Ridgway, Ed., 264-364 (1810)(Reprinted 1974).

the power was raised to the level of a right.[130] This rights versus powers dichotomy has persisted to this day, in both British and American law.

The court was not unanimously in support of Lord Mansfield's doctrine. Justice Willes, in dissent, specifically defended the right of jurors to judge the law.

> I believe no man will venture to say they have not the power, but I mean expressly to say they have the right. Where a civil power of this sort has been exercised without control, it presumes — nay, by continual usage, it gives — the right. It is the right which jurors exercised in those times of violence when the Seven Bishops were tried, and which even the partial judges who then presided did not dispute, but authorized them to exercise upon the subject-matter of the libel; and the jury, by their solemn verdict upon that occasion, became one of the happy instruments, under Providence, of the salvation of this country. This privilege has been assumed by the jury in a variety of ancient and modern instances, and particularly in the case of Rex v. Owen, without any correction or even reprimand of the court. It is a right, for the most cogent reasons, lodged in the jury, as without this restraint the subject in bad times would have no security for his life, liberty or property.[131]

The question of whether the discretion of a juror in libel cases amounted to a right or a power quickly gained the attention of Parliament. In 1791 a bill was introduced to clarify and resolve the intractable dilemma which had arisen over the past one hundred and fifty years, by explicitly granting jurors the right to decide whether a publication was in fact libelous. Mr. Fox's Libel Act,[132] named after its author, Whig statesman Charles James Fox, was intended to eliminate the confusion and litigation that had arisen as a result of seventeenth and eighteenth century libel doctrines. The bill was hotly debated, and engendered a large tract literature of its own. Thomas Leach argued for the bill on the grounds that the jury had the prerogative of determining the criminality of a libel, that the truth of an alleged libel was a legitimate defense, and finally on the grounds that restraining criticism of government prohibits the discussion necessary for understanding and improving public administration.[133] Other tracts, including an entire series written by John Bowles, warned of the "Alarming Con-

---

130. *Rex v. Shipley, supra* note 127, 1033.

131. *Id.* at 1040-1041 (1785). *See also* Sparf et al. v. United States, 156 U.S. 51, 133-134 (1895).

132. St. 32 Geo. III c. 60 (1792).

133. *See* THOMAS LEACH, CONSIDERATIONS ON THE MATTER OF LIBEL SUGGESTED BY MR. FOX'S NOTICE IN PARLIAMENT OF AN INTENDED MOTION ON THAT SUBJECT (1791).

sequences Likely to Ensue, if the Bill now before the Legislature should Pass into Law."[134] Mr. Fox personally argued for the bill on the grounds that

> '[I]f a power was vested in any person, it was surely meant to be exercised'; that 'there was a power vested in the jury to judge the law and fact, as often as they were united, and, if the jury were not to be understood to have a right to exercise that power, the constitution would never have intrusted them with it'; 'but they knew it was the province of the jury to judge of law and fact, and this was the case, not of murder only, but of felony, high and of every other criminal indictment'; and that 'it must be left in all cases to a jury to infer the guilt of men, and an English subject could not lose his life but by a judgment of his peers.'[135]

The final bill adopted most of the positions that Justice Willes had argued for in *Rex v. Shipley*. Fox's Libel Act acknowledged the right of the jury to judge the whole matter at issue including intent and maliciousness, and

> [T]herefore declared and enacted that on every such trial the jury sworn to try the issue may give a general verdict of guilty or not guilty upon the whole of the matter put in issue upon such indictment or information; and shall not be required or directed, by the court or judge before whom such indictment or information shall be tried, to find the defendant or defendants guilty, merely on the proof of the publication by such defendant or defendants of the paper charged to be a libel, and of the sense ascribed to the same in such indictment or information.[136]

Fox's Libel Act was adamantly contested in Parliament and in the House of Lords, and credit for its passage must go largely to Lord Camden. The passage of this bill was one of the last acts of Lord Camden's long career, and became a personal crusade. Camden argued that the distinction between law and fact in libel cases was an illusion. He saw no difference between intent and malice in libel and in murder, and maintained that they must as necessarily be proven in one as in the other for a conviction to be obtained. And, as malice and intent were questions of fact, they had to be determined by the jury and could not be proclaimed by the judge. He went so far as to contend that:

> [T]he jury had an undoubted right to form their verdict themselves according to their consciences, applying the law to the fact. If it were otherwise,

---

134. John Bowles, A Letter to the Right Hon. Charles James Fox, (1792). *See also* A Second Letter to the Right Hon. Charles James Fox, (1792), Brief Deductions from First Principles applying to the Matter of Libel, (1792).

135. *Sparf et al., supra* note 131, 136, citing 29 Parl. Hist. 564, 565, 597.

136. *Supra* note 132.

the first principle of the law of England would be defeated and overthrown. If the twelve judges were to assert the contrary again and again, he would deny it utterly, because every Englishman was to be tried by his country; and who was his country but his twelve peers, sworn to condemn or acquit according to their consciences? If the opposite doctrine were to obtain, trial by jury would be a nominal trial, a mere form; for, in fact, the judge, and not the jury, would try the man. He could contend for the truth of this argument to the latest hour of his life, *manibus pedibusque*. With regard to the judge stating to the jury what the law was upon each particular case, it was his undoubted duty so to do; but, having done so, the jury were to take both law and fact into their consideration, and to exercise their discretion and discharge their consciences.[137]

With all the dissension and acrimony on both sides of this debate, it is worthwhile to note that the act was considered, in retrospect at least, merely declaratory of the existing law. Lord Holt, in his work entitled *The Law of Libel*, described Fox's Libel Act:

The statute of 32 Geo. III chap. 60, is the only act of parliament which at all touches the question of the liberty of the press since the 10th Geo. II. This statute is generally considered as restorative of the common law, and therefore merely declaratory. It enacts, that in an indictment or information for a libel, where issue is joined on the defendant's plea of not guilty, the jurors may give a general verdict on the whole matter, and the judge shall not require them to find the defendant guilty, merely on the proof of publishing, and on the sense ascribed to the supposed libel in such complaint or information. The statute is wholy silent as to actions of scandalum magnatum, or for a libel.[138]

The century and a half battle for British jury rights in libel cases ended with, if not a resounding one, at least a partial victory on the side of the jurors. Fox's Libel Act was relatively conservative and said nothing about a juror's right to nullify an unjust law, but merely re-established the right of juries to render a general verdict in libel cases as in all other criminal cases. The act held closely to the reasoning of *Bushell's Case*, granting jurors the right to bring in a general verdict free of coercion and undue influence from the bench. But it was easily acknowledged (and in some quarters looked on with marked trepidation) that jurors could with impunity refuse to convict libelers, merely out of sympathy or due to a shared antipathy towards the Crown or the policies being impugned.

The legacy of the Libel Act, however, was not one of allowing libelers to escape with impunity. It probably came as a marked surprise to Lords Mansfield, Thurlow, Kenyon and other opponents of the bill that convic-

---

137. *Sparf et al., supra* note 131, 139, citing 29 PARL. HIST.1535, 1536.
138. FRANCIS L. HOLT, THE LAW OF LIBEL, 44 (2d ed., 1812)(Reprinted 1978).

tion rates in prosecutions for libel actually increased after passage of the Act. It is not unlikely that advocates of free speech, having exhausted their resources in obtaining the passage of Fox's Libel Act, were no longer able to mount strong defenses for those accused of maligning the crown, or that the recent loss of the American Colonies united Britons in defense of their government and its officials. It is also possible that many unpopular cases were simply never prosecuted.

In any case, Fox's Libel Act represents a clear case where independent jurors, in conjunction with a relentless campaign to publicize their rights and authority, forced the government of England to change what had previously been considered to be an uncontroversial legal rule supported by a long line of precedent. These juries, by exercising the power implicit in the delivery of the general verdict, had demanded and received official recognition of their right to judge whether an alleged libel was in fact false, malicious and intentional.

Chapter Three

Revolutionary Times

> *The execution of laws is more*
> *important than the making of them*
> *Thomas Jefferson*

Georgia v. Brailsford:
A Unanimous Supreme Court Instruction

In America, the legacy of the *Zenger* case survived long after the Revolutionary War. Colonial Americans had a long history of using independent juries as a method for peacefully opposing arbitrary British rule. In response to this history, the Crown transferred entire classes of cases from the common law courts to the maritime courts, where a defendant had no right to trial by jury.[1] British misuse of maritime courts finally led colonists to include into the Declaration of Independence a complaint against the Crown "For depriving us, in many Cases, of the Benefits of Trial by Jury."

But there were many reasons other than history to explain why the rights of jurors were strictly defended following the Revolution. Judges were likely to be poorly trained in the law, if in fact they could boast of any legal education whatsoever.[2] Concepts of natural law and natural right remained very much a part of the popular legal culture, implying that a well-intentioned citizen should be able to derive a just and perfectly legal result without too much supervision, instruction or interference from the bench. One author has commented that:

> Underlying the conception of the jury as a bulwark against the unjust use of governmental power were the distrust of 'legal experts' and a faith in the ability of the common people. Upon this faith rested the prevailing political philosophy of the constitution-framing era: that popular control over, and participation in, government should be maximized. Thus John Adams stated that 'the common people...should have as complete a con-

---

1. *See* Albert W. Alschuler and Andrew G. Deiss, *A Brief History of Criminal Jury in the United States*, 61 U. CHI. L.REV. 867, 874-875 (1994).

2. LAWRENCE M. FRIEDMAN, HISTORY OF AMERICAN LAW, 125-126 (1985).

trol, as decisive a negative, in every judgment of a court of judicature' as they have, through the legislature, in other decisions of government.[3]

Perhaps even more importantly, a history of British domination made early American jurors insistent upon popular control over how the law was to be applied. Colonial Americans had found jury service to be one of their most effective protests against the unjust laws imposed by Parliament, and they had only limited confidence in their own legislature and public officials. American citizens had recently fought a victorious war against the most powerful nation on earth in order to gain the right to govern themselves, and concerns over the presidency turning into a monarchy had not been completely put to rest. It was unlikely that these citizens would be too willing to hand over their legal system to a political and judicial elite without retaining some authority to judge the results and veto any potential acts of usurpation, tyranny or oppression.

The Sixth Amendment itself implicitly recognizes the right of criminal trial jurors to judge the law. Although it does not mention that power explicitly, it can logically be assumed that the definition of a jury used in that document would be consonant with the prevailing definition in the legal dictionaries of the period. The most common legal dictionary in Colonial Virginia was the British *Jacob's Law Dictionary*;[4] and within the encyclopedic definition given in *Jacob's*, the word 'jury' is defined as:

> Jury (jurata, from the LAT. jurare, to swear) Signifies a certain number of men sworn to inquire of and try the matter of fact, and declare the truth upon such evidence as shall be delivered them in a cause: and they are sworn judges upon evidence in matter of fact.
>
> The privilege of trial by jury, is of great antiquity in this kingdom; some writers will have it that juries were in use among the Britains; but it is more probably that this trial was introduced by the Saxons: yet some say that we had our trials by jury from the Greeks; (the first trial by a jury of twelve being in Greece.) By the laws of King Ethelred, it is apparent that juries were in use many years before the Conquest; and they are, as it were, incorporated with our constitution, being the most valuable part of it; for without them no man's life can be impeached, (except by parliament) and no man's liberty or property can be taken from him...
>
> Juries are fineable, if they are unlawfully dealt with to give their verdict; but they are not fineable for giving their verdict contrary to the evidence, or against the direction of the court; for the law supposes the jury may have some other evidence than what is given in court, and they may not

---

3. Note, *The Changing Role of the Jury in the Nineteenth Century*, 74 YALE L.J. 170, 172 (1964).

4. WILLIAM HAMILTON BRYSON, CENSUS OF LAW BOOKS IN COLONIAL VIRGINIA, XVI (1978).

only find things of their own knowledge, but they go according to their consciences. Vaugh. 153, 3 Leon 147.

If a jury take upon them the knowledge of the law, and give a general verdict, it is good; but in cases of difficulty, it is best and safest to find the special matter, and to leave it to the judge to determine what is the law upon the fact. I Inst. 30.[5]

The right of jurors to judge "according to conscience," then, was implicit within the word "jury" as the drafters of the Bill of Rights understood it. This was the trial by jury the Founders knew, and this was the trial by jury they intended to pass on to their progeny. The first American dictionary of the English language, published by Noah Webster in 1828, also defined petit juries as having the power to judge both law and fact, at least in criminal trials. The first edition of Webster's *Dictionary of the English Language* defined the word 'jury' as follows:

JU•RY, n. (Fr. *jure*, sworn, L. *juro*, to swear.) A number of freeholders, selected in the manner prescribed by law, empanneled and sworn to inquire into and try any matter of fact, and to declare the truth on the evidence given them in the case. *Grand juries* consist usually of twenty four freeholders at least, and are summoned to try matters alledged in indictments. *Petty juries*, consisting usually of twelve men, attend courts to try matters of fact in civil causes, and to decide both the law and the fact in criminal prosecutions. The decision of a petty jury is called a *verdict*.[6]

The contemporaneous definitions of the word "jury" have largely been neglected by courts seeking to determine the powers intended for the jury by the authors of the Sixth Amendment. However, little can be added to Chief Justice Marshall's basic rule of constitutional interpretation, spelled out in his dissent in the case of *Ogden v. Saunders*,[7] for evaluating the strength of this dictionary evidence:

To say that the intention of the instrument must prevail; that this intention must be collected from its words; that its words are to be understood in that sense in which they are generally used by those for whom the instrument was intended; that its provisions are neither to be restricted into insignificance, nor extended to objects not comprehended in them, nor contemplated by its framers; — is to repeat what has been already said more at large, and is all that can be necessary.[8]

The founders of this country were in agreement as to the value of the trial by jury as an essential means of preventing oppression by the gov-

---

5. Jacob's Law Dictionary (1782).

6. Noah Webster's Dictionary of the English Language (1st ed.,1828).

7. 25 U.S. 213 (1827).

8. *Id.* at 332. *See also* United States v. Fisher, 6 U.S. (2 Cranch) 358, 390 (1805).

ernment. Their primary concern was more with the radical true law-finding power of the jury than with the jury's power of amelioration. The Penn and Mead trial, *Bushell's Case*, and *Rex v. Zenger* provided prominent and relatively recent examples of juries intervening between the power of government to impose the criminal sanction, and the conscience of the community. Theophilus Parsons, a member of the Massachusetts Constitutional Convention who later became the Chief Justice of the Massachusetts Supreme Court, unequivocally endorsed the jury as a means of limiting the ability of legislators to exceed their rightful powers:

> But, Sir, the people themselves have it in their power effectually to resist usurpation, without being driven to an appeal to arms. An act of usurpation is not obligatory; it is not law; and any man may be justified in his resistance. Let him be considered as a criminal by the general government, yet only his fellow-citizens can convict him; they are his jury, and if they pronounce him innocent, not all the powers of Congress can hurt him; and innocent they certainly will pronounce him, if the supposed law he resisted was an act of usurpation.[9]

Parsons was far from alone in his approval of the powers of the criminal jury. John Adams, in 1771, espoused the theory that "It is not only [the juror's] right, but his duty...to find the verdict according to his own best understanding, judgment, and conscience, though in direct opposition to the direction of the court."[10] Thomas Jefferson placed more faith in the jury than in the legislature as a safeguard of liberty: "Were I called upon to decide, whether the people had best be omitted in the legislative or judiciary department, I would say it is better to leave them out of the legislative. The execution of laws is more important than the making of them."[11] But it was Jefferson's philosophical and political rival, Alexander Hamilton, who was to invoke some of the most powerful Revolutionary era arguments for juror independence. During his service as defense counsel in the 1804 libel case *People against Croswell*,[12] Hamilton defended Harry Croswell, who had been convicted of libelling then President Thomas Jefferson.[13]

In *Croswell*, the court, apparently following English precedent from before Fox's Libel Act, had instructed the jury that in libel cases the jury

---

9. 2 Debates On The Adoption Of The Federal Constitution, J. Elliot, Ed., 94 (1888).

10. C.F. Adams, The Works of John Adams, 253-255 (1856).

11. *Letter of Jefferson to L'Abbe Arnond*, July 19, 1789, in 3 Works of Thomas Jefferson, 81, 82 (1854), quoted in Mark DeWolfe Howe, *Juries as Judges of Criminal Law*, 52 Harv. L.Rev. 582 (1939).

12. 3 Johns. Cas. 336 (1804).

13. *Id.* at 337-338.

was restricted to delivering a special verdict.[14] One of the grounds the defense attorneys claimed in their motion for a new trial was that the judge had misdirected the jury that they were not judges of the law in cases of libel; and that the intent of the accused was a matter of law that was not for the consideration of the jurors.[15] Hamilton argued that

> The Chief Justice misdirected the jury, in saying they had no right to judge of the intent and of the law. In criminal cases, the defendant does not spread upon the record the merits of the defence, but consolidates the whole in the plea of not guilty. This plea embraces the whole matter of law and fact involved in the charge, and the jury have an undoubted right to give a general verdict, which decides both law and fact... All the cases agree that the jury have the power to decide the law as well as the fact; and if the law gives them the power, it gives them the right also. Power and right are convertible terms, when the law authorizes the doing of an act which shall be final, and for the doing of which the agent is not responsible.[16]
>
> It is admitted to be the duty of the court to direct the jury as to the law, and it is advisable for the jury in most cases, to receive the law from the court; and in all cases, they ought to pay respectful attention to the opinion of the court. But, it is also their duty to exercise their judgments upon the law, as well as the fact; and if they have a clear conviction that the law is different from what is stated to be by the court, the jury are bound, in such cases, by the superior obligations of conscience, to follow their own convictions. It is essential to the security of personal rights and public liberty, that the jury should have and exercise the power to judge both of the law and of the criminal intent.[17]

After the prosecution had countered that "It is the right of the jury to decide the fact, and only the fact; and it is the exclusive province of the court to decide the law in all cases, criminal as well as civil. A jury is wholly incompetent... to decide questions of law; and if they were invested with this right, it would be attended with mischievous and fatal results,"[18] Hamilton again argued forcefully for the right of the jury to judge the law, in terms reminiscent of the earlier Hamilton in *Rex v. Zenger*:

> The jury ought, undoubtedly, to pay every respectful regard to the opinion of the court; but suppose a trial in a capital case, and the jury are satisfied from the arguments of counsel, the law authorities that are read, and their own judgment, upon the application of the law to the facts, (for

---

14. *Id.* at 340-341.
15. *Id.* at 341-342.
16. *Id.* at 345.
17. *Id.* at 346.
18. *Id.* at 350-351.

the criminal law consists in general of plain principles,) that the law arising in the case is different from that which the court advances, are they not
bound by their oaths, by their duty to their creator and themselves, to
pronounce according to their convictions? To oblige them, in such a case,
to follow implicitly the direction of the court, is to make them commit
perjury, and homicide, under the forms of law. The victim is sacrificed;
he is executed; he perishes without redress.[19]

[I]n the general distribution of power, in any system of jurisprudence, the
cognizance of law belongs to the court, of fact to the jury; that as often as
they are not blended, the power of the court is absolute and exclusive.
That, in civil cases, it is always so, and may rightfully be so exerted. That,
in criminal cases, the law and fact being always blended, the jury, for reasons of a political and peculiar nature, for the security of life and liberty,
are intrusted with the power of deciding both law and fact.

That this distinction results, 1. From the ancient forms of pleading, in
civil cases; none but special pleas being allowed in matters of law; in criminal, none but the general issue. 2. From the liability of the jury to attaint,
in civil cases, and the general power of the court, as its substitute, in granting new trials, and from the exemption of the jury from attaint, in criminal cases, and the defect of power to control their verdicts by new trials;
the test of every legal power being its capacity to produce a definitive
effect, liable neither to punishment nor control.

That, in criminal cases, nevertheless, the court are the constitutional advis-
ers of the jury, in matters of law who may compromit their consciences by
lightly or rashly disregarding that advice; but may still more compromit their
consciences by following it, if, exercising their judgments with discretion and
honesty, they have a clear conviction that the charge of the court is wrong.[20]

Hamilton's argument left the court divided. Although the prosecution
was entitled to move for a judgment, no motion was ever made.[21] In separate opinions, Justices Kent and Thompson concluded that Croswell ought
to be granted a new trial; Chief Justice Lewis and Justice Livingston thought
the earlier conviction should be affirmed. Justice Kent, in an opinion joined
by Justice Thompson, supported Hamilton's view of the role of the jury
in judging the law:

In every criminal case, upon the plea of not guilty, the jury may, and indeed
they must, unless they choose to find a special verdict, take upon themselves
the decision of the law, as well as the fact, and bring in a verdict as com-
prehensive as the issue; because, in every such case, they are charged with
the deliverance of the defendant from the crime of which he is accused.[22]

---

19. *Id.* at 355-356.
20. *Id.* at 361-362.
21. *Id.* at 362-363.
22. *Id.* at 366.

But while the power of the jury is admitted, it is denied that they can right-fully or lawfully exercise it, without compromitting their consciences, and that they are bound implicitly, in all cases to receive the law from the court. The law must, however, have intended, in granting this power to a jury, to grant them a lawful and rightful power, or it would have provid-ed a remedy against the undue exercise of it. The true criterion of a legal power, is its capacity to produce a definitive effect liable neither to censure nor review. And the verdict of not guilty, in a criminal case, is, in every respect, absolutely final. The jury are not liable to punishment, nor the verdict to control.[23]

I am aware of the objection to the fitness and competency of a jury to decide upon questions of law, and especially, with a power to overrule the directions of the judge. In the first place, however, it is not likely often to happen, that the jury will resist the opinion of the court on the matter of law. That opinion will generally receive its due weight and effect; and in civil cases it can, and always ousght to be ultimately enforced by the power of setting aside the verdict. But in human institutions, the question is not, whether every evil contingency can be avoided, but what arrangement will be productive of the least inconvenience. And it appears to be most consistent with the permanent security of the subject, that in criminal cases the jury should, after receiving the advice and assistance of the judge, as to the law, take into their consideration all the circumstances of the case, and the intention with which the act was done, and to determine upon the whole, whether the act done be, or be not, within the meaning of the law. This distribution of power, by which the court and jury mutu-ally assist, and mutually check each other, seems to be the safest, and con-sequently the wisest arrangement, in respect to the trial of crimes ... To judge accurately of motives and intentions, does not require a master's skill in the science of law. It depends more on a knowledge of the pas-sions, and of the springs of human action, and may be the lot of ordinary experience and sagacity.[24]

Chief Justice Lewis, who had presided over the original trial, not sur-prisingly found no error in his instructions to the jury. Curiously, Lewis disparaged *Bushell's Case* and claimed that it had not been followed, and that "[c]ertainly, [Justice Vaughan's] reasoning in that case would not be received as law at this day."[25] Justice Lewis did not cite any cases over-ruling or limiting that precedent. Lewis claimed that "[t]he right here spo-ken of, is nothing more than the right of insisting upon their verdict being received and recorded, though it be general, where it ought not to be so. But is this a species of right, which shall impose it upon a judge, to inform

23. *Id.* at 368.
24. *Id.* at 376.
25. *Id.* at 404.

them that they may exercise it, though they violate their oaths? Surely not."[26]

What Justice Lewis was arguing for, though, was for the use of special verdicts in criminal trials. It has never been the practice of American courts to insist on special verdicts in criminal trials. In fact, requiring the jury to return a special verdict in a criminal trial can violate the Sixth Amendment right of the defendant to a trial by jury.[27] Lewis failed to cite any precedent where an American jury had been punished for delivering a general verdict according to conscience, and without them Lewis was reduced to expounding on what he believed the law should be, and not on the law as it stood in 1804, and still stands today.

Justice Kent's opinion in *People against Croswell* led to a statute similar to Fox's Libel Act being passed by the New York legislature in 1805, in which truth became a defense to the offense of criminal libel.[28]

The right of early American jurors to deliver a general verdict according to conscience was not a controversial issue during the early years of this country. Chief Justice John Jay, in a rare jury trial in front of the Supreme Court, affirmed the right of jurors to judge the law in the instructions he gave to the jury in *Georgia v. Brailsford.*[29] In what is probably among the most quoted jury instructions of all time, Justice Jay instructed the jurors that:

> The facts comprehended in the case are agreed; the only point that remains, is to settle what is the law of the land arising from those facts; and on that point, it is proper, that the opinion of the court should be given. It is fortunate, on the present, as it must be on every occasion, to find the opinion of the court unanimous: we entertain no diversity of sentiment; and we have experienced no difficulty in uniting in the charge, which it is my province to deliver.
>
> It may not be amiss, here, Gentlemen, to remind you of the good old rule, that on questions of fact, it is the province of the jury, on questions of law, it is the province of the court to decide. But it must be observed that by the same law, which recognizes this reasonable distribution of jurisdiction, you have nevertheless a right to take upon yourselves to judge of both, and to determine the law as well as the fact in controversy. On this, and on every other occasion, however, we have no doubt, you will pay that respect, which is due to the opinion of the court: For, as on the one hand, it is presumed, that juries are the best judges of fact; it is, on the

---

26. *Id.* at 405.

27. United States v. Spock, 416 F.2d 165, 180-183 (1st Cir. 1969). In limited circumstances, some appellate courts have approved the use of special verdicts in criminal cases, so long as they do not lead the jury to its conclusions "by a progression of questions each of which seems to require an answer unfavorable to the defendant." *Id.* at 182.

28. MARK DEWOLFE HOWE, READINGS IN AMERICAN LEGAL HISTORY, 376 (1949).

29. 3 U.S. (3 Dall.) 1 (1794).

other hand, presumable, that the court are the best judges of the law. But still both objects are lawfully within your power of decision.[30]

These carefully crafted instructions have been so often cited for several reasons. One reason is that the Court unanimously agreed that the jury had a right to "determine the law as well as the fact in controversy." The second, and more profound point, is the way in which they meticulously delineated the roles of the bench and the jury.

The Court instructed the jury on a *general* rule, which allowed for *exceptions*. They admonished the jury to take the instructions of the court seriously and with respect, and to be appropriately circumspect in deciding the case against the instructions of the bench. The Court rightfully acknowledged that both law and facts were within the jury's right to decide, but that the jury should presume that the court was a fair and impartial judge of the law. The instruction was designed to foster juror independence and responsibility; not jury lawlessness or wanton disregard for the rights of the parties.

Those instructions were certainly not anomalous. Other cases from the same period expressed the same conception of the role of the jury. Not long after *Georgia v. Brailsford* was decided, Supreme Court Justice James Iredell endorsed the same notion of jury autonomy in *Bingham v. Cabot*:

> It will not be sufficient to remark, that the court might charge the jury to find for the Defendant; because, though the jury will generally respect the sentiments of the court on points of law, they are not bound to deliver a verdict conformably to them.[31]

The *Fries* Case and the Chase Impeachment Trial

The right of jurors to judge the law has frequently arisen in cases with political implications. The 1800 treason trial of *United States v. Fries*[32] and seditious libel trial of *People v. Callender*[33] not only led to constraining jury instructions, but helped foster the 1805 impeachment proceedings against Supreme Court Justice Samuel Chase.[34] The earlier of the two cases was first tried with Federal District Judge Richard Peters and Supreme

---

30. *Id.* at 3-4.

31. 3 U.S. (3 Dall.) 19, 33 (1795).

32. 3 U.S. 515 (1799), 9 F.Cas. 924 (D. Pennsylvania 1800).

33. 25 F.Cas. 239 (D. Virginia 1800).

34. Francis Wharton, State Trials of the United States during the Administrations of Washington and Adams, with References Historical and Professional and Preliminary Notes on the Politics of the Times, 612-627, 718-720 (1849)(Reprint 1970).

Court Justice Iredell presiding, and ended in a conviction against Fries.[35] The trial took nine days, more than a week of which was devoted to defense attorney Alexander James Dallas's citation of English precedents in an attempt to convince the jury it was within their discretion to decide whether Fries' actions had amounted to treason.[36]

Peters instructed the jury that "[i]t is treason to oppose or prevent by force, numbers or intimidation, a public and general law of the United States, with intent to prevent its operation or compel its repeal." Justice Iredell stated that his opinion on the law did "absolutely coincide" with that of Peters.[37] The jury convicted Fries, perhaps, as Professor Stephen B. Presser has noted, because "the federal marshall, who had some discretion in picking the jury, was careful to choose members sensitive to the need for peace and good order."[38] It became apparent that the jury so chosen was biased against the defense. On the defendant's motion for new trial, it was established that one of the jurors had declared before the trial that Fries should be hanged. Iredell set the conviction aside and ordered a new trial.[39]

Justice Iredell died before the new trial. Justice Chase and Judge Peters presided over the retrial, with the other participants being the same.[40] Due to a heavy caseload and his concerns over Dallas' long arguments to the jury, Chase decided to shorten the trial by giving his written opinion on the law to the defense, prosecution, and jury before trial. He also limited the discretion of the defense to cite precedents and argue the law to the jury.[41] When Justice Chase delivered his written rulings on the law, Dallas was absent. William Lewis, the other member of Fries' defense team, refused to read the opinion.[42] The following day, Dallas and Lewis both resigned as defense counsel, in spite of Chase's willingness to withdraw the ruling and allow them to conduct their defense as they had planned.[43] The attorneys were adamant that the jury had already been affected by the court's opinion, and that their defense of their client had been fatally undermined. Their defense was based on an argument of law; if the court's opinion had

---

35. *Fries, supra* note 32.

36. Jane Shaffer Elsmere, Justice Samuel Chase, 105 (1980). *See also* Stephen B. Presser, *A Tale of Two Judges: Richard Peters, Samuel Chase, and the Broken Promise of Federalist Jurisprudence*, 73 N.W. Univ. L. Rev. 26, 86 (1978).

37. Presser, *supra* note 36, 86.

38. *Id.* at 87

39. Elsmere, *supra* note 36, 105-106.

40. *Id.* at 107.

41. *Id.* at 107-108.

42. *Id.* at 108.

43. *Id.* at 109, Ellis, The Impeachment of Samuel Chase, 60, from American Political Trials, Michael R. Belknap, Ed. (1981).

already been accepted by or imposed upon the jury, then Fries would certainly be convicted.[44]

Dallas and Alexander were also gambling that if Fries went to trial without representation, his chances of getting a Presidential pardon would be greater.[45] Their assessment of the situation proved accurate. Fries was convicted after a brief jury deliberation, sentenced to execution by hanging, [46] but was later pardoned by President John Adams.[47]

The seditious libel trial of James Thompson Callender was even more contentious than the Fries trial. Callender was accused of violating the Alien and Sedition Acts by libeling President John Adams in a piece of campaign literature entitled *The Prospect Before Us*.[48] Callender, a second-rate journalist with a sordid past, had completed his pamphlet under the tutelage of then-Vice President Thomas Jefferson, who provided him with political information designed to further the prospects of the Democratic Party.[49] Chase considered Callender's trial to be a test of wills between the Virginia Democrats and himself:

> [E]ven before the trial, affidavits were circulated in which it was stated that upon reaching Richmond, Judge Chase had publicly announced that 'he would teach the lawyers in Virginia the difference between the liberty and the licentiousness of the press'; and that he had told the marshal 'not to put any of those creatures called Democrats on the jury'.[50]

Callender's defense team, consisting of renowned lawyers William Wirt,[51] George Hay and Philip Nicholas, began by challenging the methods used to assemble the jury, which had been hand-picked by their Federalist opponents. Chase allowed the defense to question each juror as to whether they had already formed an opinion concerning "the charges contained in the indictment," but, paradoxically, would not allow them to inform the jurors as to what charges the indictment contained.[52] This Kafkaesque technique forced Callender to trial before a packed jury.

---

44. ELSMERE, *supra* note 36, 109.

45. *Fries, supra* note 32, 940.

46. *Id.* at 931-934.

47. *Id.* at 944.

48. ELSMERE, *supra* note 36, 114.

49. *Id.* at 115-116. *See also* Ruth Hedgwood, *The Revolutionary Martyrdom of Jonathan Robbins*, 100 YALE L.J. 229, 283 (1990).

50. *Callender, supra* note 33, 258.

51. William Wirt was later to serve as Attorney General under President James Monroe from 1817-1825, and under President John Quincy Adams from 1825-1829.

52. GODFREY LEHMAN, WE, THE JURY: THE IMPACT OF JURORS ON OUR BASIC FREEDOMS, 198-199 (1997).

The defense then sought to have the trial postponed, ostensibly due to the unavailability of certain material witnesses, and because the defense had insufficient time to prepare for trial.[53] More likely, their real motive was to postpone the case until a later session of the circuit court, when a Justice less openly hostile to their cause than Chase would preside.[54] These motions for postponement were denied. The defense was required to submit the questions they intended to ask the missing witnesses to the court for approval; Justice Chase then ruled that the trial should not be postponed because the testimony sought from the absent witnesses was insufficient to disprove the charges against Callender.[55]

Denied their material witnesses and the chance to disprove the allegations against Callender in a piecemeal fashion, the defense attempted to argue to the jury that the law under which the defendant had been indicted was unconstitutional.[56] They were, in effect, creating a new extension of the radical law-judging view ascribed to juries by Andrew Hamilton and John Lilburne; they were contending that the power of juries to judge the law extended to all laws, that the Constitution, being the supreme law of the United States, was by definition a law, and therefore it was within the discretion of the jury to judge the effects of the Constitution.[57] Chase became so obstreperous in his disagreement that Callender's defense counsel, aware that no argument of theirs was going to be heard by either court or jury, simply packed their books and papers and left the courtroom.[58]

Chase then concluded the case with a long opinion that limited the law-judging role of juries to the application of the facts to the law as expounded by the courts. Chase grounded his arguments on several points: he confessed that the jury could determine what the law was in the case before them, but they could not determine whether the law as given them by the court was constitutional. He claimed the powers of juries emanated from either the Constitution or the common law, and that neither gave jurors the right to judge the constitutionality of the law itself. He added that regional differences among juries would discourage consistency between areas of the nation with respect to the laws of Congress. Chase also argued that the oaths taken by judges requiring them to uphold the Constitution made them the sole judges of the constitutionality of the laws, whereas the oaths taken by jurors made them only the judges of the facts. Finally, he

---

53. *Callender, supra* note 33, 241-243.
54. ELSMERE, *supra* note 36, 120.
55. *Callender, supra* note 33, 250-252.
56. *Id.* at 252-254.
57. *Id.* at 252-253.
58. FREDERICK TREVOR HILL, DECISIVE BATTLES OF THE LAW, 24-26 (1906).

asserted that the power of appellate courts to correct judicial errors could not extend to decisions made by jurors on points of law.[59]

Many of Chase's arguments can be refuted in the full context of the trial and of the history of the development of the criminal trial jury. The rights of jurors may have been ratified by the Constitution and by common law, but it is disingenuous to claim that the Constitution granted any rights to the people. The Constitution was intended to define the powers delegated by the people to government, not to define or limit the rights of the people. The Constitution was considered "the people's law," as has recently been recognized by the constitutional law scholar Akhil Reed Amar:

> [W]e have lost the powerful and prevailing sense of 200 years ago that the Constitution was *the people's law*. Even if juries generally lacked competence to adjudicate intricate and technical "lawyer's law", the Constitution was not supposed to be a prolix code. It had been made, and could be unmade at will, by We the People of the United States—Citizens acting in special single-issue assemblies (ratifying conventions) asked to listen, deliberate, and then vote up or down...If ordinary Citizens were competent to make constitutional judgments when signing petitions or assembling in conventions, why not in juries too?[60]

The citizens who ratified the Constitution considered themselves capable of determining whether an individual statute passed by Congress fit within the power the citizens had delegated to Congress. The people claimed their rights as inalienable. While governments may violate those rights, they could neither grant them nor add to them. These rights were a product of the same Natural Law which Chase himself paid homage to in *Calder v. Bull*, writing that

> An act of legislature (for I cannot call it a law), contrary to the great first principles in the social compact, cannot be considered a rightful exercise of legislative authority...it is against all reason and justice, for a people to entrust a legislature with such powers; and therefore, it cannot be presumed that they have done it.[61]

---

59. *Callender, supra* note 33, 255-258. Other reasons are given by Chase in his opinion that seem to be either derivative from the arguments stated above or inconsequential in comparison to them. Notably, Chief Justice John Marshall was in the courtroom during Callender's trial, where many of the arguments Marshall later made in his opinion in Marbury v. Madison, 5 U.S. 137 (1803) were anticipated by Justice Chase.

60. Akhil Reed Amar, *The Bill of Rights as a Constitution*, 100 YALE L.J. 1131, 1193 (1991).

61. 3 U.S. (3 Dall.) 386 (1798).

Apparently, Chase considered the federal judiciary the sole authority on what authority the people had entrusted to the federal legislature, but he fails to reconcile this inconsistency within the rest of his opinion.

At the time Chase issued his opinion in *Callender*, under the Judiciary Act of 1793 the Supreme Court lacked the authority to review criminal cases decided by circuit courts.[62] In light of that, Chase's arguments concerning consistency fall flat. Congress' authority to make exceptions to the appellate review of the Supreme Court still allows for inconsistency between circuit courts.[63] It would appear that Chase overemphasized the judicial value of consistency in a nation that, even in 1800, prided itself in tolerance, independence and diversity. It is not clear that what made good law in Massachusetts would necessarily make good law in Virginia.

The oaths taken by judges serve a purpose entirely different than the oaths taken by jurors. The Constitution was "the people's law." The judges and other public officials were servants of the people, in a way that jurors were not. To require judges to pledge adherence to the restraints put on them by the Constitution served as a necessary constraint, giving authority to the Constitution itself. As the jurors were "the people," it would have been absurd to have required the same oath from them as was required from the judiciary. If the people did not have the authority to judge the limits that existed on the powers of Congress, they would not have had the authority to grant those powers in the first instance; and therefore they would not have had the authority to create or ratify the Constitution itself. This argument of Chase's, closely examined, is shown to rest upon a non-sequitur.

Finally, the authority of a jury to hold a statute unconstitutional only applies to the particular case at issue. If a jury makes an error of law it does not set a precedent that extends to future cases. The need for appellate review is not as great. The power of jurors to judge the law is reinforced, not contradicted, by the inability of appellate courts to review acquittals. The power argued for is the power of the jury to find the law contrary to the direction of the court, which would be meaningless if it did not extend to the appellate courts and even to the Supreme Court itself. If the error is limited to an individual case, then one conviction has been avoided, and at worst one guilty person has been erroneously acquitted.[64]

---

62. *See* Amar, *supra* note 60, 1192.

63. *Id.*

64. While the possibility of an erroneous conviction undoubtedly exists, the convicted retains the right to appeal. It is also the duty of the trial court judge to set aside a conviction contrary to evidence or to grant a new trial. The trial judge should enter a judgment of acquittal upon proper motion by the defendant before the case ever reaches the jury if the evidence is insufficient to justify a conviction. *See* United States v. Wilson et al., 28 F.Cas. 699, 712 (E.D. Pennsylvania 1830):

But if the so-called error is widespread, then it is a sign that the public either does not support or cannot understand the law involved, and the legislature is duty-bound to act affirmatively to change the law.

Article I of Chase's 1805 impeachment charges was directly related to his denial of the right of the jurors in *Fries* to judge the law as well as the facts. The third specific charge accused Chase of misconduct "In debarring the prisoner from his constitutional privilege of addressing the jury (through his counsel) on the law, as well as on the fact, which was to determine his guilt or innocence, and at the same time endeavoring to wrest from the jury their indisputable right to hear argument, and determine upon the question of law, as well as the question of fact, involved in the verdict which they were required to give."[65] Chase's defense was not that the jury did not have the right to determine the law as well as the fact; his attorney acknowledged specifically that the jury possessed this right and denied that Chase's actions were an attempt to limit it:

> As little can this respondent be justly charged with having, by any conduct of his, endeavored to 'wrest from the jury their indisputable right to hear argument, and determine upon the question of law as well as the question of fact involved in the verdict which they were required to give.' He denies that he did at any time declare that the aforesaid counsel should not at any time address the jury, or did in any manner hinder them from addressing the jury on the law as well as on the facts arising in the case. It was expressly stated, in the copy of his opinion delivered as above set forth to William Lewis, that the jury had a right to determine the law as well as the fact: and the said William Lewis and Alexander James Dallas were expressly informed, before they declared their resolution to abandon the defence, that they were at liberty to argue the law to the jury.[66]

By making this defense, Chase again confessed and defended the right of jurors to judge the law. The rule in the early federal courts was unequivocal; it was admitted on all hands that jurors in criminal trials were the rightful judges of both facts and law. That federal law continued to recognize the right of the jury to judge the law in criminal cases well after the Revolution is shown by Justice Van Ness' instruction to the jury in *United States v. Poyllon*: "...this was in its nature and essence, though not in

---

> If your verdict acquits the prisoner, we cannot grant a new trial, however much we may differ with you as to the law which governs the case; and in this respect jurors are the judges of law, if they choose to become so....But if a jury find a prisoner guilty against the opinion of the court on the law of the case, a new trial will be granted. No court will pronounce a judgment on a prisoner against what they believe to be the law.

65. *Fries, supra* note 32, 934.
66. *Id.* at 940.

its form, a penal or criminal action; and they were therefore entitled to judge both of the law and the fact, and that the enforcing act could not apply in this case,"[67] and by Chief Justice John Marshall's instructions to the jury in *United States v. Hutchings*: "That the jury in a capital case were judges, as well of the law as the fact, and were bound to acquit where either was doubtful."[68]

Jury Independence in the State Courts

The view that juries were the legitimate judges of law was not limited to the federal courts. According to one report, the earliest state decision in this country that jurors were not to judge the law came from the 1843 New Hampshire case of *Pierce v. State*,[69] although the trend towards limiting the right of jurors began almost fifteen years earlier.[70] Still, for almost five decades following the adoption of the Bill of Rights, the right of jurors to judge both law and fact was uncontroversially accepted. In Post-Revolutionary Massachusetts, the right of jurors to judge the law was unanimously supported by the Massachusetts Supreme Court. Chief Justice Theophilus Parsons, in the civil case of *Coffin v. Coffin*, wrote that:

> Both parties had submitted the trial of this issue to a jury. The issue involved both law and fact, and the jury must decide the law and the fact. To enable them to settle the fact, they were to weigh the testimony: that they might truly decide the law, they were entitled to the assistance of the judge. If the judge had declined his aid in a matter of law, yet the jury must have formed their conclusion of law as correctly as they were able. But the judge was officially obliged to declare to the jury his opinion of the law. If this be denied, as a matter not within the jurisdiction of the Court, it must also be denied that the jury were legally authorized to decide on the law; the consequence of which would be, that, when any defendant representative should plead his privilege in bar, whether the plea be true or false cannot be inquired into, because every such plea must involve both law and fact; and the judge must send the parties out of Court.[71]

Later Massachusetts cases obtained essentially the same opinions, at least until the middle of the nineteenth century. In the 1826 case of *Com-*

---

67. 27 F.Cas. 608, 611 (D.C.D.N.Y. 1812).

68. 26 F.Cas. 440, 442 (C.C.D.Vir. 1817).

69. 13 N.H. 536, 554, 566 (1843), discussed in Dierdre A Harris, *Jury Nullification in Historical Perspective: Massachusetts as a Case Study*, 12 SUFF. UNIV. L.REV. 968, 973 n. 29 (1978).

70. *See* Montee v. Commonwealth, 26 Ky. (3 J.J. Marshall) 132 (1830).

71. 4 Mass. 1, 25 (1808).

monwealth v. Worcester,[72] the defendant objected to the court's having left the interpretation of a law up to the jury, but Justice Wilde rebuffed the complaint on the ground that the "judge gave his opinion as to the construction of the by-law, which was adopted by the jury, and the construction was correct. Besides, in criminal prosecutions the jury are the judges of both law and fact."[73] In the 1830 case of *Commonwealth v. Knapp*, Justice Putnam limited the power of jurors to judge the law only in regards to their ability to rule on the admissibility of evidence or the propriety of their arraignment:

> The proposition that the jury are judges of the law as well as of the fact, is not true in its broadest sense. It requires some qualification.
>
> As the jury have the right, and if required by the prisoner, are bound to return a general verdict of *guilty* or *not guilty*, they must necessarily, in the discharge of this duty, decide such questions of law as well as of fact, as are involved in this general question; and there is no mode in which their opinions upon questions of law can be reviewed by this Court or by any other tribunal. But this does not diminish the obligation resting upon the Court to explain the law, or their responsibility for the correctness of the principles of law by them laid down.
>
> The instructions of the Court in matters of law, may safely guide the consciences of the jury, unless they *know* them to be wrong. And when the jury undertake to decide the law (as they undoubtedly have the power to do) in opposition to the advice of the Court, they assume a high responsibility, and should be very careful to see clearly that they are right.
>
> Although the jury have the power, and it is their duty to decide all points of law which are involved in the general question of the guilt or innocence of the prisoner, yet when questions of law arise in the arraignment of the prisoner, or in the progress of the trial, in relation to the admissibility of evidence, they must be decided by the Court, and may not afterwards be reviewed by the jury.[74]

In neighboring Connecticut, Chief Justice Swift admonished that "It is in criminal cases that juries are considered to be the guardians of the rights of the people against the tyranny and oppression of the government."[75] In *Harrison Dance's Case*, the Virginia Supreme Court declined to rule on whether the failure of the Clerk of Courts to execute a bond as required by statute required him to forfeit his office. The Court recognized the independence of a criminal trial jury and recognized that the issue should be decided by a jury in a criminal court, and "the Jury, in that Court, would

72. 3 Pick. 462 (1826).

73. *Id*. at 475.

74. 10 Pick. 477, 496 (1830).

75. Bartholomew v. Clark, 1 Conn. 472, 481 (1816).

pass upon the whole case, including law and facts, the decision of this Court not excepted."[76]

The Supreme Court of Maine overruled a trial court in *State v. Snow* stating that:

> [T]he presiding Judge erred, in determining that in criminal cases, the jury are not the judges of the law as well as the fact. Both are involved in the issue, they are called upon to try; and the better opinion very clearly is, that the law and the fact are equally submitted to their determination. It is doubtless their duty to decide according to law; and as discreet men, they must be aware, that the best advice they can get upon this point, is from the Court. But if they believe they can be justified in deciding differently, they have a right to take upon themselves that responsibility.[77]

In Rhode Island, where knowledge of the law was not considered a requirement for judicial office, juries were not given any instructions on the law by the court until the 1830s.[78] One author quotes the 1833 murder trial of Ephraim K. Avery: "Until the statute, passed within a few years, making it the duty of the presiding judge to charge the jury upon the law, no court in this state had adopted the practice of instructing the jury upon the application of the law to the facts."[79] The Supreme Court of Vermont ruled in 1829 that in all criminal cases, the jury indubitably were judges of law as well as of fact:

> This is the true principle of the common law, and it is peculiarly appropriate to a free government, where it is unquestionably both wise and fit, that the people should retain in their own hands as much of the administration of justice as is consistent with the regular and orderly dispensation of it, and the security of person and property. This power the people exercise in criminal cases, in the persons of jurors, selected from among themselves from time to time, as occasion may require; and while the power, thus retained by them, furnishes the most effectual security against the possible exertion of arbitrary authority by the judges, it affords the best protection to innocence.[80]

It should come as no surprise that in the state named after William Penn, whose own life had been spared by an independent jury in 1670, jurors were expected to judge the law as well as the facts. If an earlier jury had not exercised that prerogative there would have been no Pennsylvania. In *Kane v. Commonwealth*, the Pennsylvania Supreme Court explic-

---

76. 19 Va. (5 Munford) 349, 363 (1817).

77. 18 Me. 346, 348 (1841).

78. Amasa M. Eaton, *The Development of the Judicial System in Rhode Island*, 14 YALE L.J. 148, 153 (1905).

79. *Id.*

80. State v. Wilkinson, 2 Vt. 480, 488-489 (1829).

itly declared that jurors had not only the power but the right to deliver a verdict contrary to the legal instructions of the judge. The court held that the trial judge was obliged to instruct the jury, and that the jury should consider the judge's instructions as strong evidence of what the law was. Nevertheless, following the state Constitution, the court upheld the "power of the jury to judge of the law in a criminal case [as] one of the most valuable securities guaranteed by the Bill of Rights."

> Judges may be partial and oppressive, as well from political as personal prejudice, and when a jury are satisfied of such prejudice, it is not only their right but their duty to interpose the shield of their protection to the accused. It is as important in a republican as any other form of government, that, to use the language of the constitution of 1776, "in all prosecutions for criminal offences," a man should have a right "to a speedy public trial by an impartial jury of the country, without the unanimous consent of which jury he cannot be found guilty."[81]

The role of the jury in criminal trials remained uncontroversial until the approach of the Civil War. Juries were empowered to formulate their own judgment as to the law as well as the facts. Almost every decision written in the first decades of the nineteenth century was in agreement with this doctrine; although a few dissenting opinions began to surface.

---

81. 89 Pa. 522, 527 (1879).

Chapter Four

The Development of the Modern View

Law is nothing unless close behind it
stands a warm living public opinion
Wendell Phillips

Resolving Tensions Between Judge and Jury

By the mid-nineteenth century the prevalence of jury instructions charging jurors with the responsibility for reviewing both law and fact began to give way to increasingly constrained instructions. There were several factors influencing this trend, one of which manifested itself in the *Fries* and *Callender* cases: the more power given the jury, the less remained to the judge. Judges have always had their own views on what the law is, or what the law should be. Reducing the power of the jury to determine the law gave the trial court judges greater control in determining case outcome. In turn, appellate control over trial courts allowed control over the development of the common law itself.

Another factor was the reduced perception of a need for jury independence. Americans no longer had unjust laws foisted on them by a foreign power across the sea. American legislators were elected by the people, and very possibly the high level of scrutiny which had been given to foreign legislation was no longer considered a necessity. The Revolutionary power of the musket had given way to the electoral power of the ballot. The intervening power of the jury was considered to be less imperative, now that Americans were free to "vote the rascals out."

An additional consideration was that jury nullification instructions may have seemed redundant. Most early American jurors were already aware of their power to judge the law. Over 160 years had passed since Justice Vaughan's decision in *Bushell's Case* before Supreme Court Justice Joseph Story, riding circuit in Massachusetts, rendered the first major American court opinion limiting the role of juries, in *United States v. Battiste*.[1] Jury independence was part of the American legal culture; although it was rarely

---

1. 24 F.Cas. 1042 (D. Massachusetts 1835).

employed, and most Americans thought it should only be used to curtail gross excrescences of the criminal sanction. No other American court had previously dared to deny the dormant power of juries to trim back the acts of the legislature. Story believed that informing juries about their power to deliver an independent verdict increased the likelihood for frivolous and unwarranted nullification of the law.

Battiste involved a capital charge of piracy against a mate on a ship that transported slaves between ports in Africa. Story was more concerned that the Massachusetts jury would enter an unwarranted conviction than he was that the jury would acquit out of sympathy or prejudice. These concerns may have been prompted by the fact that Massachusetts was the first state to abolish slavery, and remained the center of the abolitionist movement until the passage of the Thirteenth Amendment brought the institution to an end. This reading, which flows logically from the arguments Story puts forward in summing up the case to the jury, seems misplaced. It was the defense attorneys who urged the jury to judge the law in this case, and they were thus assuming any risk for an unwarranted conviction. But perhaps this case merely provided Story an opportunity to make his views on this subject part of the record, as this issue is one on which he "had a decided opinion during [his] whole professional life."[2]

> My opinion is, that the jury are no more judges of the law in a capital case or other criminal case, upon the plea of not guilty, than they are in every civil case, tried upon the general issue. In each of these cases, their verdict, when general, is compounded of law and of fact; and includes both. In each, they must necessarily determine the law, as well as the fact. In each, they have the physical power to disregard the law, as laid down to them by the court. But I deny, that, in any case, civil or criminal, they have the moral right to decide the law according to their own notions, or pleasure. On the contrary, I hold it the most sacred constitutional right of every party accused of a crime, that the jury should respond to the facts, and the court to the law. It is the duty of the court to instruct the jury as to the law; and it is the duty of the jury to follow the law, as it is laid down

---

2. *Id.* at 1043. Fifteen years earlier, Justice Story had foreshadowed *Battiste* when he excused two potential jurors on a *sua sponte* order because their Quaker religion would not permit them to impose the death penalty:

> To insist on a juror's sitting in a cause when he acknowledges himself to be under influences, no matter whether they are from interest, from prejudice, or from religious opinions, which will prevent him from giving a true verdict according to the law and evidence, would be to subvert the objects of a trial by jury and to bring into disgrace and contempt, the proceedings of courts of justice. We do not sit here to procure verdicts of partial and prejudiced men; but of men, honest and indifferent in causes.

United States v. Cornell, 25 F.Cas. 650, 655-656 (C.C.D. R.I. 1820).

by the court. This is the right of the citizen; and it is his only protection. If the jury were at liberty to settle the law for themselves, the effect would be, not only that the law itself would be most uncertain, from the different views, which different juries might take of it; but in case of error, there would be no remedy or redress by the injured party; for the court would not have the right to review the law as it had been settled by the jury. Indeed, it would be almost impracticable to ascertain, what the law, as settled by the jury, actually was. On the contrary, if the court should err, in laying down the law to the jury, there is an adequate remedy for the injured party, by a motion for a new trial, or a writ of error, as the nature of the jurisdiction of the particular court may require. Every person accused as a criminal has a right to be tried according to the law of the land; and not by the law as a jury may understand it, or choose, from wantonness, or ignorance, or accidental mistake, to interpret it. If I thought, that the jury were the proper judges of the law in criminal cases, I should hold it my duty to abstain from the responsibility of stating the law to them upon any such trial. But believing, as I do, that every citizen has a right to be tried by the law, and according to the law; that it is his privilege and truest shield against oppression and wrong; I feel it is my duty to state my views fully and openly on the present occasion.[3]

Story's reasoning requires some analysis. Story begins by denying the moral right of juries to deliver a verdict according to conscience, and holds that the Constitution guarantees criminal defendants the right to be tried according to set rules and procedures. Although Story does not deny the jury's legal power of the jury to bring in an independent verdict, he is claiming for the defendant a legal right to be judged strictly according to the court's interpretation of the law, because only then can an appellate court discover what interpretation of the law was applied and overturn it if incorrect. These arguments may apply if a jury convicts in opposition to the court's instructions of law; it is not at all clear that they apply if the jury acquits.

If this, then, is his argument, it may be answered by allowing the defense to make the decision whether or not to instruct the jury on their power to judge the law. In *Battiste*, the defense was arguing for a nullification instruction. Because this request came from the defense, the danger of a jury convicting against the law was a tactical risk which the defense could have avoided simply by foregoing their right to request such an instruction.

Story errs in asserting that allowing juries to deliver independent verdicts would eliminate the power of appellate courts to free the wrongly convicted. As Judge Baldwin was clear to point out in the jury instructions in *United States v. Wilson et al.*:

---

3. *Battiste, supra* note 1, 1043.

> If your verdict acquits the prisoner, we cannot grant a new trial, however much we may differ with you as to the law which governs the case; and in this respect jurors are the judges of law, if they choose to become so.... But if a jury find a prisoner guilty against the opinion of the court on the law of the case, a new trial will be granted. No court will pronounce a judgment on a prisoner against what they believe to be the law.[4]

If the court does "pronounce a judgment on a prisoner against what they believe to be the law," the defendant can still appeal, on the grounds that the law was misapplied, or that the facts established are not sufficient to support the conviction. The evils Story apprehends in jury independence are not established by his argument that the court's sole discretion over the law is the defendant's "only protection" and "his privilege and truest shield against oppression and wrong."

Justice Story repeats the position held by Justice Chase, that the power of appellate courts does not extend to decisions made by jurors on points of law. There is no justification for this assertion. Judges are responsible for granting new trials or acquittals in cases where a jury might wrongfully have convicted an innocent defendant, or where the evidence established at trial would be insufficient to justify the conviction.

Further, Story fails to establish how defendants are to be protected from being judged according to the jury's understanding or interpretation of the law. No matter how faithfully the jurors may wish to follow judicial instructions, they are still limited by their understanding, accidental mistakes, ignorance and interpretations. And the truly wanton jury will never be constrained by either conscience or the instructions of any court. Perhaps Story's interpretation stems from his belief that jury law-judging relieves the judge of any responsibility in advising or instructing the jury. But with very few exceptions this has never been the practice in this country, nor did the defense in *Battiste* request that the court refrain from instructing the jury on the law.

Story assumes that if juries can rightfully and irreviewably acquit in opposition to the direction of the court, their convictions would have to be equally inviolable. But there is no requirement for symmetry in the criminal law. Acquittals are not reviewable; convictions are. It is not true that fairness requires the defense and prosecution to be treated identically.[5] While in some particulars the criminal justice system grants an advantage to the defense, there are certain prerogatives reserved for the prosecution

---

4. 28 F.Cas. 699, 712 (E.D. Pennsylvania 1830).

5. *See* Katherine Goldwasser, *Limiting a Criminal Defendant's Use of Peremptory Challenges: On Symmetry and the Jury in a Criminal Trial*, 102 Harv. L.Rev. 808, 821-826 (1989).

as well. (For example, the defense can not grant its witnesses immunity from prosecution.[6]) There is no *a priori* reason to assume, as Story does, that the discretion of the jury must operate symmetrically.

Battiste was influential in several states, and a trend towards limiting the power of jurors began. Some states converted to the new doctrine quickly; in others, legislatures fought vigorously against the courts to protect the right of jurors. New Hampshire evidenced the new trend in the 1843 case of *Pierce v. State*.[7]

Pierce contains what may be two of the most well-reasoned discussions opposing the jury's right to judge the law. In the opinion of Justice Gilchrist, and the concurring opinion of Chief Justice Parker, jury law-judging would violate the constitutional right of defendants to be judged according to predetermined and knowable laws.[8] Their conclusion is necessitated by the methodology that both justices employ, which is to insist that the same jury powers must apply in civil as in criminal cases,[9] and to analyze the principle of jury independence in the light of demurrers, directed verdicts, and new trials as applied in civil cases.

Both justices, but Parker most strikingly, confound jury independence with giving the jury the final say in determining the law.[10] Parker argues that a conviction based on a defective indictment could not be set aside if the jury were to judge the law, because

> The jury must be supposed to have found the defendant guilty of some crime...It would be absurd to say that those who had not only the power, but the right, to judge, had tried and convicted him; and then to call upon another branch of the judiciary, which had not the right of judging, but merely that of advising, to say that he had been convicted of nothing for which he could be sentenced.[11]

---

6. United States v. Turkish, 623 F.2d 769, 773-774 (2d Cir. 1980). *See also* Dr. Nancy Lord, *Reconstruction of Closing Argument: United States vs. Rodger Sless, June 6, 1994* (a segment of this argument follows Chapter 10):

> Jurors swear that they will not give greater credibility to the Government and Government witnesses than to the defendant and his. But, in the atmosphere of the trial the awesome majesty of the government frequently seems to sway the jury against the undistinguished defendant. Why? Well, we argue in the Government's courtroom, according to Government rules, staffed by the Government's employees, and listen to the Government's well-paid, professional witnesses testify against the Defendant's volunteer witnesses. They have all the advantages.

7. 13 N.H. 536 (1843).
8. *Id.* at 551, 558.
9. *Id.* at 542, 558.
10. *Id.* at 548, 567-571.
11. *Id.* at 568-569.

The argument proves too much. If the jury, as judges of law, were necessarily irreviewable, then trial judges would also be irreviewable. Just as a conviction can not stand unless the appellate court and the trial court concur in judgment of law, neither can one stand without the concurrence of the trial judge and the jury. If there is no evidence to support a conviction, or if the judge suspects that the jury convicted out of spite or confusion, it is his duty to either grant a new trial, dismiss, direct an acquittal, or otherwise overrule the verdict. Giving trial judges this power of review does not make them the judges of fact; it merely adds an additional safeguard against an erroneous conviction. The British legal scholar Sir Patrick Devlin explained that the discretion of the jury only went so far as to allow them to be merciful: "[w]henever there is a trial by jury, the condemnation must be by a judgment which is both lawful and the judgment of the country. If his countrymen condemn a man and they exceed the law, he shall go free: if the law condemns him and nevertheless his countrymen acquit, he shall go free."[12]

Parker's claim that "[i]f the court are merely to advise the jury as to the matters of law, there would be no more propriety in setting aside the verdict on account of erroneous advice, than there would be in setting it aside because there had been an erroneous argument of counsel,"[13] does not follow from the arguments for jury independence. It is the duty of the court to advise the jury on the law; and in the vast majority of cases it is presumable that the jury will follow the judge's advice faithfully. Should the court allow tainted evidence into consideration by the jury, if significant new evidence is discovered, or if perjury by a crucial witness is proven, it would be the duty of the court to rescue the hapless defendant from what would otherwise be an unjust and unjustifiable conviction. As the judge has a duty to give the jury evidence of what the law is, that evidence is under the same level of scrutiny as any other evidence the judge allows into the case. And just as the jury can decide the weight to be given to any other evidence, it can decide what weight to give the court's opinion of the law.

The issue is not whether the courts are under an obligation, to the best of their abilities, to instruct juries on the law as they understand it, but whether juries are to be bound to follow those instructions, regardless of the consequences. Defendants, if convicted, have adequate grounds for appeal if either the evidence fails to support their convictions (which would be the case if the jury found the law adversely to the defendant, against the instructions of the court) or if the charge of the court is prejudicial against the defendants' case.

---

12. SIR PATRICK DEVLIN, TRIAL BY JURY, 3rd ed., 89 (1966)(Reprinted 1988).
13. *Pierce, supra* note 7, 568.

What the justices in *Pierce* overlook is that jury independence serves a distinct purpose in criminal cases, which it does not serve in ordinary civil cases: to protect the accused from injustice or oppression on the part of government. Justice Parker recognizes that jury law-judging had served this purpose in the past; but denied that Americans had need of a buffer between themselves and their government in the enlightened 1840s:[14]

> It is obvious, from this brief review of some portion of our early jurisprudence, that it cannot furnish a rule for the action of the courts at the present day. It may be true, that it was then declared from the bench, that the jury were the judges of the law, as well as the fact, in criminal cases; although such a declaration must have been nearly gratuitous, as we have already seen, for they were practically so in civil cases also. It has undoubtedly been so said, at a later date. But this, only as a remark indicating the individual opinion of the judge who made it...In fact, it can hardly be said to have indicated what should be designated as an opinion; for after the practice had been adopted of setting aside verdicts in civil cases, for error of law occurring in the course of the trial, the court also granted new trials in criminal cases, for like error, where the defendant had been convicted.[15]

Pierce set forth a new rule of law in New Hampshire, upsetting earlier precedents. Twenty-five years later, in the case of *State v. Hodge*,[16] Justice Doe, even while approving the *Pierce* doctrine, recognized that before *Pierce* jurors in New Hampshire criminal trials had been the rightful judges of law and fact:

> In that case, on the question whether the jury are the judges of the law in criminal cases, the common law, as universally understood and practiced in New Hampshire from the first jury trial ever held in the State down to 1842 (excepting the change of Judge PARKER'S opinion, stated by him in *Pierce v. State*, 13 N.H. 561), was held to be illegal and unconstitutional, and the new doctrine was announced that the jury are not the judges of the law in criminal cases. That doctrine was one of the most startling legal novelties ever introduced into this State, although the only wonder now is that there ever could have been any doubt of its soundness.[17]

In other states, similar degradations of jury power were urged by the bench. The Massachusetts Supreme Court, sitting in the same state where *United States v. Battiste* was decided ten years earlier, declared against the right of the jury in *Commonwealth v. Porter*.[18] In *Porter*, the defense attor-

---

14. *Id.* at 557-560.
15. *Id.* at 560.
16. 50 N.H. 510 (1869).
17. *Id.* at 523.
18. 51 Mass. (10 Met.) 263 (1845).

ney had been prohibited by the court from arguing that the laws his client had been accused of violating were invalid. The judge charged the jury that

> [It] was their duty to adopt and follow the said several rulings and decisions of the court, for the purposes of the trial. But...they possessed the power of rendering a verdict in opposition to the said rulings and decisions, whereby [the court] would be in fact overruled and reversed; and that, if the jury should do so,...they would in no way be amenable to punishment by the law, or responsible, in any form, to any legal accusation or animadversion, for such proceeding."[19]

In spite of what many modern attorneys would consider a very liberal interpretation of the role of the jury, the defense attorney appealed on the grounds that the jury had the right to determine both law and facts, and consequently it had been improper to prohibit him from arguing his interpretation of the law to the jury.[20] Chief Justice Lemuel Shaw held that although the defense attorney had a right to argue the law, the jury had no right to decide the law. The purpose of allowing the defense to argue the law to the jury was not to persuade them to the defendant's views of the law, but to give them a fuller and more complete exposition of the law,[21] and the failure of the trial court to allow the defense to argue the law justified granting a new trial.[22]

But Shaw would not grant that the jury had the right to determine the law. In fact, Shaw ruled enigmatically that it was

> [A] well settled principle and rule, lying at the foundation of jury trial, admitted and recognized ever since jury trial has been adopted as an established and settled mode of proceeding in courts of justice, that it is the proper province and duty of judges to consider and decide all questions of law which arise, and that the responsibility of a correct decision is placed finally on them; that it is the proper province and duty of the jury, to weigh and consider evidence, and decide all questions of fact, and that the responsibility of a correct decision is placed upon them....It would be alike a usurpation of authority and violation of duty, for a court, on a jury trial, to decide authoritatively on the questions of fact, and for the jury to decide ultimately and authoritatively upon the questions of law.[23]

Shaw's ruling was the emerging majority opinion, and he believed recent developments had proven the wisdom of his rule. But for him to claim that there was no real controversy riding on the question seems more than

---

19. *Id.* at 266.
20. *Id.* at 266-267, 269-275.
21. *Id.* at 283-285.
22. *Id.* at 287.
23. *Id.* at 276.

a little far-fetched. The confidence Shaw displays in this passage does not seem to survive until the end of his opinion.

If in fact the judge was the sole authority on the law, there is no solid ground for allowing the attorneys to argue the law to the jury. A Note in the 1964 *Yale Law Journal* suggests that "[a]pparently, Shaw was unwilling to overrule what was concededly the well-established practice in the state; but the logic of his position suffered for it."[24] In fact, in the penultimate paragraph of his opinion, Shaw conceded that an

> Address to the jury, upon questions of law embraced in the issue, by the defendant or his counsel, is warranted by the long practice of the courts in this Commonwealth in criminal cases, in which it is within the established authority of a jury, if they see fit, to return a general verdict, embracing the entire issue of law and fact.[25]

This paragraph flatly contradicts Justice Shaws' "well settled principle and rule." The right of jurors "to return a general verdict...embracing law and fact" is irreconcilable with a rule "that it is the proper province and duty of judges to consider and decide all questions of law which arise." Caught on the crest of a rising tide of change in the roles of judges and juries, it does not seem that Justice Shaw had a clear view of whether the jury could, or could not, rightfully "embrace the entire issue of law and fact."

The Vermont Supreme Court, which in 1829 had ruled decisively in favor of the juror's right to review the law, reiterated its earlier opinion in *State v. Croteau*,[26] but a long and passionate dissent served as a harbinger of things to come. The trial court in *Croteau* instructed the jury that "it was their duty to receive the law from the court, and to conform their judgment and decision to the instructions which the court had given them... it was not within the legitimate province of the jury to revise the decision of the court in regard to the matters of law...but it was their duty faithfully to conform to such instructions."[27] The defendant was convicted.

Justice Hall, writing the majority opinion for the Vermont Supreme Court, granted Croteau a new trial. His decision supported the law-finding role of the jury on two separate grounds. First, he diligently reported the historic role of the jury as a protection against oppression by biased or corrupted judicial authority, evoking images of Lord Jeffries and the Star Chamber in the process.[28] Secondly, he disputed the dichotomy between jury powers and jury rights, arguing that

---

24. Note, *The Changing Role of the Jury in the Nineteenth Century*, 74 Yale L.J. 170, 176-177 (1964).

25. *Porter, supra* note 18, 287.

26. 23 Vt. 14 (1849).

27. *Id.* at 16.

28. *Id.* at 30-33.

The power of juries to decide the law as well as the fact involved in the issue of not guilty, and without legal responsibility to any other tribunal for their decision, is universally conceded. In my opinion, such power is equivalent to right.[29]

[W]hen political power is conferred on a tribunal without restriction or control, it may be lawfully exerted; that the power of a jury in criminal cases to determine the whole matter in issue committed to their charge, is such a power, and may therefore be lawfully and rightfully exercised; in short, that such a power is equivalent to, or rather is itself, a legal right.[30]

Justice Hall pointedly criticized both Story and Shaw for failing to take account of "the principal reason for the establishment and maintenance of this right of juries,—the preservation of the liberty of the citizen, and the protection of innocence against the consequences of the partiality and undue bias of judges in favor of the prosecution,"[31] and ends his opinion with a refreshing note of judicial humility: "It may be, that there is not in this state, at present, any undue bias in the court in favor of the government, in criminal prosecutions. But of this, it does not perhaps, become the judges to speak."[32]

Dissenting Justice Bennett (who also happened to have been the trial judge) argued that even if the instructions to the jury had improperly infringed on the jury's domain, they did not constitute grounds for a new trial, because they were substantively correct: the defendant had been convicted upon a correct interpretation of the law.[33] "If this court open the case, it should be, I conceive, for an injury done to the respondent himself, and not because it may be thought the court below advanced an untenable opinion, as to who were the ultimate judges of the law. This case was not brought up, I take it, for the purpose of redressing any wrong done to the jury, by the court having invaded their province."[34] What Justice Bennett fails to acknowledge is that if these instructions were not grounds for a mistrial, then the trial court would be given free rein to continue to infringe on the right of juries to veto oppressive prosecutions. Moreover, if the jury has a right to judge both law and fact, then the defendant was deprived of his right to trial by a jury empowered to perform their full role. Justice Hall had implicitly recognized a due process right to a trial by jury empowered to judge fact and law, a right Justice Bennett had completely overlooked.

---

29. *Id.* at 45.
30. *Id.* at 47.
31. *Id.* at 21.
32. *Id.* at 47.
33. *Id.* at 48.
34. *Id.*

It is likely that the jury would have considered the law Croteau was convicted of violating oppressive. As in the cases of *State v. Pierce* and *Commonwealth v. Porter*, Croteau had been convicted of violating a state liquor licensing statute. These statutes were not popular, and it is possible that courts feared juror resistance to liquor taxes and licensing. There is little reason to argue for the right of jurors to judge the law when the law is a popular one, carrying what are considered by most people to be just punishments. The issue of jury independence usually surfaces where there are laws which are unpopular, especially when those laws are widely applied. The liquor statutes, while not as controversial as the libel statutes of the seventeenth and eighteenth centuries, were sufficiently onerous to the people of New England to give juries an adequate incentive to exercise their prerogative to judge the law.

The Unconstitutionality of Slavery: Spooner's Influence on Jury Independence

The laws establishing and protecting the institution of slavery and punishing those who aided fugitive slaves struck many Americans—including substantial numbers of Southerners—as cruel, unjust and fundamentally un-American. Indeed, many Americans as far back as the Colonial era believed the "peculiar institution" of slavery could never be reconciled with America's constitutional principles. Juries in Massachusetts, which was later to be considered the center of the Abolitionist movement, had begun ending slavery as early as 1765, when the slave Jenny Slew sued for her freedom. After losing before a panel of judges in the Inferior Court of Common Pleas at Newburyport, Slew refiled her case so that she could bring it before a jury. In turn, the jury awarded Slew with not only her freedom, but four pounds in damages and court costs as well. Following Slew's liberation, at least seven other Massachusetts slaves sued for an acknowledgement of their right to freedom in the years from 1765 to 1773. Only one, the unfortunate Amos Newport, was returned to slavery. Several were awarded damages to compensate them for their term of bondage.[35]

In 1781, a slave named Quock Walker[36] sued Nathaniel Jennison for injuries sustained when Jennison attempted to recapture Walker. Jennison claimed in turn that he had only administered appropriate discipline towards a runaway slave. Walker had absconded from Jennison and taken

35. GODFREY LEHMAN, WE, THE JURY: THE IMPACT OF JURORS ON OUR BASIC FREEDOMS, 211-215 (1997).

36. Quock has variously appeared as Quarco, Quack, Quaco, Quocks, and Quork in different reports and texts.

employment with the brother of his original master, a Mr. Caldwell. Walker had been inherited by Mrs. Caldwell, who had gone on to marry Jennison. Jennison, in turn, claimed to have inherited Walker upon the death of his wife. Walker claimed that Mrs. Jennison had promised him his freedom when he turned twenty-five, and moreover that slavery was illegal under the United States and Massachusetts Constitutions. The Massachusetts Constitution contained the guarantee that "[a]ll men are born free and equal, & have certain natural, essential, and unalienable rights; among which may be reckoned the right of enjoying and defending their lives and liberties..."[37]

The status of Walker was debated in a series of civil jury trials, culminating in the decision that "The said Quock Walker is a free man and not the proper slave of the defendant," and awarding him damages for his injuries.[38] Since Walker was a free man, however, Jennison had committed the offense of assault and battery in attempting to take Walker back into slavery. In 1783, a criminal trial jury found Jennison guilty of assaulting Walker, and fined him forty shillings for his crime, in the case of Commonwealth v. Jennison.[39]

The heroism of the criminal trial jury cannot be given all the credit for the verdict. Chief Justice William Cushing, in his charge to the jury, instructed them that

> As to the doctrine of slavery and the right of Christians to hold Africans in perpetual servitude, and sell and treat them as we do our horses and cattle, that (it is true) has been heretofore contenanced by the Province Laws formerly, but nowhere is it expressly enacted or established...But whatever sentiments have formerly prevailed in this particular or slid in upon us by the example of others, a different idea had taken place with the people of America, more favorable to the natural rights of mankind, and to that natural innate desire of Liberty, with which Heaven (without regard to color, complexion, or shape of noses — features) has inspired all the human race. And upon this ground our Constitution of Government, by which the people of this Commonwealth have solemnly bound themselves, sets out with declaring that all men are born free and equal — and that every subject is entitled to liberty, and to have it guarded by the laws, as well as life and property — and in short is totally repugnant to the idea of being born slaves. This being the case, I think the idea of slavery is inconsistent with our conduct and Constitution; and there can be no such thing as perpetual servitude of a rational creature, unless his liberty is forfeited by some criminal conduct or given up by personal consent or contract...[40]

---

37. LEHMAN, *supra* note 35, 215-217.

38. *Id.* at 220.

39. *Id.* at 222.

40. ALBERT P. BLAUSTEIN & ROBERT L. ZANGRANDO, CIVIL RIGHTS AND AFRICAN AMERICANS, 45-46 (1991).

The jury, however, retained the final decision as to whether slavery could exist under the Constitution of the Commonwealth of Massachusetts. As numerous cases already cited show, they were entirely capable of acquitting Jennison, and recognizing the existence of slavery. The jury of white male landowners freely chose to convict, heralding the end of slavery in Massachusetts and delivering a fatal blow to the institution throughout the Northeast. It is perhaps unfortunate that Cushing's instructions so controlled the jury as to deprive their verdict of the independent moral weight it deserved.

Although slavery was abolished early on in some states, it flourished in others. The abolition of slavery became a burning issue throughout the country, as the Southern states, where the vast majority of slaves were held, fought to preserve their "peculiar institution" from what they saw as unwarranted Yankee meddling. Abolitionists, on the other hand, frequently urged that they wished to be part of no Union wherein slavery was tolerated. William Lloyd Garrison, founder of the American Anti-Slavery Society, urged a program of continual agitation to turn public opinion decidedly against slavery.

The manifest injustice of chattel slavery presented abolitionists with a special incentive to argue the right of jurors to judge the law. In 1845, the influential abolitionist and philanthropist Gerrit Smith[41] financed the writing and publication of Lysander Spooner's *The Unconstitutionality of Slavery*, in which Spooner argued that slavery was repugnant to the Constitution, and had never had a legal existence in the United States.[42] Spooner's work was to lead to one of the most thorough jury revolts in history, a period during which jurors were, in the words of Harry Kalven and Hans Zeisel, "totally at war" with the law.[43]

Spooner's landmark argument was based on natural law, history, precedent and strict rules of constitutional interpretation. He argued that 1) slavery, while tolerated, had never had a *legal* existence in the Colonies, because none of the Colonial charters had authorized it, and because the Colonies had no authority to establish laws that were repugnant to the laws of England,[44] and those Colonial statutes that attempted to institute slavery were illegally vague as to who was considered a slave;[45] 2) neither

---

41. Smith was elected to the U.S. Congress in 1852, but only served one term.

42. *See also*, Lysander Spooner, *Has Slavery in the United States a Legal Basis?*, MASSACHUSETTS QUARTERLY REVIEW, June, 1848, I, pp 273-293 (reprinted in CHARLES M. HAAR, THE GOLDEN AGE OF AMERICAN LAW, 271 (1965)).

43. HARRY KALVEN AND HANS ZEISEL, THE AMERICAN JURY, 291 (1966).

44. LYSANDER SPOONER, THE UNCONSTITUTIONALITY OF SLAVERY, 21-31 (7th Ed., 1860).

45. *Id.* at 32-35.

the Declaration of Independence nor the state Constitutions of 1789 recognized slavery;[46] 3) the sole passage in the Articles of Confederation [Art. V, § 1] that could be deemed to recognize slavery failed to do so for the same reason that Art. 1, § 2 of the Constitution fails to do so, which is that the word 'free' refers to freeholders and not non-slaves;[47] and 4) the three passages of the Constitution that are purported to recognize slavery fail to do so because they are all susceptible to other interpretations more consistent with the general spirit and intent of the Constitution[48] and because, as slavery had no *legal* existence prior to the passage of the Constitution, it could only be established by positive legislation of such "irresistible clearness, to induce a court of justice to suppose a design to effect such objects."[49] Therefore, Spooner concluded that

> [S]lavery neither has, *nor ever had* any constitutional existence in this country; that it has always been a mere abuse, sustained, in the first place, merely by the common consent of the strongest party, without any law on the subject, and, in the second place, by a few unconstitutional enactments, made in defiance of the plainest provisions of their fundamental law.[50]

It should be acknowledged that many of Spooner's arguments were foreshadowed by William Goodell, in the 1844 work *Views of American Constitutional Law, in It's Bearing Upon American Slavery.* According to historian Charles Shively,[51] Spooner believed Goodell plagiarized his work in later editions of his *Views.* Goodell, however, responded by acknowledging that the weakness of his work was that he depended primarily on religious and moral principles, whereas Spooner relied almost exclusively on legal reasoning.

Spooner's arguments were widely disseminated both in print and by orators such as Fredrick Douglass.[52] Spooner's book was delivered to every member of the Congress of 1855, courtesy of William Goodell's American and Foreign Anti-Slavery Society.[53] In 1847, Spooner came out with a second part to his book, in order to answer the criticisms which the New England abolitionist Wendell Phillips published in *The Anti-Slavery Stan-*

---

46. *Id.* at 36-51.

47. *Id.* at 51-54.

48. *Id.* at 54-114.

49. *Id.* at 18-19, quoting United States v. Fisher, 6 U.S. (2 Cranch) 358, 390 (1805).

50. *Id.* at 20.

51. CHARLES SHIVELY, 4 COLLECTED WORKS OF LYSANDER SPOONER 7 (1971).

52. "To credit Douglass with being an original legal thinker would be an error; his arguments were those of Lysander Spooner and William Goodell as he acknowledged at the time of his change of heart about the Constitution in 1851." WILLIAM S. MCFEELY, FREDRICK DOUGLASS, 205 (1991).

53. SHIVELY, *supra* note 51, 11.

dard in 1845 and later reprinted as a separate pamphlet entitled *Review of Lysander Spooner's Essay on the Unconstitutionality of Slavery.* Spooner's work appeared in at least six editions by 1860.[54]

Spooner's treatise proved surprisingly difficult to oppose. United States Senator Albert G. Brown from Mississippi was reported in *The Congressional Globe* as having said, on Dec. 2, 1856, that "If [Spooner's] premises were admitted, I should say at once that it would be a herculean task to overturn his argument."[55] The premise Senator Brown would not admit was that slaves could be considered human beings under the Constitution.[56]

The passage of the Fugitive Slave Act of 1850 revealed that Congress had not addressed Spooner's arguments. This act was probably one of the most infamous pieces of legislation ever passed by any United States legislature. By its terms, a person accused of being a fugitive slave could, without due process, be brought before a quasi-judicial commissioner for a summary hearing without a jury. If the commissioner was convinced of the claimant's veracity the 'slave' would be returned to bondage. The defendant 'slave' was not allowed to testify. Should the commissioner return the 'slave' to bondage, he was to be paid a fee of ten dollars. The fee for rejecting the claim was only five dollars.

The Fugitive Slave Act of 1850 provided that any person who interfered with the recovery of fugitive slaves, or who rescued or harbored fugitives, could be fined up to one thousand dollars and imprisoned for up to six months. Furthermore, they were liable to the slave owner, in the sum of one thousand dollars per slave, for every slave that successfully escaped with their assistance. Any person with black skin could be seized as an escaped slave wholly on *ex parte*[57] testimony. Finally, the Act deprived those arrested under its auspices of the writ of *Habeas Corpus,*[58] the same writ whose power had successfully ended the privilege of bringing slaves into England less than a century earlier.[59]

Naturally, abolitionists were not pleased with the expanded protection given to chattel slavery by the Fugitive Slave Act. Spooner in particular

---

54. *Id.* Spooner's work (along with the work of Joel Tiffany) has also received credit from at least one authority with originating the concept of national citizenship later incorporated in the Fourteenth Amendment. *See* JACOBUS TENBROCK, THE ANTISLAVERY ORIGINS OF THE FOURTEENTH AMENDMENT, 86-91 (1951).

55. Dec. 2, 1856, *The Congressional Globe*, p. 14.

56. SHIVELY, *supra* note 51, 8-9.

57. *An ex parte* hearing is a hearing where only one side is heard. The person alleged to be a slave had no right to put on evidence under the Fugitive Slave Act of 1850.

58. A writ of *Habeas Corpus* is a method of challenging the legality of one's imprisonment.

59. *See* Somerset against Stewart, 98 Eng. Rep. 499 (1772).

responded first in *A Defence of Fugitive Slaves,* published in 1850, and finally by writing what is considered his masterpiece, *An Essay on the Trial by Jury,* published in 1852. While the constitutional arguments against the Fugitive Slave Act made in *Defence* are beyond the scope of this work, a lengthy appendix was aimed directly at the power of jurors to refuse to apply a law which they believed to be unjust or unconstitutional. The appendix begins by summarizing the arguments made in *The Unconstitutionality of Slavery* in Part A. In parts B–D, however, Spooner initially drafted the arguments he would more fully develop two years later in *An Essay on the Trial by Jury.*

Whether because of Spooner's works, or because of the indigenous rebelliousness and sense of righteousness of mid-nineteenth century trial jurors, it is clear that jurors frequently refused to convict those who harbored or assisted fugitive slaves. One source reports that "violence against slave-catchers and the refusal of jurors to convict persons who aided escaped slaves effectively nullified the federal fugitive slave law in several free states."[60] When twenty-four people were indicted for forcefully rescuing the fugitive slave William "Jerry" Henry from a Syracuse, New York police station, three out of the first four trials ended in acquittals, with the government dropping the charges against the rest of the defendants.[61]

The grand jury instructions in this case were explicit in their goal of discouraging the jurors from refusing to indict on moral or constitutional grounds. The court played on the fears of civil war that were sure to be prevalent in a Northern jury in 1851. Presiding Supreme Court Justice Samuel Nelson, charging the grand jury, instructed them that:

> It is true, New York may possess the physical power to disregard her obligation, and set the constitution at naught, and abide the consequences... Before the people of New York, or of any other Northern state, make up their minds to disregard and disobey this provision of the constitution, they will, I doubt not, look well to the consequences. Common sense, as well as common prudence and wisdom, would dictate this...
>
> Disorderly and turbulent men—the common disturbers of society—are found in every government; and occasional outbreaks against law and legal authority must be expected. They scarcely compromit the character of a people, when the violence is speedily suppressed and the guilty offenders are sternly punished. New York may thus redeem herself from the odium of suffering the constitution and laws of the Union to be trampled under foot, and from a responsibility to other members of the confederacy...

60. HAROLD M. HYMAN AND CATHERINE M. TARRANT, ASPECTS OF AMERICAN JURY HISTORY, 37, in THE JURY SYSTEM IN AMERICA: A CRITICAL OVERVIEW (Rita J. Simon, ed., 1975).

61. LEON FRIEDMAN, THE WISE MINORITY, 36 (1971). *See also* Steven E. Barkan, *Jury Nullification in Political Trials,* 31 SOC. PROBS. 28, 33 (1983).

Any one conversant with the history of the times, and with the great issue now agitating the country, and in which the perpetuity of this Union is involved, cannot fail to have seen that the result is in the hands of the people of the Northern states. They must determine it, and the responsibility rests upon them. If they abide by the constitution—the whole and every part of it—all will be well. If they expect the Union to be saved, and to enjoy the blessings flowing from it, short of this, they will find themselves mistaken when it is too late.[62]

A similar case occurred in Boston, concerning the fugitive slave Fredrick Jenkins (alias Shadrack). Shadrack had escaped in May of 1850 from John Debree, a purser in the Navy. Debree located Shadrack in February, 1851, and had an affidavit made out in Virginia. On February 15, Shadrack was arrested in Boston by a Deputy U.S. Marshal.[63]

A summary hearing ensued, during which Shadrack's six attorneys requested and received a delay of three days in order to prepare their case. After the hearing, only Shadrack, Shadrack's attorney Robert H. Morris, and the federal marshals remained in the courtroom. A large crowd, "mostly Negroes," rushed into the court and cleared the way for Shadrack's escape. Eventually, Shadrack arrived in Montreal where he married an Irish woman and opened an "eating house."[64]

Prosecution of the participants in Shadrack's rescue was dropped by the government after two acquittals and several hung juries. The government was unable to obtain a single conviction although President Fillmore himself had demanded the prosecutions, and Judge Sprague in charging the grand jury had referred to the defendants as "beyond the scope of human reason and fit subjects either of consecration or a mad-house."[65]

The second defendant acquitted, Robert Morris, was a black lawyer—an uncommon figure during the middle of the nineteenth century. According to one authority, "His lawyer told the jury that they should judge the law as well as the facts, and that if any of them conscientiously believed that the Fugitive Slave Law was unconstitutional, they should disregard any instructions by the judge to the contrary."[66] The presiding trial judge, Supreme Court Justice Benjamin R. Curtis, issued one of the most cele-

---

62. Charge to Grand Jury—Fugitive Slave Law, 30 F.Cas. 1013 (N.D. New York 1851).

63. STANLEY W. CAMPBELL, THE SLAVE CATCHERS, 148-149 (1969).

64. *Id.* at 149-150.

65. Charge of Judge Sprague to the Grand Jury, 30 F.Cas. 1015, 1017 (D. Mass. 1851). *See also* RICHARD D. YOUNGER, THE PEOPLE'S PANEL: THE GRAND JURY IN THE UNITED STATES 1641-1941, 98-99 (1963), FRIEDMAN, *supra* note 61, 37-38, Barkan, *supra* note 61, 33.

66. FRIEDMAN, *supra* note 61, 38.

brated and quoted opinions disputing the right of jurors to judge the law in *United States v. Morris*.[67] Curtis argued that:

> A strong appeal has been made to the court, by one of the defendant's counsel, upon the ground that the exercise of this power by juries is important to the preservation of the rights and liberties of the citizen. If I thought so, I should pause long before I denied its existence. But a good deal of reflection has convinced me that the argument drawn from this quarter is really the other way. As long as the judges of the United States are obliged to express their opinions publicly, to give their reasons for them when called upon in the usual mode, and to stand responsible for them, not only to public opinion, but to a court of impeachment, I can apprehend very little danger of the laws being wrested to purposes of injustice.... To enforce popular laws is easy. But when an unpopular cause is a just cause, when a law, unpopular in some locality, is to be enforced there, then comes the strain upon the administration of justice; and few unprejudiced men would hesitate as to where that strain would be most firmly borne.[68]

It does not appear the jury was entirely convinced by Justice Curtis' eloquence. The very existence of slavery and of the Fugitive Slave Act demonstrated to abolitionist jurors that there was significantly more than the "little danger of the laws being wrested to purposes of injustice" that Justice Curtis recognized. Whatever danger there was, little or great, it had been realized, and jurors of the 1850s were unwilling to turn a blind eye to it.

Morris was acquitted.[69] There is no accurate way of knowing whether the jury was influenced by the arguments of Morris' attorney that they should judge the law, or whether they were simply not convinced that Morris had participated in Shadrack's escape. For whatever reason, Robert Morris, an African-American attorney, himself the descendant of slaves, was acquitted by a jury of twelve white men of assisting in the escape of a fugitive slave.

Although we cannot be sure of the reasoning behind jury verdicts in individual cases, we do know that independent jury verdicts in Fugitive Slave Act cases were common enough that the federal judiciary regularly admonished jurors in such cases not to vote their consciences. Supreme Court Justice John McLean, an adamant dissenter in *Prigg v. Pennsylvania*[70] and arguably the Supreme Court Justice most opposed to slavery, refuted the right of jurors to bring verdicts according to conscience in at

---

67. United States v. Morris, 26 F.Cas. 1323 (D. Massachusetts 1851)

68. *Id.* at 1336.

69. FRIEDMAN, *supra* note 61, 38.

70. 41 U.S. (16 Pet.) 539 (1842).

least six Fugitive Slave Act cases[71] while serving as a trial judge. Supreme Court Justice Robert C. Grier, riding circuit and sitting alongside Judge Kane, gave similar instructions in Pennsylvania,[72] as did Supreme Court Justice Curtis in Massachusetts,[73] District Judge Conkling in New York[74] and District Judge Sprague in Massachusetts.[75] The regularity of anti-nullification instructions indicates the frequency with which jurors refused to punish violations of this particularly repugnant law.

Judge Kane in Pennsylvania eventually despaired of getting juries to enforce the Fugitive Slave Act of 1850, and resorted to other more effective means to prevent abolitionists from assisting fugitive slaves to escape.[76] Because convictions were so hard to obtain under the Act, Kane turned toward granting suspects immunity from prosecution, and compelling them to answer interrogatories from the court concerning the whereabouts of the escaped slaves. Failure to answer these questions was contempt of court, and could lead to a prison sentence of indefinite duration without the need to give the contemnor a jury trial.[77] This method of enforcement

---

71. ROBERT M. COVER, JUSTICE ACCUSED: ANTISLAVERY AND THE JUDICIAL PROCESS, 191 (1975). The cases cited are: Jones v. Van Zandt, 13 F.Cas. 1040 (C.C.D. Ohio 1843); Vaughn v. Williams, 28 F.Cas. 1115 (C.C.D. Ind. 1845); Giltner v. Gorham, 10 F.Cas. 424 (C.C.D. Mich. 1848); Ray v. Donnel, 20 F.Cas. 325 (C.C.D. Ind. 1849); Norris v. Newton, 18 F.Cas. 322 (C.C.D. Ind. 1850); Miller v. McQuerry, 17 F. Cas. 335 (C.C.D. Ohio 1853).

72. United States v. Hanway, 26 F.Cas. 105 (C.C.E.D. Pennsylvania 1851), Oliver et al. v. Kauffman et al., 18 F.Cas. 657 (C.C.E.D. Pennsylvania 1853). See also Charge to the Grand Jury—Treason, 30 F.Cas. 1047 (C.C.E.D. Pennsylvania 1851).

73. Morris, supra note 67.

74. United States v. Cobb, 25 F.Cas. 481 (N.D. New York 1857).

75. Charge to Grand Jury, supra note 65, United States v. Scott, 27 F.Cas. 990 (D. Mass. 1851).

76. United States ex rel. Wheeler v. Williamson, 28 F.Cas. 682 (E.D. Pennsylvania 1855).

77. For more on Judge Kane's judicial contributions towards the enforcement of the Fugitive Slave Act, see Kane And Williamson, THE LIBERATOR, November 9, 1855:

> The law, as far as it is established by this case, is, that a slaveholder may carry his slaves through a free State, and that if any one assist them to escape, the courts of the United States may send a writ to such person, requiring him to produce the slaves, or if that cannot be done, to give all the information in his power as to their mode of escape and place of concealment. And if he refuse to do this, he must go to prison until he will…
>
> This law is likely to be far more efficient for the purposes of the slaveholders than the Fugitive Slave Law of 1850. Under this last named law, if a man assisted a fugitive to escape, he could have a trial by jury for his offence, and could therefore hope to escape conviction; or, if convicted, he was liable only to a punish-

had an Achilles' heel, however: if the slave had already escaped into Canada, there was no realistic hope of recapture. The aggrieved slave-owner could still recover the value of the slave in a civil suit against those who helped the slave escape, and perhaps Kane thought the civil damages would be sufficient to shut down the activities of the abolitionists.

Spooner's arguments on the unconstitutionality of slavery were fully developed and well publicized by the time the Supreme Court decided *Dred Scott v. Sandford*.[78] After *Dred Scott*, it was clear the constitutionality of slavery would not be seriously considered by the Taney Court. In view of the bloody history following *Dred Scott*, Spooner's constitutional arguments seem more lucid than ever, although it is unfortunate that they have so rarely been discussed or reported with an unjaundiced eye. The prevailing wisdom in America today is that slavery was constitutional, and that the Civil War was required to rid our country of its 'peculiar institution.' The gist of Spooner's arguments has been rendered moot by history.

By the time Spooner completed his trilogy, the practice of juror resistance to fugitive slave cases was well established. It was Spooner's intention to turn this trickle into a cascade that would effectively curtail enforcement of the Fugitive Slave Act of 1850. *An Essay on the Trial by Jury* is probably the fullest nineteenth-century exposition on the power of jurors to judge the law. The arguments made in it are extremely radical, so radical that they have earned Spooner the appellation of anarchist to many who have perhaps failed to adequately comprehend his works.[79] This is unfor-

---

ment limited by the statute. But, under this new law of Kane's, whoever aids a fugitive is liable to be brought not before a jury, but before Judge Curtis, Judge Sprague, or some other judicial villain, who will try the whole case himself, and if the offender shall not produce the fugitive, or give the court satisfactory information of his method of escape and place of concealment, he will be sent to prison, not for any definite period, but until he shall 'purge himself of the contempt by making true answers to such interrogatories as the honorable court shall address to him, touching the premises.

This article is commonly attributed to Lysander Spooner.

78. 60 U.S. (19 How.) 393 (1857).

79. *See* REVOLUTIONARY RADICALISM: IT'S HISTORY, PURPOSE AND TACTICS, BEING THE REPORT OF THE JOINT LEGISLATIVE COMMITTEE INVESTIGATING SEDITIOUS ACTIVITIES, PART I, VOL. I (J.B. Lyon, 1920):

The ideas of Proudhon…have had a considerable following in the United States. The principal followers of his doctrine were Stephen P. Andrew, William Green and Lysander Spooner. A prominent position among the anarchists of the country was acquired by Benjamin R. Tucker of Boston, who started in 1881 a periodical called "Liberty," which advocated Proudhon's ideas in modified form.

Id. at 843. Spooner was a leading contributor to *Liberty* until his death in 1887.

tunate, for Spooner was not an anarchist. In the *Essay on the Trial by Jury*, as well as in his other works, Spooner makes it explicit that government has a role—albeit a constitutionally limited one—to play in the administration of justice and social affairs. But he also makes it clear that government has a responsibility commensurate with that role, and that the people have the authority to actively define and restrict the role of government:

> Practically speaking, no government knows any limits to its power, except the endurance of the people. But that the people are stronger than the government, and will resist in extreme cases, our governments would be little or nothing else than organized systems of plunder and oppression. All, or nearly all, the advantage there is in fixing any constitutional limits to the power of a government, is simply to give notice to the government of the point at which it will meet resistance...
> The bounds set to the power of the government, by the trial by jury, as will hereafter be shown, are these—that the government shall never touch the property, person, or natural or civil rights of an individual, against his consent, (except for the purpose of bringing him before a jury for trial,) unless in pursuance and *execution* of a judgment, or decree, rendered by a jury in each individual case, upon such evidence, and such law, as are satisfactory to their own understandings and consciences, irrespective of all legislation of the government.[80]

An Essay on the Trial by Jury is grounded in the history of the jury and in natural law. His exhaustive investigation of history included the Norman Conquest, the Magna Charta and the full range of legal and historical materials available at the time. Spooner's conclusions go beyond a mere recitation of the history of the doctrine, and are echoed in opinions of the most radical contemporary advocates of jury independence.

Spooner believed that the right to judge the law was inseparable from the trial by jury. If jurors were to be mere fact-finders, there was absolutely no justification for going to the expense and inconvenience of a jury trial. The role of jurors, according to Spooner, is to ensure that the government does not usurp its legitimate boundaries. The people should be alert to the ambitions of every branch of government, and should always be prepared to refuse to acquiesce to any statutes that violate the natural law rights of the people. Because no one can be punished except by the verdict of a jury chosen at random from the people, the people retain the power to effectively deny legal authority to any act of the legislature.

On the other hand, Charles M. Haar referred to Spooner as an "inexorable logician" whose "literal minded approach to the Constitution resulted in an odd individualism." HAAR, *supra* note 42, 271.

80. LYSANDER SPOONER, AN ESSAY ON THE TRIAL BY JURY, 19 (1852)

According to Spooner, any statute that contradicts natural law is of no authority. It is no law, and no one may be punished for violating it. In this view, Spooner echoed the sentiments of Theophilus Parsons' speech during the Massachusetts Constitutional Ratification Convention. Unlike Justice Curtis, Spooner was extremely distrustful of judicial authority. He explained the logic behind granting "twelve ignorant men...the power to judge of the law, while justices learned in the law should be compelled to sit by and see the law decided erroneously":

> One answer to this objection is, that the powers of juries are not granted to them on the supposition that they know the law better than the justices; but on the ground that the justices are untrustworthy, that they are exposed to bribes, are themselves fond of power and authority, and are also dependent and subservient creatures of the legislature; and that to allow them to dictate the law, would not only expose the rights of the parties to be sold for money, but would be equivalent to surrendering all the property, liberty, and rights of the people, unreservedly into the hands of arbitrary power, (the legislature,) to be disposed of at its pleasure. The powers of juries, therefore, not only place a curb upon the powers of legislators and judges, but imply also an imputation on their integrity and trustworthiness; and *these* are the reasons why legislators and judges have formerly entertained the intensest hatred of juries, and, so fast as they could do it without alarming the people for their liberties, have, by indirection, denied, undermined, and practically destroyed their power.[81]

In fact, Spooner went as far as to proclaim the absence of "any power at all [for governments] to pass laws that should be binding on a jury."[82] Whether the government is monarchical or democratic is irrelevant, because "[o]bviously, there is nothing in the nature of majorities, that insures justice at their hands."[83] It is not farfetched to connect these words written in 1852, and the Fugitive Slave Act of 1850, passed by a democratically elected Congress and signed into law by a democratically elected president. It was the ability of the jury to "veto" legislation that was not supported by "the whole, or substantially the whole" that made the jury into the "palladium of liberty."[84] In Spooner's view, the randomly chosen jury of citizens does not protect minorities, but rather allows a minority to protect itself through jury duty, thereby protecting the rights and liberties of the people from the ambitions, venality and partisanship of judges and legislators.

---

81. *Id.* at 123-124.
82. *Id.* at 200.
83. *Id.* at 206.
84. *Id.*

Further, Spooner questions the maxim that all men are presumed to know the law, and ties it explicitly to ideas of *natural* law.[85] If it were really true that ignorance of the law excuses no one, then what, ponders Spooner, excuses the errors of judges and lawyers? If all men are presumed to know the law, then why should jurors be instructed at all? What reason or logic could there be in holding defendants to a higher standard of knowledge than the judge or attorneys are held to? Only where the statute is the mere codification of natural law— "that it was so clearly law, so clearly consistent with the rights and liberties of the people, as that the individual himself, who transgressed it, *knew it to be so*, and therefore had no moral excuse for transgressing it..."[86]—can all citizens be presumed to be aware of it.

In opposition to the opinion of Justice Iredell in the 1798 case of *Calder v. Bull*,[87] that "[t]he ideas of natural justice are regulated by no fixed standard; the ablest and the purest men have differed upon the subject..." Spooner believed that it was "hardly credible...that twelve men, taken at random from the people at large, should *unanimously* decide a question of natural justice one way, and that twelve other men, selected in the same manner, should *unanimously* decide the same question the other way, *unless they were misled by the justices*."[88] In a later work, Spooner elucidated the issue of natural law:

> If there be such a principle as justice, or natural law, it is the principle, or law, that tells us what rights were given to every human being at his birth; what rights are, therefore, inherent in him as a human being, necessarily remain with him during life; and, however capable of being trampled upon, are incapable of being blotted out, extinguished, annihilated, or separated or eliminated from his nature as a human being, or deprived of their inherent talent or authority.
>
> On the other hand, if there be no such principle as justice, or natural law, then every human being came into the world utterly destitute of rights; and coming into the world destitute of rights, he must necessarily forever remain so. For if no one brings any rights with him into the world, clearly no one can ever have any rights of his own, or give any to another. And the consequence would be that mankind could never have any rights; and for them to talk of any such things as their rights, would be to talk of things that never had, never will have, and never can have an existence.[89]

---

85. *Id.* at 180-181.
86. *Id.* at 181.
87. 3 U.S. (3 Dall.) 386, 399 (1798)
88. SPOONER, *supra* note 80, 140-141.
89. LYSANDER SPOONER, NATURAL LAW; OR THE SCIENCE OF JUSTICE, 12-13 (1882).

It is difficult to assess the impact of Spooner's *Essay* and other works on the history of the doctrine of jury independence. The legal literature discussing this subject show almost no mention of Spooner, although he does figure prominently in the history of the abolitionist movement. It is worth noting that Spooner's *Essay* is currently available in four different reprint editions, and that it has rarely been out of print since it was first written. Whether his works were the cause of the wave of independent verdicts handed out by juries in Fugitive Slave Act cases, or whether Spooner was merely one of the most eloquent and prolific spokespersons for the prevailing sentiment among abolitionists, Spooner's work remains the fullest exposition available of the views of the mid-nineteenth century advocates of jury independence.

State Legislative, Judicial, and Constitutional Developments

Spooner's *Essay on the Trial by Jury* is far from the only evidence available that jurors were freely granted the power to deliver an independent verdict during the nineteenth century. Several state legislatures either inserted jury independence provisions in their state Constitutions, or passed statutes granting jurors the power to judge the law.[90] One of the most interesting and long lived constitutional provisions had its origins in the Maryland Constitutional Convention of 1850, and was adopted as Article X § 5 of the Maryland Constitution of 1851, declaring that "In the trial of all criminal cases, the jury shall be the judges of law as well as fact."

This provision was originally proposed in a motion by State Representative William A. Spencer as a response to "a [recent] decision that the jury were bound by the opinion of the judge, in matter of law."[91] It was supported on the belief of the majority of the delegates that the common law

---

90. In 1851, Maryland and Indiana revised their state Constitutions to guarantee jurors the right to judge the law. Both provisions remain in force to this day, although they have been modified in effect by court decisions and practices. Mark DeWolfe Howe, *Juries as Judges of Criminal Law*, 52 HARV. L.REV. 614 (1939). An unsuccessful attempt was made to similarly revise the Massachusetts constitution in 1853. *Id.* at 608-609.

The 1820 Revision of the Laws of Connecticut provided that the court could decide questions of law and direct the jury accordingly in civil cases, but could only state its opinion of the law to the jury in criminal cases. *Id.* at 602. The 1827 Revised Laws, prepared by the supreme court justices of Illinois, provided in § 188 of the Criminal Code, that "juries in all [criminal] cases shall be judges of the law and fact." Quoted in *Id.* at 611.

91. 2 DEBATES AND PROCEEDINGS OF THE MARYLAND REFORM CONVENTION TO REVISE THE STATE CONSTITUTION 766-767 (William M'Neir, ed. 1851).

of England and the history of Maryland had established the rights of jurors to judge the law as well as the facts, and that inconsistent practice throughout the state needed to be curtailed. The majority delegates believed that the provision merely codified existing common law, thus protecting the principle of jury law-judging from recent decisions which threatened to encroach upon the role of the jury.

The amendment was opposed on the ground that it made "jurymen judges, and judges cyphers," and that "if the jury...should...convict an innocent man, he must be hung although the judge knew that the law was perverted by the jury."[92] One delegate, Mr. Constable, noted that judges had the power "to set aside a [conviction]. They could not set aside an acquittal," and Mr. Spencer answered that he "understood the practice to have been for the jury to decide the law. He understood the court to give their opinion, but that the jury were instructed that it was merely an opinion and not instruction."[93] Another delegate remarked that the "rights of the jury had been invaded by the modern construction, and he wished to see them brought back to the old common law of England making them judges of law and of fact."[94]

The new constitutional provision does not seem to have startled the courts of Maryland, or to have made much of a change in actual practice. While denying that the provision granted Maryland juries the rights to judge the constitutionality of legislation, the Maryland Supreme Court described the provision as "merely declaratory," and asserted that it had "not altered the pre-existing law regulating the powers of the court and jury in criminal cases."[95]

The jury independence provision of the Maryland Constitution of 1851 was included verbatim as Art. XII § 4 of the Maryland Constitution of 1864, and with a minor grammatical change as Art. XV § 5 of the Maryland Constitution of 1867. In 1950, it was amended to read that "In the trial of all criminal cases, the jury shall be the judges of law as well as of fact, except that the court may pass upon the sufficiency of the evidence to sustain a conviction." Those same words are currently incorporated as Art. XXIII of the Maryland Declaration of Rights.[96] A similar constitutional provision was enacted in Indiana, providing that "[i]n all criminal

---

92. *Id.* at 767.

93. *Id.*

94. *Id.* at 768.

95. Franklin v. State, 12 Md. 236, 249 (1858). *See also* Bell v. State, 57 Md. 108 (1881).

96. In 1968, a proposed constitution which did not include this provision was defeated at the polls. *See* JOHN P. WHEELER, JR. & MELISSA KINSEY, MAGNIFICENT FAILURE: THE MARYLAND CONSTITUTIONAL CONVENTION OF 1967-1968 (1970).

cases whatever, the jury shall have the right to determine the law and the facts."[97]

In Massachusetts, an unsuccessful attempt was made to enact a jury independence provision during the State Constitutional Convention of 1853. In what has been recognized as an overt attempt to overrule *Commonwealth v. Porter*,[98] a proposed amendment was offered that "in all trials for criminal offenses, the jury, after having received the instructions of the court, shall have the right in their verdict of guilty or not guilty, to determine the law and the facts of the case."[99] The amendment was thoroughly debated, with the proponents relying on theories of natural law and justice and the comprehensibility of the criminal law,[100] and the opponents contending that public opinion was more to be feared by defendants than the biases of the court, and that the common law could not be understood by jurors without the guidance of the judge.[101]

The amendment was passed by the Convention, but was defeated at the polls as a part of an unpopular package which had received little debate on its own merits.[102] Shortly thereafter, an 1855 statute incorporating nearly identical language passed in the House by a vote of 202-106.[103] The legislative history, the almost two to one vote, and the exceptionally thorough discussion this subject had received during the Constitutional Convention would seem to have made the intent of the legislature in passing this statute clear.

In spite of this relative clarity, the statute was efficiently and thoroughly eviscerated within a year of its passage. Chief Justice Lemuel Shaw, reiterating and expanding the theories he had set forth in *Porter*, ruled in

---

97. INDIANA CONST., art. I § 19.

98. *Porter, supra* note 18, 287.

99. 3 DEBATES AND PROC. OF THE MASS. CONST. CONV. OF 1853 (1853), quoted in Howe, *supra* note 90, 608.

100. *See* Note, *supra* note 24, 178-181.

101. *Id.* at 179-182.

102. *Id.* at 182-183.

103. *Id.* at 183. The statute read:

> In all trials for criminal offences, it shall be the duty of the jury to try, according to established forms and principles of law, all causes which shall be committed to them, and, after having received the instructions of the court, to decide at their discretion, by a general verdict, both the fact and the law involved in the issue, or to find a special verdict, at their election; but it shall be the duty of the court to superintend the course of the trials, to decide upon the admission and rejection of evidence, and upon all questions of law raised during the trials, and upon collateral and incidental proceedings, and also to charge the jury, and to allow bills of exception; and the court may grant a new trial in cases of conviction.

MASS. ACTS & RESOLVES 1855, ch. 152.

Commonwealth v. Anthes that "this was a declaratory act, making no substantial changes in the law regulating the relative rights and functions of the court and of the jury, in the trial of criminal cases."[104] Furthermore, if the act was intended to confer upon the jury a right to adjudicate the law in opposition to the ruling of the court, in Shaw's opinion the act would be unconstitutional. Echoing the words of Joseph Story in *Battiste*, Shaw argued it was the right of the accused to be tried by certain and knowable laws as expounded by the Supreme Judicial Court of the State. In Shaw's view, jury law-judging contravened the guarantee of "a government of laws and not of men" that John Adams had written into Article 30 of the Massachusetts Declaration of Rights.[105]

Justice Shaw was admittedly disturbed by the failure of the court to reach a unanimous opinion in *Anthes*.[106] It was a 4-2 decision, with two cogent dissents written by Justices Dewey and Thomas.[107] Justice Dewey did not accept Shaw's contention that the statute granting jurors the right to judge the law was merely declaratory:

> [W]hether, giving proper effect to its language, and construing it by the same rules by which other statutes are to be construed, it was not the purpose and effect of the act essentially to modify and change the law as declared by this court in *Porter's case*.
>
> Legislation is usually resorted to, not to reaffirm existing laws or decisions of the court, but to correct some supposed defect or omission in former statutes, or to introduce some change in the law as administered and declared by the court.... We cannot shut our eyes to the fact, that there had been recently promulgated the decision of this court in *Porter's case*, already referred to; and that, to a certain extent, there was an opinion in the community, adverse to that decision.[108]

Justice Dewey voted to affirm the constitutionality of the statute, remarking that "there is no express provision forbidding the legislature to enlarge the powers of juries in the trial of criminal cases."[109] He went on to declare that, while the accused may benefit by having the jury find the law against

---

104. 71 Mass. 185, 187 (1855).

105. *Id.* at 233.

106. *Id.* at 236.

107. *Id.* at 237, 251. Justice Bigelow wrote a concurring opinion stating that the statute was not merely declaratory—"it was the manifest intention of the legislature to change the rule of the common law, as settled by this court in Commonwealth v. Porter" (*Id.* at 251)—but Bigelow concurred in Shaw's holding that it was unconstitutional for the legislature to grant jurors this authority.

108. *Id.* at 239.

109. *Id.* at 243.

the directions of the court, he could not be prejudiced, so long as the judge was conscientious:

> ...it can hardly be possible that an intelligent judge, conversant with the trial and the questions in issue, will not easily understand whether the rulings of the court were disregarded by the jury. But if it be otherwise, the power of the court to set aside a verdict of guilty is not confined to cases where the jury may have disregarded the instructions of the court. They are to set aside the verdict as well where it is against the evidence, or without evidence, as where the jury have erred in matter of law. The whole case is before the court—the facts, and the questions of law applicable to them; and if the case, for any reason, be it error in construing the law, or in weighing the testimony, does not authorize a conviction, the court have full authority to set aside the verdict.[110]

Justice Thomas, after a long and exhaustive examination of precedent, determined that the statute was merely declaratory of the common law as settled prior to *Porter*, and that it enlarged the power of the jury "in favor of the liberty of the subject" and therefore conflicted with nothing in the state Constitution.[111] He concluded by noting that the office of jurors was judicial; that jurors were "bound to adhere to the established principles of law," but that "the jury may so far depart from [judicial] instructions as to acquit the prisoner, if they are satisfied, either that there is no such law as that which the defendant is charged with violating, or that the facts proved do not show such violation;" and that "the accused is always entitled to the benefit of the instructions of the court, in matter of law, favorable to his cause, and that the jury cannot, against such instructions, convict him."[112] Because they believed that the independent powers of jurors went only so far as to allow them to exercise mercy, Justices Dewey and Thomas did not find any constitutional violations.

In other states, courts similarly restricted the role of jurors during the latter half of the nineteenth century, often striking down or limiting earlier precedents and statutes. In Vermont, the Supreme Court affirmed the right of jurors to judge the law in the 1860 case of *State v. McDonnell*,[113] but upheld the trial court's niggardly application of the principle:

> I have a word in regard to the jury being judges of the law, as well as the facts. That is the theory in some States and governments, while it is denied in others; and to me it is a most nonsensical and absurd theory, but for the purposes of this trial we charge you that it is the law of this State. But you probably will not think that you understand the law of this case as well

---

110. *Id.* at 245-246.
111. *Id.* at 303.
112. *Id.* at 302-303.
113. 32 Vt. 491 (1860).

as the court. And you would be amply and fully justified in relying upon the court for the law that should govern this case...[114]

Chief Justice Redfield, noting the "alleged terms of disrespect in which the judge made allusion to that rule of law now recognized in this State, that the jury may judge of the law as well as the fact, in criminal cases,"[115] noted that the rule "will scarcely be claimed to have any just application to ordinary cases."[116]

> The most which can fairly be claimed in favor of the rule is, that it is one of those great exceptional rules intended for the security of the citizen against any impracticable refinements in the law, or any supposable or possible tyranny or oppression of the courts. It has always been regarded as belonging rather to the department of governmental polity than to that of jurisprudence in the strict sense of that term, and in that view is more justly considered a political than a legal maxim.
>
> [T]he principle,... because it is an exceptional rule, will always be likely to be characterized as an absurdity by the mere advocates of logical symmetry in the law, [but] will nevertheless be sure in the long run, to constantly gain ground, and become more firmly fixed in the hearts and sympathies of those with whom liberty and law are almost synonymous, and may therefore be regarded rather as an instinct, or a sentiment, than a mere logical deduction. It is...such a power as would be less likely to be wrongly exercised by juries when it was conceded, than if kept in perpetual conflict by occasional and sometimes acrimonious denials on the part of the court.
>
> But we see no objection, where the interference of a jury is directly invoked in a criminal case, to the judge stating to the jury, in his own way, that this rule is not intended for ordinary criminal cases...[117]

Chief Justice Redfield maintained the right of juries to judge the law, but recognized that in a free state with functioning democratic institutions, jury independence would only be necessary in exceptional cases. By allowing the trial judge to use his own discretion to decide how much of a role jury independence is to play, however, it seems likely that jury independence would be most disparaged in precisely those cases where it would be most needed. In recognizing the essentially political nature of juror independence, Redfield should have been aware that one purpose of the rule was to protect the defendant from the prejudicial exercise of judicial power. What was given with one hand was just as rapidly taken away with the other: in his defense of a rule that he believed created an essential connection between law and liberty, Chief Justice Redfield allowed the scope

---

114. *Id.* at 523-524.
115. *Id.* at 531.
116. *Id.*
117. *Id.* at 531, 532.

and application of the rule to be determined by those same powers the rule itself was intended to limit.

The court noted with some prescience that the nullification powers of the jury "would be less likely to be wrongly exercised...when it was conceded..." Later case history alleging racially-motivated and biased jury nullification involved jurors who had not been informed about their right to nullify the law. While it has not been established that jury nullification was prevalent in those cases, it is likely that appropriate instructions would have reduced whatever racially-motivated nullification was involved. Courts anticipate that proper jury instructions will lead to increasingly responsible behavior on the part of juries. Justice Redfield understood that proper instructions would help guide jurors to exercise their nullification powers more responsibly as well.

In spite of Redfield's optimistic view of the future of jury power in Vermont, the practice did not long survive his opinion. The injury done to independent juries by the ruling in *McDonnell* was to prove fatal in the long run. In the 1892 case *State v. Burpee*,[118] *Croteau* and its progeny were unambiguously overruled. Justice Thompson, writing for the majority, followed the prosecution's arguments that jury law-judging was neither sound in principle nor salutary in practice, and was against the weight of authority.[119]

The Supreme Court of Pennsylvania retreated from the position they had established only twelve years earlier in *Kane v. Commonwealth*[120] in the 1891 case of *Commonwealth v. McManus*, approving the trial court's instruction to the jury that "the statement of the court was the best evidence of the law within the jury's reach; and that therefore, in view of that evidence, and viewing it as evidence only, the jury was to be guided by what the court had said with reference to the law."[121] The court held that this instruction was "entirely in harmony with Kane v. Com.," leaving jurors to "look to the court for the best evidence of the law, just as they were to look to the witnesses for the best evidence of the fact."[122] The Pennsylvania Court did not choose to discuss the trial of William Penn; nor what Penn's fate would have been had Bushell and his fellow jurors "look[ed] to the court for the best evidence of the law." Nor did the Court discuss the power of the jury to "receive" the judge's opinion as to what the law is, and yet decline to apply it to the case at hand.

In a concurring opinion, Justice Mitchell urged the court to go further and "put an end, once and for all, to a doctrine that I regard as unsound

---

118. 65 Vt. 1 (1892).
119. *Id.* at 3.
120. 89 Pa. 522 (1879).
121. 143 Pa. 64, 85 (1891).
122. *Id.*

in every point of view—historical, logical, or technical...The jury are not judges of the law in any case, civil or criminal. Neither at common law nor under the constitution of Pennsylvania is the determination of the law any part of their duty or right."[123]

The Maine precedent of *State v. Snow*,[124] set in 1841, was overruled in 1865 by *State v. Wright*.[125] The court, in a unanimous opinion, announced that the doctrine that jurors "are the ultimate, rightful and paramount judges of the law as well as the facts...cannot be maintained."[126]

> It is contrary to the fundamental maxims of the common law; contrary to the uniform practice of the highest courts of judicature in Great Britain, where our jury system originated and matured; contrary to a vast pre-ponderance of judicial authority in this country; contrary to the spirit and meaning of the constitution of the United States and of this State; con-trary to a fair interpretation of legislative enactment, authorizing the reser-vation of questions of law for the decision of the law court, and the allowance of exceptions; contrary to reason and fitness, in withdrawing the interpretation of the laws from those who make it the business and the study of their lives to understand them, and committing it to a class of men who, being drawn from non-professional life for occasional and tem-porary service only, possess no such qualifications, and whose decisions would be certain to be conflicting in all doubtful cases, and would there-fore lead to endless confusion and perpetual uncertainty."[127]

The arguments made by the Maine Supreme Court, as well as by the courts in many of the states, were moving increasingly towards the assert-ed unconstitutionality of jury law-finding. These were the arguments orig-inally developed by Justice Joseph Story in *United States v. Battiste*,[128] and had become the primary arguments against jury independence in a num-ber of cases. In *Wright*, the court makes a tightly knit attempt to prove that it is unconstitutional for jurors to judge the law, in terms vaguely rem-iniscent of Chief Justice Marshall in *Marbury v. Madison*:[129]

> The constitution of the United States confers upon the Judges of the Supreme Court the power to adjudicate and finally determine all ques-tions of law properly brought before them. To allow juries to revise, and, if they think proper, overrule these adjudications, would deprive them of

---

123. *Id.*
124. 18 Me. 346 (1841).
125. 53 Me. 328 (1865).
126. *Id.* at 329.
127. *Id.* at 329-330.
128. *Supra* note 1.
129. 5 U.S. 137 (1803).

their final and authoritative character, and thus destroy the constitutional functions of the Court.

Law should be certain. It is the rule by which we govern our conduct. To enable us to do so we must know what law is. Doubtful points ought therefore to be settled, not for the purpose of a single trial only, but finally and definitively. If each successive jury may decide the law for itself, how will doubtful points ever become settled?[130]

In practice this argument goes too far. First, if it is unconstitutional for jurors to judge the law, then it is unconstitutional or illegal for jurors to have that power which no court has denied they retain and which the Constitution guarantees: the power to render a general verdict contrary to the legal instructions of the court. Second, juries do not overrule Supreme Court decisions; they merely make an equitable decision not to apply a certain law to the facts of a certain case. The jury, in acquitting, sets no precedents and has no binding authority save as a double jeopardy bar against a subsequent accusation of the same defendant on the same charge. A jury may not create new laws or convict against the weight of the evidence. And should the trial court fear that the defendant was convicted against the evidence, the court may intervene by directing an acquittal, or ordering a new trial, setting aside the conviction. Third, it is paradoxical to argue that the constitutional rights of a defendant are violated when a jury acquits him, because they did not believe the law against him was just.

Fourth and finally, jury independence does not deprive the law of "certainty." A different person may still be charged with violating the statute that the jury chose not to enforce in a previous case; the law itself has not changed. This is all the certainty that can reasonably be obtained for the criminal law. The Maine court's complaint against independent minded juries rings hollow in the context of the reality of the practice of criminal law. The law is not applied consistently or blindly by police, prosecutors or judges, all of whom are expected to act within the limits of the discretion allowed them under the constitution and the laws.[131] Many charges are dropped by the police and not submitted to the prosecutor. Many cases are plea-bargained by the prosecution or never brought to trial. Judges may dismiss cases, make discretionary (yet often decisive) rulings on evidence, suspend sentences, or grant the defendant some form of pre-trial diversion. The competence of the defense and the prosecution attorneys and investigators, as well as dumb luck, may determine the outcome of any individual case.

---

130. *Wright, supra* note 125, 338.
131. *See* KENT GREENAWALT, CONFLICTS OF LAW AND MORALITY (1989).

The reality is that there neither is nor can there be any certainty to the enforcement of the criminal law except that where the elements of a violation can be proven, a conviction may be sought, and might be obtained, by the state. Granting jurors the same discretion all other participants in the system already enjoy may lead to some slackening in the enforcement of the law, especially where the law is unpopular or unfairly applied. If it would be unconstitutional for jurors to be informed of their powers to refuse to convict, then the exercise of merciful or equitable discretion on the part of the police, prosecutors or bench would be equally unconstitutional.

Not all states have the same common law history as the original thirteen Colonies, with the result that some of the later states to join the Union have never formally acknowledged the power of juries to judge the law. Although in general the Texas Constitution allowed for the adoptation of the common law, it never entirely "received" English law in the sense that the original Colonies did. The substantive law of Texas reflected large elements of both civil and common law.[132] Although Texas eagerly adopted the institution of trial by jury, the state has never formally recognized the doctrine of jury independence. (One exception is in certain death penalty cases, described in Chapter Eight). One of the first Texas cases to consider independent juries held that

> It was not only the privilege, but the duty of the Judge to give in charge to the jury the law of the case, without regard to what had, or had not, been read to them by counsel, either for or against the prisoner. And if, in his opinion, the counsel on either side had mistaken, or misrepresented the law to the jury, it was his undoubted province to correct the mistake or misrepresentation; to disembarrass the minds of the jury, and to inform them in respect to the law of the case...For the law, it is their duty to look to the court.[133]

The Texas Code of Criminal Procedures adopted on August 26, 1856 (effective February 1, 1857) specifically denied that juries were the judges of the law.[134] It limited juries to deciding the facts of the case, and gave the judge control of the law:

> § 592: The jury are the exclusive judges of the facts in every criminal cause, but not of the law in any case. They are bound to receive the law from the court, and to be governed thereby.[135]

---

132. LAWRENCE M. FRIEDMAN, HISTORY OF AMERICAN LAW, 170-171 (1985).

133. Nels v. State, 2 Tex. 280, 281-282 (1847).

134. GEORGE W. PASCHAL, PASCHAL'S DIGEST OF THE LAWS OF TEXAS, Art. 3058 (1866).

135. Id.

Courts in Texas followed this rule consistently.[136] Arguably, this rule was inconsistent with § 6 of the Constitution of the State of Texas, which paraphrased Fox's Libel Act in what had become almost a boilerplate provision that survives today not only in the Texas Constitution but in the constitutions of several other states as well:

> § 6: In prosecution for the publication of papers investigating the official conduct of officers, or men in a public capacity, or when the matter published is proper for public information, the truth thereof may be given in evidence. And in all indictments for libels, the jury shall have the right to determine the law and the facts, under the direction of the court, as in other cases.

In the current Texas Constitution, this same provision survives as Art. I § 8:

> § 8. Freedom of speech and press; libel
> Sec. 8. Every person shall be at liberty to speak, write or publish his opinions on any subject, being responsible for the abuse of that privilege; and no law shall ever be passed curtailing the liberty of speech or of the press. In prosecutions for the publication of papers, investigating the conduct of officers, or men in public capacity, or when the matter published is proper for public information, the truth thereof may be given in evidence. And in all indictments for libels, the jury shall have the right to determine the law and the facts, under the direction of the court, as in other cases.

Not only has this guarantee not been adequate to constitute a broad grant of jury independence, but in an 1898 case, *Squires v. State*,[137] it was held that the court was responsible for determining whether any material alleged to be libels are in fact libels within scope of the law—exactly the same role the court attempted to arrogate to itself in the Colonial case of *Rex v. Zenger*. A later libel case, purportedly following but actually further limiting the construction given to Art. I § 8 of the Texas Constitution, was decided in 1960. In that case, *Aldridge v. State*,[138] the Court of Criminal Appeals held that "[t]he jury is required to take the law from the court and be bound thereby."

---

136. *See* Taylor v. State, 3 Tex. Cr. Rep. 387 (1878), Jordan v. State, 5 Tex. Cr. Rep. 422 (1879).

137. 39 Tex. Cr. Rep. 96, 45 S.W. 147 (Tex.Cr.App. 1898).

138. 342 S.W.2d 104 (Tex. Cr. App. 1960). The court wrote that:
> There are several complaints regarding the court's charge. One complaint is that the jury was not instructed on "what is not libel", and on the whole law of libel, depriving the jury of the right "to determine the law and the facts, under the direction of the court, as in other cases" as provided in Art. I, Sec. 8 of the Constitution of Texas, and Art. 1291, Vernon's Ann.P.C. These constitutional and statutory provisions were construed in *McArthur v. State*, 41 Tex.Cr.R. 635, 57 S.W. 847, and *Squires v. State*, 39 Tex.Cr.R. 96, 45 S.W. 147. The jury is required to take the law from the court and be bound thereby.

Whether the constitutional phrase "under the direction of the court" was intended to deprive the jury of the right to consider the justice of the laws themselves, or whether it was merely intended to guarantee the jury the guidance and advice of the court, were contested issues in many states until the late nineteenth century. By the end of this period, courts in a number of states which had not specifically protected independent juries by statute or constitutional provision[139] struck down the "archaic, outmoded and atrocious"[140] practice of instructing juries that they were the judges of law as well as of fact.

Sparf et al.: The Supreme Court Rejects Jury Independence

The lower and intermediate federal courts had rejected independent juries relatively early on, beginning with Justice Story's opinion in *Battiste*.[141] A number of cases during the second half of the nineteenth century clarified the federal view and paved the way for the total denial of the right of juries to review the law. The Supreme Court had not directly confronted the issue since the revolutionary era, but the stubbornness of the doctrine, combined with inconsistent opinions from the state courts (most of which were based on conflicting views of history and the common law) made this issue ripe for Supreme Court review. In 1895, an appeal of the murder convictions of two sailors reached the Court, on the ground that the jury had been improperly instructed that there was nothing in the case to justify their returning a verdict of manslaughter instead of the capital

---

139. *See* Pierson v. State, 12 Ala. 149 (1847), Pleasant v. State, 13 Ark. 360 (1852), People v. Anderson, 44 Cal. 65 (1872), State v. Buckley, 40 Conn. 246 (1873), State v. Jeandell, 5 Del. 475 (1854), Ridenhour v. State, 75 Ga. 382 (1895), Danforth v. State, 75 Ga. 614 (1895), State v. Miller, 53 Iowa 154 (1880), Montee v. Commonwealth, 26 Ky. (3 J.J. Marshall) 132 (1830), State v. Ford, 37 La. Ann. 443 (1885), State v. Hannibal, 37 La. Ann. 619 (1885), State v. Tisdale, 41 La. Ann. 338 (1889), State v. Rheams, 34 Minn. 18 (1885), Hamilton v. People, 29 Mich. 173 (1874), Williams v. State, 32 Miss. 389 (1856), Hardy v. State, 7 Mo. 607 (1842), Parrish v. State, 14 Neb. 60 (1883), Duffy v. People, 26 N.Y. 588 (1863), Robbins v. State, 8 Ohio St. 131 (1857), State v. Dawdry, 14 S.C. 87 (1866).

140. Stedman Prescott, *Juries as Judges of the Law: Should the Practice Be Continued?*, 60 MD. ST. B.A. REP. 246, 257 (1955), quoted in Gary J. Jacobsohn, *The Right to Disagree: Judges, Juries and the Administration of Criminal Justice in Maryland*, 1976 WASH. UNIV. L.Q. 571, 576 (1976).

141. *Supra* note 1. *See also* United States v. Greathouse, 26 F.Cas. 18 (C.C.N.D. Cal. 1863), United States v. Riley, 27 F.Cas. 810 (C.C.S.D. New York 1864), United States v. Keller, 19 F. 633 (C.C.D. W. Virginia 1884).

offense of murder. This case, *Sparf et al. v. United States*,[142] gave the Supreme Court an opportunity to revisit its earlier opinions on jury independence.

In *Sparf*, the defendants had been convicted of murdering the second mate on board an American vessel while at sea, a capital offense. The defendants requested the court to instruct the jury that:

> In all criminal causes the defendant may be found guilty of any offense the commission of which is necessarily included in that with which he is charged in the indictment, or the defendant may be found guilty of an attempt to commit the offense so charged, provided that such attempt be itself a separate offense.
>
> Under an indictment charging murder, the defendant may be convicted of murder, of manslaughter, or an attempt to commit either murder or manslaughter.
>
> Under the indictment in this case, the defendants may be convicted of murder, or manslaughter, or of an attempt to commit murder or manslaughter; and if, after a full and careful consideration of all the evidence before you, you believe, beyond a reasonable doubt, that the defendants are guilty either of manslaughter, or of an assault with intent to commit murder or manslaughter, you should so find your verdict. [143]

All of these requested instructions were refused. Instead, the instructions charged the jury, among other things, that:

> What, then, is murder? There are only two kinds of felonious homicide known to the laws of the United States. One is murder, and the other is manslaughter. There are no degrees of murder. I mention this fact, gentlemen, lest your experience on State juries with the State law would lead you to confusion. Nor is it the province of a jury in the United States courts to fix the punishment for murder. That is fixed by the law, as I have already read it to you, by death. The jury's province is to pass on the facts of the case, not to fix any sentence as under the State law.
>
> There is no definition of 'murder' by any United States statute. We resort to the common law for that.
>
> By the common law, murder is the unlawful killing of a human being in the peace of the state, with malice aforethought, either express or implied.
>
> Malice, then, is an element in the offense, and discriminates it from the other crime of felonious homicide which I have mentioned, to wit, manslaughter; that is, malice, express or implied, discriminates murder from the offense of manslaughter.
>
> Manslaughter is the unlawful killing of a human being without malice, either express or implied.

---

142. 156 U.S. 51 (1895).
143. *Id.* at 59.

I do not consider it necessary, gentlemen, to explain it further, for if a felonious homicide has been committed, of which you are to be the judges from the proof, there is nothing in this case to reduce it below the grade of murder. In other words, it may be in the power of the jury, under the indictment by which these defendants are accused and tried, of finding them guilty of a less crime than murder; yet, as I have said in this case, if a felonious homicide has been committed at all, of which I repeat you are the judges, there is nothing to reduce it below the grade of murder.[144]

After over two hours of deliberations, the jury returned for clarification of these instructions, and the judge strongly discouraged the jury from returning a verdict of manslaughter:

A Juror : Your honor, I would like to know in regard to the interpretation of the laws of the United States in regard to manslaughter, as to whether the defendants can be found guilty of manslaughter, or that the defendants must be found guilty?

The Court : I will read the section to you and see if that touches the proposition. The indictment is based upon section 5336, which provides, among other things, "That every person who commits murder upon the high seas, or in any arm of the sea, or in any river, haven, creek, basin, or bay within the admiralty and maritime jurisdiction of the United States and out of the jurisdiction of any particular State, or who, upon such waters, maliciously strikes, stabs, wounds, poisons, or shoots any other person, or which striking, stabbing, wounding, poisoning, or shooting such other person dies on land or at sea, within or without the United States, shall suffer death." Hence, that is the penalty of the offense described in the indictment. I have given you the definition of murder. If you remember it you will connect it with these words: "Every person who commits murder upon the high seas, or in any arm of the sea, or in any river, haven, etc...."

A Juror : I am the spokesman for two of us. We desire to clearly understand the matter. It is a barrier in our mind to our determining the matter. The question arising amongst us is as to aiding and abetting. Furthermore, as I understand, it must be one thing or the other. It must be either guilty or not guilty.

The Court : Yes; under the instructions I have given you. I will read them to you again, as to be careful and that you may understand: Murder is the unlawful killing of a human being in the peace of the state, with malice aforethought, either express or implied. I defined to you what malice was, and I assume you can recall my definition to your minds. Manslaugh-

144. Minutes of Trial and Verdict, The United States of America v. Herman Sparf and Hans Hanson, Criminal No. 2173, 30-31 (N.D. Cal. 1893).

ter is the unlawful killing of a human being without malice, either express or implied. I do not consider it necessary to explain it further. If a felonious homicide has been committed by either of the defendants, of which you are to be the judges from the proof, there is nothing in this case to reduce it below the grade of murder.

A Juror : Then, as I understand your honor clearly, there is nothing about manslaughter in this court?

The Court : No; I do not wish to be so understood. A verdict must be based on evidence, and in a proper case a verdict for manslaughter may be rendered.

A Juror : A crime committed on the high seas must have been murder, or can it be manslaughter?

The Court : In a proper case it may be murder or it may be manslaughter, but in this case it can not be properly manslaughter. As I have said, if a felonious homicide has been committed the facts of the case do not reduce it below murder. Do not understand me to say that manslaughter or murder has been committed. That is for you gentlemen to determine from the testimony and the instructions I have given you...

A Juror : We have got to bring a verdict for either manslaughter or murder?

The Court : Do not 'understand me. I have not said so....

A Juror : If we bring in a verdict of guilty that is capital punishment?

The Court : Yes.

A Juror : There is no other verdict we can bring in except guilty or not guilty?

The Court : In a proper case a verdict for manslaughter may be rendered, as the district attorney has stated; and even in this case you have the physical power to do so, but as one of the tribunals of the country a jury is expected to be governed by the law, and the law it should receive from the court.

A Juror : There has been a misunderstanding amongst us. Now it is clearly interpreted to us, an' no doubt we can now agree on certain facts.[145]

The jury convicted both defendants of murder and the court sentenced them to death. The defense appealed, contending among other things that

---

145. *Id.* at 39-42.

the trial court's instructions to the jury improperly controlled the jury and induced them to convict of murder, instead of manslaughter. The foregoing discussion between the jurors and the bench indicates both that at least some of the jurors considered a manslaughter verdict appropriate, and that the court's instructions may have led to the murder convictions. The case required the court to directly confront the question of whether the jury should be instructed on their power to bring in a merciful verdict, against the letter of the law.

The majority opinion in *Sparf* was written by Justice Harlan, and filled 57 pages of the Supreme Court Reporter. The dissent, written by Justice Gray, occupied another 74. Both opinions draw from the same history, the same precedents, and the same texts; and reach diametrically opposite conclusions. Justice Harlan denied that juries had the right to judge the law, or that they had ever had such a right:

> Any other rule than that [binding the jury to follow the instructions of the court] would bring confusion and uncertainty in the administration of the criminal law. Indeed, if a jury may rightfully disregard the direction of the court in matter of law, and determine for themselves what the law is in the particular case before them, it is difficult to perceive any legal ground upon which a verdict of conviction can be set aside by the court as being against law. If it be the function of the jury to decide the law as well as the facts, — if the function of the court be only advisory as to the law, — why should the court interfere for the protection of the accused against what it deems an error of the jury in matter of law?
>
> Public and private safety alike would be in peril if the principle be established that juries in criminal cases may, of right, disregard the law as expounded to them by the court, and become a law unto themselves. Under such a system, the principal function of the judge would be to preside and keep order while jurymen, untrained in the law, would determine questions affecting life, liberty or property according to such legal principles as, in their judgment, were applicable to the particular case being tried.... And if it be true that a jury in a criminal case may determine for themselves what the law is, it necessarily results that counsel for the accused may, of right, in the presence of both court and jury, contend that what the court declares to be the law applicable to the case in hand is not the law, and, in support of his contention, read to the jury the reports of adjudged cases, and the views of elementary writers.... Upon principle, where the matter is not controlled by express constitutional or statutory provisions, it cannot be regarded as the right of counsel to dispute before the jury the law as declared by the court.[146]

The conclusion that counsel could not argue the law to the jury had

---

146. Sparf, *supra* note 142, 101-102.

brought a prior Supreme Court Justice to impeachment. Historically, it often was the case that the primary courtroom functions of the judge were to maintain order and to advise the jury to the best of his abilities. But times had changed, and the revolutionary zeal for independence and for citizen participation in the administration of justice had given way to efficiency, consistency and administrative concerns.

Juries had also changed. Whether *Sparf* is in part a response to the democratization of the jury is an interesting question. The rights of blacks to freedom from discrimination in jury selection had theoretically been recognized as early as 1879, although it would be several decades before this ideal would even begin to be realized.[147] The enormous masses of late-nineteenth century immigrants were becoming citizens, and as citizens they were becoming eligible for jury duty. Economic qualifications and sex discrimination still prevailed in many jurisdictions; but the freeholder requirements of the eighteenth century had been drastically reduced due to necessity, as the system sought to obtain an adequate supply of jurors. The jury, formerly an elite group of well-educated and affluent white men who could be relied on to support the prevailing institutions and division of power, had come much closer to the hypothetical cross-section of society. As Wyoming attorney Gerry Spence noted in his 1989 book, *With Justice for None:*

> The founding fathers never dreamed that the system they invented would be expanded to include the class, ethnic, and social variety of the Nineteenth century. Once common men were given the right to sit on juries, it was no longer deemed safe to leave it to them to decide disputes involving interests of money and property. With the onslaught of the Industrial Revolution, the power of the jury had been wrested from them by the judges. But the history of the decline of the American jury has also been the history of the decline of democracy in this country, for the jury has always been at the heart of the system.[148]

Where social pressure in the Colonial era had favored allowing elite white male freeholders to veto the enactments of a foreign Parliament, by the end of the nineteenth century the pressure was to wrest control from the immigrants, blacks and other elements from all walks of life who found themselves sitting in judgment of their neighbors.[149] The melting pot had spilled over into the jury pool.

In dissent, Justice Gray, adamantly maintained that juries did have the

---

147. Strauder v. West Virginia, 100 U.S. 303 (1879). *See also* Ex Parte Virginia, 100 U.S. 339 (1879).

148. GERRY SPENCE, WITH JUSTICE FOR NONE, 87-88 (1989).

149. Note, *supra* note 24, 191-192:

> The criticism was particularly pointed…when numerous commentators began to argue that juries had "developed agrarian tendencies of an alarming character,"

right to judge the law; and that without that right there was no valid reason for continuing to try criminal cases before a jury:

> It is our deep and settled conviction, confirmed by a re-examination of the authorities under the responsibility of taking part in the consideration and decision of the capital case now before the court, that the jury, upon the general issue of guilty or not guilty, in a criminal case, have the right, as well as the power, to decide, according to their own judgment and consciences, all questions, whether of law or of fact, involved in that issue.[150] There may be less danger of prejudice or oppression from judges appointed by the president elected by the people than from judges appointed by an hereditary monarch. But, as the experience of history shows, it cannot be assumed that judges will always be just and impartial, and free from inclination, to which even the most upright and learned magistrates have been known to yield,—from the most patriotic motives, and with the most honest intent to promote symmetry and accuracy in the law,—of amplifying their own jurisdiction and powers at the expense of those intrusted by the constitution to other bodies. And there is surely no reason why the chief security of the liberty of the citizen—the judgment of his peers—should be held less sacred in a republic than in a democracy. Upon these considerations, we are of opinion that the learned judge erred in instructing the jury that they were bound to accept the law as stated in his instructions, and that this error requires the verdict to be set aside as to both defendants.[151]

In Justice Gray's opinion, the historical and logical role for the jury was to serve as a buffer between the accused and unjust application of the law. In this case, the jury should have been allowed to interpose its view of justice in favor of the defendant, and the instructions they were given precluded their doing this. Gray recognized the historical right of jurors to ameliorate the letter of the law by finding the defendant guilty of reduced charges, especially in capital cases.[152] Therefore, denying the right of jurors to determine the justice of the sentence their verdict would cause to be

---

and that damage suits invariably went in favor of individuals and against corporations. Many influential members of the bar evidently objected to the jury because it would be hostile to their clients and sympathetic to poor litigants. The quote is from THOMPSON, CHARGING THE JURY, vi (1880).

150. Sparf, *supra* note 142, 114.

151. *Id.* at 176-177.

152. Juries may also ameliorate by finding a defendant guilty of only one of a number of pending charges, which may lead to inconsistent verdicts, such as occurred in Dunn v. United States, 284 U.S. 390 (1932)(defendant found guilty of nuisance for possessing illegal liquor, but not guilty of possessing the liquor). For more recent cases affirming this doctrine, *see* United States v. Powell, 469 U.S. 57 (1984). *See also* United States v. Robins, 978 F.2d 881, 885 (5th Cir. 1992).

imposed deprived the jury of its rightful place in the administration of justice, and constituted reversible error.

If British common law had not been determined decisively in favor of the right of jurors to judge the law, it had certainly never been determined against that right. Jurors could not legally be bound to the court's interpretation of the law—if they could, there need be no scruples against directed convictions where no material facts were disputed. Both Justices Harlan and Gray recognized that jurors have the legal power to bring in a verdict contrary to the instructions of the court. Justice Harlan thought that this power was never intended to be exercised.[153] But as Professor Lawrence Friedman has noted, "This type of behavior has been called jury lawlessness; but there is something strange in pinning the label of "lawless" on a power so carefully and explicitly built into the law. Jury power meant that a measure of penal "reform" could take place without formal change in legal institutions."[154]

It is important to recognize the narrowness of the holding in *Sparf*. Justice Harlan suggested no way of eliminating the power of juries, *sua sponte*, to nullify the law. The case determined only that federal judges were not obligated to inform jurors of their power to bring in a verdict based on the juror's own judgment of the law. The case did not hold that federal judges could not give jurors such an instruction, or that they must disingenuously inform jurors that they were bound to follow the courts instructions. In fact, Justice Harlan specifically noted that where the states so provided, either by statute or by constitutional provision, jurors would be considered judges of the law. Because of the procedural posture of the case, all the Court decided—and all the Court could decide—was that the refusal of the court to inform the jury that they could rightfully bring in an ameliorated verdict was not reversible error.

During the closing decade of the nineteenth century, American courts were being filled with labor movement cases to an unprecedented degree. While the most famous labor-related case, *People v. Spies et al.*,[155] ended in the conviction of the eight Chicago anarchists accused of the Haymarket Square bombing (although not until after the state had thoroughly packed the jury in order to obtain that result),[156] the prosecution was finding it increasingly difficult to prevail in labor cases as the twentieth century approached. Dating back at least to the 1805 *Philadelphia Cordwainers Case*,[157] charg-

---

153. Sparf, *supra* note 142, 101-102.

154. FRIEDMAN, *supra* note 132, 285.

155. 122 Ill. 1 (1887). *See also* FREDERICK TREVER HILL, DECISIVE BATTLES IN THE LAW, 240-267 (1906).

156. *See* LEHMAN, *supra* note 35, 287-314.

ing union organizers and members with criminal conspiracies in restraint of trade had been an effective tool against labor unrest.[158] The prosecution of Eugene V. Debs for his organization of the Pullman Strike of 1894[159] was about to end in an ignominious defeat for the government when the fortuitous illness of one juror caused a mistrial to be declared, against the protests of defense attorney Clarence Darrow.[160] The case was dropped, and the government contented itself with Debs' earlier conviction on contempt of court charges for defying an injunction issued against the American Railroad Union (ARU). This allowed the government to imprison Debs while avoiding the necessity of a jury trial.[161]

It has been suggested that countering the reluctance of juries to convict in labor cases was one factor motivating the decision in *Sparf*, or perhaps leading to the Court's decision to hear this otherwise unimportant homicide case at all.[162] The government had shown high level interest in defeating the labor movement. U.S. Attorney General Richard Olney personally argued the government position in Debs' *Habeas Corpus* motion,[163] and the notedly conservative Fuller court (which had just decided *United States v. E.C. Knight Co.*[164]) could be presumed to favor the railroads over the unions. *Sparf* would have been an ideal case to choose to limit the discomfiting tenacity of independent juries.

The *Sparf* decision had only a marginal effect on the labor movement. Opponents of labor, observing the success of their efforts against the ARU, turned from pursuing criminal conspiracy prosecutions against union leaders, and increasingly sought injunctions against labor organizations after 1894. According to Felix Frankfurter and Nathan Greene, in 118 labor injunction cases in a twenty-seven-year period (representing the minority of the injunctions covered by reported opinions), "seventy *ex parte* restrain-

---

157. 3 COMMONS & GILMORE, DOCUMENTARY HISTORY OF AMERICAN INDUSTRIAL SOCIETY 59-248 (1910-1911). *See also* Schwartz v. Laundry & Linen Supply Drivers' Union, Local 187, 339 Pa. 353, 403 (1940)(Maxey, J., dissenting)(citing Commonwealth v. Pullis, Jan. Session, Court of Quarter Sessions of Philadelphia (1806)).

158. FRIEDMAN, *supra* note 61, 52.

159. United States v. Debs, 63 F. 436 (N.D. Ill. 1894).

160. *See* DANIEL NOVAK, THE PULLMAN STRIKE CASES: DEBS, DARROW AND THE LABOR INJUNCTION, in BELKNAP, AMERICAN POLITICAL TRIALS, 143 (1981). Darrow left his position as a corporate lawyer at the Chicago and Northwestern Railroad Company in order to argue Debs' case, which began his career as "the attorney for the damned." CLARENCE DARROW, THE STORY OF MY LIFE, 57-65 (1932).

161. United States v. Debs, 64 F. 724 (N.D. Ill. 1894).

162. Barkan, *supra* note 61, 33.

163. In Re Debs, 158 U.S. 564 (1895).

164. 156 U.S. 1 (1895).

ing orders were granted without notice to the defendants or opportunity to be heard. In but twelve of these instances, was the bill of complaint accompanied by supporting affidavits; in the remaining fifty-eight cases, the court's interdict issued upon the mere submission of a bill expressing conventional formulas, frequently even without a verification."[165]

Some opponents of labor injunctions decried insulating the opponents of labor unions from the necessity of first convincing a jury. In *Hopkins et al. v. Oxley Stave Co.*,[166] injunctions were upheld against several union organizers in Kansas City who had been enjoined from organizing a boycott against the appellee's machine-hooped barrels. Circuit Judge Caldwell dissented, defending the appellants' right to have their actions judged not by a court alone but by a jury of their peers. In Judge Caldwell's opinion (paraphrasing the initial verdicts in the William Penn trial), a jury would quite likely have found the defendants "[g]uilty of refusing to purchase the plaintiff's barrels and the commodities packed in them, only."[167]

Whether suppression of union activism, or trepidation over the changing composition of juries, or an actual commitment to the holding expressed, lay behind the decision in *Sparf et al. v. United States* is hard to know. What we can be sure of is that depriving jurors of the right to review the law was at most marginally effective in holding back the growth of the labor movement, although it did serve to forestall the influence of the rapidly changing American citizenry on the administration of the law.

Vices, Crimes, and the National Prohibition Act

Jury independence is a sunspot in the law, appropriately flaring up when the criminal law exceeds the limits of social consensus, dying away when the law has been reformed, only to flare up anew when legislative ambition again overtakes its legitimate bounds. Alcohol prohibition criminalized a social custom that was — and is — deeply ingrained and widely accepted in American culture. The right to be let alone; the right to do what one will with one's own life so long as one does not harm others; the right of every single individual American to go to the devil in the manner of his or her own choosing; these were all involved in the prohibition of alcohol. The results of this "noble experiment" are still debated. What is not debated is that the laws were routinely rejected by independent American juries.

---

165. Felix Frankfurter and Nathan Greene, The Labor Injunction, 64 (1930).

166. 83 F. 912 (8th Cir. 1897).

167. *Id.* at 939-940.

Unfortunately, there are few appellate court records concerning the National Prohibition Act and jury independence. There were certainly no cases brought directly challenging the holding in *Sparf et al.*, and the finality of acquittals resulting from *sua sponte*[168] jury nullification has made the record almost barren of any arguments concerning the jury independence doctrine directly associated with Prohibition. Those cases that are reported show juries frequently nullified some charges while inconsistently convicting on other, related charges. This nullification reduced the impact of the law, and left unambiguous evidence that juries reached independent verdicts.

In some areas of the country, as many as sixty percent of alcohol-related prosecutions ended in acquittals.[169] In their landmark work *The American Jury*, Harry Kalven and Hans Zeisel report that "the Prohibition era provided the most intense example of jury revolt in recent history."[170] In the 1929-1930 period, twenty-six percent of the National Prohibition Act (or "Volstead Act") cases filed in federal courts nationwide ended in acquittals.[171] The cases Kalven and Zeisel researched involved production, sales and transportation of alcoholic beverages. The Prohibition Act did not criminalize consumption, purchase or possession. If it had, it is likely that the conviction rate would have been even lower than it was. Prohibition has been described as a "crime category in which the jury was totally at war with the law."[172]

In spite of widespread jury intransigence in Prohibition Act cases, there does not appear to have been any effort made to organize jurors to resist Prohibition laws. There is no historical record of any tracts or literature urging nullification in alcohol cases. Such tracts were common during the seventeenth and eighteenth century libel prosecutions in England and the Colonies, and saw at least some popularity during the 1850s battle against the Fugitive Slave Act. The lack of a consensus of support behind Prohibition would likely have ensured any tracts of that sort a wide and enthusiastic audience. Jury independence, however, was still a strong aspect of American culture and many jurors were aware of their powers and willing to exercise them when appropriate.

Most statistics concerning the effects of Prohibition are unrevealing. Health statistics for this period are inherently misleading, because of the long period of alcohol consumption usually associated with serious alcohol-related disease.[173] Although murder rates during prohibition increased,

---

168. *Sua sponte* means, literally, of itself, as where a court moves for a mistrial on its own motion.

169. KALVEN & ZEISEL, *supra* note 43, 292 n.10.

170. *Id.* at 291.

171. *Id.* at 292 n10.

172. *Id.* at 76.

they did so more slowly than they did during the first decade of the twentieth century. Recognizing the underlying ambiguity of the statistics, one source has reported that "under Prohibition the crime rate either worsened or improved, and the pace of change may or may not have been a result of alcohol legislation."[174]

We can be sure that Prohibition was a boon to organized crime, and to the growth of a national law enforcement bureaucracy.[175] By 1939 one out of three federal prisoners serving sentences of one year or more were incarcerated for alcohol offenses, in spite of the slack conviction rate.[176] Buffalo, New York attorney James Ostrowski has noted that "convictions under the National Prohibition Act rose from approximately 18,000 in 1921 to approximately 61,000 in 1932. Prison terms grew longer and were meted out with greater frequency in the later years of Prohibition."[177] In spite of unprecedented efforts being taken to enforce this unpopular law, the blue-ribbon Wickersham Commission, appointed by President Hoover in 1929, concluded two years later that "There is as yet no substantial observance or enforcement," and urged that enforcement budgets be "substantially increased." [178]

Widespread violations of the law and public disrespect for the law go hand in hand. Vigorous attempts at enforcing unpopular laws, through complacent, ignorant or intimidated juries, inevitably creates tension between law enforcement and members of the community. In the case of Prohibition, this tension turned deadly. According to Richard Miller, "[t]rigger-happy Prohibition agents killed at least 200 innocent citizens; U.S. Senator Frank L. Greene barely survived wounds he received."[179] New York

---

173. RICHARD MILLER, THE CASE FOR LEGALIZING DRUGS, 135 (1991).

174. *Id.*

175. Historian Lawrence Friedman has noted that:

On the whole, Prohibition proved to be a costly failure. But it led to mammoth changes in the system of criminal justice. Prohibition filled the federal jails; it jammed the federal courts. In the 19th century, criminal justice was as local as local could be. It was a matter primarily for the cities and towns, secondarily for the states, for the federal government, hardly at all. Until the 1890s, the federal government did not own or run any prisons. The few federal prisoners were lodged in state prisons; the national government paid their room and board. After Prohibition, the idea of a national police force became no longer unthinkable.

FRIEDMAN, *supra* note 132, 656.

176. *Id.* at 136.

177. James Ostrowski, *The Moral and Practical Case for Drug Legalization*, 18 HOFSTRA L. REV. 607, 645-646 (1990).

178. *Id.* at 646.

179. MILLER, *supra* note 173, 136.

State Senator Joseph Galiber has commented that by repealing the National Prohibition Act through the Twenty-first Amendment in 1933:

> This country thus sensibly acknowledged the inevitable, and took limited steps to eliminate unnecessary damage caused, not by alcohol consumption, but by the laws enacted to prohibit it. Today, no innocent pedestrian is caught in a shoot-out between alcohol bootleggers; no innocent family is executed by vengeful mobs trafficking in booze; no unwitting casual drinker dies from scotch adulterated with wood alcohol by unscrupulous underground distillers; no "revenuer" kicks down the front door of a citizen's house in search of a forbidden fifth of rye.[180]

Even the low conviction rates for Prohibition offenses fail to tell the whole story. Where juries did convict, they often delivered "compromise verdicts" which resulted in reduced sentences for the accused. Just as earlier British and American juries often found items stolen to be of a trivial value in order to save defendants from the death penalty,[181] juries in Volstead Act cases sometimes found that liquor was transported which was not possessed.[182] In *Dunn v. United States*,[183] the Supreme Court affirmed a conviction for maintaining a common nuisance by keeping liquor for sale, although the jury acquitted the defendant on charges of possession and sale. Justice Holmes, quoting Judge Learned Hand's opinion in *Steckler v. United States*[184] wrote:

> The most that can be said in such cases is that the verdict shows that either in the acquittal or the conviction the jury did not speak their real conclusions, but that does not show that they were not convinced of the defendant's guilt. We interpret the acquittal as no more than their assumption of a power which they had no right to exercise, but to which they were disposed through lenity.[185]

---

180. Sen. Joseph L. Galiber, *A Bill to Repeal Criminal Drug Laws: Replacing Prohibition with Regulation*, 18 HOFSTRA L. REV. 831, 834-835 (1990).

181. *See* South Carolina v. Bennet, 3 S.Car. 514 (1815).

182. *See* Loomis v. United States, 61 F.2d 653 (9th Cir. 1932).

183. *Supra* note 152. *See also* Bilboa v. United States, 287 F. 125 (9th Cir. 1923)(acquittal on nuisance charge not inconsistent with conviction for unlawful possession or sale).

184. 7 F.2d 59, 60 (2d. Cir. 1925). *See also* Seiden v. United States, 16 F.2d 197 (2d Cir. 1926)("If they will, jurors may set at defiance law and reason and refuse to find the accused guilty; when they do, he escapes, however plain his guilt.").

Learned Hand's opinions did not change with the end of Prohibition. *See* United States ex rel. McCann v. Adams, 126 F.2d 774, 776 (2d Cir. 1942), rev'd on other grounds, 317 U.S. 269 (1942)(stating that trial by jury "introduces a slack into the enforcement of law, tempering its rigor by the mollifying influence of current ethical conventions").

185. Dunn, *supra* note 152, 393.

During Prohibition, John Henry Wigmore defended trial by jury on several grounds: that it prevented popular distrust of official justice, provided necessary flexibility in legal rules, educated the citizens of the country about the administration of the laws and improved verdicts by requiring the reconciliation of various minds and temperaments.[186] His views reflect that, even after the decision in *Sparf et al.*, juries were deciding cases based both on judicial instructions and on their own views of equity:

> Law and justice are from time to time inevitably in conflict. That is because law is a general rule (even the stated exceptions to the rules are general exceptions); while justice is the fairness of this precise case under *all* its circumstances. And as a rule of law only takes account of broadly typical conditions, and is aimed on average results, law and justice every so often do not coincide.
>
> Everybody knows this, and can supply instances. But the trouble is that *Law cannot concede* it. Law — the rule — *must* be enforced — the exact terms of the rule, justice or no justice . . .
>
> So that the judge must apply the law as he finds it alike for all. And not even the general exceptions that the law itself may concede will enable the judge to get down to the justice of the particular case, in extreme instances. The whole basis of our general confidence in the judge rests on our experience that we can rely on him for the law as it is.
>
> But this being so, the repeated instances of hardship and injustice that are bound to occur in the judge's rulings will in the long run injure that same public confidence in justice, and bring odium on the law. We want justice, and we think we are going to get it through "the law", and when we do not, we blame "the law."
>
> Now this is where the jury comes in. The jury, in the privacy of its retirement, adjusts the general rule of law to the justice of the particular case. Thus the odium of inflexible rules of law is avoided, and popular satisfaction is preserved . . .
>
> That is what the jury trial does. It supplies that flexibility of legal rules which is essential to justice and popular contentment.[187]

That one of America's most respected legal scholars was this enthusiastic about jury independence, thirty years after *Sparf et al. v. United States,* might indicate why there was no widespread jury education movement associated with Prohibition, as there was in England during the seventeenth and eighteenth centuries. American jurors knew of their power to bring in an independent verdict, and exercised it often enough to amelio-

---

186. John H. Wigmore, *A Program for the Trial of Jury Trial,* 12 J. AM. JUD. SOC. 166, 169-171 (1929).

187. *Id.* at 170.

rate the harshness of the law. It is difficult to imagine that a scholar of Wigmore's redoubtable stature[188] could have been oblivious to the fact that American jurors were "totally at war" with Prohibition. From the tone of his writing, it appears that Wigmore most likely considered the refusal of jurors to enforce the National Prohibition Act to be a positive aspect of trial by jury. Perhaps, like many Americans of his day, he personally enjoyed an occasional drink, and applauded each acquittal as a blow against an unjust regime.[189]

If the National Prohibition Act proved anything, it was that unpopular legislation could only be enforced, if at all, through draconian punishments, excesses by the police,[190] and most importantly, through complacent or approving juries. Judicial opposition to jury independence first gained prominence on the state level in state liquor control cases, such as *Pierce v. State*,[191] *Commonwealth v. Porter*,[192] and *State v. Croteau*.[193] That American juries would provide a bulwark against Prohibition came as no surprise to Clarence Darrow. America's most famous criminal defense lawyer of the period was a vocal opponent of Prohibition, which he claimed was "an outrageous violation of individual freedom against which all lovers of liberty should protest. That in fact, it is not a part of the land

---

188. John H. Wigmore, who served on the faculty of Northwestern University School of Law from 1893 to 1943 (including twenty-eight years as Dean,) was the author of more than 100 books and 800 law review articles. *See* Albert Kocourek and Kurt Schwerin, *John Henry Wigmore: An Annotated Bibliography*, 75 NW. U. L. REV. 19 (1981).

189. For an interesting (if not completely objective) look at the opposition Prohibition faced from well-educated, professional people, *see* H. L. MENCKEN, A CHOICE OF DAYS, 307-320 (1980). Other influential opponents of Prohibition included Dorothy Parker, Clarence Darrow, Fiorello La Guardia, Albert Knopf, Robert Benchley and Alexander Woolcott. Even Albert Einstein believed that the National Prohibition Act was destructive of civil government:

> The prestige of government has undoubtedly been lowered considerably by the Prohibition law. For nothing is more destructive of respect for the government and the law of the land than passing laws which cannot be enforced. It is an open secret that the dangerous increase of crime in this country is closely connected with this.

ALBERT EINSTEIN, MY FIRST IMPRESSION OF THE U.S.A. (1921).

190. *See* Olmstead v. United States, 277 U.S. 438 (1928)(Court sanctions police use of wiretaps without first obtaining a warrant), People v. Sorrells, 287 U.S. 435 (1932)(National Prohibition Act conviction overturned because federal agent resorted to entrapment).

191. *Supra* note 7.

192. *Supra* note 18.

193. *Supra* note 26.

but has been defied and neglected and cannot become a part of recognized law. I have found no one who believes it ever will be enforced, or can be enforced."[194]

Still, as late as 1931, Darrow had little hope that Prohibition could be repealed by normal methods. He believed that the supermajority needed to repeal the Eighteenth Amendment would be impossible to obtain.[195] Therefore, Darrow relied on the power of jurors and legislators to refuse to enforce Prohibition:

> Most men and women readily approve the great mass of laws that are passed by the legislative bodies. In fact, they are entirely too ready to let others tell them what they must or must not do. A small minority cannot nullify a law, but where a statute is considered tyrannical and unjust it always meets with protest. Refusal to be bound by it is such a protest. If protest is so great as to interfere with enforcement of it by ordinary methods, it is plain that it has no place in the law of the land. Since men began making laws, the favorite form of repeal is by non-observance. It was in this way that Christianity conquered the Roman Empire. If Christians had obeyed the laws of Rome their religion would have died in its birth. It was this procedure that modified the brutal laws of England that punished with death some two hundred so-called crimes, not more than a hundred and fifty years ago. It was by this same method that the laws against witchcraft were destroyed. It was by non-obedience that the horrible persecutions of heresy no longer terrified the earth. Even in America juries refused to convict for witchcraft before the laws could be wiped out. And witchcraft and heresy have put to death more victims than all other criminal statutes men ever passed.[196]

Darrow's pessimism notwithstanding, Prohibition ended with the 1933 passage of the Twenty-First Amendment to the U.S. Constitution. America's noble experiment ended a grand failure, with tens of thousands of

---

194. FORREST REVERE BLACK, ILL-STARRED PROHIBITION CASES, 10 (Foreword by Clarence Darrow) (1931).

195. DARROW, THE STORY OF MY LIFE, 293, 294 (1931):
> The prohibitionists loudly talk of the impossibility of getting rid of prohibition without changing the Constitution. Every one knows that to get a majority of two-thirds of Congress to submit the repeal of the Eighteenth Amendment to the States, and have this ratified by three-fourths of the States of the Union, is almost impossible. It would not come about unless nine-tenths of the people of the United States were in favor of such legislation...
> The prohibitionists laugh of any attempt to change the law. They say the Constitution is sacred, and it were better that tyranny and despotism should reign than that the Constitution should be ignored. Men have created an instrument so strong that it cannot be changed, and the document is more important than the citizen. The creature has destroyed the creator.

196. *Id.* at 296

people imprisoned, killed, blinded or poisoned by bathtub gin, and millions of dollars channeled into organized crime and the pockets of corrupt law enforcement officials.

If Prohibition had been enforceable, it is doubtful that it would have been repealed in 1933. If juries had not been "totally at war" with the law, Prohibition might have been enforceable. There might not have been the consensus necessary to pass the Twenty-First Amendment, and the violence and boon to organized crime engendered by the National Prohibition Act might have been prolonged, perhaps indefinitely. The verdicts of independent juries again contributed to a change in the law.

Chapter Five

The Modern Era

> *The law that will work is merely
> the summing up in legislative form
> of the moral judgment that the
> community has already reached.*
> Woodrow Wilson

State Legislative, Judicial, and Constitutional Developments Revisited

Many of the states which did not attempt to restrict the role of juries before *Sparf et al. v. United States*[1] did so during the early twentieth century. Those states with statutory or constitutional provisions protecting the role of the jury reinterpreted those provisions in order to dilute the information given jurors. In states with a common law history of instructing jurors about their right to return an independent verdict, judges modified their instructions in order to attempt to bind the jury to the instructions of the court. Some states in which courts had not spoken definitively or consistently about jury independence came into line with the prevailing viewpoint as expressed in *Sparf*.

The Pennsylvania Supreme Court clarified its opposition to jury independence in the 1923 case of *Commonwealth v. Bryson*, by affirming a trial court instruction that the jury was "to take the law from the court as the proper source of information."[2] This case furthered the more limited holding in *Commonwealth v. McManus*[3] that had been set in 1891, which left jurors free to "look to the court for the best evidence of the law, just as they were to look to the witnesses for the best evidence of the fact."[4] In *McManus*, the court was to be the best evidence of the law; in *Bryson*, the court arrogated to itself the power to be the *sole* source of evidence on the law. In spite of this, *Bryson* only declared the judge's authority to

---

1. 156 U.S. 51 (1895).
2. 276 Pa. 566, 570 (1923).
3. 143 Pa. 64 (1891).
4. *Id.* at 85.

tell the jury what the law is; it did not require the jury to deliver a conviction against their conscience.

The Supreme Court of Illinois ruled in 1931 that an 1827 statute[5] making jurors the judges of both law and fact was unconstitutional, because it denied the right of trial by jury as 'heretofore' enjoyed as guaranteed in Article 2 § 5 of the Illinois Constitution of 1870. In *People v. Bruner*,[6] the court held that a statute "which makes juries in all criminal cases judges of the law as well as the facts, therefore abrogates an essential attribute of the trial of a criminal case by a jury as known to the common law..."[7] It is not clear that the Illinois Supreme Court independently investigated the common law power of jurors to judge the law. Almost every case or text cited directly echoed Justice Harlan's opinion in *Sparf et al.*

The Illinois Court proceeded to find jury law-finding unconstitutional because "[s]ection 1 of article 6 of the Constitution vests the judicial powers in a Supreme Court and certain subordinate courts. The grant of judicial power to the department created for the purpose of exercising it is an exclusive grant, and exhausts the whole and entire power."[8] This reasoning assumes that the office of a juror is not a judicial one. This is erroneous. To judge the facts of a case is to exercise a judicial power. If jurors cannot be empowered to judge the law because only the bench has the authority to exercise judicial powers, then jurors cannot have the judicial power to judge facts, either. Either the office of a juror is not a judicial office, or the judicial power granted to the courts is not exclusive.[9]

Justice Duncan, writing in dissent, stressed that juries had been considered the judges of law and fact in Illinois since at least 1827,[10] and that no previous decision had doubted the wisdom or constitutionality of that practice.[11] Duncan pointed out that the constitutional provisions Justice

---

5. Smith-Hurd Rev. St. 1929, c. 38, § 741.

6. 343 Ill. 146 (1931). The instruction given by the trial court was that "[t]he court is the sole judge of the law in the case, and it becomes the duty of the jury to follow the law as it is given to it by the court in his instructions,' and that 'you have no right to disregard it, or disregard any portion thereof, but you are bound to take the whole of it as it is given to you by the court, and apply it to this case." *Id.* at 174.

7. *Id.* at 156.

8. *Id.* at 157.

9. *Id.* at 173.

10. *Id.* at 173:

> If it be admitted to be the fact (I deny that it is the fact) that the statute of 1827 which provided that the jury in a criminal case should be the judges of the law and the fact did make a change in the law as it had theretofore existed, it does not follow that the statute is unconstitutional.

11. *Id.* at 162.

De Young held were violated were all enacted long after jury law-finding
had become explicitly accepted in Illinois:

> The statutory provision that the jury in a criminal case should be the
> judges of the law and the fact had been in force and recognized as valid
> in this state for over forty-two years at the time the Constitution of 1870
> was drafted and adopted. The members of the Constitutional Convention
> knew of that law, and it cannot, it seems to me, be said with any reason
> that they intended that the adoption of section 5 of article 2 should oper-
> ate to destroy that statute, as substantially held by this court in its deci-
> sion of this case.[12]

The meaning of Art. 2 § 5 of the Illinois Constitution had to be determined with reference to the law as it stood in Illinois in 1870, when that
provision was drafted.[13] The right of trial by jury as 'heretofore enjoyed'
could only have meant the right to trial by jury as it had been practiced in
Illinois before that particular constitutional provision was adopted. Justice Duncan pointed out that juries in Illinois before the decision in *Bruner*
had the duty to judge both law and fact.

In neighboring Indiana, the right of jurors to judge both law and facts
had been explicitly provided for in the state Constitution since 1850.[14]
This guarantee was interpreted into a nullity by the Indiana Supreme Court
in *Beavers v. State*.[15] This was an unusual case in that the *Beavers* Court
stated it was simply enforcing the right of jurors to judge the law, even
while it approved trial court instructions that wrested the exercise of these
rights from the jury:

> The constitution of this state makes the jury the judge of the law as well
> as the facts. But this does not mean that the jurors may wilfully and arbi-
> trarily disregard the law, nor that they make and judge the law as they
> think it should be in any particular case. It means that the jurors, under
> their oaths, should honestly, justly and impartially judge the law as it
> exists, and as it is found upon the statutes of our state, in each particular
> case. It does not mean that the jurors may so judge the law in any case as
> to make it null and void and of no force, but that they shall so judge the
> laws as to give them a fair and honest interpretation, to the end and to
> the effect that each and every law, in each and every case, may be fairly and
> honestly enforced. Any other interpretation of the law would weaken the
> safeguards erected by society for its protection; for by the non-enforce-

---

12. *Id.* at 167.

13. Professor Mark DeWolfe Howe described this decision as concluding that "the legislature in 1827 had, accordingly, violated the constitution of 1870." Mark DeWolfe
Howe, *Juries as Judges of Criminal Law*, 54 HARV. L.REV. 582, 613 (1939).

14. INDIANA CONST. art. I § 19.

15. 236 Ind. 549 (1957).

ment of the law and its penalties in all criminal cases where it is shown by the evidence, beyond a reasonable doubt, to have been violated, contempt for the law is bred among the very class that it is intended to restrain. The facts must be so judged and found by the jury from a careful consideration of all the testimony given by the witnesses in the case, and under your oaths, you have no right to arbitrarily disregard either the law or the facts in the case, without just cause, after a fair and impartial consideration of both.[16]

The court found it necessary to reinterpret the constitutional provision granting jurors to the right to judge the law, because unlike a statute it could not simply be declared unconstitutional. After pejoratively (and erroneously) noting that "Indiana and Maryland are today the sole survivors of this archaic constitutional provision that a jury may determine the law in criminal cases,"[17] the Indiana Court announced its opinion that

Juries should be bound by their conscience and their oaths, and not be in substance told they may act capriciously upon a whim or prejudice. To follow their oaths and conscience is a good and wholesome admonition and certainly will not hinder, but rather aid them in their constitutional function of determining the law and the facts in a criminal case.[18]

In brief, although the Indiana Constitution explicitly guaranteed the right of jurors to judge law, the Indiana Supreme Court was willing to allow trial judges to instruct jurors that their duty was to follow the court's instructions in determining that law. The court did not acknowledge that a juror's conscience could conflict with a literal interpretation of her oath. The *Beavers* decision fails to provide any guidance to courts or jurors in cases where such conflicts occur. The only residual power left to the jury was to apply the law according to the judge's instructions, to the facts as proven at trial. The history, purpose and spirit of the constitutional provision was unequivocally ignored.

The Maryland Constitution acknowledges the right of jurors to be "Judges of Law, as well as of fact."[19] This right was interpreted not to extend to verdicts based on conscientious scruples concerning the law in the 1975 case of *Thomas v. State*.[20] In *Thomas*, the defendant's attorney "was denied permission to inform the jury in closing argument of the mandatory

---

16. *Id.* at 554-555.

17. *Id* at 556. This is not true; the State Constitutions of Georgia and Oregon contain similar provisions.

18. *Id* at 559.

19. MARYLAND CONST., DECLARATION OF RIGHTS, art. 23.

20. 29 Md.App. 45 (1975).

five-year sentence, with no possibility of suspension."[21] The attorney's hope was that, in light of the harsh sentence, the jury would nullify the law. The court refused to "read into the jury function...any such broad prerogative."[22] The court held that the jury's role was to "resolve conflicting interpretations of the law and to decide whether the law should be applied in dubious factual situations," and not to "repeal or ignore clearly existing law as whim, fancy, compassion or malevolence should dictate, even within the limited confines of a single criminal case."[23]

The role of juries was further limited in the 1981 case *Montgomery v. State*.[24] There, the Maryland Supreme Court held that jury independence instructions should only be given to the jury in

> Those instances...when the jury is the final arbiter of the law of the crime. Such instances arise when an instruction culminates in a dispute as to the proper interpretation of the law of the crime for which there is a sound basis...[C]ounsel may not in their arguments attempt to persuade the jury to enact new law or repeal or ignore existing law. However, in those circumstances where there is no dispute as to the law of the crime, the court's instructions are binding on the jury and counsel as well."[25]

This instruction allows the court to refuse to instruct the jury about its role as "judge of the law as well as of the facts" in cases where the defendant is anticipating that the jurors may have conscientious objections to the law as stated by the court. The Court would only allow a jury independence instruction in cases where there was a good faith dispute over the proper interpretation of the law. Further, the defense would be forbidden from addressing the jury as to the law except in those cases where such a good faith dispute exists. This interpretation eviscerates the protections that the Maryland Constitutional Convention of 1851 carefully drafted into the Maryland Constitution, and denies that jurors have a role to serve as "the conscience of the community."

In 1974, the Supreme Court of Iowa held in *State v. Willis* that "a district court jury is obliged not only to receive but to follow the court's

---

21. *Id.* at 51.
22. *Id.*
23. *Id.*, *cf.* United States v. Datcher, 830 F.Supp. 411 (M.D.Tenn. 1993)(holding that the jury, as conscience of the community, could be informed by the defendant of the lengthy mandatory minimum sentences the defendant faced if convicted of attempted distribution of controlled substances, where the defendant's purpose in informing the jury was the hope that they it nullify the law).
24. 292 Md. 84 (1981).
25. *Id.* at 89.

instructions on the law. The instructions are binding, not merely advisory."[26] The situation in Iowa, however, was unusual, if not unique, because in that state the role of juries was spelled out by statute.[27] The defense did not attempt to argue that the statute defining the role of jurors was unconstitutional.

Kansas trial court judges decided, as late as 1971, to draft a model instruction explaining the right of jurors to judge the law (to be given only if the defendant concurred). The model instruction read that:

> It is presumed that juries are the best judges of fact. Accordingly, you are the sole judges of the true facts in this case.
> I think it requires no explanation, however, that judges are presumed to be the best judges of the law. Accordingly, you must accept my instructions as being correct statements of the legal principles that generally apply in a case of the type you have heard.
> The order in which the instructions are given is no indication of their relative importance. You should not single out certain instructions and disregard others but should construe each one in the light of and in harmony with the others.
> These principles are intended to help you in reaching a fair result in this case. You should give them due respect. Moreover, justice will ordinarily be done by applying them as a whole to the facts which you find have seen proven. You should do just that if, by doing so, you can do justice in this case.
> Even so, it is difficult to draft legal statements that are so exact that they are right for all conceivable circumstances. Accordingly, you are entitled to act upon your conscientious feeling about what is a fair result in this case, and acquit the defendant if you believe that justice requires such a result.
> Exercise your judgment without passion or prejudice, but with honesty and understanding. Give respectful regard to my statements of the law for what help they may be in arriving at a conscientious determination of justice in this case. That is your highest duty as a public body and as officers of this court.[28]

---

26. 218 N.W.2d 921, 924 (Iowa 1974).

27. *Id.*

28. PATTERN INSTRUCTIONS FOR KANSAS § 51.03 (1971), 36-37, as quoted in JON M. VAN DYKE, JURY SELECTION PROCEDURES : OUR UNCERTAIN COMMITMENT TO REPRESENTATIVE PANELS, 241 (1977). Van Dyke goes on to quote the "Notes on Use":

> Arguably, the above instructions should bring into play the underlying value of trial by jury; the application of community conscience. If extenuating circumstances make an otherwise culpable act excusable, a jury should feel empowered to so find. Community standards are more apt to be applied if the jurors are told they are free to do what, overall, seems right to them.

Id. at 241-242.

After two years and little usage, the Supreme Court of Kansas rejected this instruction, holding that

> The instruction which we disapprove stresses the conscience of the jury as a basis for acquittal but fails to properly consider the effect of the instruction as to a conviction. The injustice which could result from adopting such an instruction when an accused is charged with a heinous crime is apparent. The administration of justice cannot be left to community standards or community conscience but must depend upon the protection afforded by the rule of law. The jury must be directed to apply the rules of law to the evidence even though it must do so in the face of public outcry and indignation. Disregard for the principles of established law creates an anarchy and destroys the very protection which the law affords an accused.[29]

The concern the court expresses over the risk of an unjust conviction as a result of a jury independence instruction is difficult to accept, so long as the defense has the right to refuse the instruction in every case. This makes it the defendant's option — and thus the defendant's strategic risk — whether to invoke jury independence or not. It is unlikely such instructions would be requested in cases involving heinous crimes. The Kansas court explicitly acknowledged that Kansas judges retained the power to grant new trials, or to set aside verdicts, where the evidence was insufficient to sustain a conviction or where the court suspected a conviction based on an erroneous interpretation of the law.[30] Defendants who have been wrongly convicted retain, of course, the right to appeal. The courts fears that resorting to "community standards or community conscience...creates an anarchy and destroys the very protection which the law affords an accused," are contradicted by the court's own admission that jury independence instructions have been given in Georgia, Maryland and Indiana without resultant anarchy or destruction.[31]

Professor Jon M. Van Dyke has written that the rejected Kansas jury instruction "does not authorize the jury to proceed lawlessly, but instead tries to impress upon the jury, in as careful a fashion as possible, the jury's role as the ultimate decision-maker on the question of whether a general law can be equitably applied to the particular fact situation presented to the jury."[32] The instruction, which was apparently patterned after the instructions given in *Georgia v. Brailsford*,[33] was designed to foster respon-

---

29. Kansas v. McClanahan, 212 Kan. 208, 216 (1973).
30. *Id.* at 212.
31. *Id.* at 213. *See also* Gary J. Jacobsohn, *The Right to Disagree: Judges, Juries, and the Administration of Criminal Justice in Maryland,* 1976 WASH. U. L.Q. 571 (1976).
32. VAN DYKE, *supra* note 28, 242.
33. 3 U.S. 1 (1794).

sible jury decision-making, not anarchy or lawlessness. The Kansas Supreme Court, in rejecting the trial judge's model instruction, was doing Kansas jurors a great disservice by denying them the guidance they needed to exercise wisely the powers they (concededly) retained. It stretches logic too far to claim that *sua sponte* jury nullification is a necessarily more valid exercise of juror discretion than jury nullification exercised as an informed and enlightened choice.

The Vietnam War Cases: A Preference for Sua Sponte Nullification

A preference for *sua sponte* nullification is precisely what the federal courts expressed in *United States v. Moylan*[34] and *United States v. Dougherty*.[35] The defendants in *Moylan* had been convicted of destroying government property, mutilation of government records and interference with the administration of the Selective Service System for their role in the break-in and ransacking of a military draft office during the height of the Vietnam war. One of the points the defense raised on appeal was specifically "[t]hat the trial judge should have informed the jury that it had the power to acquit the defendants even if they were clearly guilty of the offenses, or at least, that the court should have permitted their counsel so to argue to the jury."[36] Judge Sobeloff, writing for a unanimous panel of the Fourth Circuit Court of Appeals, acknowledged that

> If the jury feels that the law under which the defendant is accused is unjust, or that exigent circumstances justified the actions of the accused, or for any reason which appeals to their logic or passion, the jury has the power to acquit, and the courts must abide that decision.[37]

Judge Sobeloff conceded that this power of the jury is not always contrary to the interests of justice:

> However, this is not to say that the jury should be encouraged in their "lawlessness," and by clearly stating to the jury that they may disregard the law, telling them that they may decide according to their prejudices or consciences (for there is no check to insure that the judgment is based upon conscience rather than prejudice), we would indeed be negating the rule of law in favor of the rule of lawlessness. This should not be allowed.[38]

34. 417 F.2d 1002 (4th Cir. 1969).
35. 473 F.2d 1113 (D.C. Cir. 1972).
36. *Moylan, supra* note 34, 1004.
37. *Id.* at 1006.
38. *Id.*

The *Moylan* court ruled that juries may nullify, and that it is occasionally a good thing when they do so. Acknowledging that, the court ruled that jurors could not be informed of this power. The court recognized that jury independence is one of the strengths of the American legal system; but ruled that jurors must reinvent this particular wheel in every case where the prosecution is so egregious as to shock their collective conscience.

The *Dougherty* case was an appeal on behalf of seven members of the "D.C. Nine," who ransacked offices of the Dow Chemical Company to protest the use of napalm in the Vietnam war. The decision in *Dougherty* closely mirrored that in *Moylan*. Judge Leventhal, writing for the majority, held in *Dougherty* that the jurors should be instructed in such a way that they must feel so strongly as to establish an independent conscientious mandate before they can be moved to nullify the law.[39] He expressed concern that "This so-called right of jury nullification is put forward in the name of liberty and democracy, but its explicit avowal risks the ultimate logic of anarchy."[40] Even so, Judge Leventhal recognized that

> The pages of history shine on instances of the jury's exercise of its prerogative to disregard uncontradicted evidence and instructions of the judge. Most often commended are the 18th century acquittal of John Peter Zenger of seditious libel, on the plea of Andrew Hamilton, and the 19th century acquittals in prosecutions under the fugitive slave law.[41]

The crux of Judge Leventhal's argument was that informing jurors about their power to refuse to enforce an unjust law would encourage jurors to nullify the law. Where the juror's consciences were shocked by the law, they would nullify at their own initiative. An analogy offered by the Judge compared jury power to speed limits: although they are laid down as inviolable rules, drivers know that there is a 10-15 m.p.h. window of tolerance before the laws will be enforced. If speed limit signs merely stated that the recommended top speed was 55 m.p.h., there would be no limit to how fast some motorists might drive.[42]

This analogy falls apart on many points, as Chief Judge Bazelon pointed out in dissent. Motorists are aware of the tolerance applied to the enforcement of speed limits. Judge Leventhal's optimistic claim about the knowledge of the American jury pool may be in doubt:

> "The jury knows well enough that its prerogative is not limited to the choices articulated in the formal instructions of the court. The jury gets its understanding as to the formal arrangements of the legal system from

---

39. *Dougherty, supra* note 35, 1136-1137.
40. *Id.* at 1133.
41. *Id.* at 1130.
42. *Id.* at 1134.

more than one voice. There is the formal communication from the judge. There is the informal communication from the total culture—literature (novel, drama, film, and television); current comment (newspapers, magazines and television); conversation and of course history and tradition. The totality of input generally conveys adequately enough the idea of prerogative of freedom in an occasional case to depart from what the judge says."[43]

It is far from self-evident that this is at all true. Jurors may not be aware of their power to render a verdict according to conscience, or that they are immune from prosecution if they do so—particularly if they are under the impression that their oath binds them to enforcing the law as given in the court's instructions. Further, in many cases, jurors are not aware of or in control of the penalties to be imposed on the defendant if he is convicted, which deprives them of the ability to render an informed conscientious verdict ameliorating what they may consider to be an excessive or unjust punishment.

Several recent studies call into question Judge Leventhal's assumption that criminal trial juries are aware of their powers to nullify the law. For example, after conducting several surveys into this question, David C. Brody concluded that "[g]enerally, findings indicated that the public is unaware of its power and right."[44] Brody also points out that considering the "public's lack of knowledge of science, civics, and geography ... [a] policy impacting a proceeding as important as a criminal jury trial should not rest on such a speculative, hopeful assumption."[45] These studies raise the troubling possibility that some jurors may go into deliberations harboring uncorrected misconceptions concerning jury nullification which could affect proceedings in random, unpredictable ways.

Judge Bazelon thought that the trial court's treatment of jury independence "not only ... concealed [the doctrine] from the jury, but also effectively condemned [it] in their presence."[46] In his opinion, he openly displayed skepticism towards the majority view that "the spontaneous and unsolicited act of nullification [would be] less likely, on the whole, to reflect bias and a perverse sense of values than the act of nullification carried out by a jury carefully instructed on its power and responsibility."[47]

---

43. *Id.* at 1134-1135.

44. David C. Brody, *Sparf & Dougherty Revisited: Why the Court Should Instruct the Jury of its Nullification Right*, 22 Am.Crim.L.Rev. 89, n. 146 (1995); David C. Brody & Craig Rivera, *Examining the Dougherty 'All-Knowing Assumption': Do Jurors Know About their Nullification Power?*, 33 Crim.L. Bull. 151 (1997).

45. Brody, *supra* note 44, 109-110.

46. *Dougherty, supra* note 35, 1140.

47. *Id.* at 1141.

It seems substantially more plausible to me to assume that the very opposite is true. The juror motivated by prejudice seems to me more likely to make spontaneous use of the power to nullify, and more likely to disregard the judge's exposition of the normally controlling legal standards. The conscientious juror, who could make a careful effort to consider the blameworthiness of the defendant's action in light of prevailing community values, is the one most likely to obey the judge's admonition that the jury enforce strict principles of law.[48]

Informed jurors, in Judge Bazelon's view, were more likely to be responsible jurors. He rejected the view that pre-existing knowledge, implicit information or subliminal messages from court proceedings are sufficient to inform jurors of their role. Jurors should be informed of their right to acquit if in their view the law is unconscionable. Although Judge Leventhal considered this an onerous additional burden to place on the jury,[49] Judge Bazelon considered jury independence a necessary release for the jury. Jurors should not have to choose between "following the law" and "doing what's right."

The reluctance of juries to hold defendants responsible for violations of the prohibition laws told us much about the morality of those laws and about the "criminality" of the conduct they proscribed. And the same can be said of the acquittals returned under the fugitive slave law as well as contemporary gaming and liquor laws. A doctrine that can provide us with such critical insights should not be driven underground.[50]

Even though *Dougherty* has been so often cited, it is interesting to note that the *Dougherty* court was probably poorly advised to go into the nullification issue at all. The case was reversed because the defendants had been improperly denied their rights of self-representation. Accordingly, the entire discussion of nullification in *Dougherty* is probably best considered as dicta, and not even legally binding upon the district courts in the D.C. Circuit. It is a long standing rule of appellate law that courts should not discuss constitutional issues that are not necessary for the decision. Thus, the *Dougherty* court carefully concentrated on the historical context and almost completely avoided reaching the constitutional implications of their nullification discussion. *Dougherty* is simply not as strong a precedent as it has been made out to be, yet it is one of the most cited cases on this subject.

---

48. *Id.*
49. *Id.* at 1136:
> To tell him expressly of a nullification prerogative, however, is to inform him, in effect, that it is he who fashions the rule that condemns. That is an overwhelming responsibility, an extreme burden for the juror's psyche.
50. *Id.* at 1143-1144.

The *Moylan* and *Dougherty* courts were giving voice to a preference for *sua sponte* nullification that had been developed through several United States Supreme Court cases following *Sparf et al.* In any number of cases, the federal courts had been unwilling to either endorse "jury lawlessness," as it had become known, or to take any measures that would eliminate the power of juries to deliver a verdict according to conscience. It was haphazardly left up to the jury to discover and apply the doctrine of jury independence on its own initiative.

In order to prevent juries from delivering independent verdicts, a Massachusetts federal district court, trying the well-known child development author Dr. Benjamin Spock, along with co-defendants Rev. William Sloane Coffin, Jr., Michael Ferber and Mitchell Goodman, chose to submit special interrogatories to the jury for its decision in addition to the regular general verdict of "guilty" or "not guilty" normally used in criminal cases.[51] Special interrogatories, also referred to as special verdicts or special questions, are specific factual questions put to the jurors to be answered "yes" or "no." Although they are routinely used in civil cases, they are almost unknown in criminal law. The defendants were charged with conspiracy to counsel, aid and abet draft resistance during the height of the Vietnam war.

The First Circuit was apparently incensed at this innovation by the trial judge. The appellate court recognized that the trial judge was concerned that the jury would nullify, but asserted that the use of special interrogatories would destroy the purpose of the criminal trial jury:

> Of more substantive importance is the fundamental difference between the jury's function in civil and criminal cases. In civil trials, the judge, if the evidence is sufficiently one-sided, may direct the jury to find against the defendant even though the plaintiff entered the case bearing the burden of proof. In a criminal case a court may not order the jury to return a verdict of guilty, no matter how overwhelming the evidence of guilt. This principle is so well established that its basis is not normally a matter of discussion. Put simply, the right to be tried by a jury of one's peers finally exacted from the king would be meaningless if the king's judges could call the turn. In the exercise of its functions not only must the jury be free from direct control in its verdict, but it must be free from judicial pressure, both contemporaneous and subsequent. Both have been said to result from the submission of special questions.[52]

The court was primarily concerned with the "subtle, and perhaps open, direct effect that answering special questions may have upon the jury's ultimate verdict."[53] A series of questions, posed so as to lead inexorably to

---

51. United States v. Spock, 416 F.2d 165, 180-183 (1st Cir. 1969).

52. *Id.* at 180-181.

53. *Id.* at 182.

a pre-determined result, would completely deprive the defendant of the reasoned moral judgment of the community, by forcing the jury to follow the path of reasoning the judge felt appropriate. The court feared that "[b]y a progression of questions each of which seems to require an answer unfavorable to the defendant, a reluctant juror may be led to vote for a conviction which, in the large, he would have resisted. The result may be accomplished by the majority of the jury, but the course has been initiated by the judge, and directed by him through the frame of his questions."[54]

Interestingly, the court was upset that special interrogatories would prevent the jury from considering the moral implications of their verdict. At some contrast to the *Moylan* and *Dougherty* courts, this court argued that:

> Uppermost of these considerations is the principle that the jury, as the conscience of the community, must be permitted to look at more than logic. Indeed, this is the principle upon which we began our discussion. If it were otherwise there would be no more reason why a verdict should not be directed against a defendant in a criminal case than in a civil one. The constitutional guarantees of due process and trial by jury require that a criminal defendant be afforded the full protection of a jury unfettered. Here, [where] some of the defendants could be found to have exceeded the bounds of free speech, the issue was peculiarly one to which a community standard or conscience was, in the jury's discretion, to be applied. Whether we agree with defendant's position or not, this was not a case to be subjected to special limitations not sanctioned by general practice.[55]

Not only did the *Spock* court specifically call on the independent powers of the jury to determine whether the law should be applied in this case, but they founded that decision on the constitutional protections of the Fifth and Sixth Amendments. They asserted that due process requires that a jury not be impeded from rendering an independent verdict as a matter of conscience, and the constitutional fault of special interrogatories was that they interfered with that due process protection provided by the jury. If due process forbade the use of special interrogatories in criminal cases, then it would appear that *Spock* created a *per se* rule against their use, at least in the First Circuit.

The Third Circuit in the 1982 case of *United States v. Desmond*,[56] however, found special verdicts permissible where they do not harm the defendant, or where they are not objected to at trial.[57] Although recognizing

---

54. *Id.*

55. *Id.* at 182-183.

56. United States v. Desmond, 670 F.2d 414 (3rd. Cir. 1982).

57. *Id.*; *see also* United States v. Palmeri, 630 F.2d 192 (3rd. Cir. 1980); United States v. Frezzo Brothers, Inc., 602 F.2d 1123 (3rd Cir. 1979). *But see* United States v. Childress, 746 F.Supp. 1122 (D.D.C. 1990)(approving special interrogatory verdict form in multi-defendant drug conspiracy case, saying "[t]he verdict form employed by the Court was

that as "a general proposition, special verdicts are generally disfavored in criminal cases,"[58] and that "[u]nderlying this aversion is the feeling that denial of a general verdict might deprive the defendant of the right to a jury's finding based more on external circumstances than the strict letter of the law,"[59] the court, over one impassioned dissent, has not been willing to prohibit the use of special verdicts in criminal cases, at least in situations where the defense had not objected to their use at trial. Judge Aldisert, in dissent, would have banned special interrogatories altogether except at the motion of the defense showing good cause to justify their use, or where they are required by law:[60]

> My view is that there has been sufficient experimentation by the district courts with this discredited practice, and we now have the solid experience. We are now in a position to enunciate a controlling principle severely restricting the use of special verdicts and special interrogatories in criminal cases. The majority opinion carefully sets forth the history and the reasons for our disenchantment, with a procedure that seeks to catechize a jury and thus infringe upon its power to deliberate freely as the conscience of the community.[61]

The most significant jury rights case decided by the Supreme Court following *Sparf* was probably *Duncan v. Louisiana* in 1968.[62] *Duncan* was the appeal of a black man who had been convicted of simple assault after having touched a white 'victim' on the elbow in an attempt to break up a racial altercation between two black males and three white males. Duncan was denied a trial by jury under Louisiana law, which only granted jury trials in felony cases. The Supreme Court remanded Duncan's case for a new trial by jury, holding that "the Fourteenth Amendment guarantees a right of jury trial in all criminal cases which—were they to be tried in a federal court—would come within the Sixth Amendment's guaran-

---

consistent with the Court's duty to remind the jury of its obligation to reach a verdict based on an application of the law to the evidence seen and heard in the courtroom during the trial and not based on extraneous influences.")

58. *Desmond, supra* note 56, 416.

59. *Id.* at 418.

60. U.S. CONST. art. III, § 3(1) requires a special finding that two witnesses have testified to the same overt act of treason before a defendant can be convicted. *See* Kawakita v. United States, 343 U.S. 717 (1952). *See also* United States v. Uzzolino, 651 F.2d 207 (3rd Cir. 1981)(a determination of certain facts may be required in conspiracy cases, but may be obtained by submitting special interrogatories to jury after they have returned a general verdict of guilty).

61. *Desmond, supra* note 56, 421.

62. 391 U.S. 145 (1968).

tee."[63] Justice White, writing for the majority, explicitly recognized the role of the jury as a buffer between the government and the accused:

> The guarantee of jury trial in the Federal and State Constitutions reflects a profound judgment about the way in which law should be enforced and justice administered. A right to jury trial is granted to criminal defendants in order to prevent oppression by the Government. Those who wrote our constitutions knew from experience that it was necessary to protect against unfounded criminal charges brought to eliminate enemies and against judges too responsive to the voice of higher authority. The framers of the constitutions strove to create an independent judiciary but insisted upon further protection against arbitrary action. Providing an accused with the right to be tried by a jury of his peers gave him an inestimable safeguard against the corrupt or overzealous prosecutor and against the compliant, biased, or eccentric judge. If the defendant preferred the common-sense judgment of a jury to the more tutored but perhaps less sympathetic reaction of the single judge, he was to have it. Beyond this, the jury trial provisions in the Federal and State Constitutions reflect a fundamental decision about the exercise of official power—a reluctance to entrust plenary powers over the life and liberty of the citizen to one judge or to a group of judges. Fear of unchecked power, so typical of our State and Federal Governments in other respects, found expression in this insistence upon community participation in the determination of guilt or innocence. The deep commitment of the Nation to the right of jury trial in serious criminal cases as a defense against arbitrary law enforcement qualifies for protection under the Due Process Clause of the Fourteenth Amendment, and must therefore be respected by the States.[64]

This dicta in *Duncan* is significant on several counts. Most importantly, the Court recognized that the criminal trial jury's role is to "prevent oppression by the government." Obviously, the legislature is as much a part of the government as the executive or judicial branches. If the jury is to prevent oppression by the government, it must have as much ability to buffer defendants from the excesses of the legislature as from those of the judiciary. If the defendant was to have meaningful access to "the common-sense judgment of a jury" instead of "the more tutored but less sympathetic reaction of the single judge," the jury could not be hamstrung by the bench. It must have the rightful authority to interpose its independent judgment as a protection to the accused.

White goes on to recognize that "when juries differ with the result at which the judge would have arrived, it is usually because they are serving some of the very purposes for which they were created and for which they

---

63. *Id.* at 149.
64. *Id.* at 155-156.

are now employed."[65] The purposes for which juries were created under common law dating back to before the Magna Charta include reviewing the law. Justice White is plainly referring to the ability of the jury to refuse to convict on conscientious grounds. No other interpretation presents itself. But, under *Sparf*, the jurors must either be aware of their power to judge the law before they enter the courtroom, or re-invent it from whole cloth during their deliberations. The judge is not obliged to inform them, and the defense attorney is usually not allowed to.

Duncan was followed by *Taylor v. Louisiana*,[66] which was decided six years later. In *Taylor*, the Court held that the Constitution required that a jury be selected from a representative cross section of the community. The Court struck down Louisiana constitutional and statutory provisions which exempted all women from jury service unless they had filed a written request to serve as jurors. Although the Court recognized reasonable administrative flexibility, allowing the states to grant hardship exemptions and to prescribe reasonable qualifications for jury duty, they held that "jury wheels, pools of names, or venires from which juries are drawn must not systematically exclude distinctive groups in the community and thereby fail to be reasonably representative thereof."[67]

The Court insisted on representative panels because the protective functions of the jury "are not provided if the jury pool is made up of only special segments of the populace or if large, distinctive groups are excluded from the pool."[68] The defendant was entitled to the judgment of a cross-section of the community. The Court went on to declare that

> Community participation in the administration of the criminal law, moreover, is not only consistent with our democratic heritage but is also critical to public confidence in the fairness of the criminal justice system. Restricting jury service to only special groups or excluding identifiable segments playing major roles in the community cannot be squared with the constitutional concept of jury trial.[69]

As in *Duncan*, the *Taylor* Court did not discuss the role jurors had in judging the law. It is plain, however, that the role the Court described cannot be fairly performed by a jury whose sole function is that of fact-finders. That "community participation in the administration of the criminal law," which the court found to be "critical to public confidence," is a shallow concept where that participation is not accompanied by the informed

---

65. *Id.* at 157.
66. 419 U.S. 522 (1974).
67. *Id.* at 537.
68. *Id.* at 530.
69. *Id.*

exercise of rightful discretion. The court seems willing to allow the jury to serve as the voice of the community, and is positing a mandate of constitutional dimensions that that voice be heard. However, they would not recommend, much less require, that jurors be informed of their discretionary powers. Hence, in *Duncan* and *Taylor* the Supreme Court implicitly enunciated the same irrational preference for *sua sponte* nullification that has become characteristic.

This preference is irrational because jurors who are aware of their power to nullify are more likely to exercise it responsibly and appropriately than those who are not. Two studies by psychologist Irwin Horowitz[70] have shown that juries instructed that they are the judges of the law are more likely to convict defendants they considered dangerous (drunk drivers) and less likely to convict defendants whose behavior they considered understandable, excusable or merciful (illegal weapons possession and euthanasia cases).[71] Consistent with the opinion of Judge Bazelon, there was no difference in the results obtained in murder cases.[72] These studies present evidence that a particular group of defendants—those who have done the least harm—are prejudiced by the refusal of the court to inform the jury of its powers. The jurors in Horowitz' studies were apparently unaware, before entering the study, of the power they had; if they had been aware they would not have been so influenced by the changes in the instructions. It is illogical to assume that jurors would be greatly affected by being told what they already know.[73] Counting on jurors to come to court aware of their hidden powers runs counter to what little empirical evidence exists.

There is another reason for rejecting any preference for *sua sponte* nullification. Psychological studies indicate that a juror may be willing to convict and impose a cruel sentence if the legal system supports and applauds his actions, because judicial instructions have deprived him of any personal moral responsibility for his verdict. A study made by psychologist Stanley Milgram in 1963 tested the willingness of college students to inflict pain on test subjects in a simulated "learning experiment."[74] Subjects were told to administer electrical shocks of increasing severity to a test subject

70. Irwin A. Horowitz, *Jury Nullification: The Impact of Judicial Instructions, Arguments, and Challenges on Jury Decision Making*, 12 LAW & HUM. BEHAV. 439 (1988); Irwin A. Horowitz, *The Effect of Jury Nullification Instructions on Verdicts and Jury Functioning in Criminal Trials*, 9 LAW & HUM. BEHAV. 25 (1985).

71. Horowitz, *Jury Nullification, supra* note 70, 450-452.

72. Horowitz, *The Effect of Jury Nullification Instructions, supra* note 70, 33.

73. There is some chance that reaffirmation of one's knowledge could have an effect, but it is likely to be a positive effect-leading to more responsible jury deliberation.

74. *See* Stanley Milgram, *Behavioral Study of Obedience*, 67 J. ABNORMAL & SOC. PSYCHOL. 371 (1963).

whenever they received a wrong answer to a word-matching test. The simulated shock generator was labeled from 15-450 volts in thirty steps, from "Slight Shock", through "Intense Shock" and "Danger: Severe Shock" to the ominous "XXX" over the 435 and 450 volt levels.

The "victim," a confederate of the test administrator, was strapped into a chair; he could not escape. In spite of the victim's protests and refusal to answer questions above the 300 volt level, 65% of the test subjects administered shocks up to the maximum level. (No actual shocks were administered, but the subject was ignorant of this fact.) Subjects were willing to follow the director's admonitions to continue, even though "[t]o disobey would bring no material loss to the subject; no punishment would ensue."[75] Test subjects routinely administered what they thought were dangerously severe shocks to defenseless victims on the basis of a wrong answer to a word game, on the authority of an experimenter operating on a college campus. Is it then outrageous to speculate that jurors, unaware of their power to legally do otherwise, might also impose outrageous punishments for minor or negligible infractions, based on the (presumably much stronger) authority of a robed judge in an austere courtroom? Milgram noted that his test subjects violated their own conscientious scruples in proceeding as far as they did; and that it was their willingness to obey authority that induced them to play the role of willing torturers of innocent victims:

> It is clear from the remarks and outward behavior of many participants that in punishing the victim they are often acting against their own values. Subjects often expressed deep disapproval of shocking a man in the face of his objections, and others denounced it as stupid and senseless. Yet the majority complied with the experimental commands.[76]

Among the factors Milgram identified as contributing to the obedience of the test subjects was that the experiment took place "on the grounds of an institution of unimpeachable reputation," that the experiment was "designed to attain a worthy purpose," that "certain features of the procedure strengthen the subject's sense of obligation to the experimenter," and perhaps most importantly for jury independence purposes, that "there is a vagueness of expectation concerning what a psychologist may require of his subject, and when he is overstepping acceptable limits.[77]

There is a similar ambiguity over what a judge (or the law itself) can legitimately require a juror to do. Can a juror be asked to impose a draconian penalty on a well-meaning defendant because of a *de minimis* vio-

---

75. *Id.* at 376.
76. *Id.*
77. *Id.* at 377.

lation of the law? Can a juror be required to ignore the dictates of conscience and enforce the law, even when it seems "stupid and senseless" to do so? The juror does not have ready answers to these questions. He deserves, and should receive, candid instructions from the court. He should not be told, as Milgram's subjects were when they balked: "You have no other choice, you must go on."[78]

This judicial preference for *sua sponte* nullification did not prevail in every Vietnam War protest case. Occasionally, the arguments of the protesters and their lawyers prevailed, and jurors were given information on their rights to acquit against the evidence, when it would be unjust to enforce the law. The 1973 trial of the "Camden 28" was one such case.[79] In that case, an F.B.I. informant had supplied the defendants with tools, supplies and transportation needed to break into a Selective Service Office in order to steal and destroy draft records. The informant, Robert Hardy, made the following statement in his pretrial affidavit:

> I provided 90% of the tools necessary for the action. They couldn't afford them, so I paid and the F.B.I. reimbursed me. It included hammers, ropes, drills, bits, etc. They couldn't use some of the tools without hurting themselves, so I taught them. My van was used on a daily basis (the F.B.I. paid the gas). I rented trucks for the dry runs and provided about $20 to $40 worth of groceries per week for the people living at Dr. Anderson's. This, and all my expenses, were paid for by the F.B.I.[80]

Judge Clarkson S. Fisher initially told the jury that it was bound to follow the law according to his instructions, but later reversed himself, informing the jury that "if you find that the overreaching participation by Government agents or informers in the activities as you have heard them here was so fundamentally unfair as to be offensive to the basic standards of decency, and shocking to the universal sense of justice, then you may acquit any defendant to whom this defense applies."[81] Further, Judge Fisher went so far as to allow defense attorney David Kairys to explain the doctrine of jury nullification to the jury.[82] The defendants were acquitted.

---

78. *Id.* at 374.

79. United States v. Anderson et al., 356 F.Supp. 1311 (D.N.J. 1973).

80. Roger Park, *The Entrapment Defense*, 60 MINN. L. REV. 163, 188 (1976).

81. VAN DYKE, *supra* note 28, 238-239.

82. United States v. Anderson et al., Transcript, 8386-8394. Kairys' argument is reproduced at length in VAN DYKE, *supra* note 28, 239-240. A few excerpts follow:

> Now, I'd like to move on—and I am almost done now—to the second reason why I think this case is not simple and why I think these defendants should be acquitted. And that's jury nullification.
>
> Now, the term "nullification" I think is a bad term. It's used to describe the power of a jury to acquit if they believe that a particular law is oppressive, or if they

The Vietnam war protest cases inspired a wealth of articles on jury independence. Two of the most important were written by University of Michigan law professor Joseph L. Sax and Manhattan criminal defense attorney William M. Kunstler. Professor Sax published his article *Conscience and Anarchy: The Prosecution of War Resisters*[83] in a general interest publication, *The Yale Review,* instead of in a law review or professional publication. In this forum Sax managed to reach a wider audience of potential jurors and opinion makers, instead of focusing solely on legal professionals.

---

believe that a law is fair but to apply it in certain circumstances would be oppressive…

This power that jurors have is the reason why we have you jurors sitting there instead of computers. Because you are supposed to be the conscience of the community. You are supposed to decide if the law, as the Judge explains it to you, should be applied or if it should not. Nothing the Judge would say to you is inconsistent with this power.

…You decide, considering the circumstances of the case, should you brand the defendants as criminal. And it's very important in that regard, that you are only required to say guilty or not guilty. That's what people call the general verdict. You don't have to give reasons. You don't have to give specifics. You don't have to justify what you did; and if you say not guilty, it can't be reviewed by any Court…Are they deserving of the community's scorn—you being the community—or are they not deserving of the community's scorn? That's what the question is.

Now, the defendants have violated the law, and they've destroyed property, and they've explained to you how they did this, to preserve life and to preserve liberty. Now, as I indicated in my opening statement, that may sound radical, but I submit that it's in the best American tradition. And it starts, of course, with George Washington, Thomas Jefferson, and Benjamin Franklin, all of whom violated the law to preserve life and liberty.

The Boston Tea Party, the people who did that violated the law to preserve life and liberty, and I explained some New Jersey Tea Parties that were here. One of them involved someone from Cumberland County [New Jersey] to whom there is a statue in a square in a town in Cumberland County. He became the Governor after he did that and after a jury refused to indict or convict him.

[The next several paragraphs described the defendants on trial and their particular decision to commit an act of civil disobedience.]

…You must judge who went too far. Did the Government go too far in prosecuting the war? Did the defendants go too far? Did the F.B.I. go too far? And I think those kinds of judgments really require you to look at and in some sense judge yourself. The prosecution is asking you to publicly brand these people as criminals; and if that's done it will be done in your name. No one else's.

I urge you to say no to the prosecution, say no to this horrible war, way no to the F.B.I.'s manufacture of a crime, and say yes to some hope for the future. Say yes for life. Thank you.

83. 57 YALE L. REV. 481 (1968).

Sax argued that allowing juries to pass judgment on the law as well as the facts provides a sensible compromise between allowing every individual to be the sole judge of his or her own conduct, and requiring a conviction whenever a law has been broken. In terms reminiscent of John Henry Wigmore, Sax argued that jury independence "indicates the ability of a viable legal system to accommodate itself to those situations in which violation of the law should be viewed as justifiable."[84] This flexibility is especially important, says Sax, when political pressures make the normal constraints on the discretionary decision-making of the police, prosecutors and judges unreliable. Such political pressures are at their greatest when the alleged crimes themselves are by-products of a political protest. They indicate that the system has broken down; independent juries can provide the correction.

> [P]olitical prosecutions...are...generally directed to acts that are rather trivial (such as trespass); or are largely symbolic in their nature, and usually at the periphery of free speech; or urge passive resistance as a means to press for changes in the law...[I]t will sometimes be necessary to protest an unjust law by violating it and putting the question of justification to one's fellow citizens.[85]

The defendant who breaks a law, with his only hope of acquittal being that the jury will approve of his behavior, is taking a huge risk. The jury might just as easily approve of the law, and condemn him with pleasure. Vietnam War protesters were willing to take the risk of leaving the verdict up to the "conscience of the community." They were willing to hazard their freedom on their confidence that public opinion approved of their acts. The courts and the prosecutors were rarely so confident in the public's support of their position.

William Kunstler's viewpoint was similar to that expressed by Sax, but his writing was directed towards a more technical audience of legal professionals.[86] Professor Sax did not give citations or references; Kunstler's article is written in standard law review format, including full "blue-book" citations. But Kunstler also wrote with the voice of experience. He had served as defense counsel in several leading war protest cases, and had unsuccessfully attempted to raise jury independence arguments in several of them.[87] After reviewing the history behind jury independence, Kunstler asserts that

---

84. *Id.* at 487.

85. *Id.* at 493.

86. William M. Kunstler, *Jury Nullification in Conscience Cases*, 10 Va. J. Int'l. L. 71 (1969).

87. *See* United States v. Dellinger, 472 F.2d 340 (7th Cir. 1972), *cert. denied* 410 U.S. 970 (1973), United States v. Berrigan, 283 F.Supp. 336 (D. Md. 1968).

To support jury nullification is not to maintain that men are free to pick and choose with impunity what laws they will or will not obey. This is not and has never been the historical standard. However, when such choices are made, it is not too much to demand that juries must be let in on the closely guarded secret that they are, in the final analysis, the consciences of their communities and, as such, are free to acquit those, like John Peter Zenger, who, under ordinary circumstances, are indeed guilty of breaking the law in question. This is a far cry from insisting that all men who follow the dictates of their consciences must go free on that account, alone.

Unless the jury can exercise its community conscience role, our judicial system will have become so inflexible that the effect may well be a progressive radicalization of protest into channels that will threaten the very continuance of the system itself. To put it another way, the jury is, both by original design and by the nature of its own inherent structure, the safety valve that must exist if this society is to be able to accommodate itself to its own internal stresses and strains. If the jury can negate both law and fact, then it can express the deep desires of the community it represents as to whether it feels that, under certain circumstances, some laws should indeed be broken with impunity. In this manner, this ancient institution can significantly affect or even determine whether men shall survive or perish, eat or go hungry, or live in liberty or as slaves.[88]

Sax and Kunstler's unabashed advocacy of jury independence was widely discussed in academic and professional circles, and led to the publication of a number of articles on jury independence, in law reviews and elsewhere. One of the first to take up the gauntlet was Michael E. Tigar, who had worked briefly with Kunstler on the Chicago Seven conspiracy trial.[89] Tigar urged much broader participation by both defendants and jurors in the trial process, in order to circumvent the excessive formality and ritual of criminal procedure:

The "men of the country" become increasingly important as the system itself becomes suspect, for they are presumably less tempted to manipulate clients and concepts for their own benefit. A judgment by the community, moreover, seems inherently more trustworthy than one rendered in a contest of champions. With regard to the role of both defendant and jury, then, there is needed an assault on the old procedural forms, to see whether the courtroom can accommodate the sensibilities of those who are most profoundly affected by what goes on there.[90]

---

88. Kunstler, *supra* note 86, 83.

89. *Dellinger, supra* note 87. Tigar had been retained to draft pre-trial motions.

90. Michael E. Tigar, *The Supreme Court—Foreword*, 84 HARV. L. REV. 1, 27 (1970).

Tigar went beyond the usual arguments for jury law-judging and insisted that jurors should be encouraged to "participate in the questioning of witnesses, clarifying any lingering uncertainties or doubts."[91] Tigar later wrote a play extolling jury independence in the context of the John Peter Zenger trial, *The Trial of John Peter Zenger, A Play in Five Scenes*. The play was originally performed at the annual meeting of the American Bar Association on August 10, 1986.[92]

Another author, Professor Jon M. Van Dyke, took on the jury independence arguments directly, arguing that the jury is inherently a political institution.[93] His sentiments were echoed two years later by Professor Alan Scheflin,[94] who had been one of the attorneys in *United States v. Dougherty*. The number of articles published on the subject was increasing in both number and stature.[95] Most of the published articles were either supportive or neutral towards jury independence, and initially focused (at least implicitly) on the right of jurors to acquit political protesters in anti-

---

91. *Id.*

92. For a review of the play *see* James M. Treece, *Look To Your Hearts As Well*, 66 Tex. L. Rev. 715 (1988).

93. Jon M. Van Dyke, *The Jury as a Political Institution*, 16 Cath. Law. 224 (1970), reprinted from 3 Center Magazine 2 (March, 1970).

94. Alan Scheflin, *Jury Nullification: The Right To Say No*, 45 S. Cal. L. Rev. 168 (1972).

95. Some of the law review articles discussing jury nullification in 1993 include Elizabeth T. Lear, *Is Conviction Irrelevant?*, 40 U.C.L.A. L. Rev. 1179 (1993); Todd Barnet, *New York Considers Jury Nullification: Informing the Jury of Its Common Law Right to Decide Both Facts and Law*, 65 Nov. N.y. St. B.J. 40 (1993); Hon. Jack B. Weinstein, *Considering Jury "Nullification": When May and Should a Jury Reject the Law To Do Justice*, 30 Am. Crim. L.Rev. 239 (1993); Michael J. Saks, *Judicial Nullification*, 68 Indiana L.Rev. 1281 (1993); M. Kristine Creagan, *Jury Nullification: Assessing Recent Legislative Developments*, 43 Case W. Res. L.Rev. 1101 (1993); James L. Cavallaro, *The Demise of the Political Necessity Defense: Indirect Civil Disobedience and United States v. Schoon*, 81 Cal. L.Rev. 351 (1993); Lt. Comm. Robert E. Korroch & Major Michael J. Davidson, *Jury Nullification: A Call for Justice or An Invitation to Anarchy?*, 139 Mil. L.Rev. 131 (1993); George C. Thomas and Barry S. Pollack, *Saving Rights from a Remedy: A Societal View of the Fourth Amendment*, 73 B.U. L. Rev. 147 (1993); Colleen P. Murphy, *Integrating the Constitutional Authority of Civil and Criminal Juries*, Geo. Wash. L.Rev. 723 (1993); Joseph L. Galiber, et al., *Law, Justice and Jury Nullification: A Debate*, 29 Crim. Law Bulletin 40 (1993); Elena Luisa Garella, *Reshaping the Federal Entrapment Defense: Jacobson v. United States*, 68 Wash. L.Rev. 1993 (1993); William H. Simon, *The Ethics of Criminal Defense*, 91 Mich. L. Rev. 1703 (1993); Richard A. Rosen, *On Self-Defense, Imminence, and Women Who Kill Their Batterers*, 71 N.C. L. Rev. 371 (1993). *See also Proceedings of the 53rd Judicial Conference of the District of Columbia Ckt.*, 145 F.R.D. 149 (1993).

war demonstration cases. Opponents of jury rights had won the immediate battle in the courts and had little incentive to publicize a theory they opposed, if only to refute it.

The publicity the doctrine of jury independence received after the Vietnam War ended represents a new phenomenon. When John Lilburne printed pamphlets advocating jury rights in the seventeenth century, he did so with regard to a specific cause. When the cause was over, the pamphlets disappeared. A quarter of a century later, when William Penn and the Quakers ceased to be subject to the punishments of the Conventicles Act, the pamphlets they had been distributing urging jury rights ceased to be published as well. The dozens of tracts written urging jury nullification in libel cases evaporated when Fox's Libel Act was passed. Even Lysander Spooner's *Essay on the Trial by Jury* was written with a specific law in mind—the Fugitive Slave Act of 1850. With the passage of the Thirteenth Amendment, Spooner's *Essay* was to become a novelty.

By the early twentieth century, it seemed that jury independence had become a doctrine of the past, anachronistically surviving in a few isolated jurisdictions and watered down and disparaged where it remained. Rejected by the federal courts and most state courts, it served as interesting fodder for an occasional law review article.[96] Jury independence was not advocated openly, nor had it been a particularly lively topic of discussion since the demise of slavery and the repeal of the Fugitive Slave Act of 1850. The political nature of jury independence allowed the doctrine largely to hibernate until the 1960s when the Vietnam war cases brought it to the forefront as a tool of social protest.

However, as the last quarter of the twentieth century approached, the rapidly increasing number of academic law journals[97] required an increas-

---

96. For representative early Twentieth century articles on jury rights, *see* Amasa M. Eaton, *The Development of the Judicial System in Rhode Island*, 14 YALE L.J. 148 (1905); Roscoe Pound, *Law in Books and Law in Action*, 44 AM. L. REV. 12 (1910); Sunderland, *The Inefficiency of the American Jury*, MICH. L. REV. 302 (1915); Morgan, *A Brief History of Special Verdicts and Special Interrogatories*, 32 YALE L.J. 575 (1923), John H. Wigmore, *A Program for the Trial of Jury Trial*, 12 J. AM. JUD. SOC'Y 166 (1929); Norton, *What a Jury Is*, 16 VA. L. REV. 261 (1930); Farley, *Instructions to Juries — Their Role in the Judicial Process*, 42 YALE L.J. 194 (1932); Mark DeWolfe Howe, *Juries as Judges of Criminal Law*, 52 HARV. L. REV. 582 (1939); Samuel Dennis, *Maryland's Antique Constitutional Thorn*, 92 U. PA. L. REV. 34 (1943).

97. LAWRENCE FRIEDMAN, HISTORY OF AMERICAN LAW, 693 (1985):
    The few university law reviews of the 19th century had grown to an incredible number by the 1980s. There were probably on the order of one hundred and fifty. Virtually every law school, no matter how marginal, published a review as a matter of local pride. Somehow, all of these thousands of pages filled up with words.

ing number of articles, in order to fill the equally increasing number of pages. Articles on jury independence found their way onto many of those pages. For the first time in 800 years of history, the doctrine of jury independence had established a life of its own, apart from any particular issue or policy. The gauntlet handed down by Sax and Kunstler was picked up by hundreds of authors, ranging from state and federal judges[98] to community college instructors.[99]

A popular, amorphous attitude of distrust and contempt towards government became characteristic among many segments of the American people during this period, and jury independence arguments dovetailed with this new attitude perfectly. The proportion of eligible voters who chose to stay home on Election Day approached—and occasionally surpassed—fifty percent. Watergate, runaway budgets, a stagnant economy and standard of living, special-interest legislation, confiscatory taxation and a general sense that Congress had become its own favorite constituency weakened the confidence many Americans had in their government, their courts and in their law. A growing number of moderates and conservatives began urging jury independence, on the same grounds that the 'radical' William Kunstler had. The system was widely perceived as out of control, and independent juries became a rallying cry among diverse elements of both the left and the right. Even though the Vietnam War was over, many reasons still existed to urge juries to pass an independent judgment on the laws they were called upon to enforce.

---

98. *See* David L. Bazelon, *The Morality of the Criminal Law*, 49 S. CAL. L.REV. 385 (1976); Frank A. Kaufman, *The Right of Self-Representation and the Power of Jury Nullification*, 28 CASE W. RES. L.REV. 269 (1978); Noel Fidel, *Preeminently a Political Institution: The Right of Arizona Juries to Nullify the Law of Contributory Negligence*, 23 ARIZ. ST. L.J. 1 (1991).

99. Russell Richardson, *Jury Nullification: Justice or Anarchy?*, 80 CASE & COM. 30 (1975). Richardson was an instructor at East Arkansas Community College.

Chapter Six

The Current Debate

> *There are not enough jails, not enough policemen, not enough courts to enforce a law not supported by the people.*
> *Hubert Horatio Humphrey*

Why Juries Still Refuse to Convict

Criminal laws that are supported by a wide consensus of the population are in little danger of being rejected by the average trial jury. When a defendant is considered violent or dangerous, there is little likelihood that a jury selected from the community will want to put that defendant back on their own streets. Jury independence is a doctrine of lenity, not of anarchy. Where twelve people chosen at random are likely to be unanimous in supporting the law, the law will be enforced. Where a given law does not enjoy a broad consensus of community support, chances are increasingly good that the perogative will be exercised for "juries to acquit out of compassion or compromise or because of their assumption of a power which they had no right to exercise, but to which they were disposed through lenity."[1]

Many of the defendants facing trial in criminal courtrooms across America are no threat to their neighbors. They are harmless violators of victimless crime laws, tax laws, regulatory laws, licensing laws, or political protesters. They are mercy killers who have assisted a loved one to end his or her suffering, only to be put through a second round of torture as their personal tragedy is played out in court and in the press. They are peaceful gun owners who wish to be equipped to protect themselves, if need be. They are cancer, AIDS, glaucoma and muscular sclerosis (MS) patients who grow and smoke marijuana in order to alleviate their suffering. They are battered women who after years of abuse, stand up to their batterers. These are not the people who prey upon society; in the eyes of many jurors, these are the people society preys upon.

One recent example is the California case of Samuel Skipper. In October, 1993, Skipper was acquitted on two felony counts of marijuana cul-

---

1. Standefer v. United States, 447 U.S. 10, 22 (1980)(internal quotation marks omitted).

tivation by a San Diego Superior Court jury, even though he admitted growing more than 40 plants which had been seized from his home. His sole defense was that smoking and eating marijuana alleviated the nausea and weight loss associated with AIDS. Skinner freely admitted growing and using marijuana; but he contended that as a dying man, he had a basic human right to use the medication most effective in helping him survive. Jurors reportedly believed Skipper was justified in growing and using marijuana out of medical necessity, and that the prosecutor, in bringing the case to trial, had abused his discretion. They chose not to apply the law.[2]

Skinner's case is not unusual, although most exercises of jury veto power in drug cases do not involve AIDS or medical use, but simply disagreement with the drug laws themselves or the ways in which they are applied. Dr. Robert Goodman, a New York biochemist, reports serving as a juror on a "buy-and-bust" case tried in the Southern District of New York in November, 1989. The defendant was arrested in the Bronx by a New York tactical narcotics team, but the case was transferred to federal court because of congestion in the state and city courts. The charges were possession of cocaine, and possession of heroin with intent to sell. The public defender claimed that the defendant was a drug user, but not a dealer, and that he had been arrested by mistake because he resembled a drug dealer the police had been targeting.

Dr. Goodman was convinced that the case represented a gross miscarriage of justice. He hung the jury eleven to one because, in his words, "trying this case in federal court was just wasting the jury's time and taxpayers money."[3] The jury had originally been split eight to four in favor of

---

2. *Jury Gives Go Ahead for AIDS Sufferer to use Marijuana*, REUTER GENERAL NEWS, Oct. 16, 1993. *See also* Thom Mrozek, *Group Seeks to let Juries Nullify Laws*, L.A. TIMES, May 11, 1994 at B2.

Marijuana has been claimed to be an effective medical treatment for glaucoma, chemotherapy and AIDS related nausea and loss of appetite, and the spasms associated with muscular sclerosis and amputations. *See* Alliance for Cannabis Therapeutics v. Drug Enforcement Administration, 930 F.2d 936 (D.C. Cir. 1991), Alliance for Cannabis Therapeutics v. Drug Enforcement Administration, 15 F.3d 1131 (D.C. Cir. 1994). *See also* Robin Elizabeth Margolis, *Marijuana Cannot be Prescribed for Therapeutic Purposes*, 11 No. 3 HEALTHSPAN 19 (1994), Gregg A. Bilz, *The Medical Use of Marijuana*, 13 HAMLINE J. PUB. L. POL'Y 117 (1992).

Synthetic THC, the pharmaceutically active component of marijuana, is produced by Unimed under the brand name Marinol. The cost is about $150 to $180 for a one-month supply, which is significantly higher than the cost of marijuana. The synthetic drug is also reported to be slower, harder for patients to control and less effective. Bob Groves, *Pot vs. The Pill: An Illegal Therapy Has Found Support*, RECORD (NORTHERN NEW JERSEY) March 28, 1994 at B1.

3. Telephone interview with Dr. Robert Goodman (July 23, 1994).

conviction. Several of the jurors had doubts about the reliability of the police testimony. Three of Dr. Goodman's fellow jurors were willing to set aside their reasonable doubts and change their votes in order to reach a unanimous verdict. When several jurors wrote the judge a note after becoming upset at Dr. Goodman's intransigence, he was called into court and asked whether he could put his conscientious feelings aside and deliver a verdict based solely on the facts. After maintaining that he could, he continued deliberating but still voted for acquittal, insisting that he did not believe the police were telling the truth.

The day after this verdict was delivered Dr. Goodman was scheduled to return to the jury pool, when he was asked to come into the office of the Jury Administrator. He wanted to know how anybody could have delivered a not guilty verdict in the case. Didn't Dr. Goodman listen to the evidence? The public defender even admitted that the defendant was a drug user. Dr. Goodman explained that he did not have to believe what the lawyer said, and that there was no way the lawyer, a federal public defender, could have known first hand what the facts were. Besides, the lawyer was not under oath.

The Federal Jury Administrator then attempted to intimidate Dr. Goodman. He asked if a trial for perjury would inconvenience Dr. Goodman in his career, to which Dr. Goodman responded "I guess so." After offering Dr. Goodman a chance to make any further statement he cared to (which offer was declined, in light of the jury administrator's threatening attitude), Dr. Goodman was dismissed from any further jury service. Dr. Goodman has not been called back for city, state or federal jury service since.

In spite of arrogant attitudes like those of the federal jury administrator in this case, a vocal minority of judges have insisted that jurors should have access to whatever information they need in order to reach a conscientious verdict. Judge Jack B. Weinstein believes that "[n]ullification is but one legitimate result in an appropriate constitutional process safeguarded by judges and the judicial system. When juries refuse to convict on the basis of what they think are unjust laws, they are performing their duty as jurors."[4] In Judge Weinstein's view, judges should allow the defense to present evidence that is not strictly relevant but which reflects upon the defendant's motivation and the ethical dilemma involved in enforcing the law. Although he would not urge explicitly informing jurors of their powers, he believes that jurors should be given information that may lead to *sua sponte* nullification. Jurors should be empowered to follow the demands of conscience:

> When jurors return with a "nullification" verdict, then, they have not in reality "nullified" anything: they have done their job...Juries are charged

---

4. Hon. Jack B. Weinstein, *Considering Jury "Nullification": When May and Should a Jury Reject the Law to do Justice?*, 30 Am. Crim L. Rev. 239, 240 (1993).

not with the task of blindly and mechanically applying the law, but of doing justice in light of the law, the evidence presented at trial, and their own knowledge of society and the world. To decide some outcomes are just and some are not is not possible without drawing upon personal views.[5]

Although Judge Weinstein's views may be the exception and not the rule, they are not unique among federal judges. District Court Judge Thomas Wiseman, in the Middle District of Tennessee, allowed a defendant accused of attempted distribution of controlled substances to inform the jury, through his attorney, of the "draconian sentences hanging over his head."[6] The judge noted that "[this] is an argument for the right of the jury to have that information necessary to decide whether a sentence should be nullified. This is not an argument for the right to have the jury instructed on jury nullification."[7] Because "the essential feature of a jury obviously lies in the interposition between the accused and his accuser of the commonsense judgment of a group of laymen, and in the community participation and shared responsibility that results from that group's determination of guilt or innocence...a defendant's right to inform the jury of that information essential "to prevent oppression by the Government" is clearly of constitutional magnitude...Indeed, to deny a defendant of the possibility of jury nullification would be to defeat the central purpose of the jury system."[8]

Judge Wiseman went on to say that:

> Argument against allowing the jury to hear information that might lead to nullification evinces a fear that the jury might actually serve its primary purpose, that is, it evinces a fear that the community might in fact think a law unjust. The government, whose duty it is to seek justice and not merely conviction, should not shy away from having a jury know the full facts and law of a case. Argument equating jury nullification with anarchy misses the point that in our criminal justice system the law as stated by the judge is secondary to the justice as meted out by a jury of the defendant's peers. We have established the jury as the final arbiter of truth and

---

5. *Id.* at 244-245.

6. United States v. Datcher, 830 F.Supp. 411, 412 (M.D. Tenn. 1993), discussed in Kristen K. Sauer, *Informed Conviction: Instructing the Jury About Mandatory Sentencing Consequences*, 95 Colum. L.Rev. 1232 (1995)("The criminal jury, through its nullification power, is intended to function, in significant part, as a political check on the government's power to promulgate unpopular laws and overly harsh punishments").

7. *Datcher, supra* note 6, 412-413.

8. *Id.* at 414-415, quoting Williams v. Florida, 399 U.S. 78, 100 (1970).

justice in our criminal justice system; this court must grant the defendant's motion if the jury is to fulfill this duty.[9]

In spite of his belief that preventing oppression by nullifying bad law is "the central purpose of the jury system," Judge Wiseman would not instruct the jury on that power. Although he rebutted the fears of jury nullification leading to anarchy, Judge Wiseman still contended that "this remedy is one that should be reserved for only those cases where criminal law and community norms greatly diverge."[10] He does not explain why it would be impossible to fashion an instruction that would simultaneously explain the doctrine to the jury, while cautioning them to restrict its use to exceptional cases. A good example of such an instruction would be the short-lived Kansas instruction discussed earlier, or the jury instruction given by a unanimous Supreme Court in *Georgia v. Brailsford*. While Judge Wiseman allowed the defense to present to the jury information concerning mandatory minimum sentences and federal sentences guidelines, announcing "[t]he court finds no good reason for opposing candor,"[11] the judge still opposed candor concerning the power of the jury to nullify.

It is informative to contrast Judge Wiseman's opinion with that of Massachusetts Supreme Court Chief Justice Lemuel Shaw in *Commonwealth v. Porter*.[12] *Porter* has been criticized by courts and commentators alike for Justice Shaw's opinion that the defense could argue to the jury that the law was unconstitutional, even though the jury had no right to decide such questions. Judge Wiseman in *Datcher* produces a similarly fractured opinion in ruling that the defense may present information concerning the operation of sentencing guidelines to the jury, but that the jury cannot be instructed on what they may do with that information.

It is possible that Judge Wiseman was more concerned with the imposition of sentencing guidelines than he was with "candor." The oversight of the jury, according to Judge Wiseman, "restores some of the discretion and particularized justice taken away by the Guidelines, but it represents only a minimal yet necessary intrusion on Congress' work."[13] In various places in his opinion, the mandatory minimums are referred to as "draconian," "overly harsh," and "arbitrary," and he refers to the sentencing guidelines as "wholly unaccountable."[14] Jury independence could have

---

9. *Datcher, supra* note 6, 414-415 (citations omitted).

10. *Id.* at 417.

11. *Id.* at 418.

12. 51 Mass. 263 (1845).

13. *Datcher, supra* note 6, 416.

14. *Id.* at 412, 416, 417.

been used by the judge to circumvent what he viewed as unjust and oppressive legislation and interference with his judicial role. This interpretation explains the inconsistency in Judge Wiseman's opinion on the issue of candor, and also anticipates that future decisions concerning sentencing information will be subject to the judge's view of the equity of the minimum sentencing guidelines in that particular case.

Other courts have been less open about giving jurors information concerning sentencing. The Supreme Court has said that, unless the jury is involved in sentencing the defendant, as they would be in a capital case, jurors should be instructed not to consider the sentencing implications of their verdict during deliberations.[15] The Court has also strongly discouraged trial courts from allowing jurors to be informed of the sentence the accused could face if convicted, claiming that providing sentencing information "invites [jurors] to ponder matters that are not within their province, distracts them from their factfinding responsibilities, and creates a strong possibility of confusion."[16] Even the Sixth Circuit Court of Appeals, which has appellate jurisdiction over Judge Wiseman's court, has asserted that where jurors have no sentencing function, they should not be informed of the sentencing consequences of their decisions.[17] The Sixth Circuit has argued that "[i]ndeed, the only possible purpose that would be served by informing jurors of the mandatory sentence would be to invite jury nullification of the law."[18] However, the ultimate decision is still left to the sound discretion of the trial judge, who can still allow such information to be given to the jurors if he or she believes it would be in the interest of justice to do so.

The *Datcher* opinion is considered generous by modern standards, especially considering the effect that jury knowledge of sentencing guidelines has had in other jurisdictions. Drug cases are exceptionally susceptible to jury nullification when juries are knowledgeable concerning the sentences likely to be imposed. In Washington, D.C., juries aware of harsh mandatory minimum sentencing guidelines are acquitting defendants without any information or encouragement from the defense.[19] One federal dis-

---

15. Shannon v. United States, 512 U.S. 573, 579 (1994).

16. *Id.*, quoted in United States v. Johnson, 62 F.2d 849, 851 (6th Cir. 1995).

17. United States v. Chesney, 86 F.3d 564, 573-574 (6th Cir. 1996).

18. *Johnson, supra* note 16, 851. *See also* United States v. Lewis, 110 F.3d 417 (7th Cir. 1997).

19. *Crossfire*, October 1993, quoted in *Crossfire: Mandatory Minimums meet FIJA*, 14 THE FIJACTIVIST 1 (Winter 1994):

> Participants: Hosts Michael Kinsley and John Sununu; U.S. District Judge Stanley Sporkin, District of Columbia; and Former Attorney General William Barr
> Discussing the wisdom of mandatory minimum sentences in drug cases…
> KINSLEY: Are we getting folks that are being let off because the sentences are too

trict court, apparently frustrated that a jury had acquitted a gun supplier of conspiracy to commit robbery, noted that:

> Jury nullification of sentences deemed too harsh is increasingly reflected in refusals to convict. Jurors are aware of the huge sentences that result from conviction...This phenomenon of self-defeating overly-harsh sentences probably explains the jury's refusal to convict Castro and its lack of agreement as to Molina's guilt of most of the crimes for which he was being tried. The public apparently supports sentences less severe than those mandated by the Guidelines in cases such as this one.[20]

While jury nullification is relatively common in drug cases, homicide cases are usually immune from jury law-judging. There are few circumstances that would lead a normal jury to conclude that the ultimate crime should go unpunished. The well publicized May, 1994 trial of Dr. Jack Kevorkian represented an exception to that rule. Dr. Kevorkian had been accused of assisting Thomas Hyde, a 30 year old victim of Lou Gehrig's disease, to commit suicide. Assisting suicide was a felony punishable with up to four years in prison and a $2,000 fine under Michigan law.[21] Although Dr. Kevorkian had admitted placing a mask connected to a cannister of carbon monoxide on Hyde's face, and placing a string to release the gas in Mr. Hyde's hand, he was acquitted by a jury.

Lou Gehrig's disease is an unspeakably painful and debilitating nerve disorder. There is no known cure; the disease is invariably fatal. Hyde had chosen to end his life with dignity, and had sought Dr. Kevorkian's assistance. A Michigan jury refused to punish Dr. Kevorkian for his role in helping Thomas Hyde commit suicide. As one of the jurors in the case, Gail Donaldson, said "I don't think it is our obligation to choose for someone else

---

tough?

JUDGE SPORKIN: Absolutely. Every day in the District of Columbia. The juries there who understand what's going on now are acquitting people that should be convicted. And that's another problem that you have. And there's nothing you can do about it. There's no appeal to that. And it's happening every single day.

BARR: Jury nullification is a problem in many jurisdictions,

KINSLEY: Well, what are you going to do about it?

BARR: Well, I, I...

SUNUNU: Isn't the jury taking care of the concerns you've raised? Aren't they, as representatives of the people, doing what you want to do?

SPORKIN: No, nobody is saying that these people ought not to go to jail. But two years, three years, not 15, not 20 years.

20. United States v. Molina, 963 F.Supp. 213, 214 (E.D.N.Y. 1997).

21. Janet Wilson, Michael Betzold and David Zeman, *Kevorkian's Case will put Suicide Law on Trial*, DET. FREE PRESS, April 16, 1994 at 1A.

how much pain and suffering they should endure."[22] Unfortunately, prosecutions like this have occurred hundreds of times nationwide.

In 1991, Wanda Bauer was suffering from the final stages of terminal cancer. She had been told that she had less than two weeks to live. She asked her forty-nine-year-old son, Dick Bauer, to get her gun for her. When she had first been diagnosed with cancer, she had "made him promise that when she asked for the gun—when the suffering got to be too much—he would get it for her."[23] There was no question in her son's mind what his mother intended to do with her gun. After trying unsuccessfully to change her mind, Dick Bauer kept his promise. He said at trial that his mother would have hated him if he had broken his promise.[24]

In Colorado, where the Bauers lived, assisting another person in committing suicide was illegal. Dick Bauer was indicted and tried, but after an hour and a half of deliberation, the jury returned an independent verdict of "Not Guilty." Many similar cases have been reported.[25] Not all defendants have been as fortunate as Jack Kevorkian and Dick Bauer.

Seventy-three year old Emily Gilbert suffered from Alzheimer's disease and osteosoporosis. When her prolonged suffering finally became unbearable, she repeatedly begged her husband—and anyone else who would listen—to end her life. Emily Gilbert's condition was so bad that Roswell Gilbert, her seventy-five year old husband, could not find a nursing home or hospital willing to accept her. He was concerned that the only care she could be given would be in a state hospital where "they'd have to strap her down. She'd be dehumanized."[26]

Roswell Gilbert shot his wife twice in the back of the head. He was tried and convicted of first-degree murder by a Fort Lauderdale, Florida jury of ten women and two men. Gilbert pleaded not guilty. Friends of the couple testified that Emily Gilbert had pleaded for an end to her suffering. But to no avail. The jury conscientiously applied the law according to the judge's instructions. As one of the jurors said after the trial, "We had no choice. The law does not allow for sympathy."[27]

Assisted suicide and euthanasia cases are particularly difficult because of the understandable pain the defendant has gone through in ending the

---

22. Quoted in Richard Epstein, *Pondering the Kevorkian Question: The Right to End Suffering Belongs to the Individual*, CHI. TRIB., May 6, 1994 at 23.

23. Quoted in Bruce Hilton, *The Suicide Dilemma*, CHI. TRIB., July 16, 1992 at 7.

24. *Id.*

25. *See* Cheryl K. Smith, *What About Legalized Assisted Suicide?*, 8 ISSUES L. & MED. 503 (1993). (Ms. Smith is a staff attorney with the Hemlock Society USA.)

26. SAUL M. KASSIN AND LAWRENCE S. WRIGHTSMANN, THE AMERICAN JURY ON TRIAL, 157-158 (1988).

27. *Id.* at 158.

life of a person who is usually a very close friend or family member. Rarely is the defendant considered dangerous. Even jurors who disapprove of the defendant's actions are unlikely to fear him.[28] Jurors in these cases will inevitably be forced to choose between following their conscience or following the law. By failing to allow jurors to be informed of their powers to deliver an independent verdict if they believe the prosecution is misguided, judges make this dilemma more difficult and less predictable. The jury should know that it is up to them to decide whether or not the law is to allow for sympathy in any particular case.

Assisted suicide and euthanasia cases are not the only cases involving death in which jury independence issues arise. Cases involving women who have killed their batterers after years of abuse often end in nullification acquittals. These cases rarely involve legal claims of self-defense, because the women usually kill their tormentors at a time when they are in no imminent danger.[29] The law makes what is often an unrealistic assumption that these women can leave the abusive situation safely, even though the likelihood of being hunted down, beaten, and killed leaves these women with no reasonable alternatives. The danger to a woman from her abuser increases dramatically when she attempts to leave.[30] Professor Richard A. Rosen points out that the presumption that women are free to leave abusive relationships is often erroneous: "the time of most danger for the woman is when she attempts to leave; women are often killed when, and because, they attempt to escape."[31]

The jury is often left with a choice between unjustly convicting a woman, who is herself a victim, of homicide, or of nullifying the law.[32] It is not surprising that a number of these cases end in nullification verdicts. What is

---

28. Alan Dershowitz commented prior to Dr. Jack Kevorkian's trial that "If Kevorkian gets jurors who have relatives or friends who have suffered painful deaths, he'll get a sympathetic hearing." Wilson, Betzold & Zeman, *supra* note 21.

29. State v. Norman, 324 N.C. 253 (1989)(woman who, after 25 years of abuse, kills husband in his sleep, convicted of murder. N.C. Supreme Court rules self-defense inapplicable because defendant was under no imminent danger). *See also* Maria L. Marcus, *Conjugal Violence: The Law of Force and the Force of Law*, 69 CAL. L. REV. 1657 (1981); Donald L. Creach, *Partially Determined Imperfect Self-Defense: The Battered Wife Kills and Tells Why*, 34 STAN. L.REV. 615 (1982); Richard A. Rosen, *On Self-Defense, Imminence, and Women Who Kill Their Batterers*, 17 N.C. L. REV. 371 (1993).

30. Marcus, *supra* note 29, 1658-1702 (laws protecting women against domestic violence rarely enforced). *See also* Rosen, *On Self-Defense, supra* note 29, 375-376.

31. Rosen, *On Self-Defense, supra* note 29, 395. He argues that imminence is a surrogate for necessity; therefore when necessity can be proven directly there is no need for a requirement of imminence. *Id.* at 380-389.

32. Marcus, *Conjugal Violence, supra* note 29, 1723-1733; Creach, *Partially Determined Imperfect Self-Defense, supra* note 29, 626-630.

probably more surprising is that so many of them do end in convictions,[33] considering that most juries are reluctant to punish defendants who "have already suffered enough," or more than enough. It is not uncommon for battered women to have been subjected to years of abuse much worse than that which would be prohibited under the "cruel and unusual punishment" clause of the Eighth Amendment.

Almost every controversial area of law raises potential jury independence issues. The controversy over *Roe v. Wade*[34] has extended into the jury box, as Operation Rescue activists have attempted to inform jurors of their rights to acquit.[35] Pro-Choice activists, however, have also supported jury independence.[36] Should *Roe* be overturned, it is unlikely that independent juries would ever enforce laws criminalizing abortion.

Gun owners have increasingly turned to the jury to protect their rights against what they perceive as unconstitutional infringements of their right to keep and bear arms. Charges against professional "deprogrammers" and family members accused of kidnapping and assaulting cult "victims" have been dismissed in at least one case because "no jury of 12 persons is ever going to unanimously agree on guilty verdicts."[37]

There are other categories of cases in which independent juries are likely to either acquit or ameliorate the conviction by finding the defendant guilty of a lesser degree of the crime committed than the facts themselves would otherwise require. Cases which lead the jury to believe that the law is not being applied uniformly or fairly may lead to acquittals or hung juries. This group of cases includes prosecutions the jury believes are politically motivated or over-reaching. Recent cases on point include the 1989 prosecution of Marion Barry for possession of cocaine[38] and the prosecu-

---

33. Maria L. Marcus, *Conjugal Violence, supra* note 29, 1725 n. 314.

34. 410 U.S. 113 (1973).

35. Michael Granberry, *Abortion Protest Juries Told to Ignore Nullification Ad*, L.A. TIMES, January 27, 1990 at B1; Michael Granberry, *NOW Urges Advertisers to Drop Reader*, L.A. TIMES, February 3, 1990 at B1.

36. Stephen J. Adler, *Courtroom Putsch? Jurors Should Reject Laws They Don't Like, Activist Group Argues: Adherents Are a Diverse Lot*, WALL ST. JRL., January 4, 1991 at A1.

37. Tom Gorman, *All Charges in Brown Kidnap Case Dismissed; Courts: The Charges never should have come to trial, the judge tells stunned attorneys on both sides in the religious deprogramming kidnap on Ginger Brown*, L.A. TIMES, January 13, 1990 at B1.

38. Stephanie Saul, *Barry Play: 'Persecution Defense'*, NEWSDAY, June 5, 1990 at 17. (...many Washington residents believe the charges against [Barry] were racially motivated, part of a vendetta by the white power structure...there is a belief among many here, and Barry himself has claimed, that the government, which had investigated Barry for years, was overzealous in snaring him—a view that could lead to his acquittal, or jury

tion of Oliver North for lying to Congress during the 1989 investigation of the Iran-Contra scandal. As one reporter noted:

> An innocent verdict could hinge on jury nullification "rather than the juror's dispassionately applying laws to the facts of the wrongdoing," predicted John F. Banzhaf, a professor at George Washington University's National Law Center who has observed the trial....As Judge Gesell's instructions to the jury indicated, a defendant cannot justify illegal acts by claiming he was obeying orders from his superiors, Mr. Banzhaf said. But these arguments could sway jurors to use their inherent powers to acquit a defendant if they think a conviction would be unfair or not in the public interest.[39]

Even though most courts adamantly refuse to inform juries of their powers to reach an independent verdict, there clearly exists a large group of cases in which juries not infrequently reject the written law in favor of a merciful verdict based on their own concepts of justice and equity. When the defendant has already suffered enough, when it would be unfair or against the public interest for the defendant to be convicted, when the jury disagrees with the law itself, when the prosecution or the arresting authorities have gone "too far" in the single-minded quest to arrest and convict a particular defendant, when the punishments to be imposed are excessive or when the jury suspects that the charges have been brought for political reasons or to make an unfair example of the hapless defendant, the jury is likely to refuse to convict.

---

nullification).

See also Bruce Fein, *Judge, Jury...and the Sixth*, WASH. TIMES, November 8, 1990 at G3. (Judge Jackson...insisted that the prosecutor's case against Mr. Barry was "overwhelming" on at least a dozen counts, that the credibility of the defense witnesses was "thoroughly impeached," and that the declination of some jurors to vote to convict the mayor except for a single misdemeanor count of cocaine possession exhibited not a search for guilt or innocence but "their own agendas.") Alan Dershowitz, *Barry Employs a Redneck Trick: Jury Nullification Play Appeals to Racist Instincts*, BUFFALO NEWS, June 9, 1990 at C3. (Jury nullification is a double-edged sword. It is sometimes used, in a nonracist manner, to counter the unfairness of particular laws...But jury nullification also has an ignoble and racist history. And, unfortunately, Marion Barry has turned to that ignoble and racist tradition in his desparate effort ot salvage his political career). Victor Volland, *'Bill of Jury Rights' Sought by Lawyers*, ST. LOUIS POST DISPATCH, November 12, 1990 at 1B. (Despite laws requiring them to consider only the evidence presented, juries often have based decisions on their own interpretation of "justness"—as...in the drug trial of Washington Mayor Marion Barry, who was acquitted of the most punitive charges because the jurors believed that he was unfairly entrapped by police).

39. Bob Dart, *North Is Guilty, Alternate Juror Claims: Sequestered Panel to Spend Its Saturday at Work*, ATLANTA CONST., April 22, 1989 at A07.

Political Developments and Renewed Interest in Independent Juries

The inevitable response to unpopular laws is that juries, once informed of their powers, will at least occasionally refuse to enforce them. In the early days of this country, juries were selected from the elite white male property-owning classes, and were well aware of their powers before jury selection began. Further, judges regularly reminded jurors of their powers, so that a juror unaware that he could acquit if he thought the law unjust was quickly disabused. Because of the elite nature of early juries, jurors were selected from the same small class of citizens who wrote and enforced the laws. This helps explain the low rate of jury resistance in early American history, although where the laws were unfairly enforced or had been passed with a slim majority, jurors would still occasionally rebel.

Today, juries are supposed to represent a random cross section of the community in which the case is tried. The federal jury selection statutes demand as much:

> It is the policy of the United States that all litigants in Federal courts entitled to trial by jury shall have the right to grand and petit juries selected at random from a fair cross section of the community in the district or division wherein the trial convenes. It is further the policy of the United States that all citizens shall have the opportunity to be considered for service on grand and petit juries in the district courts of the United States, and shall have an obligation to serve as jurors when summoned for that purpose.[40]

Such a cross section can and should include all classes, genders, ethnic groups and occupations. These jurors do not necessarily have the same close connection with those who write or enforce the laws that early jurors had. Their sympathy for the law may be muted or absent, and their empathy with the defendant may be much greater than existed in the eighteenth century.

Probably less than ten percent of these potential jurors can be expected, however, to be aware of their powers as jurors, or knowledgable enough to exercise them reliably *sua sponte*.[41] We have seen, through Milgrams' studies, that many modern Americans are terrifyingly willing to obey authority figures even when what they are being ordered to do goes against

---

40. 28 U.S.C.A. § 1861.

41. *See* David C. Brody & Craig Rivera, *Examining the Dougherty 'All-Knowing Assumption': Do Jurors Know About their Nullification Power?*, 33 CRIM.L. BULL. 151 (1997).

their most deeply held convictions.[42] Charging jurors with unquestioningly applying the law, as laid down by the judge, strips them of the essential element of personal responsibility for the verdict they deliver. As a result, modern jurors may play their role as if the fate of the defendant were an abstract intellectual challenge, divorced from the flesh and blood life of a real human being. By not allowing their conscientious scruples to impact on their verdict, they may deny the defendant his constitutionally guaranteed right to be judged by the conscience of the community, the judgment of his peers as envisioned by the framers of the Constitution.

Denying the power of jurors to judge the law also strips the law of legitimacy. One of the purposes of the criminal jury trial is to test the criminal law against the judgment of the community. Where the law is not subjected to such a test (and where the court, by refusing to subject the law to such a test implicitly acknowledges that the law cannot survive it) the law itself is placed under a cloud of distrust and apprehension.

Occasionally, jurors feel they have been coerced into returning an unjust conviction. The jury that heard the case of Darlene and Jerry Span provides a shocking example. On April 7, 1988, the Spans were questioned by two federal marshals concerning the location of a 63 year old Indiana fugitive named Mickey Michael Span. They had a brother by the same name, but their brother was only 39 years old. He was obviously not the man the marshals were looking for.

After informing the marshals of that fact, Jerry and Darlene went on about their business. The marshals did not believe them and attacked them from behind. When their mother and another brother photographed the assault the marshals grabbed their cameras and ground the film into the dirt, striking Jerry and Darlene's mother in the process. The elderly Mrs. Span incurred injuries that resulted in a trip to the hospital.

Jerry and Darlene Span were accused of resisting arrest, even though the marshals admitted at trial that they had no probable cause for arresting them. U.S. District Court Judge Robert Broomfield instructed the jurors that:

> Federal officers engaged in good faith and colorable performance of their duties may not be forcibly resisted, even if the resister turns out to be correct, that the resisted actions should not, in fact, have been taken. The statute requires him to submit peaceably and seek legal redress thereafter. [43]

Several of the jurors were reportedly in tears when they delivered the only verdict they believed possible under the judge's instructions. Many of them

---

42. Stanley Milgram, *Behavioral Study of Obedience*, 67 J. ABNORMAL & SOC. PSYCHOL. 371 (1963).

43. J. Huston, *U.S. v. Span: A Sad Case in Point*, THE CORRESPONDENT (Missoula, MT) May 16, 1990.

signed a statement that "such a law is completely unfair and against every-thing that the United States stands for."

Five members of the jury later supplied affidavits saying they believed the Spans were innocent. The jurors said they had voted against their beliefs because of the judge's instructions. One of the jurors, Sally Osborne, wrote a letter to the judge pleading that "[i]t seems so unfair that U.S. marshals can attack a citizen and get away with it, and the innocent have to pay."[44] The judge, however, did not grant the Spans a new trial or take the concerns of the jurors into account to reduce their sentences. Darlene Span was fined $6,000 and sentenced to 36 months of probation, with special conditions that she serve three months in a community treatment center and three months under house arrest; Jerry Span was fined $1,000 and sentenced to 30 months of probation, with the special condition that he serve four months under house arrest.[45]

After an unsuccessful appeal filed by Alan Dershowitz of Harvard Law School, the Spans filed a *pro pers* petition for *Coram Nobis*, which is an attack on the legality of their conviction. The *Coram Nobis* petition was denied in the United States District Court where the Spans had originally been convicted, then appealed to the Eleventh Circuit Court of Appeals. The appellate court vacated their convictions. Although the case against the Spans was eventually reversed, theirs is a classic case of justice delayed being justice denied. It was not until February 2, 1996 — almost eight years after their arrest — that the convictions against Darlene and Jerry Span were vacated.

When jurors feel they have been coerced into returning an unjust con-viction, or when they feel obliged to implore the court to be merciful because they believe the defendants have been treated unfairly,[46] the jury

---

44. James Coates, *A Challenge to Marshal's Use of Force*, CHI. TRIB., Sept. 8, 1991 at 21.

45. United States v. Span, 970 F.2d 573, 574 (9th Cir. 1992).

46. Sarah Bain, the forewoman of the jury that tried the survivors of the 1993 raid on the Mount Carmel Branch Davidian compound, wept openly when the defendants were sentenced to serve maximum sentences of 40 years. Bain said that "jurors thought the weapons charge, carrying 5- or 25- year terms, would bring a mere "slap on the wrist. If the Davidians receive the maximum, somebody will have to escort me out weeping. It's just too severe a penalty." Mark Potok, *Branch Davidian Defendants Ask For Leniency: Sentencing Begins Today in San Antonio*, USA TODAY, June 17, 1994 at 02A.

Bain wrote the judge a letter explaining that the jury was confused and that she had been "incredulous" to discover the length of the sentences the defendants faced. She wrote that "Even five years is too severe a penalty for what we believed to be a minor charge." William Cheshire, *Law and Order in the Land of the Free and the Home of the Brave*, ARIZONA REPUBLIC, June 23, 1994 at B4.

See also Benedict D. LaRosa, *The Branch Davidian Trial Jury: An Interview with Sarah Bain, Forewoman*, 16 THE FIJActivist, 14, 15, 18, 21 (Summer 1994).

has not been empowered to truly perform the function for which juries are intended: to protect the accused against an oppressive act of government.[47] The Span jury believed that it was unjust to convict Darlene and Jerry Span. The financial and emotional drains of eight years of litigation could have been largely avoided, if their jury had known about its power to do the job for which it was intended.

Only a small proportion of today's jurors appear to be aware of their unquestionable power to judge the law as well as the facts. One recent survey conducted in the Albany, New York area asked potential jurors eight questions about the rights and powers of trial jurors. Only 6% of college students could answer all eight questions correctly. When the same poll was conducted using a smaller number of randomly selected citizens, not a single one could give the correct answer to all eight questions.[48] Professor Irwin Horowitz' experiments have established both that jurors are not aware of their discretionary powers, and that juror awareness of these powers can lead to significant differences in the quality of their verdicts.[49] The examples already discussed support the notion that there exist several significant categories of cases where jurors would be likely to reject current criminal laws on conscientious grounds, if they were aware of their power to do so. In 1989, an organization was formed to educate potential jurors of their latent powers to judge the law.

Larry Dodge and Don Doig founded the Fully Informed Jury Association (FIJA), to educate Americans about the concept of jury independence on a national scale. The first project of the nascent organization was a proposed Fully Informed Jury Act, which was drafted by Dodge, Doig and friends in Helmville, Montana. The act would have required judges to inform jurors, both before the trial began and again in the charge to the jury, of their right to deliver an independent verdict.

FIJA, headquartered in Dodge's tiny home town of Helmville, Montana (population: 28) had coordinators in fourteen states within six months of their initial meeting.[50] Within another three months that number had reached twenty,[51] and by Spring of 1991, thirty-six with contacts in anoth-

---

47. Duncan v. Louisiana, 391 U.S. 145, 155-156 (1968).

48. Brody & Rivera, *supra* note 41.

49. *See* Irwin A. Horowitz, *The Impact of Jury Nullification Instructions on Verdicts and Jury Functioning in Criminal Trials*, 9 LAW & HUM. BEHAV. 25 (1985); Irwin A. Horowitz, *The Impact of Judicial Instructions, Arguments and Challenges on Jury Decision Making*, 12 LAW & HUM. BEHAV. 439 (1988); Irwin A. Horowitz and Thomas E. Willging, *Changing Views of Jury Power: The Nullification Debate, 1787-1988*, 15 LAW & HUM. BEHAV.165 (1991).

50. 2 THE FIJACTIVIST 2 (January-February 1990).

51. 3 THE FIJACTIVIST 8 (Spring 1990).

er eight.[52] By this time the quarterly *FIJActivist* newsletter was going out to a mailing list of several thousand. Many legal scholars and authors such as Massachusetts School of Law Dean Lawrence Velvel, law professors Alan Scheflin, Steve Herzberg and Jon M. Van Dyke, attorney William M. Kunstler, historian Godfrey Lehman, several active and retired judges (including retired Washington Supreme Court Justice William C. Goodloe and retired Arkansas Supreme Court Justice John I. Purtle), and several dozen politicians had expressed support for Fully Informed Jury legislation and/or principles.[53]

FIJA state activists at first promoted jury independence primarily by distributing literature from tables in public areas. Early FIJA literature consisted mainly of its newsletter, *The FIJActivist*, some reprints of newspaper articles and quotes from cases and history books. At one unattended street table in Butte County, California, Dixianne Hawks picked up an early FIJA newsletter which interested her. At the time, Ms. Hawks' son was facing charges for possession and sale of LSD.

Dixianne Hawks photocopied some historical quotes from the FIJA literature and distributed it to five of the jurors hearing her son's case. Although the son was later convicted of the charges against him, the Butte County District Attorney's office decided to prosecute Ms. Hawks on five counts of felony jury tampering for distributing the literature. Hawks' attorney John Wolfgram argued that Hawks' actions were a legal exercise of her rights to political expression under the First Amendment.[54]

The case against Dixianne Hawks was eventually dismissed "in the interests of justice," when the defendant refused court-appointed counsel and refused to submit to psychiatric examination without the attorney of her choice being present. But from Dixianne Hawks' efforts to reach the jury in her son's case, FIJA learned the technique of leafleting outside courthouses.[55] During the same period, George Washington University Professor of Law and Legal Activism John F. Banzhaf suggested the same technique in a letter to the *Washington Times*, responding to an article about FIJA:

> The new organization could achieve its goals...simply by printing and distributing to jurors pamphlets describing how they may disregard a judge's charge and return a verdict of "not guilty" because of governmental misconduct or overreaching, or because a conviction would be fundamentally unfair.

---

52. 7 The FIJActivist 17 (Spring 1991). As another sign of FIJA's growth, issue #7 was twenty pages long; issue #2 was four pages long.

53. *Id.* at 16.

54. *Id.* at 1, 5.

55. 10 The FIJActivist 2 (Winter 1992).

Any attempt to prevent distribution of the pamphlets would raise a clear First Amendment issue: Can Americans lawfully be punished for telling jurors what the courts have repeatedly held is a power they have under our legal system?[56]

FIJA produced a tri-fold *"True of False?"* brochure designed to inform jurors of their powers, using legal and historical references. FIJA activists distribute these brochures around courthouses on jury selection days, concentrating on controversial or high-profile cases. FIJA volunteers attended the prosecution of Branch Davidian survivors; Idaho survivalist Randy Weaver; Michigan right-to-die advocate Dr. Jack Kevorkian; New Mexico vitamin wholesaler Rodger Sless; and the trial of Hollywood madam Heidi Fleiss.[57]

The streets around a courtyard are traditional "free speech zones" according to United States Supreme Court precedent.[58] The FIJA pamphlets are clearly legal political speech. However, in 1979, the 10th Circuit Court of Appeals upheld a federal conviction for "knowingly and corruptly endeavoring to influence, impede and obstruct the due administration of justice" concerning the distribution of a jury nullification pamphlet. The case involved tax protester Tim Z. Ogle from Colorado, who had allegedly sent an agent out to give a mutual friend a pamphlet entitled "A Handbook for Jurors," which urged the jury nullification doctrine. The friend was serving as a juror in a federal felony tax law violation case. The juror rejected the pamphlet and informed the judge, and Ogle was prosecuted.[59]

Ogle sought to contact a person he knew was serving as a juror in a particular case, with the intent to influence that individual juror's verdict. That puts him in a far different position from a FIJA pamphleteer who hands pamphlets to all individuals, jurors, judges, prosecutors, defendants, and passersby, indiscriminately. Ogle was not engaged in free political speech aimed at the general public, but in a focused effort to influence a juror. FIJA pamphleteers believe that this distinction should save them from prosecution.

One thing which has helped FIJA, according to co-founder Larry Dodge, is that "it pushes everybody's hot button. There are very few people in the country who have not been intimidated by government...gun owners, home schoolers, health food shop owners, bikers, etc. Most Americans have had a brush with the law, or have had some other reason to fear the law at some point."[60] In addition to the groups mentioned, FIJA has received

---

56. John F. Banzhaf III, *Oliver Wendell Holmes said it was quite OK*, WASH. TIMES, November 29, 1990 at G2.

57. 16 THE FIJACTIVIST 1, 26 (Summer 1994), 15 THE FIJACTIVIST 1 (Spring 1994), 12 THE FIJACTIVIST 8 (Fall/Winter 1992/1993).

58. United States v. Grace, 461 U.S. 171 (1983).

59. United States v. Ogle, 613 F.2d 233, 233-235 (10th Cir. 1979).

60. Interview with Larry Dodge, August 25 1994.

support from the Congress on Racial Equality (CORE), the U.S. Justice Foundation, the National Organization for the Reform of Marijuana Laws (NORML), and many other organizations, from all points on the political spectrum.

FIJA, however, has not been without its detractors. Although the *Wall Street Journal* had originally reported very favorably about the organization,[61] in 1995 that newspaper published a harshly critical story by Wade Lambert, associating FIJA with anti-semitism and the extreme right-wing militia movement. Among other things, Lambert's article asserted that:

> [Beckman's] 1984 book "The Church Deceived" describes Jews as followers of Satan who today control "our government, our major media, our banks and legal profession." The book, which is listed for sale in some FIJA brochures, says: "They talk about the terrible holocaust of Hitler's Nazi Germany. Was that not a judgment upon a people who believe Satan is their god?"
>
> Mr. Beckman contends that his views aren't anti-Semitic. "I have a serious problem with any religion that would rule the world," he says. "I have more disagreements with Baptists than I do with the Jews."
>
> FIJA's ties to the far right are most conspicuous in its home state of Montana. Driving through Billings in his Dodge van, past newly painted swastikas on the walls of the Billings Visitor Center and another building, Mr. Beckman says that abuses of power by the federal government have driven people into the militia movement. "The militias are made up of victims," he says. "They see the handwriting on the wall."[62]

This line of attack was quickly picked up by the *Village Voice*[63] and several others. FIJA has also been included in Morris Dees' Southern Poverty Law Center "Klanwatch" list as a "false patriot" organization, in a snowballing example of "guilt by association." Because Larry Dodge has expressed public gratitude towards Beckman, who first introduced him to the concept of jury nullification, the Fully Informed Jury Association has been repeatedly tied in with Beckman's religious views. Beckman has also been invited to speak at FIJA conferences held in Missouri, Texas and Utah.

Members of the organization insist that FIJA is not connected with or responsible for Beckman's decidedly misguided religious opinions. FIJA

---

61. Adler, *supra* note 36.

62. Wade Lambert, *More Angry Men: Militias Are Joining Jury-Power Activists To Fight Government; Tax Protesters, Survivalists Benefit from Message: Juries Can Ignore law; "Red" Beckman's Revenge*, WALL ST. JRL., May 25, 1995.

63. James Ledbetter, *Press Clips: A Jury Of One's Fears*, VILLAGE VOICE, June 13, 1995 (Ledbetter claims that "…the FIJA's leading theorist wrote a book in 1984 that calls Jews followers of Satan who control the government, media, banks, and the law").

activists claim that their main goal is to see justice done in individual cases, and that FIJA has no broader political agenda. FIJA believes that a jury informed of its power to deliver a verdict according to conscience assures that the punishment fits the crime. Where no harm has been done, where the defendant was acting in a responsible manner, any criminal conviction on the defendant's record is too great a punishment. If the jurors believe that it would be unjust to convict, they claim that jurors are within their rights to refuse to do so.

Larry Dodge explains that juries are a feedback loop that improves the democratic process.[64] Legislators and other elected officials are responsible for writing, revising and modifying laws until the criminal code matches community consensus. The surest way to measure community values is to see what the people do when they are called on to judge their neighbors according to the legislature's statutes. A pattern of hung juries, nullification acquittals or ameliorated convictions is a sure sign to the legislature that the law needs to be changed.

Because Dodge and Doig believe that many Americans do not support victimless crime legislation, they argue that statutes criminalizing acts that are merely "malum prohibitum" would rarely be enforced by fully informed juries. Certainly, under the present system such laws are among the most frequently nullified. It is difficult to predict whether a change in jury instructions would result in massive increases in acquittals and hung juries in such cases. Although trial judges usually view hung juries as little more than a waste of valuable court time, Dodge does not consider hung juries to be anything more than a temporary problem. In FIJA's *Jury Power Information Kit*, he explains that

> There is a backlog of laws that have escaped jury review since the Supreme Court in 1895 allowed judges to withhold information about the right of jurors to judge both law and fact. That may be why America leads the world in the percentage of population in prison, and why there could be many hung juries following pasage of FIJA. A temporary surge in the number of hung juries should be regarded positively, as a necessary part of adjusting our legal and moral priorities.
>
> Juries hung because some of their members disagree with the law are actually performing a service for society: they are sending messages to lawmakers in a peaceful, routine and institutionalized way that it is time for changes in the law. When those changes have been made, hung juries will again be rare.
>
> The wrong way to deal with discrepancies between current moral standards and the law is to avoid hung juries by allowing juries to convict

---

64. Dodge, *supra* note 60.

without reaching unanimity. This threatens the individual rights of minorities, and fosters tyranny of the majority.[65]

The national headquarters of FIJA is listed as a § 501(c)(3) non-profit educational organization. Because of its status, FIJA can not participate in lobbying or political activity. The state FIJA groups, however, can and do lobby, sponsor ballot initiatives, and endorse candidates. The National organization has no control over the state organizations, but functions as an information clearinghouse, a publicity office and as a source of materials on the subject of jury independence.

It is difficult to assess the effectiveness of FIJA in promoting jury independence. Surveys do not support the contention that a significant number of people have become aware of jury independence.[66] The results in certain cases can be shown, through post-verdict juror interviews, to have been influenced by the fact that the jurors were informed of their powers through FIJA pamphlets before *voir dire*.[67] Many other cases might have been similarly affected. FIJA volunteers report defense attorneys and jurors have thanked them for their pamphlets, and have told them that the information had made the difference between a conviction and either a hung jury or an acquittal.[68]

But the relative number of cases FIJA volunteers can directly reach are miniscule. It is by receiving media attention that FIJA hopes to reach large numbers of potential jurors, and FIJA has been remarkably successful in obtaining media attention. Over 1,000 newspaper, magazine and newsletter articles about the organization and its activities have been catalogued by the National FIJA,[69] including the large, relatively laudatory article on the front page of the *Wall Street Journal*.[70] FIJA and its proposals have

---

65. JURY POWER INFORMATION KIT, 12 (Fully Informed Jury Association, 1991).

66. Brody & Rivera, *supra* note 41.

67. *Voir dire*, also referred to as jury selection, is the part of a trial in which prospective jurors are questioned concerning their biases and opinions in order to determine their qualifications for jury service.

68. Dodge, *supra* note 60. *See also* 16 THE FIJACTIVIST 1 (Summer 1994) (discussing the case of United States v. Aguirre):

> It turns out that the forewoman of the Aguirre jury, Mara Taub, not only publishes the Coalition for Prisoner's Rights Newsletter, but has been on the FIJA mailing list for some time. She has told us that the verdicts were very much jury nullification verdicts, made possible by the "contamination" of the jury with FIJA's forbidden knowledge.

The nine defendants in the Aguirre case were on trial for possession of several thousand pounds of marijuana. Three of the defendants were acquitted, and the jury hung with regard to the other six.

69. Interview with Don Doig, August 25, 1994.

70. Adler, *supra* note 36.

been discussed in law review articles[71] and on talk radio, cable television and news programming. For an organization with no full time employees and a paltry annual budget of only $100,000, FIJA has achieved uncommon success.

Still, Fully Informed Jury Acts have not been passed in any state where they have been introduced. Such acts were twice passed by the State House in Arizona (1991 and 1993), but failed when brought before the State Senate.[72] In Oklahoma, a Fully Informed Jury Act passed the House in 1993, but was scuttled in the Senate Appropriations Committee and never considered by the full State Senate.[73] A similar act was passed by the Oklahoma House in 1994, but the Senate Judiciary Committee refused to consider it. New York State Senator Joseph Galiber proposed FIJA legislation in 1991, but did not make any progress in getting it through the New York Senate.[74] FIJA legislation has also been introduced in Washington, Massachusetts, Louisiana, Tennessee, Texas, Utah, Georgia, Montana, Vermont and Connecticut.[75] Nevertheless, FIJA expects to see a Fully Informed Jury Act passed in the near future.

---

71. Examples in 1993 include Weinstein, *supra* note 4; Michael J. Saks, *Judicial Nullification*, 68 IND. L.J. 1281 (1993); M. Kristine Creagan, *Jury Nullification: Assessing Recent Legislative Developments*, 43 CASE W. RES. L. REV. 1101 (1993); Lieut. Commander Robert E Korroch, Major Michael J. Davidson, *Jury Nullification: A Call for Justice or an Invitation to Anarchy?*, 139 MIL. L. REV. 131 (1993); Todd Barnet, *New York Considers Jury Nullification: Informing the Jury of its Common Law Right to Decide Both Law and Facts*, 65 Nov. N.Y. ST. B.J. 40 (November, 1993).

72. *See* William P. Cheshire, *Why Juries Ought to Know Their Rights*, ARIZONA REPUBLIC, March 21, 1993 at C1; Richard Romley, *Informed-Jury Act Would Neuter Courts, Is Bad Policy*, ARIZONA REPUBLIC, March 22, 1993 at A10; Barnett S. Lotstein, *Fully Informed Jury Act Died Well-Deserved Death in Legislature*, PHOENIX GAZETTE, April 24, 1993 at A11.

73. *See* 65 OKLAHOMA BAR JOURNAL, No. 13, March 26, 1994:

HB-1359–Key—Amends present law to provide that whenever the state or a political subdivision of the state is one of the parties in a trial by jury, the court shall inform the jurors that each of them has the inherent right to vote on the verdict according to his or her own conscience and sense of justice. Exercise of this right may include jury consideration of the defendant's motives and circumstances, degree of harm done, and evaluation of the law itself. Failure to so inform the jury is grounds for mistrial and another trial by jury; amends 22 O.S. 1991, § 834; effective September 1, 1994. Amended and Passed House—To Senate Committee on Appropriations.

74. Todd Barnet, *supra* note 71.

75. Kristine Creagan, *supra* note 71; David C. Brody, *Sparf & Dougherty Revisited: Why the Court Should Instruct the Jury of its Nullification Right*, 22 AM.CRIM.L.REV. 89, n. 8 (1995).

Especially interesting is the impact of publicity about jury nullification on instructions given to jurors, and on trial procedures, in areas where FIJA pamphleters are working. If jurors receive pamphlets explaining the doctrine from protestors before entering the courthouse; if they learn about the doctrine from listening to knowledgeable people talk about it on the radio; or if they read about it in the paper, then the judge no longer has the option of keeping them in the dark. If the judge tells the jurors that everything in the brochure is a lie, then the judge has decided to lie to the jury himself. If one juror knows better, he is likely to share what he knows with other jurors, which could cost the judge credibility. Once jurors believe the judge is lying to them, they are less likely to trust the judge or to pay close attention to judicial instructions.

If the judge decides to ignore the issue of jury nullification and inform the jury that they are bound to apply the law as he has explained it to them, then jurors may believe the judge is treating them like incompetent children. FIJA hopes that judges are going to find it increasingly difficult to empanel a jury that is ignorant of its power to judge the law. Knowledgeable juries are empowered juries; FIJA's mission is to educate jurors about their powers.

The Fully Informed Jury Association is not the only organization participating in these efforts. Many other groups, such as Operation Rescue, NORML, the American Anti-Prohibition League, the Libertarian Party and others have made their own jury information brochures, and they distribute their brochures on courthouse steps as well. Some of these brochures are scrupulously accurate; some are only modestly so, and some are downright manipulative and disingenuous.

The First Amendment is founded on the philosophy that allowing a free flow of information is the best way to counter inaccurate or misleading information. The best antidote to groups giving jurors faulty or incomplete information is not to ban the pamphlets, but for jurors to be told the truth by the judge in court. As judges find that more jurors are to some degree aware of their powers to nullify the written law, it will be up to the bench to ensure that jurors know how to use these powers in a responsible manner.

There is one noteworthy aspect of the Fully Informed Jury Association that separates it from past efforts to inform jurors of their powers. FIJA has shown no signs of going away. The organization has been in existence for several years and has experienced steady, and sometimes rapid, growth. Unlike efforts made to inform jurors of their powers in the past, FIJA is not organized around or inspired by a single issue or category of crime. Whereas the Levellers, the Quakers, the libel law opponents, the abolitionists and the Vietnam War protesters all ended their efforts to inform jurors of their powers when the laws they objected to had been repealed, FIJA is working on informing jurors of their powers as a means towards a general limitation on the scope of the criminal sanction, and not a means of nullifying any particular category or class of laws. FIJA, therefore, will not be easily mollified by any piecemeal changes in the criminal law. Instead, it represents for the first time a general effort to promote independent juries for the general benefits they offer.

Model Fully Informed Jury Act Legislation

What exactly should jurors be told, and in what cases, in order to honestly inform them of their powers while discouraging frivolous, biased or irresponsible nullification verdicts? The Fully Informed Jury Act originally proposed by FIJA has gone through several variations. The first attempts were criticized in an article by Prof. M. Kristine Creagan for making too many demands on judges, and for attempting to cover all cases, civil or criminal.[76] This was problematic both because jury nullification was unlikely to apply to the vast majority of criminal and civil cases, and because some jurors may interpret it to apply to affirmative defenses, or even the reasonable doubt standard itself.

It was thought a jury nullification instruction should only be available in cases where the government itself is a party, either as a prosecutor or as a civil litigant. Further, the government itself should never be permitted to request a nullification instruction. After all, if the purpose of jury nullification is to "prevent oppression by the government,"[77] then the government hardly needed the jury to intervene for its own protection. The Fully Informed Jury Bill Language proposed by FIJA in 1994 reads as follows:

> An accused or aggrieved party's right to trial by jury, in all instances where the government or any of its agencies is an opposing party, includes the right to inform the jurors of their power to judge the law as well as the evidence, and to vote on the verdict according to conscience.
>
> This right shall not be infringed by any statute, juror oath, court order, or procedure or practice of the court, including the use of any method of jury selection which could preclude or limit the empanelment of jurors willing to exercise this power.
>
> Nor shall this right be infringed by preventing any party to the trial, once the jurors have been informed of their powers, from presenting arguments to the jury which may pertain to issues of law and conscience, including
>
> (1) the merit, intent, constitutionality, or applicability of the law in the instant case;

---

76. M. Kristine Creagan, *supra* note 71.

77. *Duncan, supra* note 47, 155-156.

    (2) the motives, moral perspective, or circumstances of the accused or aggrieved party;

    (3) the degree or direction of guilt or actual harm done; or

    (4) the sanctions which may be applied to the losing party.

Failure to allow the accused or aggrieved party or counsel for that party to so inform the jury shall be grounds for mistrial and another trial by jury.[78]

This proposed language is intended to address the concerns of both jury independence proponents and opponents. Because jury law-judging should only take place after the defendant has been found otherwise guilty, the bill protects against reverse nullification by leaving the decision whether to inform the jury of its power with the defense. The bill is not overbroad; it is applicable only to criminal and quasi-criminal cases—those cases in which the government is a party.

There is no requirement in this model legislation for judges to inform jurors of this doctrine in all cases, regardless of the applicability of this doctrine to the case. Jurors are not likely to decide that laws against homicide, blackmail or kidnapping are unjust or unfair; there is no reason to confuse them or waste court time by reading rote instructions in cases where the defense makes no claim that the law is oppressive. There is also no point in requiring judges to give rote jury nullification instructions in cases where nobody reasonably believes those issues are relevant.

By leaving the decision as to whether to introduce jury independence issues into the trial with the defense, arguments that the law is unjust, misapplied or unfairly enforced become affirmative defenses of sorts.[79] It is the responsibility of the defense to convince the jury that the law can not equitably be applied to the defendant in the case before them. The burden of defending the law falls—as it should—on the government, and not on the court. The court's role should be to explain the law as it is written and interpreted, but not to attempt to bind the jurors to the courts' interpretation of the law.

---

78. 16 THE FIJACTIVIST 7, 13 (Summer 1994).

79. More accurately, jury nullification is the result of the affirmative defense that a conviction in the disputed case would constitute oppression of the defendant by government. *See* Roger Park, *The Entrapment Defense*, 60 MINN. L. REV. 163, 188 (1976)(jury nullification as part of a "due process" defense).

Chapter Seven

Scapegoating the Jury

> *A fox should not be of*
> *the jury at a goose's trial.*
> *Thomas Fuller*

The Bigoted Jury: Acquittals in Lynching and Civil Rights Murder Cases[1]

In spite of the proud history of independent juries in America, there remains one particularly odious charge against them: that they cannot be trusted to do justice when a white person is on trial for crimes against a black victim. Intermixed within those cases which may be considered "proper" or "benevolent" uses of jury independence has run a parallel, malevolent history of all-white juries allegedly acquitting those who participated in lynch mobs or in the murders of civil rights workers. This history is the most commonly invoked argument against jury independence. Juries have been charged with routinely acquitting whites who killed or otherwise victimized blacks due to racist motivations.[2] The police officers involved in the arrest and beating of Rodney King are presumed by many to have been

---

1. My thanks goes to the Cornell Journal of Law and Public Policy, which published an earlier version of this chapter under the title "Scapegoating the Jury," and which has permitted its republication here.

2. *See* Gary J. Simson, *Jury Nullification in the American System: A Skeptical View*, 54 TEX. L. REV. 488 (1976); John P. Relman, *Overcoming Obstacles to Federal Fair Housing Enforcement in the South: A Case Study in Jury Nullification*, 61 MISS. L.J. 579 (1991); Benno C. Schmidt, Jr., *Juries, Jurisdiction and Race Discrimination: The Lost Promise of Strauder v. West Virginia*; 61 TEX. L. REV. 1401, 1455 (1983); Paul Hoffman, *Double Jeopardy Wars: The Case for a Civil Rights "Exception"*, 41 UCLA L. REV. 649, 660-669 (1994); Tony Perry, *The Simpson Verdicts: Snubbing the Law to Vote on Conscience*, L.A.TIMES, October 5, 1995 at 5A; Dick Williams, *Barry's Acquittals Signals Win For "Victim" Theorists*, ATLANTA CONST., August 14, 1990 at A27; Jim Nesbitt, *Ozark Folks Learn to Skirt Law Without Violence*, CLEVELAND PLAIN DEALER, August 13, 1995 at 13A; Thomas Eagleton, *Jury Nullification: Road to Anarchy*, ST. LOUIS POST-DISPATCH, July 30, 1995 at 03B; Michael Granberry, *Abortion Protest Juries told to Ignore Nullification Ad*, L.A. TIMES, January 27, 1990 at B1; Steve Daley, *The City of Angels is Having a Hellish Time Finding Real Justice*, CHI. TRIB., October 24, 1995 at P5; Dick Williams,

modern beneficiaries of this sort of jury independence.[3] The murderers of lynching victims and civil rights workers supposedly went free because all-white juries refused to convict.[4]

In recent years, Medgar Evers' assassin Byron de la Beckwith attempted to make a racist appeal to the community, distributing literature encouraging jury nullification in his third murder trial, after two previous trials ended in hung juries.[5] Professor Alan Dershowitz has referred to jury nullification as "a redneck trick" due to the allegedly recurrent history of white juries acquitting lynch mobs.[6] Such charges are not entirely without foundation. Juries have been asked such blatantly racist questions as "Do you think it's a crime to kill a nigger in Mississippi?"[7]

While the allegedly widespread use of jury independence[8] in defense of racist murderers seems to have passed with the major civil rights advancements of the 1960s, these cases cast a long shadow over the jury room even today. Advocates of increased jury independence find that fears of racist nullification are the most frequently raised objections to their proposals. These fears are based on an inaccurate, exaggerated or incomplete view of jury behavior in cases involving racial violence. There is very little concrete evidence or data on which one could conclude that jury independence has ever been widely or routinely used in a racist or prejudiced man-

---

Barry's Acquittals Signal Win for 'Victim' Theorists, ATLANTA CONST., August 14, 1990 at A27.

3. *See* Nancy J. King, *Postconviction Review of Jury Discrimination: Measuring the Effects of Juror Race on Jury Deliberations*, 92 MICH. L. REV. 63 (1993). *See also* Hon. Stanley J. Weisberg, *Out of the Frying Pan into the Fire: Race and Choice of Venue after Rodney King*, 106 HARV. L. REV. 705 (1993); Terence Moran, *Maybe the Jury was White?*, CONN.L.TRIB., June 15, 1992 at 1.

4. *See* Judge Bazelon's dissent, United States v. Dougherty, 473 F.2d 1113, 1143 (D.C. Cir. 1972).

5. *See* Jerry Mitchell, *Beckwith Behind Leaflets Aimed at Jurors*, CLARION-LEDGER (Jackson, Miss.) August 12, 1993; William Booth, *Bias and Race Still Pertinent As 3rd Beckwith Trial Opens*, WASH. POST, January 21, 1994.

6. Alan Dershowitz, *Barry Employs a Redneck Trick: Jury Nullification Ploy Appeals to Racist Instincts*, BUFFALO NEWS, June 9, 1990 at C3.

7. This question was asked during the *voir dire* of the jury in the first murder trial of Byron de la Beckwith. *See* MARYANNE VOLLERS, GHOSTS OF MISSISSIPPI, 161 (1995).

8. It is highly questionable whether racist jury acquittals can properly be characterized as jury independence verdicts. According to Professor Alan Scheflin, jury nullification only occurs when 1) the jury has found that the defendant has met all elements of the offense and is therefore technically guilty, but 2) then decides to acquit based on conscientious grounds, because they believe that the law is either unjust or misapplied. *See* Alan Scheflin, *Jury Nullification: The Right to Say No*, 45 S. CAL. L. REV. 168 (1972).

ner. Historically, independent juries have more often been agents of change opposed to racism than the tools of racists.

Commentators and observers have exaggerated the amount of racist nullification by jurors, and implicitly exculpated the police, prosecutors and judges who frequently played as great or greater a role in exonerating lynch mobs and racist murderers. These cases plainly represent miscarriages of justice. But the unanswered questions remain. Why did justice miscarry? What parties must share in the responsibility? How widespread was racist nullification? Finally, what reforms can help eliminate similar miscarriages of justice in the future? There are several factors to take into consideration before we can answer these questions.

The above questions are vitally important because of the enormous power and responsibility bestowed upon juries. The power of juries to nullify the law, *sub rosa*,[9] is granted in part on the assumption that the community as a whole is less oppressive than government,[10] and because allowing common-sense and logic to play a role in deciding individual cases provides the flexibility necessary for the criminal justice system to function effectively.[11] The criminal trial jury has been described as the "conscience of the community." For that conscience to operate in a way in which we, as a society, can be proud, we must be confident that the community is in fact a conscientious one.[12] Unfortunately juries, like all elements of a complex society, may occasionally give us cause to question this assumption. Allowing the jury to circumnavigate the law in order to do justice merely accords with an American tradition that dates back to pre-colonial times. Allowing the jury to circumnavigate justice in order to single out a segment of society as beneath the protection of the law violates fundamental constitutional principles of due process and equal protection. If American juries are ever to regain their discretionary role in the courtroom, the role of juries in cases involving racist violence will have to be better understood.

As a starting point, we must realize that because juries do not issue written opinions, it is often impossible to know why juries chose to acquit in a given case. The Fourth Circuit Court of Appeals noted in 1969 that "the

---

9. Sub rosa literally means "under the rose." It refers here to the fact that the jury's decision is exercised secretly, privately.

10. E.g., Duncan v. Louisiana, 391 U.S. 145, 155-156 (1968).

11. Roscoe Pound, *Law in Books and Law in Action*, 44 AM.L.REV. 12 (1910); John H. Wigmore, *A Program for the Trial of Jury Trial*, 12 J. AM. JUD. SOC. 166 (1929).

12. *See* JEFFREY ABRAMSON, WE, THE JURY: THE JURY SYSTEM AND THE IDEAL OF DEMOCRACY, 62 (1994)("Once we grant jurors the right to set conscience above law, we have to live with consciences we admire as well as those we despise.")

courts cannot search the minds of the jurors to find the basis upon which they judge."[13] In many of the cases attributed to racist nullification, it appears that the jury may in fact have had reasonable doubts. Even a subsequent conviction on a federal civil rights charge does not preclude the possibility that a jury in a state case had reasonable doubts concerning the evidence presented at trial. The evidence, the sincerity of the prosecution, and the quality of the investigation and adjudication may all be vastly different in the federal case. We can collect data on cases where whites were acquitted of violent crimes against blacks; we can not collect data on cases ending in acquittal due to jury nullification. We simply have no way of knowing which cases to include in the latter category.

Second, the fact that juries do not give written opinions means that trial cases ending in acquittal remain unpublished. The absence of systematic publication makes much of the history anecdotal; sometimes persuasive but still not authoritative. Several private agencies have compiled lists of cases involving racial violence; unfortunately, the lists themselves do not always agree. In 1927, Iowa sociology professor Byron Reuter noted that:

> The number of persons done to death in the United States each year by mobs and self-appointed discipline committees can be stated with only approximate accuracy. The statistics are based chiefly upon newspaper reports and it cannot be known how many such occurrences escape the news gatherers or, if known to the reporters, fail of publication. Certainly some illegal killings escape publicity in the press. And of such happenings reported, we may not be certain that all come to the attention of reporters.[14]

Third, we do not know what improper influences may have induced the jury to acquit in those cases where non-fact based acquittals did occur, from fear of the Ku Klux Klan to pressures from the judge, prosecutors or police. We know that lynch mobs occasionally posed a threat to jurors. Justice Holmes remarked in one case involving a black defendant that "no juryman could have voted for an acquittal and continued to live in Phillips County."[15] The same threat may have applied to jurors voting to convict a member of a lynch mob. Additionally, most southern states have elected judges, sheriffs and prosecutors, who themselves are subject to the influence both of the violent mob, and of the presumably peaceable electorate. Racial oppression by the police was frequently rampant in those areas where racist nullification was reportedly widespread.[16] It may be unreal-

---

13. United States v. Moylan, 417 F.2d 1002, 1006 (4th Cir. 1969).

14. BYRON REUTER, THE RACE PROBLEM, 366 (1927).

15. Moore et al. v. Dempsey, 261 U.S. 86, 89 (1923).

16. *See* VOLLERS, *supra* note 7, 81-82, 113, 118-123, 141-145, 182-183.

istic to expect those same police and prosecutors to aggressively investigate crimes against minorities.

Finally, we cannot know to what extent improper jury selection procedures acted to influence individual cases. Trial before a racially gerrymandered jury is not the trial by jury guaranteed by the Sixth Amendment. Professor Darryl K. Brown has questioned whether a jury which is not "an impartial, representative panel of citizens" should legitimately be described as a jury at all.[17] All-white, all-male juries were the rule before the late 1960s; the likelihood of such a jury sitting on a case in the deep South are significantly less today than in 1965.[18] To the extent that we fear jury nullification because we believe such powers give vent to vicious racism, we must investigate whether better jury selection procedures will result in more responsible jury verdicts.

Repeated references to purportedly racist jury verdicts have inflamed passion and incited debate, yet have shed very little light on this problem. Few such references ever name specific cases; at best the same four or five cases are repeatedly cited, with assertions that they are "typical."[19] The idea that white Southern juries routinely nullified the law to acquit lynch mobs and the killers of civil rights workers has passed, without justification or support, into conventional wisdom. To what extent this idea is exaggerated or erroneous needs to be carefully examined, before it is accepted as a generally proven proposition against the independent jury.

The Lynching Cases

Lynching has been practiced in the United States since before the Revolutionary War. According to one source:

> Although some accounts refer to "lynch law" in fifteenth- and sixteenth-century England and Ireland, the expression of "Lynch's Law" is associated with a brand of frontier vigilantism practiced in the back-country of Virginia and North Carolina during the late eighteenth century. Colonel Charles Lynch (b. 1736) of Bedford County, Virginia, whose brother John founded Lynchburg, imposed on the region a self-fashioned rule of law in the closing days of the Revolutionary War to mitigate the disorder that surfaced in the absence of administrative courts. The punishments "Judge

---

17. Darryl K. Brown, *Jury Nullification Within the Rule of Law*, 81 Minn.L. Rev. 1149, 1192 (1981). *See also*, Holland v. Illinois, 493 U.S. 474, 494 (1990)(Marshall, J., dissenting).

18. *See* Benno C. Schmidt, Jr., *supra* note 2, 1406-1414; Jon M. Van Dyke, Jury Selection Procedures : Our Uncertain Commitment to Representative Panels, 152-160 (1977).

19. *See*, e.g., Hoffman, *supra* note 2, 661-663.

Lynch" and his companions meted out to Tory sympathizers, horse thieves, and petty criminals were controversial, and after the war they were held accountable for their actions. Among the officials who were critical of Lynch was wartime governor Thomas Jefferson. Lynch was subsequently exonerated by the Virginia legislature, but the type of justice he had practiced became known as "Lynch's Law."[20]

The practice of lynching did not take on its pronouncedly racial overtones until after 1880, by which time almost 80% of lynching victims were black. After 1900, lynchings declined slowly, with murders of blacks by Southern mobs accounting for over 90% of all lynchings.[21]

The number of lynchings started to fall rapidly after passage of the Dyer Anti-Lynching Bill by the House of Representatives in 1922. Although the bill was later killed in the Senate, discussion of the bill and the predictable public outrage that accompanied it may have been more effective in reducing lynching than passage of the bill could have been.[22] Dyer's bill was suspected even by some of its proponents to be unconstitutional. Moorfield Storey, former president of the American Bar Association and first president of the National Association for the Advancement of Colored People, wrote to a supporter of the bill that "It has seemed to me a very doubtful question whether legislation by Congress against lynching in the States is constitutional, but...It ought to be tried."[23] By the late 1930s, lynchings had become rare. "Although acts of terror against blacks in the South continued, most of them might better be described as murders, because of the small number of persons involved in their concealment, rather than as lynchings with their public participation and public rituals."[24]

Perhaps the single most startling statistic concerning jury verdicts in lynching prosecutions is their scarcity. Few members of lynch mobs have ever been brought to justice in the United States. Between 1900 and 1930, only 0.8% of all lynchings were followed by the criminal conviction of

20. Dennis B. Downey & Raymond M. Hyser, No Crooked Death: Coatesville, Pennsylvania and the Lynching of Zachariah Walker, 2 (1991).

21. Id. at 2-3; see also James Elbert Cutler, Lynch Law: An Investigation into the History of Lynching in the United States, 13-89 (1905).

22. Gunnar Myrdal, Richard Sterner and Arnold Rose, An American Dilemma: The Negro Problem and Modern Democracy, 565 (1944). See also William White, Rope and Faggot: A Biography of Judge Lynch, 196 (1929): "[A]gitation for legal weapons against the condition complained of constitutes the most effective means of creating such organized opposition to the evil."

23. White, supra note 22, 219-220.

24. James R. McGovern, Anatomy of a Lynching: The Killing of Claude Neal, 140-141 (1982).

one or more members of the mob.[25] According to Claude Shillady, then Secretary of the National Association for the Advancement of Colored People, "Sixty-three Negroes, five of them women, and four white men fell victims to mob violence during 1918 and in no case was any member of the mobs convicted in any court and in only two instances were trials held."[26] The statistics are sketchy; but do show that those in charge of the legal system were not burning with an overwhelming desire to bring lynch mobs to justice.[27]

Given the discrepancy between the number of lynchings and the number of prosecutions, we must ask not whether members of lynch mobs were brought to justice, but why they were not. On the one hand, a stronger *a priori* case can be made that juries would nullify in lynching cases than in the civil rights murders; with lynch mobs occasionally constituting several thousand members and with lynchings concentrated in poor, backwoods areas of the South,[28] it would often be practically impossible to empanel a jury for a lynching trial where no member either witnessed, participated in, or was related to a participant in the crime.

As an example, a mob approaching fifteen thousand people assembled when Ell Person, a black man, was arrested for first degree murder for beheading a sixteen-year-old white girl outside of Memphis during the spring of 1917. Two deputies delivered Person to the mob, which reportedly consisted of fifteen thousand men, women and little children. After pouring gasoline on Person and setting him afire, the crowd complained that "they burned him too quick!"[29] A mob of equal size, including the Mayor, Chief of Police, and many women and children, "witnessed the burning of a defective charged with the murder of his employer at Waco, Texas in 1916."[30] The size of the mobs and the occasional official participation in the lynchings would seem to demonstrate that lynching as a summary pun-

25. *Id.* at 11.

26. National Association for the Advancement of Colored People (NAACP), Thirty Years of Lynching in the United States: 1889-1918, 5 (1919)(Reprinted 1967).

27. McGovern noted that "Since it is unlikely that historians will ever be able to analyze the phenomenon of lynching comprehensively because of a dearth of valid empirical data, they will have to rely on theories and on those case studies where information is unusually abundant." McGovern, *supra* note 24, 15. These problems are multiplied when attempting to research those cases where jury independence and lynching were joined.

28. *Id.* at 3-5.

29. NAACP, *supra* note 26, 25-26; Frank Shay, Judge Lynch: His First Hundred Years, 131-132 (1938).

30. White, *supra* note 22, 38.

ishment for crime was condoned by the "conscience of the community," and that prosecutors may have had difficulty obtaining convictions from a local jury.

On the other hand, the prosecutor's belief that conviction would be impossible to obtain may also have contributed to the scarcity of lynching prosecutions. This sort of preemptive nullification, refusing to prosecute based on a belief that juries would refuse to convict, merely exacerbated the problem. Prosecutions of lynch mobs (where they occurred) sent a strong message to the community that lynching was simply not going to be tolerated. It also made it clear that normal legal channels had continued to function, removing the justification that lynching was an appropriate punishment for violent crimes such as rape, murder or assault. Lynching was often a response to a belief that the law was either too slow, too lenient, or otherwise inadequate.[31] Failure to prosecute lynchers gave the mob an air of presumptive legitimacy. It was an implicit statement that no real crime had been committed, justifying a pattern of shoddy investigation, lackadaisical or nonexistent prosecution, and acquittal in future cases.

While juries may have refused to convict if the lynch mobs were put on trial, it is less than honest to criticize the jurors for wrongs they never had an opportunity to commit. The lack of prosecutions shielded the community from the scrutiny necessary to encourage more equitable proceedings in the future. Acquittals caused the community where they occurred to be ridiculed in the national media. One of the organizations which collected and disseminated data on lynchings was the comparatively liberal *Chicago Tribune*. Stories on lynchings often proved an embarrassment to the South, and to the communities where lynchings occurred.[32] A popular topic among Northern cartoonists was the drunken jury, ignorant judge and bigoted prosecutor making a mockery of law and justice in cases involving racial violence.[33]

In one of the rare cases where attempts were made to convict members of a lynch mob for murder, the prosecution failed to secure a conviction even after several successive jury trials. On August 13, 1911, a lynch mob abducted and brutally killed Zachariah Walker in Coatesville, Pennsylvania. Walker, a black man, had killed a popular local police officer in a drunken stupor, and was hospitalized for injuries resulting from his attempt

---

31. *See* W. FITZHUGH BRUNDAGE, LYNCHING IN THE NEW SOUTH: GEORGIA AND VIRGINIA, 1880-1930, 27-28, 98 (1993). Fear that failure of normal legal channels to operate properly encouraged lynching is reflected in Supreme Court Justice Brewer's proposal that lynching would be reduced if the justice system were made swifter and more certain by eliminating appeals entirely in criminal cases. CUTLER, *supra* note 21, 260-261.

32. REUTER, *supra* note 14, 367.

33. *See* McGOVERN, *supra* note 24, 106; CHARLES W. EAGLES, OUTSIDE AGITATOR: JON DANIELS AND THE CIVIL RIGHTS MOVEMENT IN ALABAMA, 158, 160-161 (1993).

at suicide upon capture.[34] Walker claimed it was self-defense, yet of murdering the officer boasted that "I killed him easy." The local sheriff, Charles E. Umsted, and the deputy responsible for guarding the hospital, Stanley Howe, told the crowd they would not get in the way of a lynch mob. "It would be the devil if somebody should happen to go after that fellow... Gentlemen, allow me to say that I am not going to get hurt," Umsted remarked. After a mob approaching 4,000 people abducted Walker from the hospital, Sheriff Umsted is reported to have calmly inspected the hospital locks and doors while Walker's screams could be heard in the distance.[35]

The Coatesville lynching became a national scandal. W.E.B. Dubois, in *The Crisis,* a journal of the National Association for the Advancement of Colored People, wrote "Some foolish people talk of punishing the heroic mob... There may be a few arrests, but the men will promptly be released by the mob sitting as a jury—perhaps even as judge."[36] Nevertheless, District Attorney Robert Gawthrop almost immediately promised to prosecute, and Pennsylvania Governor John K. Tener ordered the State Attorney General's office to participate in the investigation and prosecution.[37]

As a result, a series of over a dozen trials began on October 2, 1911. Yet, even with the public outcry, all of the trials ended in acquittals. The first defendant to be tried, who had agreed to testify against the others, was acquitted at the prosecution's request. The second case, *Commonwealth v. Joseph Swartz,* proceeded to a jury trial. Only one witness, another accused lyncher, could identify Swartz as having been present at the killing. Although Swartz was allegedly one of the leaders responsible for abducting Walker, even the deputy assigned as a guard was unable (or perhaps unwilling) to identify him. In the end, the prosecution's case against Swartz—which Deputy Attorney General Jesse B. Cunningham characterized as "the strongest of them all"—consisted of was a recanted confession, and the questionable identification of Swartz by another accused lyncher.[38]

Juries cannot convict merely because they believe the defendant is probably guilty. The state is legally and morally required to prove the defendant's guilt beyond a reasonable doubt. The prosecutions related to the murder of Zachariah Walker were flimsy, as Deputy Cunningham's comment would seem to admit. Apparently the local prosecutor was only partially sincere

---

34. DOWNEY & HYSER, *supra* note 20, 16-19.

35. *Id.* at 21-24, 30-34.

36. *Id.* at 49-50.

37. *Id.* at 44-47.

38. *Id.* at 71-76, 81. Another account of this lynching appears in SHAY, *supra* note 29, 149, and disagrees with this account in many essentials, yet appears to be scantily researched and probably inaccurate.

in seeking convictions.[39] Possibly Gawthrop's enthusiasm for these prosecutions waned after a series of acquittals, especially considering that the strongest case was a weak one. It is possible Gawthrop merely wished to avoid another drawn out and embarrassing defeat. If a prosecutor in central Pennsylvania was unwilling to commit himself to obtaining a conviction against a mob that murdered a black man in 1911, it seems unlikely that prosecutors in the deep South would have shown greater enthusiasm in a similar case.

When Claude Neal was lynched in Greenwood, Florida on October 27, 1934, no members of the mob were ever prosecuted. On October 19, Neal, a black farmer and handyman, had allegedly participated in the rape and murder of nineteen year old Miss Lola Cannidy, a white girl of Jackson County, Florida. After a short police investigation Neal was arrested and later confessed.[40] In an attempt to avoid a lynching, Neal had been secret-

---

39. Downey and Hyser note that, in the trial of one of the lynchers:

"At the conclusion of testimony, Robert Gawthrop surprised the court when he rose to ask Judge Butler if there was enough substantial evidence for the trial to continue... Turning to the jury, the judge declared: "...The weight of the Commonwealth's testimony tends to but suspicion. I believe that the investigation has been conducted most properly, but I would ask of you that you render a verdict of "Not Guilty" from your seats."

DOWNEY & HYSER, *supra* note 20, 84.

40. Neal's confession, signed by a mark since he was illiterate, is recorded below. The authorities mistakenly spelled his name as "Neals."

Confession of Claude Neals.

My name is Claude Neals. I am 23 years old and have lived in Malone, Fla. for all my life.

On Wednesday night, October 17, 1934, I spent the night with my wife and came back to Mr. Cannidy's on my wagon. My wife was with me and we went to my mother's when we left Mr. Cannidy. I had been at Mr. Cannidy's that morning helping him to break a mule to the plow. We plowed up to about twelve o'clock and then went to my mother's.

When we got to my mother's, we went out in the field to hunt a sow and I met Herbert Smith out in the field. We went up alongside of the fence to a pump on the edge of Mr. Cannidy's field. When Herbert and I got to the pump, Miss Lola Cannidy was sitting by the pump cleaning out the hog trough.

She asked if I would clean it out and I said that I would. I sat down and washed out the trough and then pumped it full of water for Miss Lola.

When Miss Lola turned to go to the house, Herbert walked up and caught her by the arm. Herbert told her: "How about me being with you?" She said "You must be a fool." Herbert said, "No, won't nobody know nothing about it." She told him to go ahead and go on, but Herbert pulled her by the arm and she started calling her brother, Mr. Willford. Herbert pulled her over the fence about four or five steps away and asked me to help him put her over the fence and she stopped calling her brother. I helped him put her over

ly transferred to an Alabama jail to await trial. A large, well organized mob (reportedly consisting of one hundred men), equipped with shotguns, automatic weapons and dynamite, abducted Neal from Alabama. The mob apparently discovered Neal's whereabouts from the Florida police, and some members of the mob were wearing clothing associated with Florida state troopers. The mob brought Neal back to Florida, where they publicly invited all "concerned white citizens" to join in lynching Neal on the farm belonging to the parents of the murdered girl. Thousands of men, women and children from several states accepted the grisly invitation.[41]

---

the fence and when we got over all three of us went on down by the East and West fence to another fence running North and South and went down by the North and South fence.

When we got to the corner of the woods, about the width of 6 acres, Miss Lola said "This is far enough." Herbert said "Come on," and she said "I don't want to go into the woods for snakes will bite me. I am not going any farther."

Herbert told her "Lay down, then." She laid down with Herbert holding to her. Herbert told me to catch both of her arms and hold her and I did that. She caught my watch. Herbert pulled up Miss Lola's clothes while I held her arms and he had intercourse with her one time. She was fighting me with her hands and trying to kick Herbert off.

After he got through, Herbert said, "come on, Claude, and get yours." I told him I didn't want to do that. Then Herbert held her and I had intercourse with her.

When I got through, Herbert said, "I will fix her where she don't tell it." I told him I had been working for her brother for two years and I didn't want to do anything else to her. He said, "You are just scared as hell." I said, "Yes, I know and you do, too, what will be the consequences if this is known." Herbert said, "I'll fix her where she won't tell nobody."

Herbert then broke down a little dead oak tree and broke off a piece about 3 or 3 1/2 feet long and hit her in the head with it. She hadn't said anything from the time we made her lie down, and she breathed a few times after Herbert hit her in the head. Herbert dragged a piece of log about five feet long and as big as my thigh up side of her and I dragged up another smaller piece and we laid them on her, or by the side of her. She just was breathing when we left her, she was not quite dead at the time.

We left her and went back to the edge of the field down to the big hedgerow. Herbert walked down by the hedgerow and I haven't seen him since. I went to my mother's house and from there to my wife's aunt's place at Miss Rose Lewis's. I came back by Justice of the Peace Edgar Anderson's and talked to him.

I went back to my mother's and from there to Mr. John Daniel's. I was at Mr. Dave Daniel's house picking peas when the Sheriff came and got me.

This confession, made at Brewton, Alabama, on the 22nd day of October, 1934, in the presence of G.S. Byrne, Sheriff of Escambia County, Alabama, and W.E. Brooks, County Solicitor of Escambia County, Alabama, is made of my own free will and accord and without any threats, promises, or hope of reward, and is entirely voluntary on my part. //S//Claude X Neals. (mark)

41. McGovern, *supra* note 24, 42, 57-66, 74-77; *see also* Shay, *supra* note 29, 182-183.

During the day of October 26, 1934, a mob of seven to ten thousand anxiously waited to lynch Neal. When the mob became so rambunctious his abductors feared a melee, they tortured and murdered Neal privately, then dragged the body behind a car to the farm. The mob attacked the body; children stabbing at it with sharpened sticks. Later, Neal's mutilated body was hung from a tree by the Jackson County Courthouse. The worked up crowd then rioted, and were not calmed until Florida Governor David Sholtz illegally called out the National Guard (without the request of the local sheriff).[42]

Sheriff W. Flake Chambliss had rejected the Governor's offer of National Guard help in averting the lynching, or in quieting the riotous mob. A local deputy sheriff voiced an opinion that "the mob will not be bothered, either before or after the lynching." Although mob members made no attempt to disguise themselves or cover their license plates, no witness could identify a single participant in the riots or in the lynching.[43] The Grand Jury investigating the lynching issued no indictments but instead issued what appears to be an attempt to justify the mob's actions, reporting that:

> We have not been able to get much direct or positive evidence with reference to this matter; practically all of our evidence and information being in the nature of hearsay and rumors. However, we find that Miss Cannidy was brutally raped and murdered in this county on the 18th day of October, 1934, by Claud Neal, a negro and that Claud Neal came to his death at the hands of a small group of persons unknown to us; after being forcibly removed from the jail at Brewton, Alabama, about 175 miles from here, by persons unknown to us.[44]

No prosecutions were ever attempted. Although NAACP Secretary William White urged United States Attorney General Homer Cummings to investigate and prosecute under federal kidnapping laws, the Attorney General responded that those laws only covered kidnappings for ransom or hire.[45] State efforts to prosecute produced no results; local officials blamed the riots and lynching on the work of "outsiders," primarily Alabamians.[46]

These and other cases[47] show that the failure to bring members of lynch mobs to justice was the result of a multiplicity of forces. Jury independence could have played at most a marginal role, because only a very few

---

42. McGovern, *supra* note 24, 79-94; Shay, *supra* note 29, 184-185.

43. Quoted in McGovern, *supra* note 24, 75.

44. *Id.* at 112.

45. *Id.* at 115-121.

46. *Id.* at 95-98.

47. *See generally* Brundage, *supra* note 31. *See also* Howard Smead, Blood Justice: The Lynching of Mack Charles Parker, (1986); George C. Wright, Racial Violence in Kentucky, 1865-1940: Lynchings, Mob Rule, and "Legal Lynchings" (1990).

lynching cases ever went to a jury trial. The reluctance of officials to prosecute, protect, or investigate was certainly a much greater factor. Where attempts were made to prosecute lynch mobs, they could fairly be described as half-hearted at best—if not as outright shams. While the jury may have occasionally been implicated in this injustice, it simply was not and could not have been the primary engine of racial injustice conventional wisdom would have us envision.

Probably the most infamous lynching case involved the murder of Emmett Till in 1955. Till, a fourteen year old from Chicago, was lynched by two white men a few hours after Till had purportedly whistled at a white woman in Money, Mississippi. Roy Bryant, the woman's husband, and J.W. Milam, Bryant's half-brother, tortured and killed Till then tied his body to the fan of a gin mill and dropped it in the Tallahatchie River. Bryant and Milam were acquitted by an all-white jury. Following the acquittal, they sold their story to William Bradford Huie, writing for *Look* magazine, for $4,000. Milam described to Huie how he and Bryant killed Till when the boy refused to cry out for mercy.[48]

The acquittal of Bryant and Milam has frequently been referred to as a case of jury nullification.[49] We know that the defense attorney made a racist plea for acquittal, imploring the jury that "I know every last Anglo-Saxon one of you has the courage to acquit these men."[50] In fact, the only issue presented by the defense in the case was whether the body found in the Tallahatchie River was in fact Emmett Till. The only real identification of the body was a ring bearing the initials "L.T.," which Till had received from his father, Louis Till. Although Till's mother, Mamie Till Bradley, identified the body as that of her son, no medical testing ever verified that the badly bloated and decomposed body found in the river was in fact that of Emmett Till.[51] However, no credible version of the events could have accounted for the body not being that of Emmett Till. The defense version, that the N.A.A.C.P. had stolen Till's ring, planted it on the finger of an unidentifiable corpse, and dumped it in the river for purposes of "propaganda," was plainly implausible. As journalist Hodding Carter noted in the *Delta Democrat-Times*

> The body was identified by relatives, was accepted by the boy's mother.... Had such a murder been planned to replace another body for Till's,

---

48. William Bradford Huie, *The Shocking Story of Approved Killing in Mississippi*, LOOK, 20, January 24, 1956.

49. *See*, e.g., ABRAMSON, *supra* note 12, 111-112.

50. STEPHAN THERNSTROM AND ABIGAIL THERNSTROM, AMERICA IN BLACK AND WHITE: ONE NATION, INDIVISIBLE, 515 (1997).

51. STEPHEN J. WHITFIELD, A DEATH IN THE DELTA: THE STORY OF EMMETT TILL, 40-43 (1988).

the ring engraved 1943 L.T. (for the boy's father Louis Till), someone would have had to have been killed before the boy was abducted, the ring stolen from young Till and placed on the dead person's finger. Without the prior knowledge that Roy Bryant and his half-brother would kidnap Till, as they admittedly did, such a conspiracy defies even the most fantastic reality.[52]

The acquittal of Bryant and Milam has been presented as a classic example of racist jury nullification. The entire trial, held in Sumner, Mississippi, had been orchestrated to provide such a verdict. Tallahatchie County Sheriff Harold Clarence Strider changed his version of the events to agree with the defense shortly after the body of Till was discovered and refused to do any further investigative work for the prosecution. At trial, Sheriff Strider was to testify for the defense. Mississippi Attorney General and Democratic gubernatorial candidate James P. Coleman, himself an advocate of white supremacy, assigned Robert B. Smith III to assist with the prosecution.[53]

Tallahatchie County had a population of approximately 30,000, nearly two-thirds of whom were black. None of the black residents, not surprisingly for that era in Mississippi, were registered to vote, and therefore only whites were eligible for jury duty. The segregation in Sumner extended to the courthouse itself, with the black press given its own table, far from the bench and the white reporters. The black reporters were welcomed into the courtroom every morning by Sheriff Strider's catcall of "Hello, niggers."[54] Even black Congressman Charles C. Diggs, Jr., from Detroit was restricted to the black journalists' table. The presence of a black congressman was visibly amusing to the Tallahatchie sheriff's deputies guarding the courtroom.[55]

The chief witness against the killers was Moses Wright, a relative of Till's, who had seen Bryant and Milam kidnap Till the night of the killing. Moses Wright identified the two killers, and described their coming to his house at two o'clock in the morning demanding the "Chicago boy." The other witnesses for the prosecution, Mamie Till Bradley, Amanda Bradley and Willie Reed, were also black. The segregated courtroom, along with the racist attitude of Sheriff Strider, a key defense witness, reduced the value of these witnesses. It is inconceivable that the atmosphere of racism permeating the courtroom would not have been observed by the all-white jurors, and that it would not have acted upon them as authorization for their delivery of a racist verdict.

---

52. DELTA DEMOCRAT-TIMES, September 6, 1955 at 4, quoted in WHITFIELD, *supra* note 51, 43.

53. WHITFIELD, *supra* note 51, 30-31.

54. *Id.* at 35, 37.

55. *Id.* at 37, 38.

Another factor gravitating towards acquittal was the Northern press and organizations such as the N.A.A.C.P., which had put the case in the national (if not the international) spotlight. Residents of Sumner were protective of their community and its reputation, and parochially suspicious of "outsiders" attacking "the Southern way of life." According to one author, "[l]ocal pride and self-sufficiency were imperiled, and the capacity of Mississippi whites to govern themselves—and to live with the blacks toward whom they professed no hostility—came to be the central issues in the Till case. The primacy of states' rights became so urgent, the feelings of defensiveness so raw and exposed, that the murder of an adolescent declined in moral magnitude."[56]

As ghastly as the facts of the Till case are, they do not show that juries can not be trusted to deliver fair verdicts in cases of racial violence. Sheriff Strider, proudly racist and willing to commit perjury in order to protect Bryant and Milam, certainly did his part to avoid a conviction. The prosecution never attempted to move the case out of virulently racist Tallahatchie county. The methods of jury selection that created an all-white jury in a county that was predominantly black were never questioned. The Till case involved a racist jury, selected through racially biased methods, in a segregated courtroom in a viciously racist community. A fairly selected jury, judging the trial in a racially neutral courtroom following a full investigation and honest testimony from the local sheriff, and without the outside pressures confronting Sumner, Mississippi during the fall of 1955, might well have convicted Bryant and Milam as readily as the Sumner grand jury indicted them.

The Civil Rights Murders

The murders of civil rights workers during the 1950s and 1960s were probably more notorious, although much less numerous, than lynchings. Few civil rights murder cases ever resulted in convictions within state courts, although some of the killers were eventually tried and convicted in federal court for violations of federal civil rights law. Unlike lynchings, which usually involved relatively unknown victims in backwoods locations, the murders of Lemuel Penn, Viola Liuzzo, Jonathan Daniels, Medgar Evers, Vernon Dahmer, Andrew Goodman, James Earl Chaney and Michael Henry Schwerner occurred in larger Southern cities and involved relatively high-profile victims. For this reason alone, more information is available on these cases.

Several of the most notorious civil rights murders occurred in Mississippi. When Reverend George Washington Lee, who had registered ninety-two

---

56. *Id.* at 27.

black voters, was murdered by two shotgun blasts in the face while driving in Belzoni, Mississippi on May 7, 1955, the local sheriff attempted to blame the lead pellets in his face on dislodged dental fillings.[57] He was apparently unaware that lead is not used in dental work. When later investigations turned up a bullet in one of the tires of Lee's car, Sheriff Ike Shelton changed his theory: there must have been a woman involved. Lee was killed by a "jealous nigger," the Sheriff opined. No arrests were ever made.[58] Nor was anybody arrested when Lamar Smith was killed on the courthouse lawn in Brookhaven, Mississippi three months later. Smith was in the midst of organizing a campaign to get blacks to vote by absentee ballot.[59] The NAACP Field Secretary assigned to investigate these cases was Medgar Evers. In the early morning hours of June 12, 1963, Evers in turn was killed when Byron de la Beckwith shot him in the back.[60]

Evers' national reputation in the civil rights movement, combined with the cowardly shot in the back, made his murder a national *cause célébre*. President John F. Kennedy himself issued a statement from the White House saying that he was "appalled by the barbarity of the act."[61] "Delay" Beckwith was twice tried for the murder during 1964; both trials ended in hung juries. It was not until his third trial for murder, conducted more than thirty years after the killing, that Beckwith was finally convicted for the murder. Conventional wisdom was and remains that no Mississippi jury in 1964 would ever convict a white man for killing Evers. One chronicle of the events concluded that "[t]he mystery did not revolve around Beckwith's guilt: the evidence against him had always been overwhelming. Most people accepted that only the hold of white supremacy had allowed him to escape punishment twenty-six years before."[62]

Whatever conventional wisdom was or is, Beckwith's defense team had to work hard to procure those mistrials. Despite Beckwith's braggadocio[63] it does not appear the results were ever assured. Nor was the case against Beckwith clearly compelling. Several witnesses — including police officers — claimed they had seen Beckwith elsewhere that night,[64] there were

---

57. ADAM NOSSITER, OF LONG MEMORY: MISSISSIPPI AND THE MURDER OF MEDGAR EVERS, 44 (1994).

58. VOLLERS, *supra* note 7, 61.

59. *Id.* at 63-64.

60. *Id.* at 3.

61. *Id.* at 1, 138.

62. NOSSITER, *supra* note 57, 13.

63. Beckwith was known for his antics during his trials, handling evidence, slipping cigars into District Attorney Bill Waller's pocket, patting him on the back, and chatting with jurors during recesses. VOLLERS, *supra* note 7, 171, 175.

64. *Id.* at 190-191.

unanswered questions about Beckwith's ownership of the murder weapon,[65] and defense witnesses controverted claims that Beckwith's car was parked at a nearby restaurant.[66] As one juror claimed, "There were too many contradictions in the thing."[67]

Beckwith's case is a curious tale of racial injustice. Perhaps the most telling aspect of the case was the state's active participation in Beckwith's defense. Mississippi maintained a "Sovereignty Commission," responsible for preserving Jim Crow and independence from federal civil rights law. The Sovereignty Commission secretly investigated prospective jurors for Beckwith's defense.[68] While District Attorney Bill Waller has generally been credited with a sincere prosecution in spite of his own segregationist views,[69] it is obvious that his superiors in the state had mixed feelings. Waller's own political ambitions (he was elected Governor of Mississippi in 1971)[70] may have constrained his enthusiasm. Waller had no incentive to reach out to black voters as few Mississippi blacks were registered to vote in 1964. While racists tolerated the district attorney "just doing his job," they probably took a dim view of any real enthusiasm in this particular case. Between the contradictions in the prosecution's case, and the state's surreptitious assistance with Beckwith's defense, it is apparent that no concerted effort to convict Beckwith was being made.

Not all civil rights murders involved black victims. In Lowndes County, Alabama, two white civil rights workers, Viola Liuzzo and Jon Daniels, were killed. Liuzzo was a housewife from Detroit, Michigan, who was shot and killed while shuttling civil rights workers between Selma and Montgomery on March 25, 1965. An FBI informer was riding in the car with the three Ku Klux Klan members who shot Liuzzo as she was driving to Montgomery to pick up passengers. Collie Leroy Wilkins, who fired the fatal shots, was acquitted by an Alabama jury in his second murder trial, which followed an earlier mistrial.[71]

Similarly, Jonathan Daniels, a devoted civil rights activist, was a visiting Episcopalian seminarian from Keene, New Hampshire who was killed in Hayneville, Alabama, also in Lowndes County. When shot by Tom Coleman in the late summer of 1965, Daniels had just been released from

65. *Id.* at 172-178.

66. *Id.* at 186-187.

67. Quoted in NOSSITER, *supra* note 57, xi.

68. VOLLERS, *supra* note 7, 264.

69. NOSSITER, *supra* note 57, 145-147.; *see also* REED MASSENGILL, PORTRAIT OF A RACIST, 180-181 (1991).

70. *Id.* at 145-171.

71. EAGLES, *supra* note 33, 114-115, 254.

six days in jail, following his arrest for participating in a civil rights demonstration. The demonstration was later found to have been legal.[72] The rumor that these protestors would be freed put Tom Coleman, a local state employee, and others on guard. After their release, Daniels, accompanied by a Catholic priest, Richard Morrisroe and two black women, decided to go to a local country store to get something to eat and drink. With a shotgun in hand, Coleman met them at the store. He stood only a few feet away from Daniels when he abruptly fired his twelve-gauge shotgun at the seminarian. Coleman fired once at Daniels's chest, and then again into Morrisroe's side. Daniels died instantly but Morrisroe survived. Coleman's unlikely claim was that the clerics had threatened him. Coleman claimed that Daniels had a knife and Morrisroe a pistol. Although the weapons were never found, Coleman claimed that two black teenagers took the weapons away before police arrived.[73]

Coleman was well established in the local community. He was a special deputy sheriff, the son of a county sheriff, and the father of a state trooper. His sister was the School Superintendent. Many in Hayneville spoke well of Coleman; his personal friends included Public Safety Commissioner Colonel Albert Lingo, who was known for his violently racist views. Lingo stood firmly by Coleman and refused to cooperate with the State Attorney General Richmond Flowers or the FBI regarding investigation of the case.[74]

When the Grand Jury indicted Coleman for manslaughter instead of murder, Attorney General Flowers was incensed and attempted to postpone trial in order to seek a murder indictment. Judge T. Werth Thagard denied motions to postpone on grounds the prosecution was not ready, that the case be dismissed *nolle prosequi*,[75] and to postpone because Morrisroe was not well enough to testify. Assistant Attorney General Joseph Gantt refused to proceed under these conditions and turned the manslaughter case over to local district attorney Arthur "Bubba" Gambles, who was assisted by County Solicitor Carlton Perdue.[76] Coleman would never be prosecuted for murder.

Perdue and Gambles were less than aggressive at trial, "conced[ing] important points that not even defense witnesses had made," including a

---

72. *Id.* at 248-249.

73. *Id.* at 178-179, 237.

74. *Id.* at 186-196, 216.

75. *Nolle prosequi* is a dismissal of a charge for want of prosecution. When a case is *nolle prosequi*, the prosecution can file new charges based on the same facts at a later date, upon a new indictment or information.

76. *Id.* at 203-205, 209-211, 214-218.

77. *Id.* at 239-242.

false allegation that Daniels had brandished a knife.[77] Nobody seemed to notice that Daniels and Morrisroe had just come from jail, where they had no weapons. During closing argument, Gambles went so far as to apologize to the jury for taking the case to trial.[78] After deliberating less than two hours, the jury of 12 white men delivered the anticipated verdict, acquitting Coleman of manslaughter.[79] On his way out of court, one of the jurors reportedly asked Tom Coleman "[w]e gonna be able to make that dove shoot now, ain't we?"[80]

Just as in the lynching cases, there are reasons to question the sincerity of the prosecution and the impartiality of the tribunals in the above cases. Tom Coleman was never prosecuted for murder; we can question whether he was ever really prosecuted for manslaugher. The case was a charade, from the non-existent weapons in the hands of Daniels and Morrisroe, to the closing apology to the jury, to the *voir dire* that left Coleman's bird-hunting buddies on the jury. That sort of familiarity with the defendant is a parody of what constitutes an impartial jury.

Would a racially mixed jury have convicted in either of the above cases? Would a mixed jury have at least hung in the Coleman case, so Coleman could have shared Beckwith's fate, being retried before another jury thirty years after his crime? These questions cannot be authoritatively answered.

But we do know Coleman's defense attorneys were concerned that a mixed-race jury would not acquit. While Coleman's case was making its way to Judge Thagard's court, another case was pending in federal court which would have required the Lowndes County courts to select their jurors from mixed venire panels, including eligible black and female venire-persons. That case, *White v. Crooks*,[81] was an attempt to enjoin Lowndes County from conducting any jury trials until they had cured their persistent racial discrimination in jury selection. Although the plaintiffs in *White v. Crooks* were unsuccessful in enjoining jury trials in Lowndes county, Coleman's defense counsel publicly voiced concern that the real reason the prosecution was seeking delay was to force Coleman to be tried in front of a racially mixed jury.[82]

In any event, we still cannot conclude that an all-white jury would necessarily have refused to apply the law and convict, if the judge, police and prosecutors applied the law evenhandedly. When Andrew Goodman, James Earl Chaney and Michael Henry Schwerner were murdered by the Ku Klux Klan outside of Philadelphia, Mississippi on June 16, 1964, the killers

78. *Id.* at 241.
79. *Id.* at 243.
80. *Id.* at 244.
81. 251 F. Supp. 401 (M.D. Ala. 1966).
82. EAGLES, *supra* note 33, 199-200, 210-211.

were never prosecuted in a Mississippi state court. A federal prosecution, for conspiracy to deprive the victims of their civil rights, resulted in convictions in front of an all-white Mississippi jury. Possibly the real reasons for the different result between this case and the Tom Coleman case lay not in the jury, but in the court. When defense attorney Laurel Weir asked a black minister "Now, let me ask you if you and Mr. Schwerner didn't advocate and try to get young male Negroes to sign statements agreeing to rape a white woman once a week during the hot summer of 1964?,"[83] Judge Cox—himself a Mississippian and less than enthusiastic about civil rights litigation[84]—responded:

> I'm not going to allow a farce to be made of this trial and everybody might as well get that through their heads right now. I don't understand such a question as that, and I don't appreciate it, and I'm going to say so before I get through with the trial of this.[85]

Similarly, the Klan members who were acquitted of murdering Viola Liuzzo in an Alabama state court were later tried and convicted of civil rights violations by an Alabama jury in a federal court.[86] White Southern juries were evidently willing to convict, given sincere prosecution and impartial judges such as Judge Cox. The 1969 fire-bomb killing of Vernon Dahmer was followed by Mississippi state court convictions of the Klansmen responsible.[87] Of the jury pool, the investigators, the prosecutors, and the judge, the only factor that remained unchanged between the successful federal and the failed state prosecutions has been the jury pool, and yet it is juries that have taken the brunt of public condemnation.

Can Racist Nullification Be Discouraged or Controlled?

It is unrealistic to claim that racist juries have never been seated, or to deny the risk of a jury returning a racist verdict in occasional cases. Racist verdicts (such as the verdict in the Emmett Till case) have occurred, and

---

83. Quoted in FLORENCE MARS, WITNESS IN PHILADELPHIA, 235 (1977).

84. *Id.* at 228-235.

85. *Id.* at 151.

86. *See* Wilkins v. United States, 376 F.2d 552 (5th Cir. 1967); *cert. denied*, 389 U.S. 964 (1967). *See also* United States v. Guest, 383 U.S. 745 (1965).

87. *See* Wilson v. Mississippi, 234 So.2d 303 (Miss. 1970); Byrd v. Mississippi, 228 So.2d 874 (Miss. 1969); Smith v. Mississippi, 223 So.2d 657 (Miss. 1969); Sessum v. Mississippi, 221 So.2d 368 (Miss. 1969).

will in all likelihood occur in the future, whether by bench or jury. However, statistics and history fail to substantiate claims of the widespread use of racist jury nullification in cases involving racial violence. Nor do they show the jury as being more racist than other decision-makers in the criminal justice system — prosecutors, judges, police, attorneys. Instances of unalloyed racist nullification are extremely rare, and even these low numbers can be further reduced without affecting the jury's power to nullify in an appropriate case.

The primary tool used to guide jury decision-making has traditionally been through the instructions the jury receives from the court. We should remember that the cases we have been discussing did not involve either argument or instructions to the jury about their powers to reach an independent verdict.[88] Thus, these cases cannot be viewed as evidence against such instructions. In fact, they could present just the opposite. Appropriate instructions on the jury's nullification powers could reduce the incidence of inappropriate nullification. Just as we do not assume informing teenagers about their procreative powers encourages irresponsible fornication, we should not assume informing jurors about their nullification powers encourages irresponsible nullification. Proper instructions may channel the discretion of juries towards cases where convictions would be conscientiously untenable, thereby narrowing the class of cases where nullification is considered.[89]

The difference between the verdicts in the federal and state courts illustrates the importance of *voir dire* in controversial proceedings. While defense attorneys have often championed more extensive and thorough *voir dire*,[90] prosecutors may require incisive *voir dire* in order to ensure a jury willing to convict in cases of racial violence. The Supreme Court has deemed failure to allow defense questioning into racial or ethnic prejudice "where the circumstances of the case indicate that there is a reasonable

---

88. Note the words of Professor Steve Herzberg, *Annual Judicial Conference Second Judicial Circuit of the United States*, 141 F.R.D. 573 (1992):

> Let me just make one more point, and that is that the cases that people always use, the cases that are always used against the jurors, are always the same cases. And they are the civil rights cases in the South, where people who were charged with murdering civil rights workers were acquitted. They were acquitted with no instruction.

89. Irwin A. Horowitz, *Jury Nullification: The Impact of Judicial Instructions, Arguments, and Challenges on Jury Decision Making*, 12 L. & HUM. BEHAV. 439 (1988); Irwin A. Horowitz, *The Effect of Jury Nullification Instructions on Verdicts and Jury Functioning in Criminal Trials*, 9 L. & HUM. BEHAV. 25 (1985).

90. *See* Cathy E. Bennett, *Orientation — Voir Dire* (National College for Criminal Defense Tape, 1982).

possibility that racial or ethnic prejudice might have influenced the jury" to be a violation of due process of law.[91] There is no reason the prosecution should not also be allowed to ensure that the trial will be held in front of a jury unwilling to condone racial violence.

Unfortunately, the Supreme Court has severely limited the application of the above rule as a tool for the defense.[92] To further complicate matters, prosecution objections would have to be litigated on interlocutory appeal,[93] interrupting the proceedings and prolonging litigation. Whether courts would find the prosecution's interest in conducting *voir dire* on issues of racial or ethnic prejudice sufficiently compelling to outweigh the defendant's interest in the swift resolution of his case may depend on the skills of the advocates and on the specific facts of the case.

Clearly, courts have legal authority to address this issue on interlocutory appeal.[94] Courts should be willing to consider the racial atmosphere, history of racial violence, and racial composition of the community should this issue be raised. If the prosecution is able to show that a significant segment of the community may approve of racial violence, then appellate courts should protect the prosecutor's right to conduct whatever *voir dire* is necessary to expose the prejudice and bias of potential jurors.

Another measure courts may take is to allow for a change of venue on the motion of the prosecution when it appears that public sentiment would not allow the state a fair trial. Approximately one quarter of the states currently provide for a change of venue in limited circumstances on the request of the prosecution, primarily when local bias is such that the prosecution cannot anticipate a fair trial.[95] In some cases, however, this provision could be used to deprive the defendant of a trial by the conscience of the community. Should this provision be available in an obscenity prosecu-

---

91. Rosales-Lopez v. United States, 451 U.S. 182, 191 (1981); *see also* Ham v. South Carolina, 409 U.S. 524 (1973).

92. *See* Ristaino v. Ross, 424 U.S. 589 (1976)(the mere fact that the victim was white and the defendant black is not sufficient to invoke a requirement that the trial court allow defense questioning into racial or ethnic prejudice); Dukes v. Waitkevitch, 536 F.2d 469 (1st. Cir. 1976)(where prejudice inheres in the identities of the parties and victims and not in the specific issues, denial of defendant's request to have various questions regarding racial prejudice posed to the prospective jurors does not violate defendant's constitutional rights).

93. An interlocutory appeal is one that is heard before a final verdict is rendered. Interlocutory appeals are disfavored, but are sometimes allowed when filed by the state, as the state has no right of appeal from a final verdict of not guilty.

94. United States v. Wilson, 420 U.S. 332 (1975).

95. Wayne R. LaFave & Jerold H. Isreal, Criminal Procedure § 16.1(g)(2d ed., 1992).

tion, to move a trial from a liberal jurisdiction to a strictly religious community?

In some cases, a person may move into a community specifically because he believes his illegal acts would be understood and tolerated by his neighbors. College towns are notoriously tolerant about the personal use of marijuana and homosexuality, for example. Should a gay AIDS patient using marijuana to counteract the side effects of AZT have to risk having venue changed from the relatively liberal community he has chosen to live in, to a neighboring community markedly intolerant of both homosexuality and marijuana? Although we want to ensure that unconstitutional factors such as race are not allowed to determine the outcome in criminal cases, we do not want to open the floodgates so wide that we allow unlimited 'forum shopping' by the state. With a sufficiently high burden on the prosecution to show a specific and articulable risk that the jury will be influenced by unconstitutional factors and not merely by public dissatisfaction with the application of the law to a particular case, courts should be able to separate marginal cases where a change of venue is merely used for advantage from those cases involving mob law or grossly prejudicial pretrial publicity.

A trial may have to be moved a considerable distance in order for change of venue to have sufficient effect. Generally speaking, the Sixth Amendment prohibits venue to be transferred out of the federal district in which the crime was committed.[96] However, a defendant's venue right is not absolute, and may be forced to accommodate a sufficient governmental interest in trying the case in another district.[97] In a case involving lynching or other occurrence of mass violence, the government could have a compelling interest in prosecuting the case a considerable distance from the district where the crime was committed. While the days of mass lynchings are over, such a case would certainly present a sufficiently compelling state interest.

One of the most important measures in reducing racist nullification is to ensure that the Fourteenth Amendment's promise of racially neutral jury selection, recognized by the Supreme Court in 1879, is kept.[98] Although this promise has never explicitly been made with jury nullification in mind, it is fairly obvious that a racially mixed jury is extremely unlikely to condone racial violence. Professor Jeffrey Abramson has shown that ensuring a diverse jury serves to empower arguments that persuade across group

---

96. United States v. Abbott Laboratories, 505 F.2d 565 (4th Cir. 1974), *cert. denied*, 420 U.S. 990 (1975).

97. United States v. Stratton, 649 F.2d 1066, 1077 (5th Cir. 1981).

98. Strauder v. West Virginia, 100 U.S. 303 (1879).

99. ABRAMSON, *supra* note 12, 139-141.

lines while weakening arguments persuasive only to a select group.[99] Racist arguments are unlikely to persuade a mixed-race jury, whether such arguments are based on a racially specific perspective on the facts or on a misguided appeal to a racist conscience. The need to ensure representative jury panels is no less urgent in cases involving potential nullification issues than it is in cases presenting a fact-based defense.

Today, the primary means of enforcing the promise of racially neutral jury selection is through the rule laid down by the Supreme Court in the 1989 case of *Batson v. Kentucky*,[100] discussed in the next section. *Batson* purportedly prohibited the state from using its peremptory challenges in a racially discriminatory way. While *Batson* has been broadly expanded,[101] the Court has also made it nearly unenforceable by allowing almost any conceivable justification for peremptory challenges, however arbitrary or irrational, while ignoring evidence that such challenges were exercised in a racially discriminatory manner.[102]

Fears that increased discretion in the hands of juries will make it impossible to control racist violence are clearly misplaced. Although it would be unrealistic to claim that no jury has ever acquitted a defendant charged with a racially motivated crime of violence, in the face of a compelling case by the prosecution and an impartial tribunal, such cases were apparently few and far between. It is also true that the numbers could have been lower still, had courts taken certain reasonable and prudent precautions in order to ensure that both the state and the defendant receive a fair trial. These measures were available in the past, and are still available today. Courts willing to employ them have never been faced with widespread jury nullification in cases of racial violence.

The Impartial Jury: Black Victims, Black Defendants, and Black Jurors

Justice Sandra Day O'Connor has noted, in a dissenting opinion, that "[i]t is by now clear that conscious and unconscious racism can affect the way white jurors perceive minority defendants and the facts presented at their trials, perhaps determining the verdict of guilt or innocence."[103] It is

---

100. 476 U.S. 79 (1989).

101. Powers v. Ohio, 499 U.S. 400 (1991); Edmonson v. Leesville Concrete Co., 500 U.S. 614 (1991); Georgia v. McCullom, 505 U.S. 42 (1992); J.E.B. v. Alabama, 511 U.S. 27 (1994).

102. *See* Hernandez v. New York, 500 U.S. 352, 360 (1991); Purkett v. Elem, 512 U.S. 265 (1995).

103. *McCullom, supra* note 101, 68.

no less clear that conscious and unconscious racism can affect the way black jurors, and black or white judges, police, and prosecutors, perceive minority and majority race defendants, witnesses and victims. Race, unfortunately, does matter in the American criminal justice system, and not just in the limited context to which Justice O'Connor has alluded. Before we can consider taking any action based on Justice O'Connor's seemingly offhand analysis, we have to put whatever racism that might motivate jurors into some contextual and analytical framework.

Initially, we should recognize that it is unfair to single out jurors for criticism. Although it is unrealistic to expect any broad social reality in our complex and often divided society to be completely free of racial disparities, it does not appear that juries are exceptionally racist or biased, compared to other participants in the criminal justice system. There are many reasons to believe juries are less biased. For example, the decisions of prosecutors [104] — and sometimes judges[105] — have been statistically shown to inject more racial disparity into death-penalty cases than the decisions of jurors. Criticizing the jury for being less than perfect is intellectually dishonest, at best, without also considering whether the available alternatives may be worse.

While the jury has been frequently and popularly criticized for treating black and white defendants unequally, social science studies have shown that the verdicts of juries show fewer racial disparities than the decisions of judges. In one often-cited study critical of jurors conducted by Professor Sheri Lynn Johnson, jury verdicts came much closer to treating black and white defendants equally than did the decisions of judges.[106] Although

---

104. ABRAMSON, *supra* note 12, 209:

Although the jury is implicated in the bias, it is nowhere near primarily responsible for the race-specific ways capital punishment works. Studies consistently show that prosecutorial discretion—including the initial charging decision, the offer of a plea bargain that will permit a defendant to avoid risk of a death penalty, and the decision to seek the death penalty after a conviction—are the major points at which racial disparities skew the death sentencing process. By comparison, the jury's effect on the death penalty's racial pattern is secondary.

105. Bernard Grofman, *The Ideal of the Impartial Jury: Something More than Barstool Justice, But How Much More?*, Symposium paper, Georgetown University Law Center Conference on the Role of the Jury in a Democratic Society, October 28, 1995 at 51 (on file with author)("Yet, in Florida, where trial judges can impose a death penalty in murder cases even when juries have opted for a life sentence, judges appear even more disproportionately prone to impose a death penalty when the victim is white than are juries.") *See also* Hans Zeisel, *Race Bias in the Administration of the Death Penalty: The Florida Experience*, 95 HARV. L.REV. 456 (1981).

106. Sheri Lynn Johnson, *Black Innocence and the White Jury*, 83 MICH. L.REV. 1611, 1620-1621 (1985).

Johnson does not reach this conclusion, she does note that "both black and white judges convicted black defendants more often than white defendants but the interracial disparity was greater for white judges than for black judges."[107] Four white judges had disparities over 40%; two of those had disparities over 70%. As a much greater number of cases are disposed of by bench trial than by jury trial, it would appear that jury verdicts either failed to exacerbate or perhaps actually lessened the overall disparity between conviction rates for black and white defendants, which was 3.9%.

Johnson also fails to address other issues which may have contributed to this disparity in conviction rates, such as the quality of representation available to the defendant and the use of pre-trial diversion programs. Gunnar Myrdal noted in 1944 that:

> The strength of the counsel a man can provide depends in general upon his wealth, and Negroes, as a poor group, suffer together with lower class whites...It is true that, in criminal cases, the court will appoint a lawyer for anybody who cannot afford to provide himself with proper legal aid. The court-appointed lawyer, however, in many cases, performs only perfunctory duties. Often the court will appoint some young lawyer without much experience...[108]

A 3.9% disparity is small enough that if a portion of that disparity is attributable to sources other than racial bias, it rapidly loses significance. Considering how important some of these factors may be, the truly surprising statistic may be that the disparity between white and black conviction rates remains under 4%.

Professor Nancy J. King has surveyed a number of articles written on race and juries. Widespread racist nullification is not among her findings.[109] Black and white jurors may process information differently, filtering that information through their own life experiences. Thus, King, not surprisingly, found that "the race of jurors can and does affect jury decisions."[110] Black jurors in the aggregate may be more likely to identify with the defendant than white jurors; and they may be less trusting of the police.[111] They may also be inclined to believe that black defendants are more likely than white defendants to suffer the consequences of police dishonesty.

---

107. *Id.* at 1621 (citations omitted).

108. MYRDAL, ET AL., *supra* note 22, 548.

109. King, *supra* note 3.

110. *Id.* at 99. *See also* Elissa Krauss and Martha Schulman, *The Myth of Black Juror Nullification: Racism Dressed Up In Jurisprudential Clothing*, 7 CORNELL J. L. & PUB.POL'Y 57 (1997).

111. King, *supra* note 3, 84, 88.

Professor Douglas L. Colbert found, relying on Professor Johnson's work, that "a substantial body of empirical evidence has developed which shows that all-white juries are not impartial when deciding cases involving interracial crimes."[112] Colbert does not define what he means by "impartial," and the data he uses does not address impartiality, but only disparities between acquittal rates for white and black defendants. Neither Colbert nor Johnson accounted for legitimate factors that may cause impartial juries to have racially skewed verdicts. For example, an all-white jury may not be able to understand black slang in a trial where black witnesses are using slang, or where a black defendant takes the witness stand. This can be a problem when the defense theory revolves around the credibility of the police or the testimony of minority witnesses. In one recent case a black defendant, Byron Carter, was on trial for possession of a gun. Two police officers testified that Carter had confessed possession of the weapon by saying "I'd rather be caught in this neighborhood by the police with a gun than caught otherwise without one." Carter testified that he had said "Everybody and their mama in this neighborhood got a gun," and he denied that the weapon was his. Black jurors believed that a young black male would not have chosen the words the police quoted, and after short discussion, convinced the other jurors (three hispanics, two whites and two Asian-Americans) to acquit.[113]

Without the presence of the black jury members, Byron Carter would likely have been convicted. This is not because the white, hispanic or Asian jurors were biased against him, it was simply that their cultural experiences would not have equipped them to recognize the latent implausibility of the police officer's testimony. A failure to comprehend cultural differences does not equal a lack of impartiality, even though the consequences for the defendant may be identical.

Several other non-racial factors may be contributing to a statistical aberration between white and black conviction rates before juries:

1. Whether the conviction rates of defendants with court appointed attorneys were higher than those with private attorneys, and whether black defendants were disproportionately represented by court-appointed attorneys. And even in those cases where black defendants did utilize retained counsel, we would need to know how the

---

112. Douglas L. Colbert, *Challenging the Challenge: Thirteenth Amendment as a Prohibition Against the Racial Use of Peremptory Challenges*, 76 CORNELL L. REV. 1, 110 (1990).

113. Benjamin A. Holden; Laurie P. Cohen; Eleena De Lisser, *Color Blinded? Race Seems to Play An Increasing Role In Many Jury Verdicts*, WALL ST. JRL., October 4, 1995 at A1.

qualifications of the counsel retained by black defendants compared with counsel retained by white defendants.

2. Whether the black defendants were as likely to be out on bail while awaiting trial as the white defendants. Defendants released on bail are more likely to be acquitted than defendants who remain in jail awaiting trial. First, they are more able to assist with their own defense than a defendant who remains in jail. Second, many defense attorneys have commented on the "prison pallor," an indefinable aura of guilt and suspicion surrounding inmates, which may serve to influence both the jury and the judge in trial proceedings.

3. *Whether prosecutorial treatment of black defendants was the same as prosecutorial treatment of white defendants.* Prosecutors may be more willing to allow white defendants into pre-trial diversion programs such as deferred adjudication or deferred prosecution, thus preventing a conviction on their records.

4. Whether judges were impartial in their rulings and evidentiary decisions. Judges may also react to the race of the defendant, giving his counsel less latitude in presenting his case, or otherwise biasing the proceedings towards the prosecution.

Because the discrepancies between white and black conviction rates are so small (3.9%, according to Johnson), any one of these factors could account for the real world observations Colbert and Johnson contend prove that white jurors are not impartial. However, as Byron Carter's case demonstrates, it is not necessary for white jurors to be partial for all-white juries to be problematic. There are many areas in which white and black jurors do tend, in the aggregate, to analyze evidence differently. For the defendant to be tried by a jury truly representative of the community, it would be unfair to arbitrarily exclude those perspectives ordinarily associated with either black or white jurors, regardless of the race of the defendant, victim or counsel in the case.

If black jurors tend to be more skeptical of the police and more sympathetic towards the defendant than white jurors, then white defendants would have as much of an interest as black defendants in having black jurors hear their case. In 1991, the Supreme Court applied the *Batson*[114] rule to a case involving a white defendant, where the prosecution had peremptorily challenged all of the black venire-members without being able to give a race-neutral explanation.[115] The fact that the prosecutor chose to strike blacks from the jury in the trial of a white defendant, in a case where race was not an issue, strongly suggests that the prosecutor recognized important racial disparities in the way jurors evaluate evi-

114. *Batson, supra* note 100.
115. *Powers, supra* note 101.

dence—specifically, that black jurors tend to be more friendly towards the defense than white jurors.

However, if black jurors are in fact more likely to acquit a criminal defendant than white jurors, then we may be prompted to ask if *Batson* was wrongly decided. Should the prosecution not have the right to strike black jurors for that reason alone: that they tend (in the aggregate) to be more defense-oriented? This analysis would deprive the defendant of trial by a jury representative of the community. Reasonable doubt is a subjective standard.[116] Excluding from the jury a segment of society with a particularly strict standard of reasonable doubt would be to try the defendant by a "hanging jury."

Perhaps, in the final analysis, Justice Thurgood Marshall was correct that ending the racially discriminatory use of peremptory challenges "can be accomplished only by eliminating peremptory challenges entirely."[117] Arguing that "[m]erely allowing defendants the opportunity to challenge the racially discriminatory use of peremptory challenges in individual cases will not end the illegitimate use of the peremptory challenge," Justice Marshall believed *Batson* "left [prosecutors] free to discriminate against blacks in jury selection provided that they hold that discrimination to an 'acceptable' level."[118]

Unfortunately, Justice Marshall's fears appear to have been justified. Practicing attorneys need show only minimal creativity in order to survive a *Batson* challenge. The Supreme Court ruled in 1995 that "[*Batson*] does not demand an explanation that is persuasive, or even plausible....Unless a discriminatory intent is inherent in the prosecutor's explanation, the reason offered will be deemed race neutral."[119] Instead of setting standards for trial courts to follow in enforcing *Batson*, the Court has decided that such standards are an unattainable goal. While the Court has broadly extended the original *Batson* ruling in order to apply it not only to the prosecution's use of racially-based challenges in cases with black criminal

---

116. For example, in Texas the standard jury instruction given for reasonable doubt is:
A "reasonable doubt" is a doubt based on reason and common sense after a careful and impartial consideration of all the evidence in the case. It is the kind of doubt that would make a reasonable person hesitate to act in the most important of his own affairs.
Geesa v. State, 820 S.W. 2d 154 (Tex. Crim. App. 1991).
117. *Batson, supra* note 100, 103.
118. *Id.* at 105.
119. *Purkett, supra* note 102, 271.
120. *J.E.B., supra* note 101.
121. *Powers, supra* note 101.
122. *Edmonson, supra* note 101.

defendants but also to gender-based challenges,[120] criminal cases with white defendants,[121] civil litigants[122] and peremptory challenges made by criminal defendants,[123] they have simultaneously taken away any substantial possibility for *Batson* to be enforced.

One reason why *Batson* has proven so difficult to enforce has been the misconception that *Batson* is intended to protect the rights of jurors, not the rights of defendants.[124] Without even addressing the issue of standing, this interpretation of *Batson* ignores the very real disadvantage criminal defendants of all races are under when a cognizable group is excluded from jury service precisely because they would hold the government to its burden of proof more rigorously than the majority. As Chaya Weinberg-Brodt has pointed out, "all 'jury rights' are, in actuality, instruments to protect the defendant's rights."[125] Those rights are not protected when a significant segment of the population is arbitrarily excluded from jury duty.

Appellate courts are understandably reluctant to reverse criminal convictions for reasons that impact solely on the rights of jurors; allowing a guilty defendant to invoke these rights as a surrogate for the excluded jurors is inherently offensive to most judges. Justice demands that guilty people be punished by a justly administered sentence, not merely litigated to death through an endless series of new trials, granted for reasons having nothing to do with the defendant's guilt or innocence. For courts to see *Batson* violations as undermining a resultant conviction requires that *Batson* challenges be understood in terms of a material injustice to the defendant, not merely some abstract unfairness to the excluded jurors. This perspective requires not doctrinaire color-blindness, but a recognition that, in the aggregate, racial differences do exist and do matter. The attorneys exercising their peremptory challenges in a racially selective manner have demonstrated their recognition of this basic social reality. It is time for our courts to do so as well.

Although the Supreme Court has recognized the importance of a representative venire panel, it has never guaranteed the seating of a racially

---

123. *McCullom, supra* note 101.

124. *See* Barbara D. Underwood, *Ending Race Discrimination in Jury Selection: Whose Right Is It Anyway?*, 92 COLUM. L. REV. 725 (1992).

125. Chaya Weinberg-Brodt, *Jury Nullification and Jury Control Procedures*, 65 N.Y.U. L. REV. 825, 827 (1990).

126. *See* Taylor v. Louisiana, 419 U.S. 522, 538 (1974)(Defendants are not entitled to a jury of any particular composition, but the jury wheels, pools of names, panels, or venires from which juries are drawn must not systematically exclude distinctive groups in the community and thereby fail to be reasonably representative thereof) (citations omitted). *See also* Virginia v. Rives, 100 U.S. 313 (1880).

mixed jury in any case;[126] nor are they likely to do so. Even if the Court were to guarantee a racially mixed jury, it is not clear that any such guarantee would extend to the prosecution as well as to the defense.[127] Although some scholars have argued that merely guaranteeing racially mixed venires is a hollow gesture,[128] the Court has not been willing to make the attributions with regards to jurors and race that would justify racial quotas in the jury box.

Whether we believe white jurors are partial, or that jurors with different experiences and cultures process information differently, it is clear who sits in the jury box matters. Although the Supreme Court has failed to enunciate a cogent analysis of why racial discrimination in jury selection should be an issue of constitutional dimensions, it is clear a majority of the Court has remained convinced that it is, although not always for any single reason.[129]

The Court's jury selection jurisprudence has been designed with fact-based defenses in mind. In confronting the independent discretionary powers of the jury, the issue of who sits in the jury box can be important as well. Perhaps more important, because conscientious values are directly involved, and those values are likely to be considered differently by different segments of the community. Professor Jeffrey Abramson has argued that diverse jury panels 'enrich' jury deliberations on questions of fact.[130] But this need for diversity and enrichment is even greater when the jury is making a decision on the basis of conscience. The conscience of the community must be the conscience of the entire community, and not merely any one segment thereof. While one individual juror will always have the power to hang,[131] deliberation significantly dampens the willingness of one — or even a small number — of stubborn jurors to hang for unconscientious reasons condemned by the rest of the panel.[132] The arguments that prevail in the jury room should be those capable of forging a broad consensus of agreement across group lines.

---

127. Contrast with *McCullom, supra* note 101, which was based on the Equal Protection Clause, and gave the prosecution the right to object to discriminatory defense use of peremptory challenges as a surrogate for the excluded juror. Arguments that juries must be racially mixed are more likely to be made on Sixth Amendment grounds, and to be premised in the rights of the defendant. There is no reason to apply such arguments to the prosecution.

128. *See* Johnson, *supra* note 105.

129. *See* Underwood, *supra* note 124.

130. ABRAMSON, *supra* note 12, 139-141.

131. Except in Oregon and Louisiana, which do not require unanimous verdicts. *See Apodaca v. Oregon*, 406 U.S. 404 (1972); *Johnson v. Louisiana*, 406 U.S. 356 (1972).

132. HARRY KALVEN & HANS ZEISEL, THE AMERICAN JURY, 462-463 (1966). *See also* ABRAMSON, *supra* note 12, 88-95.

Moreover, the entire community is entitled to an assurance that the jury is acting responsibly, especially when the jury decides to return a nullification verdict. The law is not respectable when filtered through the prejudices of an unconstitutionally selected, racist jury. For a given segment of society to be arbitrarily or malevolently excluded from jury duty on account of race allows those who are so inclined to nullify, without having to justify that decision to a fair cross section of the community, as participants within a representative jury. This exclusion leads to verdicts that are inherently untrustworthy.

Although jury nullification in cases of racial violence was never as widespread as conventionally believed, an effective *Batson*-type rule may be the strongest tool against racist nullification. The lynching and civil rights murder cases are not impressive arguments against providing jurors with more information concerning their power to reach an independent, conscientious verdict. Jurors in past race cases received no more instructions or arguments on the doctrine of nullification than jurors are likely to receive in any other case today. There is no evidence or logic to show that such instructions or arguments would have increased whatever racist nullification did occur. The best defense against racist nullification is to have a fair jury, representative of a broad cross-section of the community, both willing and empowered to honestly and conscientiously evaluate the facts, the law and the equities of the case they are to decide.

Inside the Jury Room: Can Jurors Act Responsibly When Race Is an Issue?

Any first-year law student has probably gotten used to hearing the jury condescendingly criticized by his or her professors. "Do you think the jury pays attention to instructions to disregard?" "Do you really believe the average juror could possibly understand DNA evidence?" "Could a jury of laymen conceivably comprehend this contract?"[133] Neither professors nor practicing lawyers find it necessary to substantiate these attitudes towards jurors; the larval lawyer quickly learns that it sounds witty and superior to set himself above the jury. These arrogant pretensions do not long survive close examination.

Despite that fact, the internal culture of the legal profession seems to accept this sort of posturing without question, as though the incompetence of jurors is somehow a self-evident fact. We can draw some hypotheses about why these attitudes developed and what purposes they serve. It

---

133. All of these examples are culled from the author's personal experience as a law student.

is a truism that every legal case has a winner, and a loser. Human nature being what it is, the losing attorney rarely wishes to admit that he lost because he failed to prove his case. Other reasons for the loss must be found, and a few recurring possibilities present themselves:

1. The judge was biased, made incorrect rulings on evidence, or otherwise corrupted the case. Few lawyers who expect to practice before the same judge will want to make these accusations publicly, except in the context of an appeal or election.[134] Losing prosecutors do not have an opportunity to make such complaints in an appeal, because once an acquittal is rendered it is final. Also, prosecutors routinely appear in front of the same judge, so good relations with the bench are essential.

2. *The other attorney "cheated," making objectionable arguments, introducing inadmissible evidence merely in order to get the jury to hear it (even if they were instructed to disregard), etc.*[135] These arguments also blame the jury (the focus of the complaint is that jurors could not disregard information according to instructions) and the judge (who failed to control the opposing lawyer, or respond adequately to objections).

   Aggressively faulting the other attorney may be a poor career move, destroying the sense of comity between "learned members of the bar." Prosecutors and defense attorneys are repeat players in the criminal justice arena. Defense attorneys who make strong criticisms of prosecutors are likely to be faced with resistance on discovery requests, plea bargains, and other motions. Prosecutors who fault defense attorneys for tactical decisions may find themselves resisted or mistrusted in plea bargaining, with a resultant increase in the percentage of their caseload proceeding to costly, time consuming jury trials. Even more importantly, they may find well-financed campaigns opposing their future political ambitions.

3. *The jury was too stupid or ignorant to understand the evidence.* Hence, we are hearing renewed calls for special juries, juries of

---

134. During an appeal or election, the attorney is not merely trying to shift the blame for his loss.

135. *See* Mark Curriden, *Blowing Smoke: Lawyers are trained to push a jury's buttons almost any way they can*, A.B.A. JRL., October, 1995 at 4.

136. *See*, e.g., John D. Gorby, J.D., *Viewing the "Draft Guidelines for State Court Decision Making In Authorizing or Withdrawing Life Sustaining Medical Treatment" From The Perspective of Related Areas of Law And Economics: A Critique*, 7 ISSUES L. & MED. 477, 506 (1992)("A most common example would be the medical malpractice and personal injury suits being tried every day throughout the land. Perhaps decision-making could be improved by using 'blue ribbon' juries of experts in cases such as this"); Rita Sut-

experts, and juries composed of legal professionals, especially in complex cases.[136] Those least likely to make these complaints appear to be judges.[137] One counter-argument is that it is the job of lawyers to communicate the evidence to the jury; it is much easier for the lawyer to blame the jury for their lack of ability to understand, rather than to fault himself for his lack of skill as a communicator. Another is that there is no *a priori* reason to assume that judges have any greater competence to understand complex medical or financial evidence than juries.

4. The jury was biased, ideological or emotional, and disregarded the law. Thus, the losing attorney is entirely blameless, because there was nothing he could have done to win the case. For example, Los Angeles District Attorney Gilbert Garcetti, in his press conference immediately following O.J. Simpson's acquittal on murder charges, told the press that "It was clear this was an emotional trial. Apparently (the jury's) verdict was based on emotion that overcame their reason. This was not, in our opinion, a close case."[138]

Juries are uniquely available for scapegoating, because they are uniquely unavailable to speak up in support of their own verdict. Jurors scatter after a trial is over. It is a rare case where jurors can publicly defend themselves from attack.[139] While some jurors may be given an opportunity to

---

ton, *Note, A More Rational Approach to Complex Civil Litigation in the Federal Courts: The Special Jury*, 1990 U. CHI. LEGAL F. 575 (special juries, chosen for their particular knowledge or experience, could reduce problems of jury competence in complex cases). *See also* Peter Meijes Tiersma, *Reforming the Language of Jury Instructions*, 22 HOFSTRA L. REV. 37, 78 n. 37 (1993)(providing a string citation listing several articles criticizing the use of juries in complex civil cases).

137. Eighth Circuit Judge Morris Arnold publicly stated during his remarks at the Georgetown University Law Center Conference on the Role of the Jury in a Democratic Society, October 28, 1995, that in his several years on the bench, he never ran into a case so complex a normal jury was unable to understand it; he added that he did occasionally run into lawyers who were not capable of explaining the complexities of their case to the jury. *See also* Morris S. Arnold, *A Historical Inquiry into the Right to Trial by Jury in Complex Civil Litigation*, 128 U. PA. L. REV. 829 (1980).

138. Quoted in *In Wake of Simpson Trial, Garcetti Talks About Judicial Reform*, SEATTLE POST- INTELLIGENCER, November 8, 1995 at A13.

139. *See* Benedict D. LaRosa, *The Branch Davidian Trial Jury: An Interview with Sarah Bain, Forewoman*, 16 THE FIJActivist 14, 15, 18, 21 (Summer 1994); Tony Knight, *Debating Simpson Verdict: Opinion Split on Whether Acquittal Was Really Condemnation of System*, L.A. DAILY NEWS, October 16, 1995 at N1 (quoting several of the jurors explaining the reasons for their verdict); Leonard Greene, *Jury's paying the price for abiding by the rules*, BOSTON HERALD, October 5, 1995 at 6 (quoting Simpson jurors Lionel Cryer and Brenda Moran).

speak out about their verdicts in rare, sensational trials, in most cases jurors will have no access to the media after the verdict has been returned. There is simply no mechanism to give jurors the same sophisticated press relations that prosecutors or defense lawyers have; nor do jurors normally have much incentive to be heard after the close of the trial. We are usually safe in thoughtlessly criticizing the jury: due to laws guaranteeing the sanctity of jury deliberations, nobody can prove us wrong; due to the ephemeral nature of the jury itself, nobody is likely to speak up in defense of the jury's integrity after the trial is over.

Usually, we do not know what goes on in the jury room. Much of what we do know is due to statements of jurors, examinations of trial records, history, and in the end, informed speculation. It would be unrealistic to claim that no jury has ever nullified the law in any case; yet there are very few individual cases where we can be absolutely sure the jury did nullify. Statements by jurors that they nullified are hearsay, and not exceptionally reliable (a juror may not want to admit that he did not think police were telling the truth, or may think claiming to have nullified will make him seem heroic). We make our best efforts to understand what juries do, and hope that in general our answers will be roughly reliable, understanding that in any individual case we may be wrong.

We cannot evaluate the job juries have done without taking into account those participants, whose actions we usually exempt from careful scrutiny. Juries do not have an opportunity to nullify where the prosecution has failed to prove its case beyond the requisite reasonable doubt. At the very least, we cannot be sure the prosecution has proven its case without examining the trial transcripts and the jury instructions. The best we can usually do is to examine those factors which may give us reasons to trust or to suspect the sincerity of the prosecution and investigation, or the impartiality of the bench, in any particular case.

With the difficulties associated in the investigation of nullification, it is surprising that a myriad of sources have reported widespread racist nullification, both currently and in the recent past.[140] We should not be surprised, however, considering that the jury is an "easy mark" for those inclined to search for a scapegoat. We should look at these reports of widespread racist jury nullification with a great degree of skepticism, if only

---

140. Current reports are primarily about black jurors supposedly acquitting black defendants for purely racial reasons. *See* Randall Kennedy, *The State, Criminal Law and Racial Discrimination: A Comment*, 107 HARV. L. REV. 1255, 1278 (1994); Paul Butler, *O.J. Reckoning: Rage for a New Justice*, WASH. POST, October 8, 1995 at C10; Holden; Cohen & De Lisser, *supra* note 113; Joseph Perkins, *Platinum Justice Knows No Race*; ATLANTA J. & CONST., October 11, 1995 at A13; John Leo,...*A Troubling Rise in Racial "Nullification,"* NEWS & OBSERVER (Raleigh, NC), October 12, 1995 at A21.

because of their anecdotal nature and failure to adequately take other explanations for statistical disparities into account. We do not really know what juries do, and we are ambivalent over what we think juries should do.[141] But when they disagree with what we think is the "right" verdict, we are certain that whatever the jury has done, is wrong. That certainty may be a more emotional "verdict" than any a jury has ever rendered.

Violently racist communities cannot help but seat violently racist jurors. It would be unrealistic to expect otherwise. That, however, is only part of the story. Violently racist communities cannot help but elect violently racist legislators, sheriffs, judges, and prosecutors. There is no reason to expect the jury to be any worse than the other actors in the system.

There are some reasons, however, to believe juries may be better. Because they are not filtered through the electoral process, juries drawn from the community at large should at the very least include some members representing minority groups and viewpoints, those members of the community who do not approve of racist violence. The presence on the jury of those more tolerant community members may exert a moral influence serving to constrain the majority, leading to more responsible jury deliberations.

Studies indicate that many people find jury duty to be an experience that heightens their sense of personal and civic responsibility.[142] Given a diverse jury, that sense of responsibility can make it difficult to support a racist verdict through deliberations (and may also engender mutual respect among jurors of different backgrounds). The fact that jurors must deliberate to reach a verdict, at least when all jurors do not find themselves in unanimous agreement on an initial ballot, means that jurors must justify the reasoning behind their verdict to the other members of the panel. This sort of group scrutiny may make it difficult to support a racist verdict, restraining jurors from giving vent to their racism in a manner that has no parallel in the prosecutor's office or in the judges' chambers. At worst, the most stubbornly racist jurors will succeed only in hanging the jury; it is unlikely that such hung juries would ever be so common that retrial would be pointless.[143] The track record of federal prosecutions for violations of civil rights shows that a committed prosecution, with an impartial judge, can reliably obtain criminal convictions even out of fairly selected all-white juries operating in a racist environment.

And those same federal prosecutions show that the institution of the jury, while perhaps not entirely blameless, has largely been the victim of

---

141. *See* Grofman, *supra* note 105.

142. *See* KALVEN & ZEISEL, *supra* note 132, 498; *see also* Hon. Jack B. Weinstein, *Considering Jury "Nullification": When May and Should a Jury Reject the Law To Do Justice?*, 30 AM. CRIM. L.REV. 239, 241 (1993).

143. KALVEN & ZEISEL, *supra* note 132, 453-462

scapegoating. Whatever part the racist actions on the part of judges, police or prosecutors may have played in determining it, it is the jury which brings in the final verdict; therefore it is the jury which takes the public blame and condemnation for unpopular trial outcomes. But we cannot honestly blame the jury without knowing what evidence they heard, and why they delivered the verdict they did. Where the crime has not been proven at trial, even subsequent confessions by the accused do not establish that the original trial jury nullified, or even that they came to the wrong decision, *in light of the evidence presented at trial.* Juries do not judge guilt in the abstract; only guilt as proven by the prosecution in a court of law. In many cases where juries have been accused of delivering the "wrong" verdict, they may well have been delivering the only verdict consistent with the facts as proven at trial, and the only verdict consistent with the doctrine of jury nullification or the Constitution, both of which forbid convictions by jury based on anything other than the evidence.[144]

The idea that the jury delivered the "wrong" verdict implies that we have some way of knowing what the "right" verdict would have been. If we could have that knowledge, why bother with a jury—or for that matter a trial—at all? But we do insist on a trial, because we recognize that our "knowledge" of what the correct verdict is may be seriously mistaken. We should remember to be this humble when the verdict which a jury returns surprises or angers us.

Jury independence is a tool which, like any other, can be misused. That conventional wisdom has exaggerated the extent of misuse does not negate the fact that there has been misuse, and that this misuse has resulted in serious injustices. Instead of disparaging the tool of jury independence, however, we should be working to reduce the likelihood of misuse through stronger *Batson*-type rules, better and more honest guidance concerning the jury's powers, and more incisive *voir dire*. The remedy for the misuse of the nullification power of the jury, which exists at the core of trial by jury as an institution, is not to keep jurors ignorant of the existence of their powers but rather to seek to enlighten jurors so that they will be better equipped to exercise their powers with good judgment and sound reasoning. We should respect our juries for the difficult work they do, and trust them to exercise their powers, duties and discretion as responsibly, conscientiously and honorably, as they have done with remarkably few exceptions for the past 800 years.

---

144. *See* Scheflin, *Jury Nullification, supra* note 8.

Chapter Eight

The Capital Jury

*There is no crueler form of tyranny than
that which is perpetuated under the
shield of law and in the name of justice.*
Baron de Montesquieu

Early Juror Discretion in Capital Cases

Criminal trial juries have been refusing to sentence people to death since the birth of the jury as an institution. Medieval juries frequently acquitted obviously guilty defendants who would have been executed if convicted, especially when there were mitigating circumstances involved. Because the "Bloody Codes" of England punished over 200 distinct offenses with death, British juries often displayed mercy, sparing the lives of those who would otherwise have had to pay the ultimate penalty for often minor crimes such as theft of money or goods worth forty shillings or more, burglary, minor felonies and victimless offenses such as buggery or witchcraft.

Even English judges occasionally hesitated to invoke the full wrath of the Bloody Codes, and sometimes actively encouraged the jury to set them aside. Sir William Blackstone referred to jury nullification in death penalty cases as "pious perjury," explaining that "this... does not at all excuse our common law... from the imputation of severity, but rather strongly confesses the charge."[1] At times British judges were so opposed to the harshness of the sanguinary laws that they encouraged juries to ameliorate their verdict in minor crimes punishable by death:

> "Trying a prisoner at the Old Bailey on a charge of stealing in a dwelling house to the value of forty shillings, when this was a capital offense," Lord Mansfield advised the jury to find a gold trinket, the subject of the indictment, to be of less value. The prosecutor exclaimed, with indignation, "Under forty shillings, my Lord! Why, the *fashion*, alone, cost me more than double the sum." Lord Mansfield calmly observed, "God for-

---

1. Sir William Blackstone, IV Commentaries on the Laws of England, 239 (1769).

bid, gentleman, we should hang a man for *fashion's* sake!" This is a highly significant episode for Lord Mansfield was not a lenient judge.[2]

The Bloody Codes of England survived until the mid-nineteenth century, by which time growing public opposition had effectively limited imposition of the death penalty to those convicted of the most violent crimes. Various segments of society—particularly some of those whom the Bloody Codes were intended to protect—had complained at various times that the sanguinary laws offered no protection at all, because juries consistently refused to convict those who had violated them.[3] A Petition of the Corporation of London, delivered to Parliament in 1819, for example, complained that unless the Bloody Codes were repealed

> the increase of crimes must be progressive, because, strong as are the obligations upon all good subjects to assist the administration of justice, they are overpowered by tenderness for life—a tenderness which, originating in the mild precepts of our religion, is advancing, and will continue to advance, as these doctrines become more deeply inculcated into the minds of the community.[4]

Although it is usually difficult to be certain in which cases juries have nullified laws outright, this petition referred to two clearly unambiguous cases. In one, a jury found a £10 note to be worth only 39 shillings; in another, the jury "found two bills of exchange, value of £10 each, and eight Bank notes, value of £10 each, worth the same sum of 39s."[5] There is simply no explanation for these verdicts other than that the jurors mercifully decided to spare the defendants' lives.

Following similar incentives, in 1830 bankers from over 200 towns and cities submitted a petition to the House of Commons complaining that applying the death penalty to the crime of forgery was effectively preventing the conviction and punishment of forgers. They believed, through their experience, that "the infliction of death, or even the possibility of the infliction of death, prevents the prosecution, conviction and punishment of the criminal and thus endangers the property which it is intended to protect."[6] The bankers did not criticize the actions of the jurors, but believed the law needed to be reformed so as to come into accord with the morality of the times. An excessively cruel law, being unenforceable, failed to prevent or to discourage crime.

---

2. Lord Campbell, The Lives of the Chief Justices of England, Vol. III, 477-478 (1873).

3. Leon Radzinowicz, A History of English Criminal Law and its Administration from 1750, 727-732 (1948).

4. *Id.* at 729.

5. *Id.*

6. *Id.* at 730.

Approximately one in four death-eligible felonies tried in England and Wales between 1805-1810 ended in acquittals.[7] How many of those cases were the result of jury independence, and how many were the result of reasonable doubts on the part of jurors, it is impossible to know. Tellingly, however, one eighteenth-century source reported that

> The acquittals will generally be found to attach mostly to small offences which are punishable with death: where Juries do not consider the crime deserving so severe a punishment, the delinquent receives no punishment at all. If all were convicted who were really guilty of these small offences, the number of victims to the severity of the Law would be greatly increased."[8]

In a large number of cases where the defendant was convicted, the jury apparently found the defendant guilty only of a lesser-included offense, in order to avoid the death penalty. It is quite likely that the same jurors who would without hesitation have sentenced a cold-blooded killer to death would have acquitted a thief of capital charges, either through acquittal or by purposefully understating the value of the goods involved. Because amelioration often occurred in theft cases by undervaluing the property stolen, and because the majority of capital offenses during the eighteenth century were crimes against property,[9] the twenty-five percent acquittal rate no doubt greatly understates jury resistance to the Bloody Codes.

Remnants of these brutal measures carried over to Colonial America, even as they were beginning to be eliminated in England. American laws during the Colonial and Revolutionary periods often prescribed death as the penalty for those same offenses where English juries had regularly shown mercy, and American juries predictably exhibited a similar reluctance to send minor criminals to their deaths. In the 1815 case of *South Carolina v. Bennett*,[10] for example, a jury found that Bennett had stolen goods "worth less...than twelve pence," although all the testimony indicated that the goods were much more valuable. Bennett's jury acquitted him of the capital offense of grand larceny; he was convicted only of the lesser offense of petty larceny. The jury's "pious perjury" prevented Bennett's hanging. On the state's appeal, the South Carolina Court of Appeals affirmed the right of the jury to ameliorate the rigor of the law through

---

7. *Id.* at 93.

8. PATRICK COLQUHOUN, A TREATISE ON THE POLICE OF THE METROPOLIS 23-24 (4th ed., 1797), cited in *Id.* at 94.

9. RADZINOWICZ, *supra* note 3, 96. The same was true during the fourteenth century; *see* THOMAS ANDREW GREENE, VERDICT ACCORDING TO CONSCIENCE: PERSPECTIVES ON THE ENGLISH CRIMINAL TRIAL JURY 1200-1800, 59-60 (1985).

10. 3 S.Car. 514 (1815).

their verdict.[11] Jury refusal to sentence defendants to death was great enough that in 1820, Supreme Court Justice Joseph Story, riding circuit in federal district court in Massachusetts, began to utilize the now-routine practice of "death-qualifying" juries, when he disqualified two Rhode Island Quakers from sitting as jurors in a capital case. Story was concerned that their religious beliefs would result in a conscientious refusal to convict in a case where the only possible punishment was death.[12]

Because the reluctance of jurors to convict under mandatory death sentencing schemes was leading to the acquittal of a significant number of factually guilty defendants, many state legislatures created varying degrees of homicide offenses, with only first degree homicide classified as a capital crime. Pennsylvania was the first state to divide homicide into several offenses of varying degrees. In 1794, Pennsylvania designated murder in the first degree as any murder "perpetrated by means of poison, or by lying in wait, or by any other kind of willful, deliberate or premeditated killing, or which shall be committed in the perpetration, or attempt to perpetrate, any arson, rape, robbery or burglary."[13] Many states followed the example of Pennsylvania in this regard. Further, several states, although unwilling to abolish the death penalty, restricted its scope. South Carolina, which punished 165 assorted crimes with death in 1813, had only twenty-two capital crimes on its books in 1850.[14] Michigan, in 1845, became the first state to totally abolish capital punishment.[15]

Creating degrees of murder, however, merely presented lawmakers with a new problem. Juries were convicting first-degree murderers of lesser included homicide offenses, so that their lives could be spared. When it became clear that many juries were delivering ameliorated verdicts solely in order to avoid imposing the death penalty, several states began giving jurors discretion to choose between imposing the death penalty or life imprisonment in first-degree murder cases. This removed the necessity for jurors to nullify the law in order to spare the life of the accused. Tennessee, in 1837, became the first state to allow jurors unfettered sentencing discretion in capital cases; other states gradually followed suit. The exercise of this absolute discretion became integral to the role of the jury in capital cases. In 1899, the United States Supreme Court found that a jury

---

11. *Id.; see also* LAWRENCE FRIEDMAN, A HISTORY OF AMERICAN LAW, 285 (1985).

12. United States v. Cornell, 25 F.Cas. 650, 655-656 (C.C.D. R.I. 1820); *see also* United States v. Wilson et al., 28 F.Cas. 699 (1830); Logan v. United States, 144 U.S. 263, 298 (1892).

13. FRIEDMAN, *supra* note 11, 281, quoting Edwin R Keedy, *History of the Pennsylvania Statute Creating Degrees of Murder*, 97 U. PA. L. REV. 759 (1949).

14. FRIEDMAN, *supra* note 11, 283.

15. *Id.* at 282.

instruction to the effect that mitigating circumstances must be found to justify sparing the defendant's life was reversible error, because it improperly impinged on the role of the jury.[16] The federal government finally allowed jurors discretion to choose between a life sentence or the death penalty in capital cases beginning in 1897[17] — two years after the Supreme Court in *Sparf et al.* denied the right of a defendant to have the jury informed of its power to deliver a merciful verdict, sparing the life of the accused.

Giving jurors unbridled sentencing discretion, however, left at least one major difficulty remaining in capital punishment law: there were some jurors (such as Justice Story's stubborn Quakers) who would refuse to vote to execute a man under any conceivable circumstances. These jurors were sufficiently numerous as to make any provision for capital punishment which depended on jury unanimity (or even broad consensus) unworkable, unless the courts first removed all potential jurors who had substantial qualms about imposing the death penalty. Courts accordingly began to refine and regulate the process of "death-qualifying" juries through *voir dire*, in order to exclude citizens who have strong moral objections to capital punishment from sitting as jurors in capital cases. How strong a moral objection is required for a juror to be excludable, and what effect death-qualifying a jury has on jury determinations of guilt, innocence and culpability, remain debatable questions today.

Ironically, these reforms — intended to clarify the jury's discretion to act mercifully — were themselves in time objected to on the grounds that juries were imposing the death penalty so arbitrarily and capriciously as to deprive defendants of due process of law, and that to impose the death penalty under such circumstances constituted cruel and unusual punishment prohibited under the Eighth Amendment to the United States Constitution. Further, the death penalty itself was so seldom being invoked by juries as to call into question whether capital punishment still had the support of public opinion. In their role as the conscience of the community, jurors had, if not unanimously, at least overwhelmingly rejected death as an appropriate punishment for crime.

It was argued that the death penalty sentencing decision had become entirely subjective, and that there were no requirements for this profoundly weighty decision to be made on any rational or intelligible basis whatsoever. Without some cognizable and articulable procedures in place to ensure that only the worst of the worst could be subjected to the death penalty, capital defendants asserted they had been denied the right to be sentenced according to fair and ascertainable standards. Moreover, there

---

16. Winston v. United States, 172 U.S. 456, 460 (1899).
17. *See* McGautha v. California, 402 U.S. 183, 200 (1971).

seemed to be no rational way to distinguish those few cases in which capital punishment was imposed from the greater number in which it was not. Because jurors more often than not rejected capital punishment in favor of a life sentence, and because there were no meaningful standards to separate those condemned to die from those allowed to live, the condemned argued that their sentences represented the unequal and arbitrary application of the law.

A dichotomy was presented, posing a difficult balancing act. On the one hand, there is a need to have jurors make an individualized determination of whether capital punishment or imprisonment is the appropriate sentence in a given case, in order to prevent jury nullification on the question of guilt or innocence. On the other, there is a need to give juries some standards and guidance to employ in choosing either life or death in an individual case, in order to provide due process and equal protection of the law, and to avoid charges that the punishment imposed is "cruel and unusual" under the Eighth Amendment. This tension between the requirement of "individualized sentencing" and the requirement to "narrow and channel" the discretion of the jury remains the central paradox in capital punishment jurisprudence.

The powers of the independent jury affect every aspect of our capital punishment laws. Every capital punishment system operating in the United States today is premised on "narrowing" and "channeling" the discretion of the jury, in order to remedy the "arbitrariness" and "freakishness" with which capital sentences were meted out prior to 1972, when the Supreme Court handed down the landmark decision in *Furman v. Georgia*,[18] discussed below. But the Supreme Court has never held that the discretion of *juries* was the factor responsible for the unequal application of the death penalty. More recent studies have shown that while juries may exhibit some bias or arbitrariness in the choice to impose the death penalty, prosecutors bear the brunt of the responsibility.[19] As in cases involving racial violence, the jury has been blamed for problems inherent in a legal system which includes capital punishment, blamed for problems juries did not cause and which jury reforms cannot cure. And because the cause of these problems has been misidentified, those solutions which courts and legislatures have implemented to remedy the problem have not been successful.

It is also important to examine the practice of jury selection or *voir dire* in capital cases, and of the ability of prosecutors to require "death-qual-

18. 408 U.S. 238 (1972).
19. DAVID C. BALDUS, GEORGE WOODWORTH, CHARLES A. PULASKI, JR., EQUAL JUSTICE AND THE DEATH PENALTY: A LEGAL AND EMPIRICAL ANALYSIS, 327 (1990).

ified" juries, consisting of jurors who have stated under oath that if the evidence indicates it is justified, they would be willing to impose a punishment of death. It is still an open question whether a death-qualified jury can be fair and impartial on questions of guilt or innocence, or whether death-qualified juries are inherently biased towards conviction.[20]

Many courts and commentators have noted that by death-qualifying a jury, we may also be depriving the defendant of his Sixth Amendment right to be tried by a jury selected from a fair cross-section of the community. Women and minorities are excluded during the death qualification process at a much higher rate than are white males;[21] liberals at a much higher rate than conservatives.[22] Yet if we do not death-qualify juries it may be impossible for the prosecution ever to obtain a death sentence; moreover, the end of death-qualification could quite possibly lead to the abolition of capital punishment in America.

An additional insight into the role of the jury in capital cases has been raised by the United States Supreme Court itself, which, as a practical matter, has protected the power of jurors to nullify by mandating sentencing discretion in capital cases.[23] In *Penry v. Lynaugh*,[24] the Court held that the Texas capital punishment system was unconstitutional as it applied to Penry because it did not allow the jurors to properly consider and act upon mitigating evidence of the defendant's mental retardation. The Texas Court of Criminal Appeals[25] has specifically invoked the jury's power to nullify in order to remedy the constitutional deficiencies of the Texas capital sentencing system. How this reflects upon the jury's right to nullify in other cases is a question which neither the Texas Court nor any other has attempted to answer.

---

20. Although this question was not answered by the Supreme Court in Lockhart v. McCree, 476 U.S. 162 (1986), the Court did hold that the interest of the state in enforcing its death penalty overrode the interest of the defendant in an impartial jury.

21. Michael Finch and Mark Ferraro, *The Empirical Challenge to Death Qualified Juries: On Further Examination*, 65 NEB. L.REV. 21, 44-50 (1986); *see also* Robert Fitzgerald and Phoebe C. Ellsworth, *Due Process v. Crime Control: Death Qualification and Jury Attitudes*, 8 LAW AND HUM. BEHAV. 31, 46-47 (1984).

22. *See* Fitzgerald and Ellsworth, *Due Process v. Crime Control, supra* note 21, 46-47.

23. Woodson v. North Carolina, 428 U.S. 280 (1976); Roberts v. Louisiana, 428 U.S. 325 (1976); Lockett v. Ohio, 438 U.S. 586 (1978); Eddings v. Oklahoma, 455 U.S. 104 (1982).

24. 492 U.S. 302 (1989).

25. The Court of Criminal Appeals is the court of last resort for Texas criminal cases. Texas has a bifurcated system of highest courts, with the Court of Criminal Appeals having exclusively criminal jurisdiction, and the Texas Supreme Court having exclusively civil jurisdiction.

Furman and its Progeny: Resolving the Disparities in Capital Sentencing

The constitutionality of capital punishment systems which leave death sentencing decisions at the discretion of juries was examined by the Supreme Court in the 1971 case of *McGautha v. California*.[26] In *McGautha*, the defendants argued that "to leave the jury completely at large to impose or withhold the death penalty as it sees fit is fundamentally lawless and therefore violates the basic command of the Fourteenth Amendment that no State shall deprive a person of his life without due process of law."[27] The defendants in *McGautha* were not claiming that capital punishment was unconstitutional *per se*, but only that they had been deprived of due process of law because the juries which had sentenced them to die had been given unbridled discretion, and that without proper guidance the jury sentencing decisions which condemned them to death were "fundamentally lawless."

The Supreme Court rejected these arguments, noting that "in recent years, challenges to standardless jury sentencing have been presented to many state and federal appellate courts. No court has held the challenge good..."[28] The Court expressed its belief that juries were capable of rationally making the sensitive and necessarily subjective judgments involved in capital sentencing decisions. The Court quoted with approval its own language from *Witherspoon v. Illinois* that:

> One of the most important functions any jury can perform in making [a capital sentencing decision] is to maintain a link between contemporary community values and the penal system—a link without which the determination of punishment could hardly reflect "the evolving standards of decency that mark the progress of a maturing society."[29]

Thus, the Court refused to find jury discretion either so standardless or so subject to abuse as to deny a capital defendant due process of law. On the contrary, the Court expressed a profound confidence in the abilities of jurors, stating that "[t]he States are entitled to assume that jurors confronted with this truly awesome responsibility of decreeing death for a fellow human will act with due regard for the consequences of their deci-

---

26. *Supra* note 17.
27. *Id.* at 196.
28. *Id.* at 203.
29. Witherspoon v. Illinois, 391 U.S. 510, 519 (1968)(quoting Trop v. Dulles, 356 U.S. 86, 101 (1958)).

sion..."[30] Jurors, in the Court's opinion, were both competent and responsible enough to be entrusted with the "awesome responsibility" of making capital sentencing decisions. The *McGautha* Court decided that giving juries unlimited discretion in capital sentencing did not violate due process, but it was not asked in that case to consider whether other constitutional guarantees may have been violated.

Only four years later, the Supreme Court was to consider whether standardless jury sentencing in death penalty cases violated the cruel and unusual punishment clause of the Eighth Amendment—a question that was never raised in *McGautha*. Less than a month after the decision in *McGautha*, the Court granted certiorari to three capital defendants, in order to determine whether the death penalty was invoked so infrequently or arbitrarily as to become cruel and unusual in those rare cases in which a defendant was sentenced to die. The cases were grouped together under the name of *Furman v. Georgia*.[31]

The Court's decision in *Furman v. Georgia* created a tumult. The *Furman* Court held that capital punishment, as it then existed, was so arbitrarily and freakishly enforced as to be unconstitutionally cruel and unusual under the Eighth Amendment. The *Furman* decision struck down every single capital punishment scheme then in operation across America and entirely suspended execution of the death penalty. The sentences of all persons on American death rows were commuted to life imprisonment, which in turn made many of these formerly condemned prisoners eligible for parole. Following *Furman*, there was a four-year moratorium on capital punishment, as many states scrambled to draft and enact revised capital punishment schemes which would comply with the constitutional requirements the *Furman* Court had loosely identified.

That job was made more difficult, because there was no clear majority opinion or holding in *Furman*. *Furman* represents not just a split, but a splintered opinion of the Court. All nine Justices wrote separate opinions to the 5-4 decision, which commentators have grouped into three categories. Two Justices (William J. Brennan and Thurgood Marshall) concluded that the death penalty was cruel and unusual *per se*, and could never be constitutional under any circumstances. Three Justices (Byron R. White, Potter Stewart and William O. Douglas) agreed that then-current capital punishment schemes were unconstitutional, but were unwilling to commit as to whether future schemes could be developed which would comply with constitutional requirements. The dissenting members of the Court (Justices Harry A. Blackmun, Lewis J. Powell, Warren E. Burger

---

30. *McGautha, supra* note 17, 207-208.
31. *Furman, supra* note 18.

and William H. Rehnquist) believed that the death sentences at issue in *Furman* had been constitutionally rendered, and voted to uphold the death penalties pending against these defendants.

Although five of the Justices on the *Furman* Court agreed that capital punishment as it existed in 1972 was imposed in an unconstitutionally arbitrary fashion, they did not lay the blame for that arbitrariness clearly on the jury. Justice White, for example, made it clear that he did not believe the scarcity of capital sentences was the result of juries acting irrationally. On the contrary, White believed that jury reluctance to impose capital punishment was a consequence of waning public support for the death penalty itself. While he agreed that "there is no meaningful basis for distinguishing the few cases in which [capital punishment] is imposed from the many cases in which it is not,"[32] he emphasized that:

> the policy of vesting sentencing authority primarily in juries—a decision largely motivated by the desire to mitigate the harshness of the law and to bring community judgment to bear on the sentence as well as guilt or innocence—has so effectively achieved its aims that capital punishment within the confines of the statutes now before us has for all practical purposes run its course."[33]

Justice Brennan merely remarked that "[w]hen the punishment of death is inflicted in a trivial number of cases in which it is legally available, the conclusion is virtually inescapable that it is being inflicted arbitrarily. Indeed, it smacks of little more than a lottery system."[34] Still, Brennan did not find it necessary to be specific as to who was conducting this lottery, because he, like Justice Marshall, was committed to the proposition that the death penalty could never be constitutional. Likewise, neither Justices Brennan nor Marshall found it necessary to discuss the issue of randomness or arbitrariness of sentencing at any length.

Justice Stewart, although he compared receiving the death penalty with being struck by lightning,[35] and described the appellants as "among a capriciously selected handful upon whom the death penalty has been imposed,"[36] did not go so far as to claim that juries were responsible for this capriciousness. Rather, Justice Stewart indicated that the problems with the death penalty were systemic, implicitly recognizing that other participants in the criminal justice system—police, prosecutors and judges—shared

---

32. *Id.* at 313.
33. *Id.*
34. *Id.* at 293.
35. *Id.* at 309.
36. *Id.* at 309-310.

responsibility for the irrational sentencing disparities in capital cases.[37] Only Justice Douglas was willing to place the blame for any arbitrariness on the jury, criticizing the "discretionary statutes" which he believed were "pregnant with discrimination and discrimination is an ingredient not compatible with the idea of equal protection of the law that is implicit in the ban on 'cruel and unusual' punishments."[38] None of the Justices explicitly addressed the issue of whether entities other than the jury—police, prosecutors and judges—may in fact have actually played the leading role in creating the "freakishness" and "arbitrariness" surrounding capital sentencing.

Georgia, led by State Senator Lester Maddox, was one of the first states to pass a newly revised capital punishment scheme, doing so less than a year after *Furman*.[39] The Georgia bill addressed the problems the Supreme Court had identified by controlling the discretion of the jury in several ways. First, the new bill narrowed the class of defendants who were eligible for the death penalty by requiring that the jury find that one or more statutory "aggravating circumstances" was involved in the commission of the murder before the death penalty could be imposed.[40] Next, the defendant was guaranteed individualized consideration in sentencing, by instructing the jury to consider any "mitigating circumstances" presented by the defense in deciding whether a defendant should live or die.[41] And finally, the Georgia Supreme Court was required to perform a "proportionality review" of all capital sentences to ensure that the sentence of death was not the result of prejudice or arbitrariness, nor was it excessive or disproportionate to the penalty in similar cases.[42]

This new Georgia law, along with the new laws of Texas, North Carolina, Louisiana and Florida, were considered in a series of decisions which form the foundation of modern American capital punishment jurisprudence. The United States Supreme Court in 1976 considered the laws of each of these states in a group of cases, beginning with *Gregg v. Georgia*.[43] The *Gregg* case was the appeal of the death sentence of Troy Gregg, who had been convicted of armed robbery and murder.

In deciding *Gregg*, the Court first considered the question left unanswered in *Furman*, whether the death penalty was *per se* unconstitution-

---

37. *Id.* at 309.
38. *Id.* at 256-257.
39. American Civil Liberties Union, Race and the Death Penalty, 7 (1987).
40. Gregg v. Georgia, 428 U.S. 153, 196-197 (1976).
41. *Id.* at 197.
42. *Id.* at 198.
43. *Id.*

ally cruel and unusual punishment. Rejecting the argument of the petitioners in *Furman* that "standards of decency had evolved to the point where capital punishment no longer could be tolerated,"[44] the *Gregg* Court decided that "a large proportion of American society continues to regard [capital punishment] as an appropriate and necessary criminal sanction."[45] As evidence, the Court pointed to the passage of revised capital punishment laws in over thirty-five states in the four years following *Furman*.[46] The Court further validated the death penalty on grounds that it served the valid penological purposes of retribution and deterrence of capital crimes by prospective offenders.[47] Having decided that capital punishment was not cruel and unusual *per se*, the Court went on to consider whether it was cruel and unusual under the procedures which had led to Troy Gregg's death sentence.

The Supreme Court held that the new Georgia capital punishment scheme complied with *Furman*, because it adequately guided the discretion of the jury by requiring a finding of a statutory aggravating circumstance before the defendant could be considered "death eligible," and by requiring the consideration of any relevant mitigating circumstances before deciding on the appropriate sentence. In narrowing and channeling the discretion of the jury, the new Georgia capital punishment laws complied with the requirements of *Furman*.[48] Because adequately defined statutory guidelines were in place, providing the jury with a rational framework within which to make the capital sentencing decision according to articulable standards, the Court found no violation of *Furman* in the Georgia capital punishment law. "Guided discretion" became the benchmark for capital punishment schemes following *Gregg*; the Court holding that:

> [W]here discretion is afforded a sentencing body on a matter so grave as the determination of whether a human life should be taken or spared, that discretion must be suitably directed and limited so as to minimize the risk of wholly arbitrary or capricious action.[49]

Proffitt v. Florida[50] considered whether the revised Florida death penalty procedures, which were quite different from those adopted in Georgia, also complied with *Furman*. The Florida capital sentencing jury makes only an advisory opinion as to whether the defendant should be sentenced

---

44. *Id.* at 179.
45. *Id.*
46. *Id.* at 179-180.
47. *Id.* at 183.
48. *Id.* at 206-207.
49. *Id.* at 189.
50. 428 U.S. 242 (1976).

to life imprisonment or death. The trial judge has the authority to override the jury's recommendation. (Only three other states—Alabama, Indiana and Maryland—presently allow for similar judicial overrides of jury sentencing recommentations). Although in *Gregg*, the Court noted that "jury sentencing has been considered desirable in capital cases in order to maintain a link between contemporary community values and the Penal system,"[51] in *Proffitt* the Court paradoxically noted that:

> [This Court] has never suggested that jury sentencing is constitutionally required. And it would appear that judicial sentencing should lead, if anything, to even greater consistency in punishment, since a trial judge is more experienced in sentencing than a jury, and therefore is better able to impose sentences similar to those imposed in analogous cases.[52]

These assumptions are called into question by later studies of judge-sentencing in capital cases, which show greater racial bias in capital sentencing decisions made by judges than those made by jurors.[53] This issue will be discussed at greater length below.

As in Georgia, the new Florida law required the sentencing authority to consider certain aggravating and mitigating factors in making the decision whether to impose the death penalty.[54] Because the discretion of the sentencing decision-maker—in Florida, the trial court judge—was guided and channelled by a statutorily prescribed framework, the Florida law was found to pass muster under *Furman*. The Court held that it is not necessary that the jury be the entity to decide between life and death, so long as the discretion of the sentencing authority is exercised along rational, statutorily defined guidelines.

Jurek v. Texas[55] examined the Texas scheme. The Texas plan was significantly different from those of either Georgia or Florida. First, capital murder was made a distinct offense in Texas; the jury had to find the defendant killed under one or more of a limited number of statutory aggravating circumstances in order to elevate a homicide to capital murder. If the aggravating circumstances were not found the greatest offense the defendant could be convicted of was murder, a non-capital offense. The same sorts of aggravating factors which were thus considered in the sentencing

---

51. *Gregg, supra* note 40, 190.

52. *Proffitt, supra* note 50, 252.

53. *See* Linda Foley & Richard Powell, *The Discretion of Prosecutors, Judges, and Juries in Capital Cases*, 7 CRIM. JUST. REV. 16-22 (1982); Hans Zeisel, *Race Bias in the Administration of the Death Penalty: The Florida Experience*, 95 HARV.L.REV. 459 (1981).

54. *Proffitt, supra* note 50, 253.

55. 428 U.S. 262 (1976).

stage of the trial in Georgia and Florida were considered in the guilt/innocence stage of the trial in Texas.

Secondly, at the punishment stage of the trial, Texas jurors were required to answer a set of factual "special issues" reflecting on the moral culpability of the accused. The special issues, as they existed at the time of Jerry Lane Jurek's trial, required the jury to answer "yes" or "no" to:

> (1) whether the conduct of the defendant that caused the death of the deceased was committed deliberately and with the reasonable expectation that the death of the deceased or another would result;
> (2) whether there is a probability that the defendant would commit criminal acts of violence that would constitute a continuing threat to society; and
> (3) if raised by the evidence, whether the conduct of the defendant in killing the deceased was unreasonable in response to the provocation, if any, by the deceased.

If the jury unanimously found that the special issues were true (voted "yes"), the judge was required to sentence the defendant to death. If the jury did not unanimously find that all the special issues were true, then the judge was required to sentence the defendant to life in prison.

The Texas law represents an apparent exception to the "guided discretion" principle. Because the Texas "special issues" require the jury to find specific facts to be true or false, the jury is given the absolute minimum amount of discretion possible. However, in *Jurek*, the Supreme Court held that the new Texas law complied with *Furman* by requiring statutory aggravating circumstances under which a homicide qualifies as capital murder, and by requiring a jury finding that the defendant would pose a risk of future dangerousness if not executed. The Court reasoned that the Texas statute guided and focused the discretion of the jury by requiring the assessment of any mitigating evidence presented in the sentencing stage (through the future dangerousness special issue), while narrowing the class of death-eligible defendants at the guilt/innocence stage.[56] The Supreme Court counted on the Texas Court of Criminal Appeals to give the Texas special issues an adequately broad interpretation so as to allow the jury to consider whatever mitigating evidence the defense raised, including the defendant's prior criminal record, age, and mental or emotional state.[57] How these issues were to be given an adequately broad interpretation so as to allow the jury to consider and give effect to any and all potentially

---

56. *Id.* at 273-274.
57. *Id.* at 272-273.

relevant mitigating evidence was not discussed, in light of the factual, true/false nature of the special issues the jury was to answer.

In the two remaining companion cases to *Gregg*, the Court struck down capital punishment schemes as unconstitutional because instead of "narrowing" and "channeling" the jury's sentencing discretion, they eliminated it entirely. In *Woodson v. North Carolina*,[58] the Court struck down a statute under which any defendant found guilty of first degree murder was automatically sentenced to die. A plurality of the Court found this mandatory capital punishment scheme failed to give the defendant "particularized consideration of relevant aspects of [his] character and record before the imposition upon him of a sentence of death."[59] The Court determined that "in capital cases, the fundamental respect for humanity underlying the Eighth Amendment requires consideration of the character and record of the individual offender and the circumstances of the particular offense..."[60] Perhaps more importantly here, the Supreme Court repeatedly recognized that a mandatory death penalty can function as a virtual open invitation for juries to nullify the law, if they believe that death is an inappropriate punishment in the case they are called upon to decide.[61]

Again, in *Roberts v. Louisiana*[62] the Court found that "the constitutional vice of a mandatory death sentence statute—lack of focus on the circumstances of the particular offense and the character and propensities of the offender"[63] were present in the Louisiana mandatory death penalty statute. If the jury did convict the defendant of murder under the Louisiana statutes, death was the only possible sentence. However, in order to mediate the harshness of this rule, the Louisiana law required juries to be instructed on lesser included offenses in all first degree murder cases, *whether or not such instructions were justified by the evidence.*

The Supreme Court determined that the Louisiana law was a clear invitation for juries to nullify the law and "choose a lesser offense whenever they feel the death penalty is inappropriate."[64] There were no other mechanisms for the jury to show mercy, or to allow for the consideration of mitigating evidence. The only way to spare the life of the defendant was to be through the jury's option of amelioration, convicting him of a lesser

---

58. *Supra* note 23.
59. *Id.* at 303.
60. *Id.* at 304.
61. *Id.* at 290-293, 299-300, 302-303.
62. *Supra* note 23.
63. *Id.* at 333.
64. *Id.* at 335.

included offense whatever the facts of the case might be. Yet the jurors were to be solemnly sworn that they would not do this during the death qualification *voir dire*. Louisiana was attempting to have it both ways.

Even more objectionable under *Gregg*, the Louisiana jury was to receive no guidance in when it would be appropriate to place other considerations above their oath, and when they should follow the letter of the law. Thus, the Louisiana statutes inadvertently left juries with the same degree of discretion the Court found objectionable in *Furman*, and expected them to exercise it through the legally-unmentionable mechanism of jury nullification. The Louisiana statute required the jury's exercise of its independent powers to be surreptitious and entirely unguided, and therefore this statute failed to comply with the requirements of *Gregg*. Clearly, the Supreme Court intended to preserve for the sentencing authority—whether it be the judge or the jury—some measure of discretion in sentencing in capital cases. How that discretion is intended to be exercised, guided, narrowed, focused and channelled remain among the central questions in capital punishment law.

Gregg and its companion cases were based on the assumption that it was jury decision-making which was responsible for the arbitrariness and randomness with which capital sentences had previously been imposed, and thus that controlling the discretion of juries would resolve the constitutional difficulties the Court recognized in *Furman*. This assumption was never explicitly made by a majority of the Court in *Furman*, and it is certainly not supported by what statistical research presently exists. The *Furman* opinion shows that a good part of what troubled the Court was the existence of disparities in the way black and white defendants were being treated in factually similar cases.

A pair of extensive and sophisticated statistical studies of capital sentencing in Georgia, conducted by Professor David C. Baldus and others in the late 1970s until the mid 1980s, include findings which dispute the perception that it is the jury which is primarily responsible for racial disparities in capital sentencing.[65] The Baldus studies were directly at issue in the 1987 Supreme Court case of *McCleskey v. Kemp*.[66] *McCleskey* was the unsuccessful death row *habeas corpus* petition of Warren McCleskey, sentenced to death for killing a white Georgia police officer during an armed robbery.[67] McCleskey did not argue that his death sentence was disproportionate to his crime. He did, however, argue that the statistics shown in the Baldus studies proved that as a black man convicted of killing

---

65. BALDUS, WOODWORTH & PULASKI, *supra* note 19, 327.
66. 481 U.S. 279 (1987).
67. *Id.* at 283.

a white, juries were disproportionately likely to sentence him to die, thus depriving him of equal protection of the law.[68]

The Baldus studies showed that the single most important factor in predicting whether a capital defendant would live or die was the race of the victim. Slayers of whites were 4.3 times as likely to receive the death sentence as slayers of blacks.[69] Blacks who killed whites were even more likely to be sentenced to die than whites who killed whites.[70] McCleskey's argument that this aggregate level of racial disparity violated the Constitution was never addressed by the Court, because he could not prove that racial considerations contributed to the capital sentence delivered by the jury in his particular case.[71]

Although juries have some culpability in the racially skewed manner in which the death penalty is applied, the Baldus studies clearly showed that this disparity was overwhelmingly the result of the misuse or abuse of prosecutorial discretion. Whereas juries are approximately 40% more likely to sentence the killer of a white to die than the killer of a black, prosecutors are 200% more likely to seek the death sentence against the killer of a white.[72] Similar levels of racial disparity have been found in other studies.[73]

Although it is prosecutorial discretion which introduces the overwhelming majority of racial bias into death penalty law, in general defense counsel have little leeway in which to attack the charging decisions of prosecutors. Following the Supreme Court's decision in *Bordenkircher v. Hayes*,[74] prosecutors have nearly unbounded discretion to charge as they see fit absent a clear showing of purposeful or deliberate discrimination. In run-of-the-mill criminal cases, this loose standard is appropriate in order to protect the independence of the executive branch (of which the prosecutor is a part) against intrusion or manipulation from the judicial branch of government. However, it is neither self-evident nor generally true that the same standards that are appropriate in run-of-the-mill cases are also appropriate in capital cases. Death is different from incarceration—different in severity, in finality, and in its societal implications. Accordingly, we allow capital defendants increased due process protections in many ways.

To date, however, the Supreme Court—which has been more than willing to micro-manage the decision making process of the jury in capital

---

68. *Id.* at 286-287.

69. *Id.* at 287; *see also* BALDUS, WOODWORTH & PULASKI, *supra* note 19, 316.

70. BALDUS, WOODWORTH & PULASKI, *supra* note 19, 328.

71. *McCleskey, supra* note 66, 292-293.

72. BALDUS, WOODWORTH & PULASKI, *supra* note 19, 327.

73. Michael L. Radalet and Glenn L. Pierce, *Race and Prosecutorial Discretion in Homicide Cases*, 19 LAW AND SOC'Y REV. 587, 613 (1985).

74. 434 U.S. 357, 364 (1978).

cases—has not been willing to make any decisions to control or guide the discretionary decision most responsible for arbitrary racial disparities in capital cases: the prosecutor's charging decision. Nor has it addressed the problems of discrimination from the bench. In Florida, for example, where judges may override the jury's recommendation of life in order to impose a death sentence, judges show a significantly greater amount of racial bias in their sentencing decisions than juries do.[75]

In sum, while the Supreme Court's decisions focus upon an alleged or assumed need to "narrow and channel" the discretion of the trial jury, those actors who have most abused their discretion—prosecutors and judges—have retained their power to act with as great a degree of bias, capricousness and arbitrariness as ever. *Furman* and its progeny have been attacking the wrong problem. The dilemma of persistent and unconstitutional racial bias in the application of the death penalty will remain intractible, so long as judges and prosecutors retain unlimited discretion to choose which defendants will face a risk of death, and in the case of Florida, Alabama, Indiana and Maryland judges, which ones will actually die.

The Death-Qualified Jury

The risk of racial bias in jury capital sentencing decisions may be greatly exacerbated by the unique methods of jury selection employed in capital cases. Capital juries tend to be more white and more male than noncapital juries, due to the death-qualification procedures employed during *voir dire*. In eliminating jurors with serious moral or religious qualms about the death penalty, minorities and women are removed at a much higher rate than are white males.[76] The jury which results is not a jury representative of the community as a whole; even worse, it may be seriously biased against the defendant in both guilt and punishment.[77]

Death-qualification of juries began as a means of controlling independent juries. We have already discussed how Justice Joseph Story began death-qualifying juries in capital cases in 1820, by removing two Quakers from a capital jury because of their conscientious refusal to sentence the

---

75. Foley & Powell, *supra* note 53, 16-22; Zeisel, *supra* note 53.

76. Fitzgerald & Ellsworth, *supra* note 21, 46-47.

77. *See* Samuel R. Gross, *Determining the Neutrality of Death-Qualified Juries: Judicial Appraisal of Empirical Data*, 8 LAW AND HUM. BEHAV. 7 (1984); Claudia L. Cowan, William C. Thompson and Phoebe C. Ellsworth, *The Effects of Death-Qualification on Jurors' Predisposition to Convict and on the Quality of Deliberation*, 8 LAW AND HUM. BEHAV. 53 (1984).

defendant to die.[78] In more recent years, a large number of cases have attempted to define when a potential juror may be disqualified due to his or her conscientious objections to the death penalty, as the Supreme Court continues to experiment with death qualification procedures.

In 1968 the Supreme Court, in *Witherspoon v. Illinois*,[79] decided that a state court could not automatically disqualify potential jurors merely because they "might hesitate to return a verdict inflicting [death]."[80] While the Court saw no problems with disqualifying those jurors who would simply refuse to impose or consider the death penalty,[81] or those whose determinations of guilt or innocence would be affected or colored by the specter of the executioner,[82] they held that removing all potential jurors who had any reservations about capital punishment denied the defendant his right to have his punishment considered by the "conscience of the community."[83] The Court explained:

> Just as veniremen cannot be excluded for cause on the ground that they hold such views, so too they cannot be excluded for cause simply because they indicate that there are some kinds of cases in which they would refuse to recommend capital punishment. And a prospective juror cannot be expected to say in advance of trial whether he would in fact vote for the extreme penalty in the case before him. The most that can be demanded of a venireman in this regard is that he be willing to *consider* all of the penalties provided by state law, and that he not be irrevocably committed, before the trial has begun, to vote against the penalty of death regardless of the facts and circumstances that might emerge in the course of the proceedings. If the *voir dire* testimony in a given case indicates that veniremen were excluded on any broader basis than this, the death sentence cannot be carried out even if applicable statutory or case law in the relevant jurisdiction would appear to support only a narrower ground of exclusion.
>
> We repeat, however, that nothing we say today bears upon the power of a State to execute a defendant sentenced to death by a jury from which the only veniremen who were in fact excluded for cause were those who made unmistakably clear (1) that they would *automatically* vote against the imposition of capital punishment without regard to any evidence that might be developed at the trial of the case before them, or (2) that their attitude toward the death penalty would prevent them from making an impartial decision as to the defendant's guilt. Nor does the decision in this case affect the validity of any sentence *other* than one of death. Nor, final-

---

78. *Cornell, supra* note 12.
79. *Supra* note 29.
80. *Id.* at 513.
81. *Id.* at 513-514.
82. *Id.* at 513.
83. *Id.* at 519.

ly, does today's holding render invalid the *conviction*, as opposed to the *sentence*, in this or any other case.[84]

Witherspoon was decided four years before *Furman v. Georgia*. Juries in 1968 still possessed completely unfettered discretion to impose a sentence of either life or death in any death-eligible case. By 1980, in consideration of the reduced discretion given the capital jury following *Gregg, Proffitt* and *Jurek*, the Court was willing to give prosecutors wider berth to eliminate jurors with conscientious scruples about capital punishment. In the 1980 case of *Adams v. Texas*,[85] the Court maintained that "jurors whose only fault was to take their responsibilities with special seriousness or to acknowledge honestly that they might or might not be affected"[86] by trying a capital case were not "so irrevocably opposed to capital punishment as to frustrate the State's legitimate efforts to administer its constitutionally valid death penalty scheme."[87] The *Adams* Court held that a juror was not disqualified "based on his views about capital punishment unless those views would prevent or substantially impair the performance of his duties as a juror in accordance with his instructions and his oath."[88] The language concerning "substantial impairment" was an expansion of the Court's holding in *Witherspoon*, which they were to develop further in the 1985 case of *Wainwright v. Witt*.[89]

In *Witt*, the Court acknowledged for the first time that the task of capital juries had changed due to the decisions in *Furman, Proffitt* and *Jurek*.[90] The Court attempted to harmonize *Adams* with *Witherspoon*, noting that the Texas capital punishment scheme at issue in *Adams* required the jury not to express the conscience of the community, but to answer specific factual questions. The conscience of the community had already been adequately expressed, in the Court's opinion, in the death penalty statute as written by the Texas Legislature:

> In such circumstances, it does not make sense to require simply that a juror not "automatically" vote against the death penalty; whether or not a venireman might vote for death under certain personal standards, the State

---

84. *Id.* at 522-523, n.21.

85. 448 U.S. 38 (1980). The defendant in this case was Randall Dale Adams, who was granted a new trial in 1989 because of prosecutorial misconduct and perjury, after coming within 72 hours of being executed. *See* Ex Parte Adams, 768 S.W.2d 281 (Tex.Crim.App. 1989). *See also* RANDALL DALE ADAMS, ADAMS V. TEXAS (1991). Adams' exoneration was prompted by the release of a documentary film, THE THIN BLUE LINE (Miramax 1988), which detailed the facts of his wrongful conviction.

86. *Adams, supra* note 85, 50-51.

87. *Id.* at 51.

88. *Id.* at 45.

89. 469 U.S. 412 (1985).

90. *Id.* at 421.

may properly challenge that venireman if he refuses to follow the statutory scheme and truthfully answer the questions put by the trial judge.[91]

Although *Woodson* and *Roberts* had held that mandatory death penalties were unconstitutional, in *Witt* the Court was willing to exclude any juror who may conscientiously refuse to give the fatal answer, if the factual answers to a set of statutory questions dictated what, to the juror's mind, may be an unjustified sentence of death. The *Witt* Court thus allowed jurors to be excluded on the chance that they may reach an independent judgment as to whether the defendant deserved to live or die. The Court did not address how the Texas capital punishment system with its true-false questions, enforced by jurors who had sworn not to make an independent judgment as to the appropriateness of death, differed from the mandatory death penalty schemes disapproved of in *Woodson* and *Roberts*. Although under Texas law a smaller category of cases qualifies for capital punishment than under the disapproved North Carolina and Louisiana laws, once the case is found to fit within the law, the defendant must be sentenced to die—unless the jury chooses to nullify the law in order to spare the defendant's life. And the Court's holding in *Witt* means that all jurors who indicate that they might consider nullification may be disqualified from jury service.

The *Witt* Court described the holding in *Witherspoon* as "limited,"[92] even though *Witherspoon* had been the leading case in capital jury selection for seventeen years. The Court believed that *Adams* presented the better rule, and held that the true touchstone of an excludable juror was the *Adams* "substantial impairment" test.[93] That is, in deciding questions of fact, a juror must not be "substantially impaired" in his decision-making by the spectre of death. While it is presumably still permissible for the juror to weigh a capital case with exceptional caution and gravity, the juror must not be materially influenced away from convicting or sentencing the defendant to die due to the severity of the punishment involved. The dividing line between "weighing the case with exceptional caution and gravity" and "being materially influenced" is vague, to say the least.

Social scientists have shown that a death-qualified jury behaves markedly differently than an ordinary criminal jury. Although the *Witherspoon* Court had commented that "It is, of course, settled that a state may not entrust the determination of whether a man is innocent or guilty to a tribunal 'organized to convict',"[94] several researchers have reported that

---

91. *Id.* at 422.
92. *Id.* at 418.
93. *Id.* at 421-422.
94. *Witherspoon, supra* note 29, 521.

death-qualified juries are far less than impartial as to conviction or acquittal, and may for all practical purposes be "organized to convict." Professors Michael Finch and Mark Ferraro, after surveying the available research on death qualified juries, concluded:

> In the seventeen years following *Witherspoon*, death qualification has been one of the most studied subjects in the area of sociological jurisprudence. The product is more than a dozen reported investigations which, in the overwhelming consensus of commentators, have confirmed three empirical hypotheses: (1) jurors excluded because of their inability to impose the death penalty are more attitudinally disposed to favor the accused than are non-excluded jurors; (2) excluded jurors are more likely to be black or female than non-excluded jurors; and (3) excluded jurors are more likely to actually acquit the accused than non-excluded jurors.[95]

Similarly, federal district Judge James McMillan has noted:

> Common sense suggests that people who favor the death penalty are more likely to convict defendants charged with capital crimes, and that people who do not favor the death penalty are less likely to convict defendants charged with capital crimes. The Supreme Court recognized those contentions... but prudently did not then adopt them as a basis for decision because of the lack of sociological testimony, juror opinion polls and other evidence.
>
> Such evidence has now been developed and occupies hundreds of pages...
> A fair jury has not been provided when the prosecutor is able to keep on the jury persons most likely to convict and to exclude from the jury for cause all those persons most likely to acquit.
>
> Nor does a jury so constituted represent, even in theory, a representative cross-section of the community.[96]

In spite of the evidence that death-qualified juries are biased, in 1992 the Supreme Court, in the case of *Lockhart v. McCree*, announced that even if death-qualification does produce juries more conviction-prone and less representative than non-death-qualified juries the Constitution does not forbid states from death-qualifying juries in capital cases.[97] First, the Court held that death-qualified juries complied with the "fair cross-section" requirements the Court had previously articulated in *Taylor v. Louisiana*[98] and *Duren v. Missouri*,[99] discussed in Chapter Five. This was because *Witherspoon-* excludables removed from the panel during death-qualifi-

---

95. Finch & Ferraro, *supra* note 21, 24-25.
96. Keeten v. Garrison, 578 F.Supp 1164, 1167 (W.D.N.C. 1983), rev'd, 742 F.2d 129 (4th Cir. 1984).
97. *Supra* note 20, 173-184.
98. 419 U.S. 522 (1975).
99. 439 U.S. 357 (1979).

cation did not form a "distinctive group" as defined in *Taylor*. The Court only recognized gender, ethnic or racial groups as being constitutionally protected.[100] "In sum," the Court announced, "'*Witherspoon*-excludables,'" or for that matter any group defined solely in terms of shared attitudes that render members of the group unable to serve as jurors in a particular case, may be excluded from jury service without contravening any of the basic objectives of the fair-cross-section requirement."[101]

The Court was apparently not concerned that this analysis clearly contradicts the Court's own plain language in previous cases, such as *Ballard v. United States*.[102] In that case, the Court explained that

> [I]t is not enough to say that women when sitting as jurors neither act nor tend to act as a class. Men likewise do not act as a class…The truth is that the two sexes are not fungible; a community made up exclusively of one is different from a community composed of both; the subtle interplay of influence one on the other is among the imponderables. To insulate the courtroom from either may not in a given case make an iota of difference. Yet a flavor, a distinct quality is lost if either sex is excluded. The exclusion of one may make the jury less representative of the community than would be true if an economic or racial group was excluded.[103]

Clearly, a "distinct quality" is also lost when vast numbers of Americans—all those with moral or religious scruples about the imposition of the death penalty—are excluded from capital jury duty. A jury stricken of all who may object to capital punishment is certainly less representative of the community as a whole than it would be if those conscientious objectors were seated. Those excluded can indeed be expected to act, as a class, differently from those who were empanelled. The fact that these conscientious objectors do not form a distinct class for other purposes (such as voting rights or employment discrimination) should be completely irrelevant to whether they form a distinct class in this context. Whether their exclusion would prevent a fair trial in a non-capital case is entirely immaterial, yet it is precisely this double standard that the Court is using. That "distinct quality" which is lost may be the possibility for a merciful verdict, and depriving the defendant of that possibility deprives him of a trial by a jury fairly representative of the community on the very issue where the conscience of that community is most urgently involved—on a matter, literally, of life and death.

---

100. *Supra* note 20, 174.
101. *Id.* at 176-177.
102. 329 U.S. 187 (1946).
103. *Id.* at 193-194.

Secondly, the *Lockhart* Court further rejected any claims that the absence of *Witherspoon*-excludables from the jury unconstitutionally slanted the jury towards conviction. Instead of addressing the defendant's arguments in terms of exclusion, the Court looked to the variety of people who actually do sit on capital juries, commenting that "[i]f it were true that the Constitution required a certain mix of individual viewpoints on the jury, then trial judges would be required to undertake the Sisyphean task of "balancing" juries, making sure that each contains the proper number of Democrats and Republicans, young persons and old persons, white-collar executives and blue-collar laborers, and so on."[104] The Court contended it made no sense to say that "a given jury is unconstitutionally partial when it results from a State-ordained process, yet impartial when exactly the same jury results from mere chance."[105]

This contention is disingenuous, because Lockhart was not demanding any particular mix of jurors in his trial. He was, instead, arguing for a fair and random selection, for judgment by a fair cross-section of the community, and for a jury which had not been selected through procedures that disproportionately eliminated minorities, women, and those who may be more likely to acquit. From 1879 on, it has been recognized that the Constitution, while not requiring any particular mix on juries, does require that no segment of society be excluded merely on account of race.[106] Lockhart was arguing for the same principle with regard to a different issue: that the state should not be able to insist on jury selection procedures that allow only the most conviction prone segments of society to sit as jurors, regardless of race.

Moreover, any possible combination of jurors can occur by chance. It would be possible to have a randomly selected jury include only members of a certain religion or profession, only members of a particular race, or only men, women, Democrats, bowlers or Ku Klux Klan members. Would the Court claim that such a jury was constitutional if it resulted from a state-ordained process, merely because "exactly the same jury [could result] from mere chance"? Certainly not—the distinction the Court is attempting to draw is meaningless. Either the jury is fairly selected, or it is not. A jury selected through a process that predisposes the jury to be biased is not fairly selected, regardless of whether a biased jury could also have been selected through fair means.

The Court's position is especially untrustworthy because ideological positions are so often used as a surrogate for race in jury selection. We know from studies of death-qualified juries that blacks tend to be eliminated

---

104. *Supra* note 20, 178.
105. *Id.*
106. Strauder v. West Virginia, 100 U.S. 303 (1879).

at a much higher rate than whites, and that women tend to be eliminated at a much higher rate then men. We also know that black jurors on average tend to be more acquittal-prone than whites.[107] This is why prosecutors quite openly made a practice of peremptorily striking blacks from juries even in cases where the defendant was white,[108] until the Supreme Court deemed that practice unconstitutional in the 1991 case of *Powers v. Ohio*.[109] Some prosecutors have continued using race as a reason for striking blacks from jury duty, even in the face of *Batson v. Kentucky*.[110]

It is undeniable that capital juries do show some racial disparity in their sentencing decisions—even if it is only one-fifth the level of racial disparity shown by prosecutors. However, this does not appear to be so much a reflection on the jury as an institution, as it is on the fact that the racial and gender mix on capital juries is distorted by the jury selection procedures peculiar to capital cases. The remedy for the racial disparities shown by juries in capital sentencing is not to reduce the protection given the accused by the trial jury or to encroach on the discretion and power of the jurors, but to reinforce the protection of trial by jury by reducing or removing the ability of the prosecution to exclude all jurors who harbor any serious conscientious opposition to the institution of capital punishment.[111]

While it is true that the will of the legislature is an important measure of public opinion, it is not the sole measure, and it may not in all instances be the most important. The level of social consensus which should be required by law in order for a human being to be put to death is understandably greater than that which should be required for the enforcement of more mundane legislative acts. It is in this sort of case, where the jury is called on to act as the conscience of the community, that the degree of social consensus is most urgently being tested. If there is insufficient consensus for a normal *voir dire*—including the liberal application of peremp-

---

107. Nancy J. King, *Postconviction Review of Jury Discrimination: Measuring the Effects of Juror Race on Jury Deliberations*, 92 MICH. L. REV. 63 (1993).

108. *See* JON M. VAN DYKE, JURY SELECTION PROCEDURES : OUR UNCERTAIN COMMITMENT TO REPRESENTATIVE PANELS, 152-153 (1977)

109. 499 U.S. 400 (1991).

110. 476 U.S. 79 (1989). *See* L. Stuart Ditzen, Linda Loyd and Mark Fazlollah, *Avoid Poor Black Jurors, McMahon Said*, PHILADELPHIA INQUIRER, April 1, 1997 at A1 (discussing Philadelphia Assistant District Attorney Jack McMahon's training video for prosecutors, made one year after *Batson*, advising them to strike blacks from jury duty.) *See also* Michael Matza and Mark Fazlollah, *Juries and justice*, PHILADELPHIA INQUIRER, April 6, 1997 at E1; Barnaby C. Wittels, *Jury selection or elimination?: Too many lawyers rely on stereotypes, conventional wisdom to seat jurors*, PHILADELPHIA INQUIRER, April 15, 1997 at E7.

111. JEFFREY ABRAMSON, WE, THE JURY: THE JURY SYSTEM AND THE IDEAL OF DEMOCRACY, 237-239 (1994).

tory challenges[112]—to remove presumably rare death penalty opponents from the panel, then perhaps the community is not as strongly in favor of the death penalty as the legislature has presumed. In matters of life and death, is it not humane, rational, and just that we allow a significant minority in the community a veto over the majority's power to kill?

Our entire edifice of capital punishment law revolves around guiding, focusing and channeling jury discretion into judicially approved channels. But in following this single-minded quest to prevent any possibility of jury nullification by micro-managing the jury, courts may be depriving defendants in capital cases of an impartial jury, of a jury selected from a fair cross-section of the community, and perhaps most importantly, from a jury determination of guilt and punishment in accordance with the conscience of the community. As one author has noted,

> In their desire to eradicate irrational acquittals and nullifications, courts have undermined the basic procedural guarantees granted to a criminal defendant. These guarantees are necessary to preserve a core value of our criminal justice system: a criminal conviction should result only upon evidence of a statutory violation and a determination by the community, speaking through a representative jury, that the defendant's conduct is blameworthy.[113]

It is impossible to preserve the other "core values" of the criminal justice system while concentrating our capital punishment jury selection procedures singlemindedly on the prevention of jury nullification. Have we really reached a point in this country where we are willing to allow human beings to be executed after a trial by a biased jury that has been stacked against them and sworn to execute? Such juries were categorically condemned by the Founders of this country, and should be rejected by Americans today.

Penry and the Requirement of Individualized Sentencing

The near-mandatory character of the Texas death penalty system was first examined by the United States Supreme Court in the 1989 case of *Penry v. Lynaugh*.[114] Johnny Paul Penry was convicted of capital murder

---

112. In Texas, the state most active in dispensing death as a penalty for crime, prosecutors have 15 peremptory strikes in death penalty cases. TEXAS CODE OF CRIMINAL PROCEDURE Art. 35.15.

113. Chaya Weinberg-Brodt, *Jury Nullification and Jury Control Procedures*, 65 N.Y.U. L. REV. 825, 870 (1990).

114. *Supra* note 24.

and sentenced to death by a Texas jury, following the rape and murder of Pamela Carpenter in her Livingston, Texas apartment. Penry, who was on parole following a prior conviction for sexual assault when the murder occurred, was quickly identified and arrested for the crime. He confessed to the crime, and was promptly convicted of capital murder and sentenced to death.

On *habeas corpus* review, defense counsel asserted that the Texas capital punishment scheme did not allow the jury to consider the mitigating evidence presented on Penry's behalf. Expert witnesses testified that Penry was mildly to moderately retarded, with an IQ falling in the range of 50–63, giving him a mental age of about six and a half years.[115] This retardation was suspected to be the result of organic damage caused to Penry's brain at birth, and was possibly exacerbated as a result of his having been repeatedly beaten over the head by his mother as a young child.[116] As a consequence of his retardation, Penry was unable to control his impulses or learn from his mistakes. The defense contended that, while Penry's retardation and brain damage mitigated his moral culpability for his actions, there was no way for the jury to give this evidence any consideration within the narrow framework of the Texas special issues.

The Supreme Court agreed, in a decision written by Justice Sandra Day O'Connor. Justice O'Connor specifically observed that:

> The mitigating evidence concerning Penry's mental retardation indicated that one effect of his retardation is his inability to learn from his mistakes. Although this evidence is relevant to the second issue, it is relevant only as an *aggravating* factor because it suggests a "yes" answer to the question of future dangerousness…Penry's mental retardation and history of abuse is thus a two-edged sword: it may diminish his blameworthiness for his crime even as it indicates that there is a probability that he will be dangerous in the future.[117]

Because "[t]he second special issue… did not provide a vehicle for the jury to give mitigating effect to Penry's evidence of retardation and childhood abuse,"[118] the Court held that it would be cruel and unusual to sentence Penry to death. The Court was concerned that the sentencing jury was not allowed to exercise its reasoned moral judgment on whether or not the defendant should be sentenced to die. The Court reiterated that "the jury must be able to consider and give effect to any mitigating evidence relevant to a defendant's background and character or the circumstances of the crime."[119]

---

115. *Id.* at 307-308.
116. *Id.* at 307-310.
117. *Id.* at 323-324 (emphasis in original).
118. *Id.* at 324.
119. *Id.* at 328.

The *Penry* decision could have effectively stricken the Texas capital punishment scheme, making it unconstitutional in any case where there was any mitigating evidence presented which was not directly applicable to the Texas special issues—and thus arguably depriving other defendants, to whom the Texas special issues could be applied, of equal protection of the law.[120] In *Jurek*, the Supreme Court had made clear that the constitutionality of the Texas special issues depended on their being given an adequately broad interpretation by the Texas courts, so as to encompass all material mitigating evidence. The *Penry* decision showed that the Texas courts failed to live up to this responsibility. *Penry* potentially undermined the constitutionality of the entire Texas capital punishment system.

What is interesting, for our purposes, is that the Texas courts specifically invoked the jury's power to reach an independent verdict in order to bring the then-existing Texas law into compliance with the Supreme Court's holding in *Penry*. The dilemma of the Texas court was caused by the very clarity of the Texas special issues. They presented a clear set of relatively unambiguous factual questions. Given the capital punishment scheme they were presented with, a Texas juror had no way to give effect to any migitating evidence not directly applicable to the three special issues. The Texas Court of Criminal Appeals itself complained, in a footnote to the case *Trevino v. State*, that

> The Supreme Court failed to understand that under Texas law the jury does not "impose the death penalty." The jury in a capital case decides three special issues and, upon an affirmative finding to each, "the court shall sentence the defendant to death." Article 37.071(e) V.A.C.C.P. As such, the high Court failed to inform this Court how the jury is to give "mitigating effect" to mitigating evidence that is not capable of being considered outside the special issues.[121]

---

120. The Texas legislature revised the Texas special issues, effective September 1, 1991, in order to give the jury an opportunity to exercise their reasoned moral judgment on sentencing without having to nullify the law. The new special issues read:

> (1) whether there is a probability that the defendant would commit criminal acts of violence that would constitute a continuing threat to society; and
>
> (2) whether the defendant actually caused the death of the deceased or did not actually cause the death of the deceased but intended to kill the deceased or another or anticipated that a human life would be taken; and
>
> (3) whether, taking into consideration all of the evidence, including the circumstances of the offense, the defendant's character and background, and the personal moral culpability of the accused, there is a sufficient mitigating circumstance or circumstances to warrant that a sentence of life imprisonment rather than a death sentence be imposed.

TEXAS CODE OF CRIMINAL PROCEDURE, Chapter 37, Art. 37.071

121. 815 S.W. 2d 592, n. 11 (Tex.Crim.App. 1991).

Giving the jury an opportunity to consider and give effect to mitigating evidence not covered by the special issues required affirmatively instructing jurors that they could nullify the law. Jurors were instructed that they could answer "no" to a question, even when the evidence relating to that question would clearly require an answer of "yes," if their consciences led them to believe a "no" answer would lead to a more just result.

It was impossible for the Texas Court of Criminal Appeals itself to fashion a way to bring Texas law into compliance with the *Penry* decision. (The Texas Court could, of course, have itself declared that the Texas capital punishment scheme was unconstitutional, thereby leaving the problem for the legislature). As an appellate court, it could only remand cases to the trial court for new sentencing hearings, when the instructions given to the jury did not allow it to consider and give effect to all the mitigating evidence presented. It was the responsibility of the trial courts to find an instruction that would comply with *Penry*.

Texas trial courts found only one way to empower juries to answer "no" to a factual question when the facts plainly led to an answer of "yes." Trial courts in capital cases began instructing juries that, if mitigating evidence made the death penalty conscientiously inappropriate in a given case, it was their duty to ignore the clear wording of the special issues, and answer "no" to one or more of the special issues. Juries were instructed that they were to go beyond merely finding facts; they were to nullify the special issues when their personal moral judgment, in light of whatever mitigating evidence was presented, led them to believe that the life of the defendant should be spared. In *Fuller v. State*,[122] the Texas Court of Criminal Appeals approved a jury instruction that

> If you find there are any mitigating circumstances, you must decide how much weight they deserve and give them effect when you answer the Special Issues. If you determine, in consideration of this evidence, that a life sentence, rather than a death sentence, is an appropriate response to the personal moral culpability of the defendant, you are instructed to answer at least one of the Special Issues under consideration "No."[123]

No provision was made for the trial court to give the jury any instruction as to which of the special issues they should answer "no" — that was irrelevant, because the effect of a "no" answer to any of the issues would result in a sentence of life imprisonment instead of death. In other words, the State of Texas specifically began instructing jurors in capital cases that, if they believed after hearing all the aggravating and mitigating evidence that

---

122. 829 S.W.2d 191 (Tex.Crim.App. 1992).
123. *Id.* at 209, n. 5.

following the law would cause an unjust death sentence to be delivered, they were not only empowered to, but actually obligated to nullify the law.

This so-called Texas "nullification instruction"[124] was not the only method Texas trial courts employed in order to comply with the requirements of *Penry*. In *State v. McPherson*,[125] the trial court employed a fourth special issue of its own invention:

> SPECIAL ISSUE NO. 4
>
> Do you find from the evidence, after considering fully the Defendant's mitigating evidence, if any, that the death penalty is a reasoned moral response to the Defendant's background his character, and to the crime of which he was convicted?[126]

The Texas Court of Criminal Appeals did not "fault" the trial judge for creating and using a fourth special issue, but clearly preferred the nullification instruction:

> [A]t the time of appellee's trial, we had not ruled on the sufficiency of an instruction to meet the demands of Penry. Clearly, the trial judge believed the Eighth Amendment and Penry required that the jury have a vehicle to consider and give effect to appellee's mitigating evidence. Having no guidance from the Supreme Court, or this Court, the trial judge chose to provide the fourth issue... [127]

Since *Fuller*, the Court has repeatedly approved the use of jury nullification instructions in order to bring the Texas capital sentencing scheme into compliance with *Penry*.[128]

The Texas Court has developed several requirements for the nullification instructions given in capital cases. The Court has determined that these instructions must 1) "clearly communicate... that evidence that has no rational bearing whatsoever on (the) special issues, or only has a ten-

---

124. Coble v. State, 871 S.W. 2d. 192, 206-207 (Tex.Crim.App. 1993).

125. 851 S.W.2d 846 (Tex Crim.App. 1992).

126. *Id.* at 850.

127. *Id.*

128. *See* Garcia v. State, 887 S.W. 2d 846 (Tex Crim.App. 1994); Goynes v. State, No. 71,387, unpublished slip op. at 3-4 (Tex Crim.App. Dec. 14, 1994); Riddle v. State, 888 S.W. 2d 1, 7 (Tex Crim.App. 1994); Wheatfall v. State, 882 S.W. 2d 829, 840 & n.11 (Tex Crim.App. 1994); Clark v. State, 881 S.W. 2d 682 (Tex Crim.App. 1994); Miller v. State, No. 70,989, unpublished slip op. (Tex Crim.App. May 12, 1993); Robertson v. State, 871 S.W. 2d 701, 710-711 (Tex Crim.App. 1993); Coble v. State, *supra* note 124, 206-207; San Miguel v. State, 864 S.W. 2d 430, 445 (Tex Crim.App. 1993); Hittle v. State, No. 71,138, unpublished slip op. at 13 (Tex Crim.App. 1993); Smith v. State, No. 71,099, unpublished slip op. at 2 & nn. 2-3 (Tex Crim.App. Feb. 24, 1993). This list is from STEVEN C. LOSCH, 1996 CAPITAL MURDER MANUAL, p. 112 (1996).

dency to militate in favor of affirmative answers, may nonetheless serve as the basis for answering one or more of the issues 'no,' in spite of the jurors' oaths to answer (the) special issues honestly, and in accordance with what they believe the relevant evidence shows"; 2) "tell the jurors that they may, should they find it appropriate in their reasoned moral judgment, use the defendant's mitigating evidence as a reason to answer the first special issue 'no,' even if they do not find that it prevented him from acting deliberately"; and 3) "tell the jurors that they can use mitigating evidence not only to answer the future dangerousness question 'yes,' but also, paradoxically, to answer it 'no.'"[129]

The Texas Court of Criminal Appeals has not addressed how its approval of a jury nullification instruction in capital sentencing proceedings reflects upon the role of the jury in other criminal cases. Texas courts have consistently denied the right of juries to render independent verdicts since the earliest reported cases.[130] In spite of this, the very constitutionality of the Texas capital punishment scheme was left to rest on the rightful authority and willingness of Texas jurors to nullify if in their "reasoned moral judgment" they do not believe the death penalty to be an appropriate sentence in the case before them.

In *Dougherty*, Justice Leventhal wrote that juries need not be instructed about their powers to render independent verdicts, because jurors are already aware of their powers, and instructing them about those powers would merely be encouraging them to nullify in inappropriate cases.[131] If this were true, there would seem to be little to gain and much to lose by giving juries nullification instructions in capital cases. Not a single Texas court, however, has been bold enough to assert that such instructions are not necessary in order to comply with *Penry*, because Texas jurors are "already aware" of their powers and how they should be exercised in the interest of justice. Time after time, the Texas courts have done exactly the opposite by mandating such instructions when the circumstances dictated them.

By explicitly turning to the independent powers of the jury in order to rescue the Texas capital punishment scheme, the Texas Court of Criminal Appeals has at least implicitly recognized the right of juries to render similarly independent verdicts in other cases. To date, however, it appears that no court in Texas has been willing to give a nullification instruction in a non-capital case, and Texas courts have hewed to the now-tradition-

---

129. Rios v. State, 846 S.W. 2d 310, 316-317 (Tex Crim.App. 1992).

130. Nels v. State, 2 Tex. 280 (1847); Squires v. State, 39 Tex. Cr. Rep. 96, 45 S.W. 147 (Tex.Crim.App., 1898).

131. United States v. Dougherty, 473 F.2d 1113, 1135 (D.C.Cir. 1973).

al formulation that "[t]he jury is required to take the law from the court and be bound thereby."[132] In fact, at least one Texas Court of Appeals has upheld a trial court's refusal to give a jury nullification instruction in a non-death penalty case without addressing either *Penry* or the cases following *Penry*.[133] Still, the Texas Court of Criminal Appeals cynical use of jury nullification in order to salvage an otherwise unconstitutional capital sentencing scheme makes it plain that in the opinion of that court a properly instructed jury may, even in the most serious of cases, responsibly consider the crime, the criminal and the law, and decide whether applying the law to the acts and the actor will result in justice being done. If juries are responsible enough to exercise this oversight power in capital cases, there can be little justification for not trusting them to exercise the same oversight power responsibly in less serious criminal prosecutions.

There can be no more important criminal cases in the American criminal justice system than those cases involving the death penalty. It is in capital punishment cases where mistakes are the least forgivable, where the consensus of the community is most sorely needed and most severely tested. Yet it is in capital punishment cases that our system is least willing to allow a fair trial before a randomly selected cross-section of the community empowered to "prevent oppression by the government." The meaning and purpose of trial by jury has been distorted in every conceivable way by modern capital punishment law.

Indeed, our courts have put so much effort into micro-managing every facet of the capital jury decision-making process that basic constitutional questions about the death penalty remain unanswerable. Although courts have recognized the discretionary role of juries by requiring individualized sentencing and by prohibiting the states from instituting mandatory death-penalty statutes, they have at the same time effectively neutralized community input, largely by increasing the power of prosecutors to death-qualify jurors, and of judges to "guide and channel" jury decision-making.

Courts have interfered with the role of the jury purportedly because juries have not uniformly punished comparably situated offenders. As in cases of racial violence, however, courts have not been willing to critically or objectively scrutinize the role of judges or prosecuting attorneys in capital cases. Those studies which have done so have determined that the lion's share of the disparities involved in capital cases are attributable to those other actors in the system, with the single largest proportion being due to disparate charging decisions made by prosecutors. While the discretion of jurors is more and more tightly guided, narrowed, channelled,

---

132. Aldridge v. State, 342 S.W.2d 104 (Tex.Crim.App. 1960).
133. Mouton v. State, 923 S.W.2d 219 (Tex.App.-Hous. (14th Dist.) 1996).

and directed, the discretion of prosecutors is almost entirely unfettered, with no effective oversight or supervision from any source.

Politicians and some pollsters claim that Americans overwhelmingly support the death-penalty. If this is true, then there should be little need to death qualify juries in order to prevent the laws from being nullified in capital cases. The normal *voir dire*, including the use of peremptory challenges, should be more than sufficient to identify and eliminate those few death penalty opponents within the jury pool. The remaining jurors can be presumed to be either neutral or supportive of the death penalty. It is telling that no state has yet shown enough confidence in public support for the death penalty to do away with death-qualification procedures. Perhaps that should tell us something important about the depth of public support for capital punishment in the first place. If the power of the state to kill people is a legitimate part of the law of the land, it should not require a complicated series of arcane and hypertechnical jury control procedures in order to function.

Chapter Nine

The Obligations of Jury Duty

*It is not what a lawyer tells me I
may do; but what humanity, reason,
and justice tell me I ought to do.*
Edmund Burke

Understanding the Juror's Oath

A common thread running through articles and court decisions critical of jury independence is the allegation that nullifying jurors are in some manner violating their sworn oaths. In *United States v. Krzyske*, the Sixth Circuit Court of Appeals approved a jury instruction warning jurors that they "...would violate [their] oath and the law if [they] willfully brought in a verdict contrary to the law given [to them] in this case."[1] In a more recent case, Judge Jose Cabranes, writing for the Second Circuit Court of Appeals urged that "a refusal to apply the law as set forth by the court" is "an obvious violation of a juror's oath and duty."[2] Neither case stated what clause of the juror's oath would be violated, or what promise the juror would be breaking if the juror delivered an independent verdict. While different courts in different states require jurors to swear to a variety of oaths, in general jurors are not required to swear that they will follow the instructions given to them by the judge regardless of how deeply it violates their personal moral or conscientious convictions.

Juror's oaths are not always defined by statute. In many states and in the federal courts, jurors oaths are "simply an old tradition judges have made up."[3] Moreover, court reporters rarely bother to transcribe the oath taken by jurors, but merely insert into the record a phrase such as "the jurors were then empannelled and duly sworn." It would seem difficult for an appellate court to discern whether jurors in fact violated an oath, when the oath taken by the jurors is not reflected in the record before them.

---

1. 836 F.2d 1013, 1021 (6th Cir. 1988).
2. United States v. Thomas et al., 116 F.3d 606, 608 (2nd Cir. 1997).
3. James Joseph Duane, *Jury Nullification: The Top Secret Constitutional Right*, 22 LITIG. #4, pp. 6, 12 (1996).

Some typical juror's oaths from states where the oath is defined by statute require jurors to affirmatively answer that:

(Texas)

> You and each of you do solemnly swear that in the case of the State of Texas against the defendant, you will a true verdict render according to the law and the evidence, so help you God.[4]

(Pennsylvania)

> You do solemnly swear by Almighty God [and those of you who affirm do declare and affirm] that you will well and truly try the issue joined between the Commonwealth and the Defendant(s), and a true verdict render according to the evidence.[5]

(Massachusetts)

> You shall well and truly try the issue between the Commonwealth and the defendant (or the defendants as the case may be) according to your evidence, so help you God.[6]

(California)

> JURY TO BE SWORN. As soon as the jury is completed, an oath must be administered to the jurors in substance, that they and each of them will well and truly try the matter in issue...and a true verdict render according to the evidence.[7]

(Ohio)

> FORM OF OATH TO JURY. In criminal cases jurors and the jury shall take the following oath to be administered by the trial court or the clerk of the court of common pleas: "You shall well and truly try, and true deliverance make between the State of Ohio and the defendant (giving his name.) So help you God."[8]

These sorts of oaths are certainly nothing new. Jurors have apparently been required to swear to some sort of oath ever since the late twelfth century, if not before. Actually, some of the ancient oaths may have constrained a juror's discretion more than those quoted above. Probably the

---

4. TEXAS CODE OF CRIMINAL PROCEDURE § 35.22.

5. PENNSYLVANIA RULES OF CRIMINAL PROCEDURE 1110(b).

6. MASSACHUSETTS PROCEEDINGS IN CRIMINAL CASES Rule 278 § 4.

7. CALIFORNIA CODE OF CIVIL PROCEDURE § 604. California courts use the same oath in civil and criminal proceedings.

8. OHIO REVISED CODE § 2945.28.

earliest oath on record was reported by Sir William Blackstone in his 1769 *Commentaries on the Law of England*, and dates back to the early eleventh century. This oath merely required that jurors "shall swear, with their hands upon a holy thing, that they will condemn no man that is innocent, nor acquit any that is guilty."[9] Blackstone noted that the oath he cited was probably given to grand jurors. Lysander Spooner disputed this, noting that "there was but one jury at the time."[10] Whether this oath constrained the jurors depends on whether the terms "guilt" and "innocence" were interpreted as possessing moral, as well as legal, meanings, in the twelfth century. Considering the strong influence religion had on the development of the law in early times, it is almost certain that twelfth century jurors would have given moral interpretations great weight.

The twelfth century *justiciar* Ranulph de Glanvill recorded an oath given to British Knights acting as compurgators in civil trials:

> The King to the Sheriff, Health. Summon, by good Summoners, those twelve Knights R. and N. (naming each) that they be, on such a day, before me or my Justices at such a place, prepared on their oaths to return, whether R. or N. have greater right, in one Hyde of Land, or in the subject matter of dispute, which the aforesaid R. claims against the aforesaid N., and of which the aforesaid N. the Tenant, has put himself upon our Assise, and has prayed a Recognition, which of them have the greater right to the thing in question; and, in the mean time, let them view the Land or Tenement itself, of which the service is demanded; and Summon, by good Summoners, N. the tenant, that he be then there to hear that Recognition, &c.[11]

Towards the end of the thirteenth century jurors were required to promise that they would "say the truth in answer to such questions as shall be addressed to them on the king's behalf and to obey orders."[12] Jurors who violated their oath—or even had the facts wrong—were occasionally subjected to extremely cruel punishments under ancient common law through the "attaint," at least in civil cases. Glanvill described the punishment jurors could face:

9. Sir William Blackstone, IV Commentaries on the Laws of England, 302 (1769).

10. Lysander Spooner, An Essay on The Trial by Jury, 86 (1852).

11. Ranulph de Glanvill, The Treatise on the Laws and Customs of the Realm of England Commonly Called Glanvill, translated from the latin by G.D.G. Hall, Book II, Chapter XV (1181) (Reprinted 1983).

12. Sir Frederick Pollock and Frederick William Maitland, A History of English Law, Vol. II. p. 645 (2nd ed., 1909).

> If the jurors shall, by due course of Law, be convicted, or, by legal Confession, be proved to have perjured themselves in Court, they shall be despoiled of their Chattels and Moveables, which shall be forfeited to the King, although by great clemency of the Prince, their freehold Tenements are spared. They shall also be thrown into prison, and be there detained for one year at least. In fine, deprived for ever after of their Law, they shall justly wear the mark of perpetual infamy. This penalty is properly ordained in order that a similarity of punishment may deter Men in such a Case, from the unlawful use of an Oath.[13]

Although jurors in criminal cases could not be subjected to an attaint, they could still be punished by the sometimes draconian contempt powers of the court. These contempt powers were probably exercised most brutally by the court of the Star Chamber, as *The Trial of Sir Nicholas Throckmorton*[14] and others demonstrated. After the abolition of the Star Chamber in 1645 and Chief Justice Vaughn's decision in *Bushell's Case*,[15] however, jurors could no longer be punished for their verdicts. Yet as much as Edward Bushell and his fellow jurors enraged the court, it does not appear that they violated their oath as jurors. A good argument can be made that a conviction would have been the true violation of their oath. When William Penn and William Mead were put to trial for "causing a tumult" by holding a Quaker meeting in Gracechurch Street, London, all their jury was required to swear was that:

> You shall well and truly try and true deliverance make betwixt our sovereigh Lord the King and the prisoners at bar, according to your evidence, so help you God.[16]

This oath, which continued to be used with little variation until at least 1769[17] (and which is still used, almost verbatim, in the State of Ohio today) certainly did not require the jurors to follow the law as they were instructed by the court, and gave the jurors a wide range of discretion to allow their conscience to be their guide. For the juror to make a 'true deliverance' between the King and the accused merely requires the juror to return a just and conscientious verdict. If the evidence showed that the accused had done nothing wrong, the jury was obliged to say so, regardless of how-

---

13. GLANVILL, *supra* note 11, Book II, Chapter IXX.

14. How. St.Tr. 1:869 (1554).

15. How. St.Tr. 6:999 (1670).

16. The Tryal of Wm. Penn and Wm. Mead for Causing a Tumult..., How. St.Tr. 6:951 (1670).

17. BLACKSTONE, *supra* note 9, 355.

ever many statutes may have been violated. And, as the Penn trial showed, some jurors interpreted their oath just that way.

The Juror's Oath in Early American History

Colonial American trial jurors were probably given at least as much latitude as seventeenth century British jurors. Reports of early cases rarely contain any citation of the exact wording of the juror's oath. In fact, the seventeen-volume set of *American State Trials*[18] is almost completely devoid of any renditions of the juror's oaths. In Colonial Virginia, an act of the assembly passed in 1705 guaranteed trial by jury in all criminal cases, and stated that the jury would be sworn.[19] The act did not specify what oath the jury would be required to swear to. Instead, Virginia courts relied on the common law of England to provide the substance of their oath.

We know that revolutionary procedure generally recognized the jury as having the final legal say upon questions of law, as *Georgia v. Brailsford*[20] so amply demonstrated. Being charged by the Court with judging both law and fact, there was no act of rebellion in a jury choosing to nullify the law, so even the strictest oath would not be violated by a jury rendering an independent verdict. One of the earliest examples of a juror's oath specified in American law comes from the State of Connecticut and dates back to 1823:

> [G]entlemen of the jury, look on the prisoner, you that are sworn, and hearken to his cause. AB stands indicted or informed against by the name of AB, (then reading the indictment he proceeds.) Upon this indictment or information he has been arraigned, and upon this arraignment he has pleaded not guilty and for his trial (in capital cases,) has put himself on God and his country, (and in other cases) on his country, which country you are, so that your charge is to enquire whether the prisoner is guilty of the crime, whereof he stands indicted, or informed against: if you find him guilty, you will say so, and say no more: if you find him not guilty, you will say so, and say no more. Now please to attend to your evidence.[21]

---

18. JOHN D. LAWSON, LL.D., ED., AMERICAN STATE TRIALS: A COLLECTION OF THE IMPORTANT AND INTERESTING CRIMINAL TRIALS WHICH HAVE TAKEN PLACE IN THE UNITED STATES, FROM THE BEGINNING OF OUR GOVERNMENT TO THE PRESENT DAYS (WITH NOTES AND ANNOTATIONS) (1915).

19. Chapter XXXII, An Act concerning Juries, ACTS OF ASSEMBLY OF VIRGINIA (1705).

20. 3 U.S. (3 Dall.) 1 (1794).

21. ZEPHANIAH SWIFT, LL.D., C.A.S., DIGEST OF THE LAWS OF THE STATE OF CONNECTICUT, 404 (1823).

In contrast, the Illinois statutes specified an oath for grand jury foremen, but only stated that trial jurors "shall be sworn by the justice to try the case according to the evidence."[22]

Following *United States v. Battiste*[23] and its progeny, the influence of the jury began to be devalued in American courts, and the power of the judge correspondingly increased. Many American jurisdictions began to demand more and more restrictive oaths of their jurors. By the second half of the nineteenth century, Kentucky jurors in Matthews F. Ward's trial for murder were given a combination of instructions and oath at the beginning of the trial, as follows:

> JUDGE KINCHELOE. Gentlemen: The defendant in this case has been arraigned and has entered a plea of Not Guilty, throwing himself upon God and his country for trial. You are to try him, according to your oaths, upon this indictment. If you find him Guilty, you will say so; if Not Guilty, you will thus return him to the Court. In case the killing shall be proved to have been done under the influence of excitement and passion, you may find him guilty of manslaughter, under this indictment, and will do so. Should it appear that the killing was done in self-defense, it was not an act of voluntary manslaughter, and you will find him Not Guilty.[24]

This combining of jurors oaths and instructions was probably never routine practice. It is not clear from the reports whether the jurors had already been given a separate oath or not. However, it is interesting to note that in this cause, the judge not only instructed the jurors that "[i]n case the killing shall be proved to have been done under the influence of excitement and passion, you may find him guilty of manslaughter," but more forcefully that the jurors "will do so." Kentucky, however, had begun officially limiting the powers of jurors twenty four years earlier, in the case of *Montee v. Commonwealth*,[25] so it may not be surprising that Kentucky courts should have required jurors to swear to follow so controlling a set of instructions.

New York jurors were apparently given an oath derived from common law, and not an oath formally prescribed by statute. In 1873, the New York Court of Appeals stated that a juror was required to "declare on oath that he verily believe that he can render an impartial verdict accord-

---

22. REVISED CODE OF ILLINOIS, An Act Concerning Justices of the Peace and Constables, § 21 (1843).

23. 24 F.Cas. 1042 (D. Massachusetts 1835).

24. The Trial of Matthews F. Ward for the Murder of William H. G. Butler, Elizabethtown, Kentucky, 3 AMERICAN STATE TRIALS, 71, 75 (1854).

25. 26 Ky. (3 J.J. Marshall) 132 (1830).

ing to the evidence submitted to the jury...the end sought by the common law was to secure a panel that would impartially hear the evidence and render a verdict thereupon uninfluenced by any extraneous consideration whatsoever."[26] Whereas this oath did not require jurors to follow the directions of the court, it did forbid them from being influenced by any "extraneous consideration." Whether this was intended to forbid the juror from considering questions of justice is simply not clear.

Juror's oaths remained both lax and vague in the years between Justice Story's opinion in *Battiste* and that of the United States Supreme Court's in *Sparf et al. v. United States*.[27] Even as the twentieth century began, jurors were still not given oaths obliging them to follow the directions of the court. In 1910, the Georgia legislature merely required criminal trial jurors to swear to "well and truly try the issue formed upon this bill of indictment, between the State of Georgia and A.B., who is charged (herein state the crime or offense) and a true verdict give, according to evidence. So help you God."[28] Whether a "true verdict...according to evidence" would require the juror to obediently follow the directions of the court is a matter of interpretation, which Georgians apparently thought was best left between the juror and his own conscience.

In 1935, the Pennsylvania Supreme Court reversed the conviction of one defendant in a multi-defendant case when the record failed to show that the jury had been duly sworn with responsibility for that defendant. Although the Court held that "[a] defendant cannot and should not be permitted to waive the swearing of the jury. The swearing of the jury is not a mere formality... This omission, affirmatively shown as a fact of record, is so vital to trial by jury that further discussion is unnecessary,"[29] it never specified what sort of oath would have satisfied them, or what a juror's oath had to contain in order to be valid. They rhetorically asked "[w]hat proceedings are more vital in a criminal case than the swearing of the jury to try the cause?...Without destroying the safeguards of trial by jury as known to the common law, we cannot presume (that the jury was properly sworn)."[30] Although the Pennsylvania Supreme Court recognized the importance of the juror's oath, their treatment of the substance or purpose of the oath was sparse indeed.

---

26. Stokes v. The People, reported in Patrick H. Cowen, 1 REPORTS OF CRIMINAL CASES DECIDED IN THE APPELLATE COURTS OF THE STATE OF NEW YORK AND OF OTHER STATES, AND IN THE SUPREME COURT OF THE UNITED STATES, WITH NOTES, 557, 561 (1873).

27. 156 U.S. 51 (1895).

28. CODE OF THE STATE OF GEORGIA § 1005 (1910).

29. Commonwealth v. Robinson et al. (Pent, Appellant), 317 Pa. 321, 326-327 (1935).

30. *Id.* at 327.

What's A Juror To Do?

It is almost impossible to tell what sort of obligation the modern juror's oath is expected to place upon a juror, both because the oath itself is so vague, and because it is exceedingly rare (if not entirely unknown) for a case involving jurors' oaths to be litigated. It is relatively difficult to say whether a juror choosing to render an independent verdict would give a prosecutor any grounds on which to proceed at all, even if there was sufficient evidence on which to convict, and the prosecution had the temerity to take such a case before a second jury. As a general rule, the privacy of juror deliberations makes it impossible to prove when a juror has chosen to nullify, although (as the cases below will illustrate) there have been rare exceptions. Only recently have any cases arisen where an attempt has been made to prosecute jurors, and those cases have not involved accusations that the juror violated his or her oath.

Probably the leading case involving the prosecution of a juror is *United States v. Clark*.[31] The juror's oath was not the subject of the *Clark* case. Instead, *Clark* involved a prosecution for criminal contempt, based upon the defendant, Genevieve Clark, concealing her previous working relationship with the accused, a William B. Foshay, during the *voir dire* stage of Foshay's trial for felony mail fraud.

Genevieve Clark had previously been employed as a stenographer by Foshay's firm. After she left that position, she worked as a cashier at the bank where Foshay kept his accounts, and where her husband was the President. Her husband no longer worked for that bank, but he and Foshay had maintained a personal relationship the Court described as "cordial."[32] While there was no evidence introduced at Clark's trial that she had ever met Foshay personally, the Court believed it was "next to impossible that her husband, who was with her in the courtroom, had refrained from telling her of his own friendship for one of the prisoners at the bar."[33]

Clark assured the trial court, during *voir dire*, that she could remain free from bias. She was asked about her past employment and told the trial court about every job she had held in the past, leaving out only her experience working for Foshay's firm. She also failed to mention her husband's friendship with Foshay, or that he was a customer of the bank where she had worked and where her husband had served as President. During jury deliberations, she refused to attempt to resolve her differences with other jurors (at times going so far as to put her hands over her ears), and she admitted to other jurors that she based her decision in significant

---

31. 289 U.S. 1 (1933).
32. *Id.* at 7-8.
33. *Id.* at 8.

part on information she received from her husband, outside of the court-room. At the end of deliberations, hers was the sole vote to acquit Foshay.[34]

The Supreme Court held that Clark had willfully and deliberately concealed information from the trial court when she failed to tell them about her employment with Foshay's firm. They further held that she had made a "positive misstatement" — lied — when she claimed her mind was free from bias.[35] The Supreme Court affirmed her conviction for contempt on the grounds that Clark had obstructed the course of justice by concealing her biases and past employment in order to gain a seat in the jury box.

The Court also held that, although as a general rule jury deliberations are confidential because "[f]reedom of debate might be stifled and independence of thought checked if jurors were made to feel that their arguments and ballots were to be freely published to the world,"[36] jury deliberations are no longer privileged "where the relation giving birth to [jury service] has been fraudulently begun or fraudulently continued."[37] The Court maintained that the privilege did not exist where the government could establish a "prima facie case sufficient to satisfy the judge"[38] that a juror had obtained her seat through some form of concealment or misconduct. The Court claimed that disallowing this corroborative evidence would be "too high a price to pay for the assurance to a juror of serenity of mind."[39] Clark was punished not for her verdict, said the Court, but for failing to forthrightly answer questions during *voir dire*, when her verdict had evidently been decided prior to trial.

There are strong parallels between the *Clark* case and the more recent Colorado case of Laura Kriho, a 33 year-old research assistant who was convicted in a Colorado County Court on contempt of court charges in 1997, for failing to volunteer information during *voir dire*.[40] Kriho was the last juror seated in the trial of *Colorado v. Michelle Brannon*[41] on May 13, 1996. Brannon was charged with possession of methamphetamines. During *voir dire*, Kriho was asked only a few somewhat cursory questions, to which she gave appropriately cursory responses. The only ques-

---

34. *Id.* at 9.
35. *Id.* at 10.
36. *Id.* at 13.
37. *Id.* at 13-14.
38. *Id.* at 14
39. *Id.*
40. Colorado v. Kriho, Case No. 96-CR-91 Division 1, Gilpin County, Colorado, Judge Harry E. Nieto, Presiding. (February 10, 1997).
41. GILPIN COUNTY COLORADO DISTRICT COURT CASE NO. 95-CR-74.

tion that Kriho was accused of failing to answer forthrightly was whether she cared to give a different answer to any of the over 300 questions that had already been asked of other venire-members. She said "No."

Of course, nobody really claims that Kriho did wish to give a different answer to any of the questions. What the prosecution claims is that Kriho would have had different answers, if she had been asked those questions. One thing that seems implicit in the prosecution of Kriho was that she did not care to give a different answer to any of the questions previously asked of the other venire-members. The prosecutions claims were thus not so much that Kriho had answered any questions dishonestly, merely that she had answered them artfully, in order not to give the court any more information than necessary to answer the questions asked of her.

Kriho failed to divulge that twelve years earlier she had been arrested on a felony drug charge. She had pled guilty to that charge and been given "deferred adjudication" probation. She had never been adjudicated guilty of that, or any other, offense. "Deferred adjudication" is a probationary scheme whereby a defendant pleads guilty and is put on a stringent term of probation while the judge "defers" making a judgment of guilt. If the defendant completes their probation without any significant violations, the case is dismissed and the defendant leaves court with a clean record. Laura Kriho completed her probation satisfactorily, and the charges against her had been dismissed.

Kriho's drug charge had occurred more than a decade before. The case had been dismissed. She had never been convicted. Kriho had been led to believe by her previous lawyer and by the nature of the earlier proceedings that her record was clean. When, during *voir dire*, she was asked if she had ever been convicted of a felony or a drug charge, Kriho answered that she had not been — which was the truth. She did, however, fail to volunteer the details of the charges that had been held against her, twelve years earlier. It was for failing to volunteer this information, as well as failing to initiate a discussion about her own opinions concerning the drug laws, that Kriho was charged with contempt of court, because the court felt that she either knew or should have known that this was information the prosecution and the court would have wanted.

Laura Kriho wanted a jury trial. She and her attorney Paul Grant wanted to put the issues involved in her case to the "conscience of the community" for judgment. However, in Colorado, a criminal defendant is only entitled to a jury trial if the prosecution seeks a punishment of six months or more. District Attorney Jim Stanley informed the court that he would not seek a punishment exceeding six months, so Laura Kriho's case was scheduled for a trial before the judge. Defense motions requesting a jury trial had been denied. In his verdict, Judge Harry E. Nieto found Kriho guilty of having "...misled the trial court and the trial attorneys about important matters during the jury selection process with the intent to remain on the jury and obstruct the legal process."

Unlike the case against Genevieve Clark, Laura Kriho had forthrightly answered all the questions that were actually asked of her. Laura Kriho was convicted on the basis of her failure to volunteer information to the court, and given a $1200 fine. While Clark was found in contempt for dishonestly answering questions, Kriho was found in contempt for failing to volunteer answers to questions that were never asked. Judge Nieto's findings of facts state the issue from his perspective:

> Ms. Kriho testified that she was able to hear all of the court proceedings from her place in the courtroom. Because it was stated clearly by the judge during his voir dire, and the other jurors who testified *clearly understood the need to volunteer information*, and because the question was asked repeatedly to all replacement jurors, this Court finds that Ms. Kriho was aware of the prior questioning and she was given an *opportunity to comment* on the topics discussed. (emphasis added).

Giving someone an "opportunity to comment" is hardly the same as mandating that they do so. Yet failing to choose to comment or volunteer information when given the opportunity to do so is precisely the strange new crime for which Laura Kriho was convicted.

Tellingly, Judge Nieto did not argue that Laura Kriho could or should be punished for "violating her oath," even if her vote on the *Brannon* case was based on jury nullification. He clearly stated that "[t]his case is not now and has never been about how Ms. Kriho voted during jury deliberations... No juror can be punished for their vote in deciding a case. Even if the juror's vote amounts to jury nullification and flies in the face of the evidence and the law, they cannot be punished in any way."

One cannot help but wonder whether Laura Kriho would have been convicted, however, if she had been an ardent advocate of the War on Drugs, had failed to say so during *voir dire*, and had been the only juror on the panel voting for conviction. If the prosecution against her was not aimed at vengefully persecuting her for her verdict, it should make no difference which way she voted. It appears that failing to divulge a strong opinion is only a criminal action when that opinion works against the state. The jurors who voted for Brannon's conviction were not investigated, prosecuted, or otherwise pursued, although during their testimony at Laura Kriho's trial several of them admitted to not volunteering equally relevant information during *voir dire*.

No juror in Gilpin County has ever been prosecuted after voting to convict. Just as the Court of the Star Chamber never prosecuted a juror who voted to convict, Gilpin County District Attorney Jim Stanley apparently only prosecutes jurors who vote to acquit.

Even more intriguing is the fact that shortly before the Kriho case came to trial another Gilpin County Court Judge, Frederic B. Rogers, published an article in the *Judges' Journal*, a publication of the American Bar Association Judicial Section, decrying jury nullification and recommending precisely the same sorts of prosecutions as occurred against Laura Kriho.[42] Rogers' article referred to jury independence advocates as "having their antecedents in the radical anti-semitic right" and recommends that judges use increasingly restrictive methods to eliminate anyone from the jury pool who is familiar with the jury nullification doctrine. Finally, he advocates prosecuting independently minded jurors for perjury or contempt of court, seemingly anticipating the prosecution against Kriho. Rogers' article was widely distributed within the Gilpin County Courts, and it is reported that Jim Stanley, Kriho's politically ambitious prosecutor, was given a draft of the article before he filed the charges against Kriho.

The real weakness of Rogers' article is his lack of scholarship on the very subject about which he writes. He misquotes Lord Willes from the case of *Rex v. Shipley*,[43] claims without any citation that juries were the dominant source of racial injustices during the lynching and civil rights eras, and makes several false statements about the Fully Informed Jury Association and other jury independence advocates. It is very likely that this article was the mold into which Laura Kriho's case was forced to fit, and that Rogers' ideas were in effect the 'game plan' for Kriho's prosecution. A rebuttal written by this author, and published in a subsequent issue of the *Judges' Journal*,[44] went unanswered by Judge Rogers.

As this is written the Kriho case is on appeal. It would be bizarre indeed to require jurors to volunteer information, when we do not require the same of witnesses testifying at trial. Witnesses are never required to volunteer information, and attorneys understand that it is their job to pose questions in such a way as to obtain the information they seek. Punishing a juror who fails to volunteer information during v*oir dire* is vindictive, harassing the juror for the failure of the prosecutor or the judge to do a competent job at questioning prospective jurors. If the question is not asked,

---

42. Frederic B. Rogers, *The Jury in Revolt? A "Heads Up" on the Fully Informed Jury Association: Coming Soon to a Courthouse in Your Area*, JUDGES' JRL. 10-12 (Summer, 1996).

43. How. St.Tr. 21:847 (1785). Rogers claimed that Willes wrote "I admit the jury have the power of finding a verdict against the law, and so they have of finding against the evidence, but I deny that they have the right to do so." In fact, Willes wrote precisely the opposite: "I believe no man will venture to say [jurors] have not the power, but I mean expressly to say they have the right (to judge the law)."

44. Letters and Comments, Clay S. Conrad, *Not Fully Informed about FIJA*, JUDGES' JRL. 40-42 (Winter 1997).

it is grossly inequitable to demand that it be answered upon punishment of contempt.

Attorneys are often reticent to ask sufficiently probing questions of venire-members during *voir dire*, because they are concerned with creating an adversarial relationship between themselves and the jurors who will eventually be trying their case. Too much pressure put on examining one venire-member may end up antagonizing the entire panel. It is easy to understand why an advocate wants to use *voir dire* to ingratiate himself with the jury, and leave it to the judge to ask the hard questions necessary to weed out any potential nullifiers.

That given, it remains unfair to require a venire-member to volunteer information which he or she may be uncomfortable discussing or may not believe is relevant, merely in order to increase the comfort level of the trial attorneys. How many people would care to blurt out the details of a 12-year old dismissed drug charge in front of a room full of strangers? Must a person receiving a summons for jury service first consult a lawyer to ascertain exactly which personal details of their life might be deemed essential to divulge? Should courts appoint lawyers to indigent venire-members to help prepare them for the demands that may be made of them during *voir dire*?

The entire Kriho case was avoidable had the prosecutor simply asked the right questions during *voir dire*. Prosecutors who fail to do their job properly in court should not be set free to bedevil jurors who do their job as they see fit in the jury room. Jim Stanley had his chance to ask Kriho whatever questions he chose to put to her. Unless he is prepared to show that Kriho deliberately gave a materially false answer to a *voir dire* question that was actually asked of her, the only honorable thing for the Colorado courts to do would be to give Kriho an apology, and thank her for her service as a juror in the case of *Michelle Brannon v. Colorado*.

Regent Law School Professor James Joseph Duane has argued that a juror's oath places no real obligation on a juror, that it is merely a hortatory ritual. Referring to arguments that nullifying jurors violate their oaths as "threadbare," Duane claims that "this ominous-sounding charge has no logical substance, although it naturally carries much emotional appeal."[45] Duane points out that most juror's oaths do not require jurors to follow the instructions given to them by the bench. Instead, they merely swear that they "will well and truly try and a true deliverance render according to the evidence, so help [me] God." Such an oath would not preclude a juror from voting to acquit if the juror found that the defendant was

45. Duane, *supra* note 3, 11.

"morally blameless." Duane goes on to question whether a juror could "well and truly try" a case and render "true deliverance," "if they had to disregard their sense of justice to convict."[46]

> If a jury refuses to convict a man because of overwhelming feelings of mercy or justice, they are not returning a "false" verdict. A verdict of "not guilty" based on a jury's notions of justice is not affirmatively declaring that he is innocent. (The same is true of an acquittal based on their conclusions that he has only been shown to be probably guilty, but not beyond a reasonable doubt). The general "not guilty" verdict is merely a shorthand way of allowing the jury to express, for reasons they need not explain, "we do not choose to condemn the accused by pronouncing him guilty."[47]

Most importantly to Duane, though, is the fact that a juror's nullification powers are constitutionally protected. Jurors' oaths, being either statutory or created by judges, cannot act to limit a power which is grounded in the Constitution:

> A jury's latitude is deliberately protected by the Constitution. Neither the tradition nor the wording of the oath administered to the jurors, on the other hand, is so dictated. In federal court it is not even prescribed by statute. It is simply an old tradition judges have made up. If the wording of the oath poses some conflict with the jury's constitutional prerogative to nullify, it is clear which one must yield the right of way. Courts simply have no business (much less lawful authority) asking jurors to swear to anything that would violate the Constitution or the jury's deeply held convictions about justice.[48]

While the juror's oath should certainly act to constrain a responsible juror and remind them of the gravity of a decision to nullify the law, the oath by itself does not and should not act to prohibit a juror from delivering an independent verdict, based on the facts, the law and his or her own conscientious judgment. An oath to "well and truly try" the defendant, as was sworn to by the William Penn jury and which is still echoed in the oaths given to jurors in many states, does not even discourage the juror from well and truly deciding that the defendant is not guilty "in the teeth of both law and facts," according to the conscientious judgment of the juror.

The juror's oath may have more impact if jurors in criminal trials were required to answer specific issues, instead of delivering a general verdict of law and fact. However, the Constitution protects the power of juries to nullify by forbidding that criminal trial juries be required to return a special verdict except in unusual circumstances.[49] Wherever a jury honestly

---

46. *Id.* at 12.
47. *Id.*
48. *Id.* at 12.

believes that the law is being misapplied, or that the law itself is unjust, the jury in many jurisdictions may well have the option to acquit within their oath. Guilt is, at least in a significant part, a moral question. And where jurors do not have that latitude under the particular oath they have taken, their discretion still remains protected under several different clauses of the United States Constitution.

It is doubtful that any attempt to punish independent jurors for violating their oaths would be constitutional, especially if the jurors, when they took their oaths, had not already decided to nullify. Punishing a juror for violating his oath would arguably interfere with the freedom of speech a juror requires in the jury room, if the juror is to be able to properly perform the job—and thus, any threats of prosecution against jurors would arguably deprive the defendant of his Sixth Amendment right to trial by jury. It is not difficult to imagine that the willingness of jurors to acquit may be significantly dampened, in a jurisdiction where jurors are regularly prosecuted by the government for verdicts displeasing to the state. Trial by jury cannot work if jurors are allowed to be menaced or intimidated by the government. A trial by a coerced jury is not a trial by jury in any meaningful sense of the term, and is certainly not the trial by jury contemplated by the Founding Fathers of this country.

Even courts hostile to the doctrine of jury independence have begun to recognize that investigating or prosecuting jurors could coerce them into convicting in cases where no nullification issues are involved, because the jurors may fear being persecuted if their verdict is not acceptable to the state. A jury cannot operate if the court or the government is allowed to pry into its deliberations or intrude itself into its processes. This is one of the reasons the Second Circuit in *United States v. Thomas et al.*[50] set such a high standard before a sitting juror bent on nullification could be excused. The *Thomas* case involved a single black juror sitting on the prolonged trial of a group of black defendants accused of federal narcotics charges in New York. "Juror No. 5," as he was referred to in the opinion, made himself obnoxious to his fellow jurors, "distracting them in court by squeaking his shoe against the floor, rustling cough drop wrappers in his pocket,

---

49. Special interrogatories are required in prosecutions for treason, as the Constitution requires that the jury find an overt act. *See* Kawakita v. United States, 343 U.S. 717 (1952). *See also* United States v. Desmond, 670 F.2d 414 (3rd Cir. 1982)(special interrogatories permitted where they do not lead jury to its conclusion by a progression of questions each of which require an answer unfavorable to the defendant, and where the defendant did not object to their use at trial); United States v. Spock, 416 F.2d 165, 180-183 (1st Cir. 1969)(special interrogatories not permitted that may catchize a jury as to the reasons for its verdict).

50. *Supra* note 2.

and showing agreement with points made by defense counsel by slapping his leg and, occasionally during the defense summations, saying "[y]eah, yes."[51]

The trial court was presided over by Judge Thomas J. McAvoy, Chief Judge of the Northern District of New York. After receiving complaints about Juror No. 5 from other members of the jury, Chief Judge McAvoy held *in camera*[52] interviews (over defense objections) with each juror, on the record, and only refrained from dismissing Juror No. 5 and seating an alternate juror because of the unanimous objections of defense counsel. McAvoy was concerned that "[j]uror No. 5's behavior, especially in light of the court's own inquiries of the jurors, might place him in an adversarial relationship with his fellow jurors as they began deliberations."[53] On balance, however, Chief Judge McAvoy was convinced that removing the sole black juror from the trial of several black defendants would be misinterpreted as having been motivated by race, and that any such actions may be reversible error, when the juror had not been disqualified as a matter of law.

However, by the end of the third day of deliberations, at least three jurors again complained of difficulties in dealing with Juror No. 5. One juror claimed that No. 5 was "predisposed." Chief Judge McAvoy again held *in camera* off the record conversations with each juror, during which several jurors complained about Juror No. 5, while a few others claimed that Juror No. 5 was being treated unfairly:

> Several mentioned the disruptive effect he was having on the deliberations. One juror described him "hollering" at fellow jurors, another said he had called his fellow jurors racists, and two jurors told the court that Juror No. 5 had come close to striking a fellow juror. The judge was also informed by a juror that, at one point, Juror No. 5 pretended to vomit in the bathroom while other jurors were eating lunch outside the bathroom door. The jurors, however, were not unanimous in identifying Juror No. 5 as a source of disruption in the jury room. One juror informed the judge that friction among the jurors had been "pretty well ironed out," and another indicated that the other jurors were in fact "picking on" Juror No. 5.[54]

Although several jurors claimed Juror No. 5 was refusing to convict out of racial solidarity or sympathy, this sentiment was not unanimous. Judge Cabranes noted that:

> several jurors recounted Juror No. 5 couching his position in terms of the evidence—one juror indicated specifically that Juror No. 5 was discussing

---

51. *Id.* at 609-610.
52. Literally, "in chambers," meaning private, not divulged to the public.
53. *Thomas, supra* note 2, 610-611.
54. *Id.* at 611.

the evidence, and four recalled him saying that the evidence, including the prosecution's witness testimony, was insufficient or unreliable. As for Juror No. 5, he said nothing in his interview with the court to suggest that he was not making a good faith effort to apply the law as instructed to the facts of the case. On the contrary, he informed the court that he needed "substantive evidence" establishing guilt "beyond a reasonable doubt" in order to convict.[55]

Following this second set of interviews, the trial judge removed Juror No. 5, over strenuous objection from the various defense counsel, finding that Juror No. 5 "was refusing to convict because of preconceived, fixed, cultural, economic, [or] social...reasons that are totally improper and impermissible."[56]

The Second Circuit Court of Appeals held, in an opinion written by Judge Jose A. Cabranes, that it was appropriate to remove a juror from deliberations if it was clear that the juror was determined to render a nullification verdict. The Second Circuit

> categorically reject[ed] the idea that, in a society committed to the rule of law, jury nullification is desirable or that courts may permit it to occur when it is within their authority to prevent. Accordingly,... a juror who intends to nullify the applicable law is no less subject to dismissal than is a juror who disregards the court's instructions due to an event or relationship that renders him biased or otherwise unable to render a fair and impartial verdict.[57]

In spite of this ruling, Judge Cabranes — in twists of logic reminiscent of *Dougherty* and *Moylan* — praised some juries which had nullified, and recognized the power of juries to do so:

> We recognize, too, that nullification may at times manifest itself as a form of civil disobedience that some may regard as tolerable. The case of John Peter Zenger, the publisher of the New York Weekly Journal acquitted of criminal libel in 1735, and the nineteenth-century acquittals in prosecutions under the fugitive slave laws, are perhaps our country's most renowned examples of "benevolent" nullification.[58]

Judge Cabranes finally compromised, it seems, between an all-out attack on jury nullification on the one hand, and explicit approval on the other. While he argued that "it would be a dereliction of duty for a judge to remain indifferent to reports that a juror is intent on violating his oath,"

---

55. *Id.*
56. *Id.* at 612.
57. *Id.* at 614.
58. *Id.*

his opinion also made it extremely—some may say, insuperably—difficult for a litigant to prove that a juror was so intent on nullifying. Judge Cabranes did not find that Juror No. 5 was intent on nullifying, so he found that the removal of Juror No. 5 from the panel was erroneous. Accordingly, the case was remanded back to Chief Judge McAvoy's court for a new trial.

Because the Second Circuit believed that "secrecy of deliberations is the cornerstone of the modern Anglo-American jury system"[59] they held that a "court must not, however, remove a juror for an alleged refusal to follow the law as instructed unless the record leaves *no doubt* that the juror was in fact engaged in deliberate misconduct—that he was not simply unpersuaded by the Government's case against the defendants."[60] (emphasis added). This is a remarkably high standard to meet before a juror may conceivably be disqualified—higher, even, than the "beyond a reasonable doubt" standard used in criminal trials, which is often claimed to be the highest standard known to law. In balancing out the risks of allowing trial courts to scrutinize jurors closely in order to prevent nullification, and of allowing nullifying jurors to proceed unchecked, the Second Circuit came down on the side of protecting the sanctity of deliberations and allowing jurors to nullify, where there was any question whatsoever about why a given juror was voting for acquittal. Only where there was no question at all would the trial judge be allowed to remove the independently minded juror from the panel.

The Context Of The Juror's Oath

It is not clear that a juror is violating his oath when he chooses to nullify. The variety of juror's oaths, and the vagueness of some of them, probably indicate that the oaths of most jurors are not violated by the delivery an independent verdict. However, even if we assume that a juror is violating his oath, then we should ask what could justify such an action on the part of a juror. Can a juror ever be justified in violating his oath?

The juror's oath is taken in a particular context, right after the jury is selected from the venire panel, but before the members take on their role as trial jurors. At this point the jury has heard some information about the case during the *voir dire*, but they have not yet heard the court's instructions on the law, nor have they heard the details of what the defendant, the police, or any other people have done. They are not swearing as to

---

59. *Id.* at 618.
60. *Id.* at 625.

what they themselves have done, but only as to what they anticipate they will do, based on the information that is available to them at that time.

When a juror takes his oath, he must base his pledge on certain assumptions, including a presumption that the law will be fair, and fairly applied. It seems reasonable to claim that a citizen, conscripted into serving his government, should be entitled to make the presumption that his government would not require him to particpate in an injustice. By asking the juror to make certain promises through his oath, the government should be willing to promise, at a minimum, that it will not put the juror in a position where his oath can not be conscientiously fulfilled. If the premises upon which a juror agrees to swear to his oath are proven to be false, then the juror should be morally and legally absolved of any responsibility under the oath. If the law is not fair, or if it has been unfairly applied, then the government has failed to live up to its end of the bargain.

Certainly, a juror could not have been committing perjury when he or she took the oath, if he or she intended on following the law at the time the oath was taken. If the reasons for violating the oath did not become known to the juror until after the oath was taken and the trial was under way, then the juror would have the right to be released from their oath. A juror in that situation would have two choices: either tell the judge and be excused from further jury service, or to refuse to convict and either hang the jury, or (if eleven other jurors were in agreement) nullify the law by delivering an independent verdict.

While the choice may seem to make a good deal of difference, in practice the end result is likely to be the same, if only one juror in the panel believes the law is unjust or unjustly applied: a hung jury, potentially followed by a retrial. In federal court, and in some states, a verdict may be returned by eleven jurors if one juror becomes disqualified during deliberations.[61] In at least one federal circuit, if a juror's decision to nullify becomes known to the court, that is considered adequate cause to disqualify that juror.[62] If two or more jurors agree that the law should not be applied, then even in those jurisdictions that allow deliberations to con-

---

61. FEDERAL RULE OF CRIMINAL PROCEDURE 23(b) provides:

RULE 23. Trial by Jury or by the Court

(b)   JURY OF LESS THAN 12. Juries shall be of 12 but at any time before verdict the parties may stipulate in writing with the approval of the court that the jury shall consist of any number less than 12 or that a valid verdict may be returned by a jury of less than 12 should the court find it necessary to excuse one or more jurors for any just cause after trial commences. Even absent such stipulation, if the court finds it necessary to excuse a juror for just cause after the jury has retired to consider its verdict, in the discretion of the court a valid verdict may be returned by the 11 remaining jurors.

62. *Thomas, supra* note 2.

tinue with only eleven jurors there will be a hung jury, regardless of whether they tell the judge of their decision or return a nullification vote.[63] Of course, if there are a series of such hung juries the law may well be too divisive to ever be consistently enforced.

On the other hand, if the injustice is so palpable that the entire jury unanimously agrees the law should not be applied, then the jurors may tell the judge and cause a mistrial, or they may acquit the accused and the prosecution will be powerless to retry the defendant. Which path the jurors choose may depend on how intensely they perceive the obligations outside the oath that touch upon them. Perhaps more important will be whether they are aware of their autonomy, or whether they feel that they have no choice but to follow the directions of the court.

Although courts are apparently very concerned with making sure jurors meet their obligations, it is very rare that courts show much concern for the rights of jurors. Jurors are probably treated more shabbily than any other participants in the criminal justice system—they are embarrassingly underpaid, often made to work hours that not one of them would choose, and given no say at all as to their working hours or conditions. They are simply told to sit down, shut up, and take orders. The only time that jurors are allowed to speak in court is during *voir dire*, when their most intimate secrets are made part of a public record. Perhaps the one right most important to jurors is the one most often violated: their right to privacy.

In 1929, a case reached the United States Supreme Court where the defendants had employed a team of fifteen private detectives to "shadow" the members of a trial jury, following them day and night, looking into their personal finances, and writing daily reports to be used to attempt to discredit one or more jurors and cause a mistrial.[64] The case went to the Supreme Court for a determination of whether the behavior of the defendants could be considered contempt of court, where no juror was aware of being followed, and no contact was made between any of the agents and any juror. The Court ruled that the defendant's behavior could constitute contempt, because the risk of corrupting the proceedings was so great. Moreover, the Court reported that:

> If those fit for juries understand that they may be freely subjected to treatment like that here disclosed, they will either shun the burdens of the service or perform it with disquiet and disgust. Trial by capable juries, in important cases, probably would become an impossibility.[65]

---

63. The number of persons refusing to convict would necessarily have to be increased in those states allowing for non-unanimous verdicts.

64. Sinclair v. United States, 279 U.S. 749 (1929).

65. *Id.* at 765.

The jurors involved in the above case had already been seated in the jury box. Venire-members, however, are often subjected to treatment very similar to that disclosed in the above case, if not worse. Jury consultants and detectives have been hired to discover as much as possible about the people who could potentially find themselves on the jury, analyzing their handwriting, their body language and the demographics of their neighborhoods.[66] According to Professor Jeffrey Abramson:

> Perhaps most alarming of all is the simple "community network," or "background check," approach. In cases where the names and addresses of potential jurors are known, some lawyers have employed field investigators or private detectives (the federal government has used the FBI) to ride through the neighborhoods of prospective jurors, interviewing acquaintances about marital problems, drinking problems, and treatment of minorities.[67]

The First Amendment protects the right of people to snoop into the backgrounds of venire-members, to some extent. But in this age of internet databases, the power to snoop into the most intimate details of the lives of potential jurors is chilling, and possibly unstoppable. The judge and the opposing side will not know if the defendant has hired a private detective to find out every venire-members' shoe size, sexual preference and social security number. Worse yet, if the opposing side has no way to know whether this has been done, it creates a prisoner's dilemma. The defense must run this sort of background check, because the prosecution very likely has. Of course, the prosecution will have to run its check for the same reason. Everybody loses a little, because nobody wants to risk losing a lot.

Jurors expect that courts will respect and protect their privacy, at least to a reasonable extent. Many people would very likely refuse to show up for jury duty if they realized their entire lives would be put on display to help decide a battle they have no interest in. Americans take their privacy rights very seriously. At least one federal appellate court has commented that "prospective jurors will be less than willing to serve if they know that inquiry into their essentially private concerns will be pressed."[68]

Very rarely do jurors stand up to protect their privacy, although courts are beginning to recognize that jury questioning can simply go too far. In

---

66. Jeffrey Abramson, We, The Jury: The Jury System and the Ideal of Democracy, 149-154 (1994).

67. Id.

68. United States v. Barnes, 604 F.2d 121, 140 (2nd Cir. 1979).

1994, a potential juror for a Denton, Texas capital murder trial marked about a dozen of over one hundred questions on a juror questionnaire "n/a" (not applicable). The inquiries covered her income, religious and political affiliations, magazine and newspaper subscriptions, medications, television viewing habits and other personal facts. When she asserted her right to privacy and refused to answer these same questions during *voir dire*, the trial judge found her in contempt of court, and sentenced her to three days in jail and a two hundred dollar fine.[69] After the Texas courts affirmed her conviction and sentence, she stubbornly took the case to the federal district court on a writ of *habeas corpus,* in the case of *Brandborg v. Lucas.*[70] The venire-member's name was Dianna Brandborg.

The *Brandborg* court recognized that jurors do have certain privacy rights, but held that they had to be balanced against the need of the litigants to an effective *voir dire*. Although the court reversed Brandborg's conviction, it did not do so because jurors had a *per se* right to privacy. Instead, it reversed her conviction because the trial court failed to inquire into whether the questions Brandborg refused to answer were either relevant or necessary to the proceedings. The court held that it is the duty of trial judges to balance the privacy rights of the jurors against the needs of the parties to adequate *voir dire*, so that they may intelligently exercise their peremptory challenges.

This left open the question of when a juror does have to answer a question, either in *voir dire* or in a juror questionnaire. In the court's opinion, "if the issue is relevant to determining the bias or prejudice of a prospective juror then the question is proper."[71] Questions which are not relevant should be rejected by the court if submitted for juror questionnaires. Further, potential jurors should be informed at *voir dire* that they have a right not to answer any questions that they think are overly intrusive until there has been a judical determination that the question is relevant.[72] If the issue is relevant but personal, the individual should be afforded an opportunity to answer the question in a private setting, with only the attorneys and the judge present. Any record of that portion of the *voir dire* should then be sealed by the court, to prevent its later disclosure. According to the court:

> If a trial court determines that a specific question is relevant and after conducting a balancing of the competing interests determines that the prospective juror's privacy rights are outweighed by the other interests, the prospec-

69. Rick Hagen, *Juror's Rights: Is the Enemy Armed?*, 24 VOICE FOR THE DEFENSE 32 (October 1995).

70. 891 F.Supp. 352 (E.D. Tex. 1995).

71. *Id.* at 358. *See also* Aldridge v. United States, 283 U.S. 308, 314 (1931).

72. *Brandborg, supra* note 70, 360.

tive juror cannot refuse to answer the question. However, the court should provide the prospective juror with the least intrusive means to provide the information.[73]

The privacy rights of jurors and the due process rights of criminal defendants will in all likelihood continue to come into occasional and inevitable conflict. The *Brandborg* court should be commended for seriously looking at this problem and for requiring that the interests of litigants and jurors be weighed by trial courts before requiring a juror to answer invasive or prying questions. Many attorneys expressed concerns that *Brandborg* would destroy their right to an effective *voir dire*, but if trial courts properly apply the balancing test that would appear to be a gross overreaction. As Rick Hagen, Dianna Brandborg's attorney, noted, "[a] juror who in good faith invokes a constitutional right might just understand it when your client does."[74]

Other Obligations Jurors Face

It is plain that the oaths given to jurors in court are not the only obligation jurors face. Although the juror's oath is explicit and is constantly referred to, a juror has an equally important—if not overridingly important—fundamental human obligation not to commit or contribute to an injustice. This nation expects jurors to remember this obligation when they step into court.

In not so distant times, this nation has assisted the world community in prosecuting, and even executing, those individuals who put their oaths to their government above their conscientious obligations, as when sitting United States Supreme Court Justice Robert H. Jackson served as chief prosecutor during the Nuremburg war crimes trials. Jurors in America are under the same moral obligation to refuse to be a part of a cruel injustice, and that obligation should be given at least as much weight as a vague and obscure oath which has developed throughout history without a significant amount of serious debate or discussion.

The Milgram studies on obedience to authority, discussed in Chapter Five, showed that Americans may all too easily set their moral responsibilities aside in compliance with the demands of authority figures. Do we want that sort of slave-like, passive response from jurors? Or do we want jurors who are willing to defy authority, if they are conscientiously convinced that what authority is demanding is unconscionable? Even those courts that have decried jury nullification seem to admit that independent juries

---

73. *Id.* at 361.
74. Hagen, *supra* note 69, 33.

are occasionally needed, and that the "pages of history shine on instances of the jury's exercise of its prerogative to disregard uncontradicted evidence and instructions of the judge."[75] Some of the proudest moments in American jurisprudence are due to juries unwilling to commit injustice, and even some of the most stubborn judges have admitted as much.

Courts in America expect jurors to remember these other obligations, and to act in accordance with them in an appropriate case. In fact, even courts that have rejected providing jurors with instructions advising them about their nullification powers anticipate that jurors will nullify, in spite of any oath, if their conscientious obligations become far weightier than their promise to the court. Probably the best explication of this "pressure-release" conception of jury independence was made by Judge Leventhal in *United States v. Dougherty*. Leventhal argued that:

> The jury system has worked out reasonably well overall, providing "play in the joints" that imparts flexibility and avoid undue rigidity. An equilibrium has evolved—an often marvelous balance—with the jury acting as a "safety valve" for exceptional cases, without being a wildcat or runaway institution.[76]

Similarly, Dean Wigmore insisted that trial by jury "supplies that flexibility of legal rules which is essential to justice and popular contentment."[77] That "flexibility" is only obtained, that "safety valve" only releases the pressure, when jurors are free to put conscientious obligations over their oaths.

How much pressure should we maintain? How flexible should the system be? At what point should jurors choose to nullify? Those are all normative questions, impossible to answer with quantitative certainty. Perhaps the question we should really ask is how flexible is the system today? Is it presently too flexible, or not flexible enough? The studies conducted by Professor Irwin Horowitz[78] indicate that jurors would probably come up with verdicts that would be more widely accepted in their communities if jury nullification were explained to them by the court. This may indicate that the safety valve has become far too tightly sealed.

Jurors necessarily have a responsibility to their neighbors and to the community. The "conscience of the community" can scarcely be effective

---

75. United States v. Dougherty, 473 F.2d 1113, 1130 (D.C. Cir. 1972).

76. *Id.* at 1134.

77. John H. Wigmore, *A Program for the Trial of Jury Trial*, 12 J. Am. Jud. Soc. 166, 170 (1929).

78. Irwin A. Horowitz, *Jury Nullification: The Impact of Judicial Instructions, Arguments, and Challenges on Jury Decision Making*, 12 Law & Hum. Behav. 439 (1988); Irwin A. Horowitz, *The Effect of Jury Nullification Instructions on Verdicts and Jury Functioning in Criminal Trials*, 9 Law & Hum. Behav. 25 (1985).

if it is forced to act in a vacuum, completely divorced from the ethical norms and values of that community. If the jurors believe that incarcerating a morally innocent defendant would cause undue hardship to his family, employer or employees, creditors, or others in the community, they may be more inclined to deliver an independent verdict, in hopes that the accused would have learned his lesson by coming so close to being convicted. If the jury, in its role as the "conscience of the community," believes that the accused contributes to the community, they are more likely to turn a blind eye to his minor and victimless transgressions.

Paul Butler, a professor at the George Washington University School of Law, has recognized the responsibility of jurors to their community, although he unfortunately colors his thinking with racial issues that may not be applicable in this context. Butler argues in particular that black jurors should be willing to acquit black defendants found guilty of non-violent, victimless crimes, because in his words:

> My thesis is that, for pragmatic and political reasons, the black community is better off when some nonviolent lawbreakers remain in the community rather than go to prison. The decision as to what kind of conduct by African-Americans ought to be punished is better made by African-Americans themselves, based on the costs and benefits to their community, than by the traditional criminal justice process, which is controlled by white lawmakers and white law enforcers...Why would a black juror vote to let a guilty person go free? Assuming that the juror is a rational actor, she must believe that she and her community are, in some way, better off with the defendant out of prison than in prison. [79]
> Any juror legally may vote for nullification in any case, but, certainly, jurors should not do so without some principled basis. The reason that some historical examples of nullification are viewed approvingly is that most of us now believe that the jurors in those cases did the morally right thing; it would have been unconscionable, for example, to punish those slaves who committed the crime of escaping to the North for their freedom. It is true that nullification later would be used as a means of racial subordination by some Southern jurors, but that does not mean that nullification in the approved cases was wrong. It only means that those Southern jurors erred in their calculus of justice. I distinguish racially based nullification by African-Americans from recent right-wing proposals for jury nullification on the ground that the former is sometimes morally right and the latter is not.[80]

Jurors, white or black, have a responsibility to consider the effects their verdicts will have on the defendant before them and on their communi-

79. Paul Butler, *Racially Based Jury Nullification: Black Power in the Criminal Justice System*, 105 Yale L.J. 677, 679, 690 (1995).

80. *Id.* at 705.

ties. Where Butler has drawn so much ire is in "argu[ing] that the race of a black defendant is sometimes a legally and morally appropriate factor for jurors to consider in reaching a verdict of not guilty or…refusing to vote for conviction."[81] Should white jurors be less willing to nullify in order to acquit a morally innocent defendant—white or black—when they have "some principled basis" to do so? Should black jurors be more willing to convict a white defendant even when there is "some principled basis" for refusing to convict? Is there any ethical principle that can justify bringing race into the calculus at all? It is unfortunate that Butler committed himself to a racial calculus of the role of the jury for which he has been criticized widely on all sides of the political spectrum, and on both sides of the nullification debate.[82]

Butler is absolutely correct in asserting that jurors should consider the effect their verdicts will have on their community, and that before delivering their verdict they should be confident their actions are not causing more harm to the community than the actions of the accused. However, if this rule is a just one, as it appears to be, then should it not more properly be applied even-handedly, regardless of the race of the defendant or the juror? An injustice does not become just if the victim does not look like "us," whatever we may happen to look like. Damage to the community does not become negligible because the damage is felt on the other side of town.

It should be very clear that jurors should take all of their obligations seriously, and the overwhelming majority of jurors clearly do. Responsible jurors should be entitled to approach their oath, and their service, anticipating that the law will be both just and justly administered by the court and the prosecution. Only when those assumptions have been dispelled should jurors begin to consider delivering an independent verdict, and they should be fully aware of the gravity of their decision to do so. However, if jury nullification is the only route to a just and sane verdict,

---

81. *Id.* at 679.

82. Harvard Law professor Randall Kennedy claimed "jury nullification…is immoral and self destructive for black people." Benjamin Weiser, *U.S. Court Orders Judges to Step In when Jurors Balk*, N.Y. TIMES, May 21, 1997 at A1. Santa Clara Law professor Alan Scheflin claimed that Paul Butler (along with Marcia Clark, prosecutor in the O.J. Simpson murder trial) has done a great deal of damage to the concept of jury nullification by seriously misinterpreting the concept and its application. *Randy Johnson Show*, KOPE Radio, Medford Oregon, May 31, 1997. *See also* Brian Graves, *Law or Justice: Some African-Americans say jury nullification only way to correct what they see as disproportionate penalties for crack cocaine convictions*, WATERLOO-CEDAR FALLS COURIER, March 16, 1997 at B1; Claude Lewis, *Jury nullification driven by bitterness*, PHILADELPHIA INQUIRER, June 5, 1997; James J. Kilpatrick, *'Jury nullification' intends to subvert the criminal justice system*, TAMPA BAY GAZZETTE, May 30, 1997; Editorial, *Should Juries be allowed to weigh social injustice?*, SEATTLE POST-INTELLIGENCER, May 1, 1997.

then jurors may be neglecting their other responsibilites if they allow their oaths to dissuade them from that course of conduct. Their oath should serve to remind them of the seriousness of the decision which lies before them, and the importance of making that decision with cool, clear minds, committed to justice, and uncluttered by prejudice, race, or bigotry of any sort.

Chapter Ten

The Lawyer's Challenge

> *It is the conscience of the jury that must*
> *pronounce the prisoner guilty or not guilty.*
> Lord Matthew Hale

Empowering the Jury[1]

Although all criminal trial juries have the power to nullify the law, few jurors enter the courtroom aware of their power, and in most cases jurors never learn of their power during the course of the trial. The lawyer who believes his client would be found "not guilty" by a jury aware of its power to return a verdict according to conscience is faced with a perplexing dilemma, especially in cases where the defendant has no persuasive factual or legal defense. While his ethical duty is to zealously represent his client, he must also comply with the rules of the court and any applicable rules of evidence. The lawyer must find a way to put this decision before the jury, surreptitiously, without himself going so far as to be cited for contempt of court. Although good criminal defense attorneys frequently do just that on an ad hoc basis, the techniques and strategies for doing so have rarely been identified or discussed.

There are many permissible strategies available for communicating this otherwise forbidden information to the jury.[2] Many of the avenues the defense can use are constitutionally protected and cannot be foreclosed by the trial court. For example, the right to cross-examine and impeach witnesses is constitutionally protected by the Sixth Amendment right of a

---

1. My thanks goes to the Texas Forum on Civil Liberties and Civil Rights, which published an earlier version of this chapter under the title *Jury Nullification as a Defense Strategy*, and which has permitted its republication here.

2. It is neither advisable nor practical to write a complete "how-to" on presenting a nullification defense. This chapter is intended to give lawyers handling cases where nullification may be appropriate a conceptual framework within which to organize their defense. A dialogue on the points raised here may be useful to the criminal defense bar, and this is an area where the published literature is incredibly sparse.

defendant "to be confronted with the witnesses against him,"[3] even though impeachment testimony may be inadmissible for other purposes. Any significant denial of the right to confront a witness is a "constitutional error of the first magnitude and no amount of showing of want of prejudice will cure it."[4] Impeachment testimony can lay the foundation for an independent verdict. The character and past record of an informant may impugn the integrity of the prosecution. Further, the informant's prison record or the fact that he has "cut a deal" to testify against the defendant may serve to inform the jury as to the draconian penalties the defendant faces if convicted.

Many of the techniques which may be used to bring about an independent verdict are simply good advocacy, of the sort good prosecutors and defense attorneys consistently rely on as part of their stock in trade. Occasionally some of the techniques that can be used to put these issues before the jury, while not *per se* inadmissible, may be disallowed at the discretion of the trial judge. The attorney has to be ready to argue and to attempt to persuade the trial judge to permit the sought-for line of inquiry.

Oftentimes, defense attorneys have ethical concerns about seeking a nullification verdict, believing that they have taken an oath to uphold the law which would be violated by a deliberate attempt to prevent the law from being enforced. However, that concern has been set aside by the courts. The Second Circuit Court of Appeals has held that a lawyer may "satisfy the *Strickland*[5] standards while using a defense with little or no basis in the law if this constitutes a reasonable strategy of seeking a jury nullification verdict..."[6] Defense attorneys not only should be aggressive in seeking nullification in an appropriate case, but may even be ethically *required* to do so where no other realistic defense exists.

This is not to say that a defense lawyer can reasonably forego viable fact or law based defenses and attempt to plead his case solely on equitable or conscientious grounds. It is certainly an unreasonable gamble with the future of a client to completely ignore other defenses and urge jury nullification alone, when more conventional defenses are available. Another of the federal circuit courts has stated that:

---

3. Davis v. Alaska, 415 U.S. 308 (1974); U.S. Const., amend. VI.

4. *Davis, supra* note 3.

5. Strickland v. Washington, 466 U.S. 668 (1984). Strickland sets out the minimum standards for attorney competence in criminal cases. If defense counsel falls below those standards, the case must be reversed and the defendant given a new trial. Deficient performance is shown when "counsel made errors so serious that counsel was not functioning as the 'counsel' guaranteed the defendant by the Sixth Amendment." *Id.* at 687.

6. United States v. Sams, 104 F.3d 1407 (D.C. Cir. 1996).

> When a defendant takes the stand in his own behalf and admits all of the
> elements of the crime, exactly in accord with the court's instructions to
> the jury, it is surely inadequate legal representation to hope that the jury
> will ignore the court's instructions and acquit from sympathy, rather than
> to raise an entrapment defense that has some support in the evidence.[7]

On the other hand, in light of *Sams*, it may also be unreasonable to
completely forego a jury nullification defense, and to concentrate solely
on an entrapment or necessity defense. Certainly, jury nullification is not
a feasible defense in every criminal case—a defendant who is likely to be
justly loathed and condemned by the community is not a likely candidate
for an appeal to conscience. However, in those cases where jury nullification is a viable defense, it may be unreasonable, unethical and unprofes-
sional *not* to employ it.

The attorney seeking a nullification verdict for his client may in some circumstances have to abandon any serious attempts to obtain a fact-based
acquittal, and essentially admit the facts of the government case, just as
he would if he were to seek an acquittal on the grounds of entrapment,
self-defense, or justification. Whether this is good advocacy will depend
on how viable the defense case on the merits may be. Jurors may sense a
conflict between claiming that one should not be convicted for one's actions
because they were motivated by conscience, and an unwillingness to proudly admit those same conscientious actions. In many of the Vietnam War
era cases where jury nullification was urged by the defense, the defendants
admitted all of the actions attributed to them by the government and asked
the jury to acquit them solely because their actions were justified by the
circumstances.[8] In a similar vein, Sam Skipper, the AIDS patient who was
prosecuted for growing and eating marijuana, went so far as to bring marijuana brownies into court in order to show the jury exactly what he was
doing.[9] The defense in these cases was forced to rest entirely upon the conscientious justifications they could offer, and on the discretion of the jury
to acquit solely on conscientious grounds.

In other situations, the defense may choose to rely on what could be
considered an otherwise flimsy or inadequate defense, hoping that for equitable reasons the jury will give such defenses more weight than they may
legally merit. Sometimes this is referred to as a "shadow defense." One

---

7. Capps v. Sullivan, 921 F.2d 260, 262 (10th Cir. 1990).

8. *See* United States v. Spock, 416 F.2d 165 (1st Cir. 1969); United States v. Moylan,
417 F.2d 1002 (4th Cir. 1969); United States v. Boardman, 419 F.2d 110 (1st Cir. 1970);
United States v. Dougherty, 473 F.2d 1113 (D.C. Cir. 1972).

9. *See Jury Gives Go Ahead for AIDS Sufferer to use Marijuana*, REUTER GENERAL
NEWS, Oct. 16, 1993.

example would be where defense counsel chooses to rely on the inability of the prosecution to prove specific intent, or to prove some other element of the crime, even though they know that the evidence is strongly against them. The defense may attempt to argue "entrapment" or "necessity," even though all the elements of those defenses may not be presented by the facts of the case. Yet by setting up this shadow defense, the jury will have a "peg to hang their hats on" should they resolve to deliver an independent verdict.

Jury nullification is often the result of successfully arguing for a shadow defense. Jurors may consciously or subconsciously decide to give these defenses far more credibility than they merit, in order to reach a comfort level with acquitting. As one recent article put it, these "collateral issues [may] act as a surrogate for the jury's true discomfort with the propriety of the conviction itself."[10]

Requests to the court that the jury either 1) be instructed concerning its nullification powers or 2) that the defense be allowed to mention those powers during *voir dire* and argument, are almost certain to fall on deaf ears barring plainly unconscionable conduct on the part of the government. Very rarely, a court may grant such a request when governmental misconduct has palpably exceeded the bounds of civilized behavior, as in the "Camden 28" case,[11] discussed in Chapter Five.

Most often, however, courts will not only refuse to allow open discussion of jury independence, but will erroneously claim that they are actually forbidden to do so.[12] While defendants are not entitled to a jury nullification instruction, it is clearly within the court's discretion to grant one.[13] Regardless, on this particular point courts almost never exercise their discretion in the defendant's favor. Whether this is good policy is, obviously, debatable, and (as we have seen) has been debated since before the Magna Charta. The defendant in any particular case is not in a good position to wait for the resolution of this interminable debate. His attorney must be prepared to appeal to the independent powers of the jury, using those tools that are available in the face of a judiciary which is openly hostile to the doctrine of jury independence. What can the advocate do to increase the possibilities of having a jury either acquit or ameliorate the charges against his client on conscientious grounds, without himself being jailed for contempt?

---

10. David N. Dorfman and Chris K. Iijima, *Fictions, Faults and Forgiveness: Jury Nullification in a New Context*, 28 U. MICH. J. OF L.R. 861, 864 (1995).

11. United States v. Anderson, 356 F.Supp. 1311 (D.N.J. 1973).

12. United States v. Sepulveda, 15 F.3d 1161, 1189 (1st Cir. 1993).

13. United States v. Grismore, 546 F.2d 844, 849 (10th Cir. 1976).

Theories and Themes of the Nullification Case

Probably the first thing a defense attorney must do in a potential nullification case, if only in order to prepare his case for trial, is to identify the moral or ethical basis on which he hopes the jury will decide to acquit. It is not enough for counsel to seek an independent verdict based solely on a general conscientious objection to the prosecution. The defense attorney must be able to clearly identify what it is about the case that he hopes the jury will object to, why he hopes the jury will find it objectionable, and what evidence he intends to introduce in order to persuade the jury that these conscientious considerations are important enough to cause them to render an independent verdict. If he is not prepared to answer these questions clearly and cogently in his own mind, he will not be able to build his case around them and communicate them to the jurors. Just as a good lawyer needs to develop a theory of the case prior to *voir dire* for any other trial, in a nullification case counsel must expand his theory to encompass those conscientious motivations he hopes will result in an independent verdict. And just as everything the lawyer does in any other trial should result from and resonate with his theory of the case, so everything the lawyer does in a nullification case should resonate with and amplify those conscientious considerations he wishes to convey to the jury.

The lawyer seeking a nullification verdict must frame the issues of the case broadly enough so that the evidence he wants to put before the jury will be admissible under the applicable rules of evidence. Evidence which is not relevant to a "legitimate" legal issue in the case will not be admitted, following a proper objection by the prosecution. However, provided it is otherwise admissible (e.g., not hearsay), evidence relevant to a legal issue should be admitted.[14] The fact that evidence may also be seen by the jury as justifying a nullification verdict will not be grounds for exclusion of the evidence, so long as the evidence is also relevant to a legally "legitimate" issue in the case. The defense should be sure that they have not foreclosed an important line of testimony by too narrowly construing their case.[15] This may be a reason to stage a shadow defense of "entrapment" or "necessity," opening up the theory of the case to allow for presentation of governmental conduct or the ethical (if not practical) necessity of the defendant's actions.

If the defense attorney attempts to present evidence whose "only purpose...would be to invite jury nullification of the law" the trial judge will

---

14. Hon. Jack B. Weinstein, *Considering Jury "Nullification": When May and Should a Jury Reject the Law To Do Justice*, 30 Am. Crim. L.Rev. 239, 251 (1993)(judges should construe relevance liberally to permit argument for nullification.)

15. I would like to acknowledge the assistance of Salt Lake City attorney Mark Besendorfer in clarifying the logic of this point.

in all probability consider such evidence inadmissible.[16] Courts have deemed that defendants have "no right to present evidence relevant only to [a nullification] defense."[17] Moreover, where the evidence sought to be introduced is only marginally relevant on one or more issues in the case, the evidence may be excluded if the trial judge deems that it is "being sought to discredit the government and obtain an acquittal based upon jury nullification."[18] The evidence must be fairly relevant upon some issue in the case other than nullification.

A shadow defense can serve to expand the scope of admissible evidence at trial. Claiming the defendant acted under duress or in self-defense opens the door to discussion of the character and past history of whoever he is claiming forced or threatened him. A defense of entrapment opens the door to the behavior and credibility of the police officers involved and any informants they used. A necessity defense opens the door to evidence of the consequences the defendant would have faced had he not taken the prohibited actions. A defense of insanity gives the defense an opportunity to put the defendant's whole life in front of the jury, instead of just the moments when he committed some criminal act. A shadow defense should be chosen that is compatible with the facts of the case, and that provides justification for admitting the broadest range of the nullification evidence necessary to the case.

Most courts will take a liberal view of admissibility, if some credible relevant grounds for admitting the evidence exists. One federal district court stated in this context that "the court in a criminal case is reluctant to substitute its judgment for a defendant's on the question whether such evidence is "necessary or critical" to a defense. It is sufficient that a compelling argument of cogency can be made."[19] The important lesson to be learned here is that an attorney presenting a jury nullification defense must become adept at framing his theory of the case broadly and finding legally relevant issues upon which the evidence he wants to use will be admissible.

In order to convince a jury to nullify the law, the lawyer must communicate several concepts to them. These concepts should be woven into the defense theory and themes, and reinforced at every possible opportunity during trial. First, defense counsel must convince the jury that this is a case where applying the law according to the court's instructions would be unjust.

---

16. United States v. Johnson, 62 F.3d 849, 851 (6th Cir. 1995).

17. United States v. Griggs, 50 F.3d 17 (9th Cir. 1995).

18. United States v. Malpeso, 115 F.3d 155, 162 (2nd Cir. 1997)(excluding defense evidence on Government objection as more prejudicial than probative, under Rule 403 of the Federal Rules of Evidence).

19. United States v. Sanusi, 813 F.Supp. 149, 160 (E.D.N.Y. 1992)

Although there are probably infinite ways to get this across, the three most common avenues used to communicate this message to the jury include: making them aware of draconian penalties attached to a conviction,[20] convincing the jury that the motives of the defendant were proper or that the law involved in the case was unjust,[21] and humanizing the defendant in order to elicit a merciful or sympathetic response from the jury.[22] These considerations, and others, may overlap to varying degrees in different cases.

Next, the defense attorney must find a way to empower the jurors by making them at least subliminally aware of their potential role as a bulwark of the defendant's liberties. This is quite likely to be the most difficult part. It is certainly where an attorney can expect to encounter the greatest resistance from the trial judge. Presenting this issue to the jury may involve long speeches on the history and justifications for trial by jury, or it may involve a simple closing statement reminding jurors that "the verdict in this case is to be your own. You just do not have to convict [the client] in this case." The more information defense counsel wants to get through to the jury, the more artfully he is going to have to work in order to prevent being silenced by the judge, and the more creatively he or she must incorporate history, precedent and law into his arguments.

The history of trial by jury is used quite often to this end. Courts are usually willing to allow defense counsel to wax eloquent about the Founding Fathers and the importance of jury duty, so long as the discussion remains either vague enough or familiar enough as not to raise any hackles. Judges are likely to think that the attorney ran out of anything important to say about the case, and that he is just trying to remind jurors to take their job seriously. Reminding jurors that "trial by jury is the cornerstone of American liberty. Every single one of our freedoms rest on the integrity and the sense of justice of twelve honest citizens, just as they did in the days when juries courageously acquitted William Penn and John Peter Zenger," may stir the lost memories of a high school civics class lurking in the recesses of one juror's mind. Dr. Nancy Lord made a masterful use of historical themes in her defense of vitamin wholesaler Rodger Sless, a portion of which is included at the end of this chapter.

---

20. *See* United States v. Datcher, 830 F.Supp. 411 (M.D. Tenn. 1993).

21. *See* James Cavallaro, *The Demise of the Political Necessity Defense: Indirect Civil Disobedience and United States v. Schoon*, 81 CAL. L.REV. 351 (1993); Martin Loesch, *Motive Testimony and a Civil Disobedience Justification*, 5 NOTRE DAME J. L. ETHICS & PUB. POL'Y 1069 (1991); Steven Bauer & Peter Eckerstrom, *The State Made Me Do It: The Applicability of the Necessity Defense to Civil Disobedience*, 39 STAN. L. REV. 1173 (1987).

22. *See* Alan Scheflin and Jon M. Van Dyke, *Merciful Juries: The Resilience of Jury Nullification*, 48 WASH. & LEE L. REV. 165 (1991).

Third, the defense must actively provoke the empathy of the jury. Jurors must be given a reason to want to acquit, to want to show the defendant mercy, a reason to share in the defendant's outrage at the injustice he is facing. It is not enough that the jurors passively recognize that a conviction would be unjust. The jurors must be given reasons to feel personally involved, and they must not only be reminded, but made to feel, their individual moral responsibility for their verdict. They must want to acquit, enough so that they are inspired to find a way to justify an acquittal. This will be essential if the jurors need to reinvent the doctrine of jury nullification *sua sponte* once in the jury room.

Once defense counsel has found the theory of the case which allows for the broadest introduction of evidence, and has found themes to communicate his theory of the case that allow him to reinforce the independence of the jury as much as possible, he is ready to begin to plan his actual trial strategy. The defense needs to stress these themes during all four stages of the jury trial: *voir dire*, opening statement, presentation of evidence, and closing argument. Each stage presents defense counsel with different goals, opportunities and obstacles, that he must be equipped to confront before they arise.

Voir Dire

The *voir dire*, or jury selection, stage of a criminal trial can be a fascinating thing to observe. It is during *voir dire* that the judge, and/or the attorneys for all sides, question prospective jurors about their qualifications, opinions, backgrounds, values and attitudes, supposedly so that unqualified or biased jurors can be removed. In reality, most attorneys will concede that they do not want an unbiased jury—they want a jury biased in their favor. In a potential nullification defense, the defense wants jurors willing to think and act independently, skeptical of government, sensitive to the conscientious issues in the case, and able to stand up to pressures.

Voir dire presents the defense with their first real opportunity to introduce the jury to the factual and legal issues in the case.[23] During *voir dire*, the defense has its first opportunity to present the jury with reasons to question whether the law can conscientiously be applied in the case before it. By asking questions designed to test the juror's value system and to probe the juror's responses to the type of situation the defendant was in,

---

23. Powers v. Ohio, 499 U.S. 400, 412 (1991) stated that "[t]he *voir dire* phase of the trial represents the 'jurors first introduction to the substantive factual and legal issues in a case.'" Quoting Gomez v. United States, 490 U.S. 858, 874 (1989).

the entire jury panel may be educated and sensitized as to the innocent reasons the defendant had for his actions, or to the harmless nature of the defendant's conduct.

Judges, in general, are given a great deal of discretion in determining how *voir dire* will be conducted.[24] In federal courts, *voir dire* is usually conducted by the trial judge, although federal trial judges have discretion to allow attorneys to conduct *voir dire* directly. The defense attorney and the prosecutor are usually required to submit proposed questions to the judge in writing, which the judge will then ask of the venire-members if he believes it is necessary or prudent to do so. State courts are slightly more liberal and normally allow the attorneys for the prosecution and the defense to conduct their own *voir dire*, yet often limit the time allowed to ask questions. Further, courts may curtail questioning at any time if they believe that questioning is straying into impermissible areas, or that further *voir dire* will serve no purpose other than to unnecessarily prolong the trial.

Voir dire can—and in a potential nullification case, probably should—be used to instruct the venire-members about the purposes of jury trial, and to find out what the venire-members think trial by jury is all about. Because courts will not generally allow the defense to raise the issue of nullification directly, the defense must find permissible or constitutionally protected ways to get this information before the venire. One of the least objectionable techniques may be to quote the Supreme Court's decisions describing the role of the criminal trial jury and to get the venire-members talking about them. For example, the defense may inform the venire that "a jury is to guard against the exercise of arbitrary power—to make available the commonsense judgment of the community as a hedge against the overzealous or mistaken prosecutor and in preference to the professional or perhaps overconditioned or biased response of a judge."[25] By reinforcing those facts which may make it impossible for the jury to conscientiously convict in the very beginning of the process, while emphasizing that "[a] right to jury trial is granted to criminal defendants in order to prevent oppression by the Government,"[26] the defense can begin the long process of assisting the jury in developing its own independent voice.

The defense attorney should be careful not to tip his hand too far. It does no good to identify the potential friendly jurors on the panel just so the prosecution can eliminate them from the sitting jury. By getting the entire panel to join in a discussion about the purpose of trial by jury, the venire-members can be educated as to their potential role in the court-

---

24. Rosales-Lopez v. United States, 451 U.S. 182 (1981).
25. Taylor v. Louisiana, 419 U.S. 522 (1975).
26. Duncan v. Louisiana, 391 U.S. 145, 155 (1968).

room. The idea is to lead the entire panel in a discussion, not to lecture them or start a debate.

Because the jury is to act as the conscience of the community, each juror is required to take his or her own personal moral sense into account in the process of applying the facts to the law. Jurors have to apply the law to the facts within the sphere of their personal moral convictions. They have to individually resolve any conflicts between law and conscience within their verdict. Although the defense attorney can not ordinarily use the word "nullification," he may talk to the jury about listening to their conscience. He needs to help the jurors to do their job by introspecting, contemplating their own thoughts and conscience, and being sensitive to any latent hesitation. He should seek to sensitize the jurors to their inherent moral responsibility, making them atuned to any latent cognitive dissonance they may be experiencing during deliberations.

Voir dire may also be used to emphasize the independent judgment required of jurors in criminal cases. Las Vegas defense attorney Nancy Lord has recommended asking venire-members whether they would be able to hold out in a case as long as they still had a reasonable doubt, if they were the only juror voting for acquittal, even if they think the defendant is probably guilty, even if the hour is late and the judge is pressuring the jury for a verdict. A venire-member who would be willing to convict under those circumstances may be dismissed on a challenge for cause, because jurors are required to vote for an acquittal if they retain a single reasonable doubt. This line of questioning can have the effect of emphasizing the independence and personal responsibility of each juror for their verdict. It should serve to empower individual jurors to remain more intransigent than they may otherwise be able to be, given social pressures inside the jury room. Most importantly, it should be used to encourage all of the jurors—those in the minority as well as those in the majority—to realize that a hung jury is "okay," that it is alright for reasonable jurors to disagree. This realization may serve to reduce the amount of pressure majority jurors put on those in the minority, and decrease the risk of a compromise verdict.

Venire-members may also be questioned on their ability to withstand pressures from the trial judge or the prosecutor. Judges may—inadvertently or deliberately—communicate their view of the case to the jury through their rulings, their demeanor, tone of voice and facial expressions, and their attitude towards the defendant or his attorney. Especially in a controversial case or a case with strong political overtones, the defense should seek to question the venire about whether, if they believed the judge thought the defendant should be convicted, that belief would influence their verdict. Once again, this line of inquiry may also be used to remind the venire-members of their independence and their autonomy from the judge, by reminding them of Justice Byron White's words that "when juries differ with the result at which the judge would have arrived, it is usually because they are serving some of the very purposes for which they were created and for which they are now employed."[27]

Informing the venire that, although counsel respects the judge, it is only the jury's verdict that matters, and that the defendant could not care less whether the judge thinks he is absolutely guilty or completely innocent, is likely to get their attention and make them aware that the ultimate power in the courtroom is in their hands. Venire-members should be aware that the jury is the only entity in the entire edifice of government with the power to convict a citizen accused of crime, and that so far as the defendant is concerned they are more powerful than Congress, the Supreme Court and the President all put together. The defendant has chosen the "common-sense judgment of the community...in preference to the professional or perhaps overconditioned or biased response of a judge,"[28] and the jurors may properly be reminded that it is their judgment, not the opinion of the judge, that matters.

The defense has to decide, prior to *voir dire*, whether to have the defendant appear either *pro se* or as co-counsel. While a competent defendant has an absolute right to appear *pro se*[29] (provided he refrains from disrupting the proceedings),[30] he may only appear as co-counsel with the permission of the court,[31] and only in those jurisdictions whose laws will allow it.[32] The pioneer jury consultant Cathy E. "Cat" Bennett pointed out that having the defendant personally conduct a portion of the *voir dire* allows the defense to humanize the defendant, which may be especially important when the defendant is accused of a brutal or senseless crime: "[i]t's amazing how it's so much more difficult to send someone to the gas chamber you have had a conversation with, that you've heard talk, that you've seen people touch."[33] When a defendant represents himself, trial judges

---

27. *Id.* at 157, referring to HARRY KALVEN AND HANS ZEISEL, THE AMERICAN JURY (1966).

28. *Id.* at 155.

29. *Pro se* means to appear in one's own behalf, to represent oneself.

30. Faretta v. California, 422 U.S. 806 (1975).

31. *Id.* at 810.

32. *Compare* O'Reilly v. New York Times Co., 692 F.2d 863, 869 (2d Cir. 1982)(decision whether to let defendant appear as co-counsel is within discretion of trial court) *with* Linnen v. Armainis, 991 F.2d 1102, 1106 n. 3 (3rd Cir. 1993)(defendant never permitted to appear as co-counsel for himself in Pennsylvania state court).

33. Cathy E. Bennett, *Orientation-Voir Dire*, National College for Criminal Defense Audio Recording, 346 (1982). Cathy Bennett was a pioneer in the jury consultant field, and the founder of Cathy E. Bennett & Associates, one of the major jury consulting orga-

often allow him a wider range of argument and questioning than legal counsel would be permitted.[34] Jurors may also identify with the non-professional *pro-se* defendant, and resent any efforts of the judge to shut down the defendant's sometimes awkward and stumbling efforts at presenting his own case.

The defense should also conduct *voir dire* on punishment wherever possible, especially in those state courts where juries may assess punishment in routine criminal cases. Asking venire-members whether they consider the stigma of conviction itself as part of the punishment for a crime may induce them to acquit, instead of merely minimizing the sentence. In federal courts, there exists the possibility, although not the right, of informing jurors about the effect of federal sentencing guidelines.[35] In some parts of the country, juries aware of how the federal sentencing guidelines work have nullified with some frequency, presumably because they believe that the guidelines are unjustifiably severe.[36]

Voir dire is unique in that it represents the only real opportunity for the attorney to have an open-ended two-way conversation with the jurors. Counsel asks the jurors questions, the jurors answer, and may ask him some questions in response. The attorney may also tell them a little about himself, his client, and the kind of case the jurors are going to decide. This is where the jurors will inevitably receive their "first impression" of the case, of the defendant and of the attorney. If the attorney wants the jurors to go out of their way to acquit his client, this first impression had better be a good one. Jurors are very unlikely to nullify if they dislike the client, mistrust the attorney, and think the judge is there to protect them from being led astray and manipulated by some sneaky defense lawyer, or if the defendant has committed a heinous crime. Defense counsel should never try to trick or manipulate a jury into nullifying. A sincere, honest, forth-

---

nizations in the country. *See* Kerry Fitzgerald, *Cathy E. (Cat) Bennett: A Tribute to a Fine Lady and a Dedicated Professional,* VOICE FOR THE DEFENSE 4 (Spring 1992).

34. *See* Hon. Frank A. Kaufman, *The Right of Self-Representation and the Power of Jury Nullification,* 28 CASE W.RES. L.REV. 269 (1978): "In a criminal or civil jury trial, the *pro se* litigant, like counsel, is subject to the contempt powers of the court. But he is not subject to the discipline and the effect of any continuing relationship with the court and the organized bar. Thus, he is not subject to the same degree of control which a court has over counsel...The result is that is is far easier for the *pro se* litigant to argue that the jury should exercise its nullification power than for counsel to do so."

35. *See Datcher, supra* note 20; *see also* Kristen Sauer, *Informed Conviction: Instructing the Jury About Mandatory Sentencing Consequences,* 95 COLUM.L.REV. 1232 (1995).

36. *See Crossfire,* October 1993, quoted in *Crossfire: Mandatory Minimums meet FIJA,* 14 THE FIJACTIVIST 1 (Winter 1994).

right approach, showing them where the equities lie, is far more effective than a barrage of legal wizardry, salesmanship, and hyperbole.

The defense attorney looking to select an independent jury should be very specific about what considerations he intends to put before the jurors to motivate them to nullify. He must be able to identify what values he wants the jury to respond to in the case, so that he can know what sort of values he wants in the jurors who eventually serve. He has to know what values he is looking for, before he can plan the questions he wants to ask the venire. If he asks the rights questions, the answers should help him determine which venire-members hold the relevant values — and which jurors hold the opposite values.

Selecting juries by stereotyped race, religion and gender classifications is just not adequate for the fine-tuned value-based responses sought for the selection of an independent jury. Although many jury consultants and attorneys have selected juries through such classifications for years, these methods often backfire and do not stress the sort of open communication with the jury that is desirable in seeking a nullification verdict.[37] The advocate should employ the highest level of psychological sophistication he can muster, in order to identify jurors most likely to respond favorably to the moral issues raised by the case. Probably second to none in understanding the relationships between the *voir dire*, values and verdicts was the late Cathy E. "Cat" Bennett, a psychologist who worked on the trials of Russell Means, William Kennedy Smith, and countless others. Her posthumously published *Bennett's Guide to Jury Selection and Trial Dynamics* (co-authored by her husband, Robert Hirschhorn) remains the definitive trial guide to psychological methods of *voir dire*.

Opening Statement

The opening statement is where the attorneys for both the government and the defense speak to the jury and tell them what they expect the evidence in the case to show. The prosecution makes the initial opening statement, and the defense follows. In many jurisidictions, the defense can wait until after the prosecution has closed its case before presenting its own opening statement. Opening statement is supposed to consist of an objective recitation of what counsel expects the facts to show, without argument. Arguing the case during opening statement is specifically forbidden, although lawyers almost always try to inject as much argument into opening statement as the court will tolerate.

---

37. *See generally,* JEFFREY ABRAMSON, WE, THE JURY: THE JURY SYSTEM AND THE IDEAL OF DEMOCRACY, 143-176 (1994).

As opposed to *voir dire*, which is ideally a dialogue between the attorney and the venire-members, the opening statement is an opportunity for the defense to tell the jury a story. As one criminal defense lawyer has pointed out, any parent — or former child — should know that a good story has both a theme and a moral.[38] Defense statements in nullification cases may revolve around themes such as "defendant as victim," "defendant acting on irresistably good impulses," "defendant has suffered enough," etc. For a nullification defense, the jury should be left offended, shocked or outraged that the defendant is facing prison for acts the jurors do not find blameworthy (or perhaps even find commendable), or that the prosecution is seeking to further torment some hapless, unfortunate defendant. Of course, the jurors should be aware that they are going to have to determine the moral of this story, whether the story is to have a happy ending.

During the opening statement, the defense needs to make the jury aware of its theory of the case, and give the jury a coherent theme or themes to which the defense will return throughout the trial. While defense counsel can not expect to be allowed to argue jury independence explicitly (and indeed, during opening statement, he probably should not be allowed to "argue" at all) he may show that his client is the "good guy" in the story, and that the prosecutor or the witnesses against his client are the "bad guys." It is during the opening statement that the jury gets its first real picture of what happened. The opening statement in a nullification case should be planned to give the jury a queasy, uneasy feeling about the conscientious aspects of convicting the defendant, and make the jurors identify or empathize with the defendant's situation.

One of the purposes of the opening statement is to build rapport with the jury, to make a favorable first impression. The defense attorney wants to make sure that he has credibility with the jurors so that they will be at least willing to consider the possibility that his client is being prosecuted unfairly, and that the government is overreaching its bounds. It is possible to concentrate on the ethical issues in the case by focusing on what the evidence will show the defendant was thinking, what his motives were, what his intent was. By focusing on evidence reflecting the defendant's state of mind, defense counsel can do a much more effective job of building empathy between the jurors and the defendant.

Prosecuting attorneys almost always try to connect with the jury by claiming to represent "the people of" the United States, or the state. One rarely used technique is for counsel to object, in front of the jury, to the prosecutor claiming to represent "the people." Objecting that the prosecutor represents the government, and that the jury represents "the people"

---

38. *See* William P. Allison, *The Winning Beginning*, 24 VOICE FOR THE DEFENSE 24 (April 1996).

achieves several objectives—it shows the jurors that the prosecution is posturing and attempting to manipulate them, and it shows them that they have an independent role to play which the prosecution is attempting to usurp. The judge will almost never grant this objection in any case, and may well chastise the attorney bold enough to make it, but in front of an appropriate jury that posture may well cost the judge credibility as well. This technique can be reinforced by being sure to refer to the prosecutor either as the "prosecutor" or as the "government" throughout the trial, and never as the "state" or "the people."

In the alternative, defense counsel may wait until his opening statement to point out that the prosecution does not represent "the people," that the jury represents the people. Here, however, the prosecution would likely be the one to object that the defense is improperly arguing during opening statement, leaving the jurors with the impression that the defense attorney is attempting to mislead and manipulate them. However he chooses to do it, defense counsel has to show the jurors that it is they who represent the conscience of the community, and that the government's concept of a just resolution to the case is not the result of the sober, unbiased deliberation of trained, trustworthy professionals, but is the product of a naked partisan interest.

Defense counsel needs to highlight whatever conscientious weaknesses exist in the prosecution's case during opening statement. If the case involves an informer with a more notorious criminal history than the defendant, the jury needs to know about it. If the prosecution is going to bring in thieves, perjurers, adulterers, hired witnesses, or people with axes to grind—counsel must let the jury know about it in advance. If the government has ulterior motives for the prosecution, if the law was enforced arbitrarily, if the defendant has not caused anybody harm, and if all these things will be brought out in the evidence, then the defense needs to bring those things out in opening statement. It is important to let the jury know, as soon as possible, that the defendant is the "good guy."

The only caveat is that whenever counsel tells the jury during opening statement that "the evidence will show that the prosecution is building its case on the testimony of a convicted child molester," he has made a promise to the jurors and must be sure that the evidence will show exactly what he has promised. If the evidence does not show what has been promised, he risks losing credibility with the jury, and the likelihood of the jury nullifying the law in his client's favor decreases. Counsel and client must remain credible, honest, and truthful with the jury. The defense is asking the jury to let the defendant go home, for reasons of equity and justice. Accordingly, defense counsel must treat the jury with the respect, openness and integrity necessary to inspire that sort of lenity.

Many attorneys and commentators have contended that the majority of jurors decide on their verdict by the end of the opening statement. This opinion is most often erroneously attributed to Harry Kalven and Hans Zeisel's book, *The American Jury*, written in 1966 at the conclusion of the Chicago Jury Project's research into jury behavior. This is a misreading of Kalven and Zeisel's work. According to University of Iowa law professor Michael J. Saks, Hans Zeisel specifically disavowed this conclusion, noting that the words "opening statement" appear nowhere in the text of *The American Jury*.[39] In fact, jurors most often base their verdicts solely on the law and on the evidence (as in the vast majority of criminal cases, they undoubtedly should).

What is true is that if the opening statements by defense and prosecution give an accurate image of the evidence that will be presented at trial, then it is only logical that the juror's views of the case at the conclusion of the presentation of evidence would be the same as at the end of the opening statement. In light of that fact, it is important for the defense to be scrupulously accurate about what the evidence will show, and give the jurors an ethical framework in which to consider that evidence. The jurors must be empowered to view the evidence from an ethical, as well as a factual, perspective, if they are to deliver an ethically-based verdict.

Presentation of Evidence

The largest portion of the trial is usually taken up with the presentation of evidence. Presentation of evidence consists mainly of the questioning of witnesses, and the introduction of physical evidence. All the facts considered by the jury are introduced during this part of the trial, and everything the defense wants to use to convince the jury that nullification is warranted must be introduced during this stage of the proceedings.

There is no limit to the types of evidence the defense may choose to present in a nullification case. The facts the defense will need to present will depend on the defense theory of the case, and the reasons the defense is hoping the jury will believe justify a nullification verdict. Commonly presented are the punishment itself, the defendant's motivations, and the conduct of the police or other officials in prosecuting the defendant.

The punishment the defendant faces if convicted is usually considered legally irrelevant at trial. The greater the punishment the defendant faces, however, the greater the injustice of an ethically unwarranted conviction. Counsel should always be alert for opportunities during trial to inform

---

39. Professor Saks expressed this point during his presentation at the Georgetown University Law Center Conference on the Role of the Jury in a Democratic Society, October 28, 1995.

and remind the jury of the potential sentence the defendant faces, especially in cases where the sentence would seem harsh and unconscionable to the jury. In most states and in all federal courts, the imposition of punishment is determined by the court and the range of punishment the defendant faces is consequently inadmissible at trial, unless this information can be admitted for some reason other than to convince the jury to nullify. Fortunately, there are frequent opportunities to do just that. Witnesses who have been granted immunity from prosecution can be questioned as to the sentences they faced for their crimes, which may be similar to or the same as the defendant's. Other witnesses who have served time in prison for similar crimes may also be used to bring out the range of punishment the defendant faces and what conditions in prison are like.

One good example of introducing otherwise inadmissible evidence about punishment was the cross-examination of government witness Kathryn Schroeder during the trial of the surviving Branch Davidians in February, 1994. The cross-examination conducted by Fort Worth criminal defense attorney Jeff Kearney detailed the potential punishments Schroeder would have faced had she gone to trial instead of testifying for the government in return for immunity. Kearney brought out from Schroeder the facts that she was charged with the same offenses the defendants were on trial for committing; that the federal sentencing guidelines mandated a life sentence without parole upon conviction; and that if she had been convicted of these charges Schroeder would never have been able to be with her children again.

In federal courts, evidence about the punishment faced by the defendant is not supposed to be admissible at trial because the jury does not decide the sentence, and they are not supposed to consider it in reaching their verdict.[40] The jury is only supposed to consider the factual guilt or innocence of the defendant, and not the ramifications of its verdict. Although the evidence concerning Kathryn Schroeder's plea bargain was ostensibly admissible solely to impeach Schroeder by showing that she had ample motive to fabricate her testimony to fit the government's case, in fact the evidence adduced also had the result of introducing before the jury the forbidden facts concerning the potential punishment (and the ramifications of the punishment) the defendants faced if convicted.

Another issue that should be developed before the jury is the defendant's motivation. Jurors may nullify the law when they approve of the defendant's motive. For example, the abused wife who kills her husband

---

40. Shannon v. United States, 512 U.S. 573, 579 (1994). *See also* United States v. Johnson, *supra* note 16, United States v. Lewis, 110 F.3d 417 (7th Cir. 1997); *but see* United States v. Datcher, *supra* note 20.

in his sleep is not motivated by a desire to kill or obtain personal gain, but to be free from future abuse.[41] While she may not be able to establish self-defense due to lack of imminent danger, it is clear that a jury nullification verdict will revolve around her motive. Dr. Jack Kevorkian has repeatedly earned acquittals by showing that his motive was not to take away life, but to relieve the suffering of terminally ill patients.[42]

Although motive is not actually an element of most crimes,[43] motive may be inseparably associated with the often critical element of intent, and can usually be discussed within the context of intent during the course of the trial. When the motives of the defendant are honorable, when in fact the jurors would be likely to respond the same way given similar incentives, the defense has gone a long way towards laying the groundwork for a nullification verdict.

Having the defendant take the witness stand is usually considered a risky move. However, when the defendant is seeking a nullification verdict it may well be essential to have him testify, especially in those cases where a just law is being misapplied to obtain an unjust result. Only the defendant may be able to communicate his motives, acts and concerns to the jury. Only the defendant may be able to humanize his position, and to allow the jurors to see and understand his actions through his own eyes. This perspective may be essential to activate their moral sensibilities, and to get them to act upon them.

This tactic may not work when the defendant hopes the jury will find the law itself unjust, as opposed to those cases where the defendant hopes they will find the application of the law unjust. The chemotherapy patient on trial for the medicinal use of marijuana may be able to gain an advantage by taking the stand and explaining what he was doing and why. The person who smokes marijuana for recreational purposes and hopes that the jury will believe marijuana should be legal will be in a much weaker position. This is because the former's personal story will add to his argument and justification; the latter defendant will have little to add to his essentially political argument.

Another important issue to examine is the behavior of the police and

---

41. Maria L. Marcus, *Conjugal Violence: The Law of Force and the Force of Law*, 69 CAL. L. REV. 1657 (1981); Donald L. Creach, *Partially Determined Imperfect Self-Defense: The Battered Wife Kills and Tells Why*, 34 STAN. L.REV. 615 (1982); Richard A. Rosen, *On Self-Defense, Imminence, and Women Who Kill Their Batterers*, 17 N.C. L. REV. 371 (1993).

42. Janet Wilson, Michael Betzold and David Zeman, *Kevorkian's Case will put Suicide Law on Trial*, DET. FREE PRESS, April 16, 1994 at 1A.

43. *See*, e.g., Bush v. State, 628 S.W. 2d 441, 444 (Tex. Crim. App. 1982)(motive is not an essential element of a criminal offense and need not be proven to establish a crime).

prosecution. When the defendant has been beaten, harassed or abused by the police, these facts should be brought before the jury. Evidence which impeaches a witness is *per se* admissible in a criminal trial. The fact that the police have offended community values — or even themselves broken the law — in a single-minded quest to arrest the defendant can be very persuasive, especially where police actions are less acceptable to the jurors than those of the defendant.[44] Understanding what sort of official misconduct may have been condoned in order to apprehend and punish the defendant puts the defendant's actions into context and allows the jurors to make a reasoned decision as to whether the police should be rewarded with a conviction upon this particular set of facts.

Closing Argument

Closing argument is the last opportunity defense counsel has to speak to the jurors. During closing argument, the prosecution gets to argue its case first. After the defense argues, the prosecution gets a second opportunity to rebut anything the defense said. The defense does not get to speak again, so defense counsel has to communicate his points effectively and powerfully enough that they are still in the minds of the jurors as they begin their deliberations. Although the range of permissible argument is very broad, in general both sides are expected to limit their argument to the evidence (including reasonable inferences to be drawn from from the evidence), pleas for effective law enforcement, the law as contained in the court's charge, and responses to the arguments of opposing counsel.

During closing argument, the defense must not only be prepared to persuade the jurors to act on their moral sensibilities (which, by now, they have been made acutely aware of), but he must also be prepared to counter both the court's instructions and the arguments of the prosecution. The defense may not stray too far from arguing the facts as they relate to the law as given in the court's "charge," or instructions to the jury. Courts often instruct jurors using words similar to these:

> It is your duty as jurors to follow the law as stated in all of the instructions of the Court and to apply these rules of law to the facts as you find them from the evidence received during the trial.
> Counsel have quite properly referred to some of the applicable rules of

---

44. *See* Darryl K. Brown, *Jury Nullification Within the Rule of Law*, 81 MINN. L.REV. 1149, 1172-1178 (1997)(discussing when official violation of the law may justify jury nullification.)

> law in their closing arguments to you. If, however, any difference appears to you between the law as stated by counsel and that as stated by the Court in these instructions, you, of course, are to be governed by the instructions given to you by the Court.
>
> You are not to single out any one instruction alone as stating the law, but must consider the instructions as a whole in reaching your decisions.
>
> Neither are you to be concerned with the wisdom of any rule of law stated by the Court. *Regardless of any opinion you may have as to what the law ought to be,* it would be a violation of your sworn duty to base any part of your verdict upon any other view or opinion of the law than that given in these instructions of the Court just as it would be a violation of your sworn duty, as the judges of the facts, to base your verdict upon anything but the evidence received in the case.[45]

Counsel treads a fine line in attempting to broaden the scope of these instructions in order to make room for a nullification verdict. If the *voir dire*, opening statement and trial evidence prepared the jury to consider the moral aspects of the case, then closing argument should concentrate on the conscientious impossibility of applying the law to the facts, and on the importance of having the jurors maintain the integrity of their independent judgment and refusal to compromise. The lawyer should focus on the lack of moral guilt of the defendant and how the police response was dramatically out of proportion to the defendant's actions; how the defendant was startled to be arrested because he had not hurt anyone; how a citizen "just like you or me" was forcibly taken out of their home to face the moral judgment of the community.

While the criminal defense lawyer cannot contradict the instructions of the court on the law, he may expand on them, giving them historical context. The lawyer may also remind the jurors that only they can decide the case; that their verdict, their opinions are the only ones that count. The more the attorney can reinforce the independence of the jury, the more empowered they will be when it comes to deciding the case. Houston attorney Randy Schaffer has argued that:

> This is a time in our country when people are questioning the necessity of maintaining many of our political institutions. It's a time when many people are distrustful of elements in our government from the highest office in the land to the lowest on the county level. But I suggest to you that the last bastion between the individual and the mighty power of the State

---

45. DEVITT ET AL., FEDERAL JURY PRACTICE AND INSTRUCTION § 12.01 (1992) (emphasis added).

46. RAY MOSES, FINAL ARGUMENT IN CRIMINAL CASES, 5-56 (1995).

is the jury system. Only the jury is the last dignified, uncorrupted body politic in this country. No one can tell a jury what to do.[46]

Criminal defense attorneys are often criticized for attempting to appeal to the emotions of the jury; jurors are just as often criticized for responding to emotion instead of reason.[47] While these allegations may seem disingenuous (prosecutors routinely emphasize the emotional aspects of cases),[48] they do call into question whether the practice of making an emotional plea to the jury is unethical.[49] Frequently, defense attorneys and prosecutors alike appeal to jurors to "send a message"; following the verdict in the O.J. Simpson murder trial defense pleas of this sort were referred to as appeals for a nullification verdict.[50] When such pleas are made by the government, they are usually referred to as "pleas for effective law enforcement," although many defense attorneys consider them "a plea to ignore your reasonable doubts." However disfavored emotional appeals may be in the media or in the law schools, the criminal defense attorney seeking a nullification verdict should seek not only to provoke but to validate the emotional responses of the jury, and to vindicate the right of the jurors to take those emotions with them into the jury room.

---

47. Los Angeles District Attorney Gilbert Garcetti, in his office's press conference following O.J. Simpson's acquittal on murder charges, told the press that "[i]t was clear this was an emotional trial. Apparently (the jury's) verdict was based on emotion that overcame their reason. This was not, in our opinion, a close case." *In Wake of Simpson Trial, Garcetti Talks About Judicial Reform*, SEATTLE POST-INTELLIGENCER, November 8, 1995 at A13.

48. Prosecutors do not shy away from emphasizing that murders are brutal, that drugs are poison, or that victims are old, young or crippled; nor are prosecution pleas to "send a message" about how the community views drug pushers, rapists or domestic violence considered unacceptable. *See* Zacharias, *Structuring The Tactics of Prosecutorial Trial Practice: Can Prosecutors do Justice?*, 44 VAND. L. REV. 45 (1991): "For every commentator who concludes that prosecutors commit misconduct by appealing to emotion, another can be found who suggests that arousing jurors is the role of summation."

49. *See* Mark Curriden, *Blowing Smoke: Lawyers are trained to push a jury's buttons almost any way then can. But now some members of the bar think they have gone too far and society is the big loser*, A.B.A. JRL. October 1995 at 55. *See also* William H. Simon, *The Ethics of Criminal Defense*, 91 MICH. L. REV. 1703 (1993).

50. *See* Tony Perry, *THE SIMPSON VERDICTS; Snubbing the Law to Vote on Conscience; History: If Simpson's acquittal was a message about racism, panelists exercised a controversial American legal tradition: jury nullification*, L.A. TIMES, October 5, 1995 at 5:

> Prosecutor Marcia Clark complained that Cochran was using a forbidden "jury nullification" argument in closing statements. Judge Lance A. Ito responded that Cochran's argument had indeed been "artful" on that point.

The possibility of making a "plea for effective law enforcement" is too often overlooked by defense lawyers in constructing their closing arguments. This plea is almost exclusively made by the prosecution, and urges that the jurors have a civic duty to enforce the law. A typical prosecution plea for effective law enforcement might go something like this:

> Ladies and gentleman of the jury, you've seen a lot of police officers come in here and testify in this case, and Officer Murphy told you about being shot at, about the kinds of risks these Officers face in their job every day. They go out there and find the bad guys, ladies and gentleman, and that is hard and dangerous work. And after they find them, we get to prosecute them, and we take them in front of a jury of twelve citizens just like you. And all the work of these Officers goes to naught if the twelve of you won't do your job, and convict criminals like Mr. Defendant here. If you are not going to do that, then all these Officers are risking their lives for nothing.

However, in a nullification case a plea for effective law enforcement can be used by the defense:

> Ladies and gentleman of the jury, you have heard a lot about the crime problem in our city, in our state. And we have all been afraid of crime, we all lock our doors when we go out and we all wonder if someone will have broken those locks before we get home again. We all know the law is here to protect us and we all want the law to do its job. We all want effective law enforcement; in fact we depend on it.
> But effective law enforcement is not what occurred in this case. Effective law enforcement means the bad guys—people who pose a threat to law-abiding citizens like the twelve of you—are sought out, caught, tried, convicted and punished, all through legal means. No, this case is not an example of effective law enforcement—it is an example of what happens when police turn their attention not against the bad guys, but against the good guys. It is an example of what happens when the police and the government cross the line and themselves become criminals. What occurred in this case is a textbook example of what no American citizen should ever have to endure…

Closing argument is the last chance for the defense to remind the jury of any points brought out earlier in the trial. If the defense counsel has objected to the prosecution referring to him or herself as representing the people, or the citizens, the jury can be informed during closing argument about why defense counsel objected to that. For example, Florida attorney Jack Blumenfeld has made the following argument:

> The prosecutor introduced himself earlier in this trial by saying "I'm (*name the prosecutor*) and I represent the State of (*name the State*)(or the people of the State, or the Citizens of our County or the United States of

America)." That is not correct. He doesn't represent the people of this State (or County or country). He works as a paid legal employee for the executive branch of the government of this jurisdiction. You ladies and gentleman of the jury, not the prosecutor, represent the citizens of this State. Only you and other citizens like you give life to what are otherwise "paper rights."[51]

It is sometimes said that cases are often lost in closing argument, but almost never won there. By the time for closing argument, the jurors have already heard the facts, the opening statements, and the *voir dire*. Closing argument, therefore, is not a time to try to inject new concepts to the jurors, but is a time to guide them in reflecting upon and evaluating all that they have already heard. If the defense theory and themes of the case have been clearly presented to the jury up to this point, closing argument should serve to wrap up the entire trial into a few, well considered conscientious issues, and to empower the jurors to act upon those issues during their deliberations and in reaching their verdict.

While some tactics aimed at obtaining a nullification verdict may be forbidden by the court, the defense attorney should always be prepared to resort to other techniques without becoming disheartened. No single technique will prevail in all cases; no trial judge will be able to forbid all possible avenues of reaching the jury with this information without eventually denying the accused a right to a fair trial by jury, and subjecting himself to a reversal on appeal. The attorney who actively seeks a nullification verdict must be prepared to test the limits of what the court will allow; he must have his law, history and logic well prepared before going into court. If the advocate explores enough paths for the presentation of this information, he stands a reasonably good chance of success.

* * *

Reconstruction of Closing Arguments in the Rodger Sless Trial

United States District Court, Albuquerque, New Mexico, June 6, 1994

This case is about a federal agency, the Food and Drug Administration, that has spun so completely out of control—out of control of the people,

---

51. MOSES, *supra* note 46, 5-54.

out of control of Congress, that they are now no more than a band of armed terrorists. That is why Rodger Sless rented the mailboxes. The FDA was perpetrating armed raids all over the country, of alternative care practitioners, health food stores, and distributors, and nobody knew where next they would strike. You do not have to believe my client. Dr. Priestley told you the very same thing.

They want their subjects—we, the people—to obey rules they haven't even made. They want you to endorse this by convicting Rodger Sless, so that they can use him as an example. And go on making important decisions without a public airing where we can hold them accountable...

* * *

I will conclude by talking a little about the role of the jury. Did you know that one of the reasons the Colonies declared independence from Great Britain was "For depriving us in many cases, of the benefits of Trial by Jury"?

Thomas Jefferson said in 1789, "I consider trial by jury as the only anchor ever yet imagined by man, by which a government can be held to the principles of its constitution." I cannot imagine a case where those words of Thomas Jefferson, written over 200 years ago, are more appropriate than in this case.

It is ironic that one often quoted complaint in the Declaration of Independence, against King George was "He has erected a multitude of new Offices, and sent hither Swarms of Officers to harass our People, and eat out their Substance."

The Articles of Confederation had problems, so we wrote the Constitution, but the Founders could not get the states to ratify it unless they guaranteed a Bill of Rights. Because they knew better then than we do today how government can get out of hand. So they wanted to prohibit government from doing certain things. It never occurred to most of them to tell the government it couldn't forbid herbs. Herbs were an integral part of the culture. Every one used herbs back then. They never even thought the government would try to do what it is doing today.

The idea of government control of medicine occurred to two people—Benjamin Rush, George Washington's personal doctor and a signer of the Declaration of Independence, and Thomas Jefferson. Benjamin Rush warned: "Unless we put medical freedom into the Constitution, the time will come when medicine will organize into an undercover dictatorship... To restrict the art of healing to one class of men and deny equal privileges to others will constitute the Bastille of medical science. All such laws are un-American and despotic and have no place in a republic... The Constitution of this republic should make special privilege for medical freedom as well as religious freedom."...

But in spite of Dr. Rush's prophetic warning, the right to freedom in our choice of health care is not part of the Bill of Rights. The founders never imagined that a trial such as this would ever take place in America. Because they never thought the federal government would even attempt to control what we keep in our medicine cabinets and kitchen cabinets. There was no such thing as the FDA until 1906, when the Pure Food and Drugs Act permitted the government to seize dangerous substances...

Law begins in philosophy. First you have the philosophy, and from that philosophy you create the constitution, the great law of the nation. And that constitution then authorizes the government to pass laws or statutes. And in our country today, though not at the last turn of the century, the statutes allow agencies to create regulations which also have the force and effect of law.

But in this case, ladies and gentlemen, they did not even create a regulation. They never tested this vitamin. They never published notice, never asked for comment, never held hearings, and never gave Mr. Sless any warning. Now they expect Rodger Sless, and others in his position, to have some clairvoyant ability to divine rules that even the FDA has yet to make or face criminal charges.

The FDA expanded its power every few decades by claiming that the public needed to be protected from one thing after another. Justice Brandeis once said, "Experience should teach us to be most on our guard to protect liberty when the government's purposes are beneficent. Men born to freedom are naturally alert to repel invasion of their liberty by evil-minded rulers. The greatest dangers to liberty lurk in insidious encroachment by men of zeal, well-meaning but without understanding."

So that is how it started. And this is how it ends. They have tried to control this courtroom as they try to control vitamins and supplements. You've seen it for yourself...

* * *

Lord chief Justice Matthew Hale said in 1665, "it is the conscience of the jury that must pronounce the prisoner guilty or not guilty." Conscience has nothing to do with determining facts: they either exist or do not. Nor does it have anything to do with the law: the law either requires something or it does not. Those are cold, unemotional determinations. Conscience deals with justice—the basic obligation of the jury...

* * *

Rodger Sless is part of what is loosely called the "alternative care movement," or the "nutritional supplement industry." For decades, this arm of the health care industry has been the first to recognize scientific realities that took years to gain acceptance by the mainstream. The government had been saying for years that there was no relationship between cancer and diet, between diet and heart disease, and the so-called "health-nuts," as they described us all were persecuted for this—including Nathan Pritikin who they tried to bring criminal charges against. Only when the paperwork was so huge that it would bury the very offices of the FDA did they concede that there was a connection.

But over recent years, alternative care began to actually cut into the profits, market, the customer base, of orthodox physicians and pharmaceutical companies. The powers that were felt threatened. They started using buzz words like "black market in unapproved new drugs" when the reality was that the bedrock of the new philosophy was to avoid the use of drugs. The basis of care was—as Joan Priestley explained, vitamins and nutrients, spirituality, exercise, and a positive attitude. And you heard how well her patients are doing. The FDA doesn't have a clue. People don't like drugs. They don't want to take them anymore. They want alternatives. And the FDA wants it to stop...

The FDA agents moved in against Rodger Sless using deadly force: firearms which they were brandishing and apparently willing to use. And they did so without even determining if he was engaged in criminal activity. This is a reckless violation of both individual rights and public safety.

If the jury endorses these acts, it will set loose a swarm of armed and dangerous agents to trample on people's rights in every health food store, vitamin distributor, and alternative clinic in the country. You heard Dr. Priestley...

* * *

In the year 1215, in England, the Noblemen got tired of King John's arbitrary tyrannical rule and they forced him at the point of a sword to sign the Magna Charta. He conceded certain rights of the people such as the right to trial by jury. Why did the Noblemen rebel? Because King John was so arrogant that he would proclaim, "the law is in my mouth"—whatever he said, was the law. The law is in my mouth...

* * *

They are hoping that you will have trouble believing that our country now has a government that will trump up a total of 15 dubious charges on one person, and will compromise by finding him guilty of something. The FDA underestimated you.

One of the great injustices a jury can make is to betray truth by attempting to compromise. Perhaps some of you believe the Defendant to be not guilty of all counts, and others of you believe that he is guilty. If you believe that the defendant is not guilty of all counts, it is a betrayal of truth to vote for conviction on any count. There is no compromise between right and wrong. Principles cannot be compromised; they can only be abandoned. You're not mixing pastels here, you're declaring the truth.

You understand how to tell the FDA that their unlawful terror tactics will not be tolerated: total acquittal—all counts, not guilty. Conviction on even one count rewards the government for terrorism. This man is not a criminal. So, why did Rodger have to keep a low profile? Because when the government becomes a lawbreaker the little guy has no remedy. He has no effective protection from a lawless government except to either hide, or appeal to a jury.

* * *

Judge Hansen will tell you that the government must prove each and every element of each count, and that the burden never shifts to Mr. Sless. Ladies and gentlemen, the government usually succeeds in cases like this by throwing so many charges against the person, causing so much confusion in the minds of the jurors, that they just finally give up and convict the poor guy of something... The purpose of the jury is to prevent oppression by the government and if the jury detects a pattern of oppression they must employ the remedy...

* * *

What's going on here?

The FDA wants you to believe that because THEY are the government, they must have acted lawfully. They do not want to acknowledge the rules and regulations which THEY are supposed to follow. Shakespeare once said: "Upon what meat do these our Caesars feed that they have grown so great?"

The law is in my mouth...

They just came rushing in 3 unmarked cars, in civilian clothes, drew their guns and hollered "PUT YOUR HANDS UP" like the renegade gestapo agents that they are, without even identifying themselves to their victims. What if Rodger Sless—mistaking the government agents for self-employed criminals—had resisted and been killed?

Justice George Sutherland wrote in 1936: "Arbitrary power and the rule of the Constitution cannot both exist. They are antagonistic and incompatible forces; and one or the other must of necessity perish whenever they are brought in conflict."

The FDA wants people to be scared. They want the vitamin sellers and the health food stores and the alternative care practitioners—like Dr. Priestley—not to know where next they will strike. No, they do not expect them to take out mailboxes under made-up names. They expect them to take products off the shelves, and stop using them, if they have any doubt as to their status with the FDA.

So when I asked Dr. Spyker if he was planning to outlaw chili pepper, I wasn't being paranoid was I? In fact, he admitted that the capsicum found in chili pepper is already on prescription—all he has to do is extend that to the chili pepper itself.

They do not want to have to determine that a product is, in fact, an unapproved new drug before they send five armed agents with guns drawn to swoop down on some befuddled small business owner and his terrified employees.

One of the reasons for this is that they know that if they had to go through notice and comment, and hold public hearings, the people of this country, and Congress would find out what they're about to do. And they don't want to be accountable.

I trust you will hold them accountable.

Justice Byron White, in 1975 wrote: "The purpose of a jury is to guard against the exercise of arbitrary power—to make available the common sense judgment of the community as a hedge against the overzealous or mistaken prosecutor."

We don't get to serve on many juries in our lives. As long as you live, you'll remember this trial and this verdict you rendered. When a person sits on a jury, John Adams said, back in 1791, "It is not only his right, but his duty to find the verdict according to his best understanding, judgment and conscience."

Your vote is your own. It belongs to only you and others cannot vote for you nor you for them. To find Rodger Sless guilty all 12 must agree. To find him not guilty, also requires all 12. If there is no agreement—you have a hung jury. You must try to convince each other, but if they cannot convince you, even if you stand alone, do not go along merely because you are tired and the hour is late.

Your vote is your own. You can't be punished for it—you can't be required to explain it, or fined for it, or go to jail.

Nothing can happen—except that your conscience will bother you if your vote is wrong. The conscience of the jury is the grandstand of justice. Just as it will eat at you if you've done wrong, it will eat at you if you've gone along with wrongdoing.

What the Food and Drug Administration is doing here is wrong, and now they hold my client as a criminal to cover up their tyranny and bureaucratic bungling.

That is what a jury trial is all about - justice. See that it be done.

The issue is squarely in your lap. By placing charges on Rodger Sless the state is saying that he's a criminal. That's the only question. Is he a criminal? Is he your neighbor, or is he a criminal?

So if you know in your heart that Rodger Sless is innocent—say so now.

And if this case bothers you, if something nags your mind, if you even have reasonable doubts, express them now. If you have reasonable doubts, speak them now. Because tomorrow will be too late.

When in doubt, juries will sometimes convict the defendant in the belief that the appeals courts can correct any error. But appeals are expensive and risky. This trial is the only time that Rodger can take his case to ordinary citizens for a common-sense determination of his guilt or innocence.

And how could you not have doubts? Of course you have doubts. How can they prove beyond reasonable doubt that Rodger Sless knew something that they didn't know themselves? If Rodger Sless even thought GH3 was an unapproved new drug, and not generally recognized as safe and effective, why did he give it to his own mother? Why has she been taking it for nine years? ...

* * *

Tell the FDA that you want them to leave Dr. Priestley and all of her colleagues in the supplement industry alone. Tell the FDA to go back to Rockville, Maryland. Tell them to take their guns and their badges with them. Tell them that the only thing in this trial that isn't safe and effective is the FDA. Remember what Dr. Priestley said. Those guns are loaded. Somebody could get hurt...

Chapter Eleven

Summary

> *The law is not an end in itself, nor does it provide ends. It is preeminently a means to serve what we think is right.*
> Justice William J. Brennan, Jr.

The Role of the Jury: A Political Question

The American criminal trial jury can trace its roots back at least to twelfth century. This extraordinarily ancient lineage should have given ample opportunity for any questions concerning its use or purpose to be completely resolved. It is clear that has not been the case, although a review of the history is the starting point towards gaining a real understanding of the institution. Honestly reviewing this history may upset the preconceived notions of many people, especially trial lawyers and judges, who have too frequently developed an ahistorical, vocational understanding of trial by jury beginning with their first experiences in law school.

It is possible that the last truly important legal decision attempting to define the legitimate range of juror discretion was *Bushell's Case* in 1670. The legal powers and independence of jurors were understood and well articulated by Chief Justice Vaughan, writing for the humble Court of Common Pleas more than three centuries ago. In all the cases and all the years that have passed since then, there is no reason to believe the rules have changed. If anything, the intervening years have clearly proven the wisdom of Justice Vaughan's decision.

Even at the time Justice Vaughan wrote his opinion in *Bushell*, many judges, lawyers and legal scholars believed that jurors had the power, but not the right, to judge the law. That had been the view of Lord Mansfield in the *Dean of St. Asaph's Case*. That was the view adopted by Chief Justice Delancey in the seditious libel trial of *Rex v. Zenger*, and this same view was later reiterated by the United States Supreme Court in *Sparf et al. v. United States*. This view has not been modified by that Court since. The *Sparf* court recognized that the power of jurors to deliver a general verdict gives jurors the raw power to deliver a verdict contrary to law and facts, veiled within the general verdict of "Not Guilty." *Sparf* also established that the officially condoned power of jurors to judge the law is lim-

ited to issues where the law is so intertwined with fact as to be inseparable. And finally, *Sparf* reaffirmed that a judge can not direct a conviction,
because the judge has no legal power to decide the facts of a criminal case,
even where none of the facts of the case are in question. In a very real
sense, nothing has materially changed since *Bushell's Case.*

Sparf et al. could be read as merely reaffirming the Justice Vaughan's
opinion. Nothing in that opinion required trial judges to inform jurors of
their nullification powers—in fact, Vaughan studiously avoided any discussion of those powers at all. Then, as now, it was up to the defendants
and the press to tell jurors about their power, and they often had to fight
the courts tooth and nail to do so.

American courts have long recognized the folly of attempting to make
judicial resolution of political questions.[1] The role of the criminal trial jury
is primarily a political question, as Justice Vaughan well understood. It is
a question that was raised in 1215, when the political power of the King
to punish his subjects at whim was limited by the guarantee of trial by
jury in the Magna Charta. It is a question that was raised by the Levellers,
led by John Lilburne (perhaps history's first radical jury rights advocate),
when the Levellers had to fight for their political and religious freedoms.
After the Levellers the question was raised by the Quakers, who were
repressed and denied any religious freedom whatsoever by the Conventicles Act.

The doctrine of jury independence was subsequently embraced by rebels
in the young American Colonies, in their struggles for political autonomy
from the Crown. Jury independence became an important political check
on the power of the fledgling government of the United States, and it saw
massive resurgence as an essentially political protest against early American libel laws and against the Fugitive Slave Acts of 1793 and 1850. Labor
activists adopted jury independence in order to gain their political and
economic freedoms, and opponents of alcohol Prohibition turned to the jury
in order to protect their personal civil liberty. Political opponents of the
Vietnam War advocated jury independence openly and often, and today,
serious citizens of all political stripes still turn to a jury of their peers as the
last and best bulwark of their liberty, when they are in danger of being
jailed for acts they believe are justified. All of these are political protests,
urging the quintessentially American right that author Jessica Mitford
described as "the most basic of all, the right not to be tried for dissent."[2]

Some of these dissidents were successful and changed the course of history. Some of them were infamous and their trials demonstrated the lack

---

1. This is referred to as the "political question doctrine," which was established in
Marbury v. Madison, 5 U.S. 137 (1803).

2. JESSICA MITFORD, THE TRIAL OF DOCTOR SPOCK, 241 (1969).

of social consensus supporting a particular group or groups of dissidents. But all of them raised issues that were fundamentally political or moral in nature, and not strictly or merely legal.

Because the extent to which jurors should feel entitled to vote their conscience is a political and not a legal question, it is not a question that can be answered, either legally or definitively, by the courts or the legislature. Because Article III, § 2, along with the Fifth, Sixth and Fourteenth Amendments to the United States Constitution give this question a constitutional dimension, this is not an issue that can be addressed through any routine act of legislation. In order to limit the power of jurors to render an independent verdict, nothing less than a long series of constitutional amendments would be required. As the Constitution currently exists, the exercise of juror independence is a question that each juror must legally and ethically address within the confines of his or her own conscience.

We must face the reality that some degree of jury independence is inevitable in our current criminal justice system. There is nothing to prevent a juror from voting his or her conscience — unless that same conscience forbids him or her from violating the judge's instructions. If the jurors feel more strongly about what they consider to be a just verdict than they do about following the instructions of the judge, their verdict will reflect that. Jurors are increasingly likely to be aware of their power to judge the law, and informed jurors may be increasingly likely to exercise their powers when they believe it is appropriate.

Courts should be willing to come to grips with the fact that jury independence is not a "problem," as too many case decisions and law journal opinions naively describe it. Instead, it is one of the most important sources of resilience within our judicial system. A rigid, unyielding system cannot survive, just as a tree would crack and splinter if it could not bend in the wind. Laws written by the legislature may not always be just. And even when a given law is just, the law, by its nature, has to be written for general application. It would be impossible and undesirable to have a specific law for every possible set of circumstances. As a result, circumstances that make enforcement of a given general law unjust or even absurd inevitably occur.

As a society, we hope that legislatures will repeal or modify laws that are unjust or unfair. Experience shows that such change, however necessary, does not always happen quickly or painlessly. The Fugitive Slave Act of 1850 remained valid law in the United States until Abraham Lincoln signed the Emancipation Proclamation. How many morally innocent people should be punished, while we wait for the legislature to correct its mistakes? And how are the legislators to know what laws are mistaken, if they are denied response from "the conscience of the community" itself?

We hope police will not make arrests, and prosecutors will not press charges, when the circumstances make it unconscionable to enforce the law in a particular case. We give police and prosecutors the discretion to filter out such cases. In practice, however, this system does not always work perfectly. Sometimes, police, prosecutors and judges believe they are "just doing their job," when in fact they ignore their discretion to do their job justly, not mechanically or reflexively. Sometimes, their idea of a just outcome may not be supported by the community at large. And that is where the jury must intervene, not only to protect the defendant, but to protect the system itself, giving it the flexibility it needs to work justly, fairly, and equitably. Without this "bulwark of liberty" in place, public discontent and distrust of the law may lead to a growing and dangerous sense of alienation. It is not surprising that discontent and alienation are often blamed for the violence and despair in the very same communities where non-violent citizens have all too often come into contact with the criminal justice system, in courts where the powers of juries to see justice done are denied, ridiculed and disparaged. The "safety valve" Judge Leventhal spoke of with approval in *U.S. v. Dougherty* has been officially eliminated. A powerful system with no safety valves can be a very dangerous thing.

This political protest on the part of jurors should be recognized for exactly what it is: proof either that the nullified law lacks adequate social support to be consistently enforced, or that the law is being misapplied by the prosecutor. Laws which are regularly nullified are laws that must change. Jury review should be understood as an essential part of the legislative process. When laws cease to be accepted by jurors, they should be either stricken or modified by responsive legislation. In this way, independent juries can reduce the lag time between social change and legal change, a problem that has always proven intractable.

Jurors should also be viewed as a feedback loop by the prosecutor's office. When a given law is frequently nullified with regard to a particular class of defendants—be it medical users of marijuana, doctors assisting terminally ill patients to end their suffering, or battered spouses who kill their abusers after years of torment—then prosecutors should reconsider how they handle those cases. Perhaps they may decide to quit prosecuting the Sam Skippers and Jack Kevorkians of the world. Perhaps they will decide that the community is wrong, and that for ethical or practical reasons the criminal justice system needs to keep "sending a message" that certain widely tolerated crimes will be taken seriously. One thing they should not do, however, is to ignore the message by denying that the messenger ever had a right to speak.

Screening out "conviction qualified" jurors for all criminal cases threatens to raise the time, cost and difficulty of *voir dire* immensely. More importantly, such a process would reduce respect and support for the criminal law, and would arguably deprive criminal defendants of an impartial jury, fairly representative of the community.[3] The credibility given to juries grows out of their image of the 'conscience of the community.' Discriminating against a sizable percentage of the population who question the wisdom of unpopular legislation is likely to result in an unfavorable and unpredictable backlash, as venire-members who feel strongly about the injustice of a particular law are likely to lie during *voir dire*, in order to obtain a seat on the jury.

Charging independent-minded jurors with perjury or with violating their oaths will only further erode respect for the system, and subject the prosecution to reasonable charges of jury tampering. Segments of the public excluded from jury duty for their views will no longer see the system as protecting their rights or representing the judgment of the community. Those targeted for exclusion will cease to trust or respect the system. Many will fail to respond to a jury summons, because they will reasonably believe that they are sure to be stricken from the panel for their views. Without citizens who believe in the system and are ready to answer a summons for jury duty, the criminal justice system can not be expected to operate. The right to a trial by jury is the right to a trial by a jury fairly selected from a random cross section of the population: attempts to circumvent the decisions of independent-minded jurors are likely to result only in a cure much worse than the disease.

The distinction between jury "rights" and jury "powers" is nonsensical, and should be discarded. A legal power that can be exercised with legal impunity is a legal right. Pennsylvania Chief Justice Sharswood stated it with absolute clarity in 1879:

> [I]t has been strongly contended that though the jury have the power they have not the right to give a verdict contrary to the instruction of the court upon the law; in other words that to do so would be a breach of their duty and a violation of their oath. The distinction between power and right, whatever may be its value in ethics, in law is very shadowy and insubstantial. He who has legal power to do anything has the legal right. No court should give a binding instruction to a jury which they are powerless to enforce by granting a new trial if it should be disregarded. They may present to them the obvious considerations which should induce them to receive and follow their instruction, but beyond this they have no right to go.[4]

The idea that jurors have the "power" but not the "right" to deliver an independent verdict does not blend well with other areas where "pow-

---

3. *See generally* Chaya Weinberg-Brodt, *Jury Nullification and Jury Control Procedures*, 65 N.Y.U. L. Rev. 825 (1990).

4. Kane v. Commonwealth, 89 Pa. 522, 525 (1879).

ers" and "rights" are set in opposition to each other. A person may have the legal "power" to breach a contract, but not the legal right—and for that reason he may be sued for damages should he in fact breach the contract. Similarly, a person may have the raw physical power to punch his neighbor in the nose, shout "fire" in a crowded theatre, or to drive his car on the wrong side of the road. None of these things are his legal right to do, however—and as a result he may be enjoined from committing them, and arrested, jailed, fined, or sued if he does them. There is simply no parallel recourse available to the state against a juror who votes for an independent verdict. Where no injunction or penalty is possible, there is no real difference between a legal power and a legal right.

Potential jurors are increasingly likely to learn about their powers from pamphlets, pulpits, protesters, newspaper articles, books, television, computer networks, talk radio or friends. Some of these sources may tend to be well informed and strictly accurate. Others may be less scrupulous, or less knowledgeable. Some of these sources may be completely misleading. Jurors will naturally look to the judge for clarifying information. If jurors do not get accurate or honest information from the judge, they may not trust his instructions on other points of law. Further, they may go into deliberations with wildly inaccurate or misinformed views concerning the doctrine of jury independence itself. In an effort to prevent jurors from nullifying, courts have simply abdicated their role with respect to supplying jurors with reliable, uniform and unimpassioned guidance concerning the jury's unquestionable power to see that justice is done. This, not jury independence, encourages anarchy.

Too often, we think of the jury simplisticly, as merely the trier of facts. But the jury also has a political function, an educational function, and a social function.[5] Today, with jury independence minimized by controlling courts and procedural rules, juries are prevented or discouraged from performing many of its essential roles. The political role of juries is minimized, as few responsible jurors feel themselves empowered to nullify bad laws or misguided prosecutions. We are not listening to our jurors; even worse, we are not allowing them to speak. Jurors are the citizen link most intimately involved in the criminal justice system. If the opinions of jurors are not worth listening to, then we can quit wondering if citizen input has any impact on our laws. We can be assured it does not.

---

5. ALEXIS DE TOCQUEVILLE, DEMOCRACY IN AMERICA, 273 (1835)(Reprinted 1969):
   [T]he jury is above all a political institution; it should be regarded as one form of the sovereignty of the people; when the sovereignty of the people is discarded, it too should be completely rejected; otherwise it should be made to harmonize with the other laws establishing that sovereignty. The jury is the part of the nation responsible for the execution of the laws...

The educational function of juries is thwarted by treating jurors like errant schoolchildren who must be kept under the strict control of the judge at all times. Jurors are dealt with as though they are too ignorant, emotional, malevolent or misguided to benefit from the training jury duty has historically provided American citizens.[6] Judges and lawyers have forgotten that they are not the only members of society capable of forming valid opinions about abstractions like "justice," "rights," or "liberty." There is no evidence that modern citizens do not possess the same capacity for civic responsibility and awareness as citizens of the eighteenth and nineteenth centuries.

The social function of criminal trial juries can not coexist with a regime of jury servility. When jurors leave courtrooms in tears after delivering convictions against their most deeply held conscientious beliefs, the trial by jury is not performing the function Madison, Adams, Jay, Jefferson and Hamilton intended it to perform. How much of our often declaimed social breakdown can be traced to a lack of trust in the criminal justice system's ability to dispense justice? When citizen jurors are not allowed any meaningful opportunity to participate in the execution of laws, it is not surprising that they lose confidence in the ability of the system to protect them or treat them fairly if accused.

Supreme Court Justice Louis D. Brandeis reportedly said that "[i]f we wish to have the law respected, we must first make the law respectable." Our courts must recognize that the best way for them to have their instructions respected is to make their instructions and their rulings thorough, honest and even handed—particularly with reference to the power, rights and discretion of the jurors themselves. Our courts should allow defendants and their counsel to tell jurors about the various points of view concerning the doctrine of jury nullification, and what purposes the doctrine serves. Judges should make clear to jurors the gravity and responsibility inherent in a decision to veto the written law, but they should also make it clear that this is a responsibility the legal system places in their hands. While it is not a responsibility to be exercised lightly, neither is it a responsibility which can be denied or ignored.

---

6. *Id.* at 275: "Juries are wonderfully effective in shaping a nation's judgment and increasing its natural lights. That, in my view, is its greatest advantage. It should be regarded as a free school which is always open and in which each juror learns his rights…"

Index